Flowers and Tombstones of a Conservation Officer, Struggles Won and Lost

Volume One

by

Terry L. Grosz

Print Edition
© Copyright 2015 Terry L. Grosz (as revised)

Wolfpack Publishing
48 Rock Creek Road.
Clinton, Montana 59825

ISBN: 978-1-62918-865-2

Table of Contents:

Chapter One...1
Chapter Two... 97
Chapter Three... 157
Chapter Four.. 195
Chapter Five.. 303

Excerpt from *Wildlife Wars*...............................527
About the Author...533

Dedication

In 1954, I was an 8th grade student in Miss Billyjean McElroy's class, a teacher who just happened to be the prettiest teacher in the whole darn school. I was a budding young man in those days, into hunting, fishing and exploring all the old California gold diggings left over from the days of the placer and hard rock miners of '49'. In short, as a young man being raised in the wilds of northeastern California high in the Sierra Nevada mountains, I had it made.

Figuring I had it 'made in the shade with a downhill pull', I sat waiting during that first day of school in 1954 in Miss Billyjean's class for roll call to be finished and for class to begin. It was at that moment in time that the front door to my classroom opened up right after the 'Pledge' had finished and in walked a new girl who was to be the newest addition to our school, class and small mountain community.

The new girl was beautiful! She was fairly tall, had reddish blond hair, was smartly dressed and had a grace about her that caught my attention more than if I had just caught a 20" German brown trout! It was at that VERY moment in time, that I felt a physical and emotional feeling sweeping over me that I swear to God never stopped until it hit my feet! Little did I realize at that time, I had just experienced a real life Heaven sent revelation!

Without hesitation, I turned to one of my best friends, Eugene Miller, saying, "I am going to marry that girl someday!" Eugene turned to me in amazement saying, "How do you know that? She is a new girl and you don't even know her name. Besides, you are just a kid, so how can you say that?"

"I don't know" I replied, still looking at the new girl in wonder. "But I do know that I will marry her someday." The lasting effects of that revelation never left me and that new girl, named Donna Larson, and I were happily married nine years later while both of us were still in college on February the 3rd, 1963!

Little did I realize throughout those years, that God had sent me an Angel. An Angel who would completely fulfill my entire life's dreams, raise our three children, teach school full time, went on to earn her Masters of Arts Degree on the side, ran the household, especially during my many long absences as a state and federal wildlife law enforcement officer, provided for all my needs, was my best friend and the total love of my life. In fact, truth be known, I loved her more than my own life…

As these words are being written in 2016, some 62 years later, I am very happily in love and still married to my "Angel." I am convinced that Donna was Heaven sent to me by the good Lord above because He knew I would need such a loving companion in order to fulfill His wishes relative to His choice of my path of destiny in His world of wildlife.

My simple and heartfelt words can never describe the wonderful life my children and I have lived because of the grace provided to all of us throughout our lives by the Angel God gave me and the one that I married.

It is to this Renaissance Woman for all seasons, the Light of my Life, the Love of my Life and the one I love more than my own life, Donna, that I dedicate this book.

Chapter One: Klamath River Follies

THE KLAMATH RIVER, GILL NETS AND YUROK INDIANS

Finding myself early one morning as a rookie fish and game warden in the Eureka Office clearing my citation books of closed cases, I could hear the sounds of a heated and vigorous exchange pouring forth through the adjacent open doorway of my captain's office. Figuring it was just another fish and game warden getting chewed out by my alcoholic and judgmental captain, I kept my mind on my citation book case-closings and filing business at hand. I had been in that same uncomfortable on the carpet position a number of times previously because my captain had a distaste for college graduates in general with degrees in wildlife management and for me in particular because I always stood my ground when right in the face of his many times off the wall criticisms.

By means of an explanation in light of me always standing my ground, I had an alcoholic father who eventually caused a family breakup and divorce early on in my young life. Shortly after that occurred, I developed an independent means and toughness early on in my life toward any adversity swirling around me. Because of the wreckage my father had left behind in the divorce and the years of a near starvation hardscrabble lifestyle that was left for my mother, sister and me to endure, I developed a low tolerance for folks like my drunken captain and his many times unfounded criticisms. Especially when the captain openly lived, espoused and flaunted his drunken lifestyle at the work place to the determent of a number of his chosen and evilly-targeted subordinates. That kind of abnormal and vindictive behavior my captain knew he could get away with because his immediate supervisor who had chosen him for that position, was somewhat of the same chemically dependent cut of the cloth. I was especially quietly intolerant because my captain never even tried to square himself away from such a chemical dependency. In living such a lifestyle, he took his alcohol induced, ill-tempered behavior out on everyone he disliked within arm's length at the work place. On many of those occasions, the good captain purposely took out his belligerence on those officers who had a backbone, which was to say, any officers who stood up to the captain in the face of his bluster or on those unfortunate rookies like myself. Rookie officers were extremely vulnerable because they were still on a one-year probationary period and could be released during that time almost without due cause.

As for the much despised college graduates, the captain automatically figured having a college degree was a stupid waste of time since he never had one. To the captain's way of thinking, if one wanted to become a lowly game warden, all he really needed was just a high school education. Since I held Bachelor's and Masters of Science degrees in Wildlife Management from nearby Humboldt State College, I quickly discovered that I was truly a marked man in the captain's eyes.

As I later discovered, the captain, who was old school law enforcement, had nothing but disdain for all the wildlife and fisheries biologists working within the fish and game department. And there I stood, a wildlife college graduate within his law enforcement squad as a fellow subordinate officer.

In fact, I had discovered his distaste for college graduates the very first day on the job as a new hire in the good captain's fish and game squad. When I first tried to introduce myself to my new captain, he refused to shake my hand and told me he had no tolerance or use for any of us college boys. He went on to say if it had been his choice and not that of the Central Office in Sacramento, I wouldn't have been chosen by him and placed into his fish and game squad. So being a survivor and a somewhat hard-headed German, I just buckled down and caught every fish and game wildlife violating son-of-a-gun that strayed across the line of legality that I could and saw to the prosecution of the same. In so doing, I politely avoided my captain's wrath at every turn in the road by keeping my physical presence working in the field or the courtroom at every opportunity.

Often times I heard him say, "I don't need any God damned fish and game biologist as a game warden in my squad." Hence, it didn't take a very survival oriented chap like me long to realize that my college degrees in wildlife management did not set me in good stead with my captain. Thankfully, all fish and game warden hiring was done out of the Sacramento Office and as a result of my successful competition among 1,400 other best qualified candidates, I was now one of 25 bright and shiny new fish and game warden types in and for the State of California. Before long and to my Germanic way of thinking, I was quickly discovering that being a wildlife officer was a dream come true. Especially when it came to the part of hunting my fellow man or, which I came to learn rather quickly, was really hunting the most dangerous game. To my way of thinking, once I had discovered what the law enforcement profession was all about, if the good captain wanted to get rid of me, he would have to pry me off like a Western deer tick from the back of a Columbian black-tailed deer.

However, in my quest to remain within the ranks as a fish and game warden, I was facing a major problem. I was still on official probation because I had less than one year of service under my belt. Captain Gray reminded me of that administrative point and that he could let me go for ANY reason at ANY time as he saw fit. So as I said earlier, I made sure I caught every fish and game violating son-of-a-gun that I could, remained highly qualified at every pistol shoot (only bested by Herb Christie in our squad), my rate of successful rate of prosecutions remained at the 100% level, and stayed the hell out of the many times vindictive captain's path, reach and drunken presence.

However, as I was soon to discover, the good captain's wrath concerned a more senior officer that morning and because of that earlier overheard heated conversation referencing a dangerous duty assignment, was quickly to discover that I would soon be touched with some rather hair-raising experiences. Moments later, I noticed the good captain's doorway filled with the huge frame of Herb Christie, the warden from the nearby Humboldt County town of Fortuna. Now to my way of thinking, there was a good man and a gifted wildlife officer if I ever saw one. Herb stood 6-foot 4-inches in height and weighed in at a solid frame packing 250 pounds. He had hands like a blacksmith and was as strong and powerful as a Clydesdale horse. However, that is where his "Man Mountain Dean" essence ended. Herb was very bright, a real catcher of wildlife outlaws, gentle as a downy duck feather floating on a morning's breeze to most everyone around him, brave as any Marine on Iwo Jima during the

Second World War and yet approachable and considerate as all get out. As I said earlier, Herb, in my eyes, was one hell of a man and was soon to become a great mentor and 'tricks of the trade' teacher to yours truly.

I had liked Herb from the very first moment I had met him but had yet to work with him on any fish and game patrol assignments. As a rookie game warden, given the chance to learn the law enforcement tricks of the trade from such a learned and respected individual, I would have done so at the drop of a hat. Well, surprise, surprise, guess what? Herb dropped that hat in my lap unexpectedly in the moments that soon followed his exit from the good captain's office.

"Tiny," (my fish and game squad nickname given to me since I stood 6-foot 4-inches tall and tipped the scales at a tad over 300 beautiful pounds in my stocking feet and Cheshire cat grin), "do you have a minute so we can talk?" Herb asked.

With an affirmative nod of my head, Herb gestured for me to follow him into another squad room where we could talk in private. Once there, he closed the door behind me, gestured for me to sit down and then began speaking quietly. "Tiny, Captain Gray has just given me one hell of an assignment and a dangerous one at that. This assignment I did not ask for nor am I interested in doing because of the unnecessary danger faced in completing such a detail. For some reason, Gray is pissed off at the Yurok Indians for gill netting on their tribal extension on the Klamath River (the Extension was not considered an official reservation in those days. Today, the Yuroks have their own reservation). Why is beyond me because the courts have yet to rule on the legality of allowing the Yurok Indians to gill net salmon on the extension (use of gill nets was illegal in California in those days unless one was a registered Native American on the Tribal Roles and only if that person gill netted on a sanctioned Indian Reservation). Going in there now before rendering that legal opinion and taking on a mess of already pissed off Indians is just asking for trouble.

Apparently, Inspector Les Lahr also has it out for the Yuroks over their gill netting on the Extension before a legal decision has been rendered. He has passed his being 'pissed off' down to his subordinate, namely Captain Gray. It seems that Lahr and Gray now want the fish and game department to challenge the Indians over their right to gill net salmon on the Yurok Extension. To me, that appears to be nothing more than a 'pissim' contest in which Les Lahr just wants to show the Yuroks who is the boss. I tried talking Gray out of such a foolish and dangerous patrol assignment but you know how pig headed the captain can be, especially when he has been drinking. This morning he is soused. So, I have been ordered to go undercover, take a boat down the Klamath River at night, document any Yurok Indians gill netting salmon before the courts have rendered a decision on the legality of such activities, seize their gill nets and take any salmon the Indians have in their possession. As such, Gray has ordered me to continue such patrols until a court decision is rendered in the favor of the State of California or the Yurok Tribe. That kind of action on our parts will sure as hell set the hair on the backsides of any Indian we treat in such a manner. I guess both Lahr and Gray want to make sure the Yuroks realize who is in charge of the state's salmon resources and understand that it is not them."

"That is where you come in. Warden Hank Marak in Willow Creek who would be my logical choice for assistance on this detail because of his level of Indian experience already has his hands full of the Hoopa Indians and their gill netting activities on the Trinity River running through that portion of their reservation. So, I can't really call on him for any help on this matter without short changing all of his on-going law enforcement efforts. All the other wardens in our squad are either too old or scrawny in size to be of any assistance on this assignment if events were to turn physical. Especially if the crap really hits the fan, like they start shooting or something else just as stupid. Of course, there is always the availability of rookie Warden Warren Duke. However, he just doesn't have what I think I will need if the going gets rough in the form of needing somebody who can get physical or is a really good shooter. As I see it, you are big enough to pull a beer wagon and eat hay, so you being physical enough if the crap hits the fan in order to take care of yourself is not a concern. You are also a damn good pistol shooter from what I have seen on the range. With that in mind, I suppose with your framing, you can hit as hard as an angry mule's kick if that is called for. So by default, rookie or not, Warden Duke is out and you are going to have to be my partner in this crazy damn dangerous Klamath River detail."

"Now before you give me your answer, this detail is not for the faint hearted. We will be using a 12-foot wooden boat to float the Klamath River at night in our efforts to catch any Yurok Indians gill netting salmon. Our work will be during the dark of the night because that is when the migrating salmon cannot see the mesh in the gill nets and will entangle themselves in it as they migrate upstream. During daylight hours, the Indian's nets will be removed because the salmon can see the net's mesh and swim around it. Additionally, other white fishermen in the area can see the nets and the Indians don't like that to happen. That is because when the 'white-eyes' passing by see those nets, they like to cut them to pieces since they are such killing machines and catch so many salmon."

"The Klamath River onto which we will be working in the dark of the night is in and of itself inherently dangerous. That is because we will be floating almost blind, there will be numerous rocky obstructions along with waterfalls, 'suck holes' and it is damn fast flowing. The Klamath River is also littered with numerous dangerous riffles, all backed up by a ton of white water and did I mention, numerous waterfalls? We will have no backup or radio contact because we will be in the backcountry and down in numerous deep river canyons where radios are useless. If either of us become seriously injured, that is probably where we will die because we will be too far away from any quick arriving medical assistance."

"Then there is the Indian factor where we will most certainly be outnumbered by numbers of pissed off Indians every time we try to take their expensive gill nets and the salmon they caught. Those Indians will more than likely be armed, many times have been drinking and when that happens, they can be damn dangerous. However, the Yuroks are generally physically smaller than many of our other North Coast Indians and that means between the two of us, we should be able to handle up to a dozen of them at one time. Any more than that and they can probably overwhelm us. That is unless those Indians we will be confronting are armed and have been drinking. Then, there are no guaranties as to our safety or being able to come home at the end of this detail. Now I know you are recently married to your wife, Donna. I suggest you keep much of this information from your bride so she is not so unduly alarmed. Welcome to the real world of wildlife law enforcement and the pool of snakes we will be standing in once this mission begins. What do you say, Tiny? Are you game?"

You know, my readers, we Germans have not won a war since about 1870. So with what Herb had to say about this detail, what did I have to lose? After all, I had been in some pretty damn life threatening scrapes before while working in Alaska during my college summer of 1962 as a seasonal employee for the Bureau of Commercial Fisheries. After those experiences, many of them life threatening, I thought I had seen it all. Especially since I found the nature of the environment in Alaska would kill you in a heartbeat unless you are at the top of your game every moment of every day. As I was soon to discover, I had not seen anything in Alaska compared to what I was about to experience on the Klamath River in the wilds of Northern California during the dark of the night...

"I will be glad to give you a hand, Herb. What will I need in the way of gear and when do we leave for this detail?" I casually asked like any other senior experienced officer. However, not to show the rookie in me, I held back with a million unanswered detail questions roaring around in my head like a swarm of Africanized honeybees.

"Tomorrow should be soon enough for us to leave and we will be living along the river on handy sandbars so you will need a sleeping bag. Put any extra clothing in a rubberized bag along with your sleeping bag in case we get inadvertently dumped into the river. And, be sure and bring your stainless steel .357 pistol as your choice of firearm. That way, if we inadvertently take a swim in the Klamath, that type of firearm won't rust up and will still be able to function and allow us to accomplish our mission. Bring a sharpened combat knife in case you somehow get entangled in a gill net and need to cut yourself free so you don't drown and at least 50 rounds of hollow point bullets for your handgun. That way, if we get into a real serious shootout, we will stand a better chance of being able to shoot our way clear and come back to our wives in one piece. Other than that, bring your regular night use law enforcement equipment and we should be set. As for chow, don't worry about that. Since you are willing to go along with me on this detail, I will supply the chow. Understand though, the food will be simple fare. We will just roast steaks over the fire and bake a spud and an onion in the coals for our suppers. For breakfast and lunch just bring along several "Snicker" or "Payday" candy bars because we won't have much room in the boat for anything else nor the time to fix it. The way I figure it, if you get thirsty and need anything to drink, you can get that from the river. Other than that, I can offer you all the steep canyon walls you can stand, lots of Type Four and Five rapids, as much white water you will want to see in a lifetime from a 12-foot wooden boat in the dark of the night, and all the pissed off Indians you can s stomach. Oh, I will also bring along a first aid kit in case we end up with a few bruises, nicks or scratches. Other than that, that should about do it as near as I can figure," said Herb.

"Any idea just how long we will be gone on this detail?" I asked.

"That will depend upon any legal action that we generate. About three days as near as I can figure after we get there and start patrolling. After that, the jungle ˜tom-toms' will be letting all the other Indians along the river know they need to pull their nets because fish and game is on patrol," quietly advised Herb. "I will let Captain Gray know that I will be taking you even though you are a rookie. Knowing how much he hated having you join the squad because of all of your wildlife management educational background, if you get screwed up while on the river that will make him happy. He will just assume if you get shot or drown while out on the Klamath, you will be out of his hair for good. Being frank, I think the two of us will make a damned good pair and a match for anything the Indians care to throw our way," he said, followed by an easy laugh.

Little did I then realize at that point in my career just how often strong men routinely laughed in the face of real danger as a stress reliever, as did Herb that day. Well to my way of thinking, laughter   wasn't the right reaction when looking at our approaching river boat patrol assignment on the mighty Klamath River. Over the subsequent years in my long career as a wildlife office, I discovered that many times on dangerous law enforcement assignments, valor in facing those types of dangers was a common virtue among the best of the badge carriers. *It is a good thing that God really does love little children, fools and us goofy damn game wardens*, I thought, as the specter of my upcoming adventure produced a grin of anticipation on my young face. However, to be frank, it was a somewhat goofy and worried kind of a look on my face as well. So much for any show of valor in my heart and soul in the face of such a dangerous assignment on the Klamath River soon to be undertaken... Over the many years that came later, I learned that officers for the most part didn't get too excited over or in the face of commonly faced dangerous assignments until after the fact. By then it was too damn late for an officer to get his 'tool kit' all wound up over such history. Bottom line, there were two things that I learned to carry with me in life. One was that death was certain and the other was that life was not. So, there was no use in getting upset about either one, just carry one's self always towards the next horizon and hope you could be around in order to see the next sunrise...

When Herb had finally finished with the trip's details, I didn't feel like laughing over what potentially could lie ahead. This detail looked to me like it had the trappings of a one-way ticket to eternity if one was not on the top of his game. Since I was just a rookie, I really hadn't had much time in which to gain a whole lot of 'game.' On the other hand, the opportunity to work with an officer like Herb Christie and boating into the unknown on the Klamath River deep in Indian country in the dead of night would bring me a world of life's experience. And in so doing, attempt to give the noble salmon a better chance to live, found me starting to get more comfortable with the upcoming challenge and the odds we would soon be facing. I guess when one is dumber than a box of river rocks as I was that day in my life, it sometimes doesn't hurt to face one's Maker all bright eyed and bushy tailed with a goofy grin splashed all across one's face.

As Herb got up to leave the room and let Captain Gray know we would be going the next day into that directed assignment, he paused and turned. "Are you a student of history?" Herb asked me right out of the blue.

"Yes, I am," I responded. However, I must have replied with more than a quizzical look on my face over being asked such a question because what followed next took care of that kind of a look.

"Custer tried something like this in his day and look what that got him. But, Custer was a wimp. I figure between the two of us, we should be able to give a few of those king salmon some relief and a lot of heartburn to those who like running their damn killin' gill nets," he quietly said with a smile. Man, let me tell you that smile befitted a senior game warden with a ton of experiences under his belt and yet, one who was as tough as a barrel of horseshoe nails. That and now that I look back on that moment in time this many years afterwards, I would say Herb said what he said with a whole lot of mischievous adventurer in him as well. I also now know that kind of 'sand' Herb showed me that day is what a good 'catch dog' within the ranks of those in the thin green line needs in order to be successful in what he or she does for a living.

Excited over the prospects of my next adventure, I hurried home and began packing up what I figured I would need for such a venture. Following Herb's earlier instructions, I gave out little information to my wife about what I was about to experience. In fact, when she reads this story some almost 50 plus years later as she edits my draft of this adventure or reads the book, that will be the first time she becomes aware of what squirrels Herb and I were about to become.

The next morning bright and early, I was at the fish and game office making final trip preparations. Going downstairs into the evidence and closed case property room to retrieve a couple of fishing poles so Herb and I would look like regular sport salmon fishermen, I grabbed what was needed for the ruse to come. Hustling back upstairs with the fishing gear, I met Herb and then the two of us took all my gear out to where he had parked in front of the fish and game office building.

There sat our 'chariot'. It was a small, four-cylinder beat up looking green Jeep with an unpainted, homemade cab. Behind it was a small towed boat trailer holding a 12-foot wooden boat. That was it! NOW, I truly knew how Custer felt back in June of 1876 on the eastern prairies of Montana on his fateful day. To the uninitiated like my rookie self, it appeared we were going into battle without everything we would really need in order to be safe and successful. Looking over at Herb for any further explanation as to how little boat-substance, based on my previous boat work experiences in Alaska, I was now seeing, I did not see any concern on his weathered face. So, I fixed my face like one of those faces on Mount Rushmore and went along with the flow (no pun intended). Brother, being young and inexperienced sure has its advantages sometimes, especially in the world of wildlife law enforcement.

We two wildlife warriors loaded up and travelled north of Eureka on State Highway 101 until we hit State Highway 299. Traveling behind slow moving logging trucks all the way, we finally turned off at the small mountain town of Willow Creek. Turning north on State Highway 96 at Willow Creek, we proceeded northerly through the Hoopa Indian Reservation to the even smaller town of Weitchpec. From there, we turned north onto State Highway 169 and soon found ourselves deep in the Yurok Indian Extension. Damn, looking around as we drove deeper and deeper into Indian Country, I couldn't help but thinking that we were so far out in the bush that *'any chickens we run across out there will have square faces*!' Shortly thereafter, we approached a small boat launching site on the mighty Klamath River where we could launch our twig of a boat and turned into the area. Man, let me tell you, looking at the surrounding deep river canyon walls and the fast moving waters now confronting us, that 12-foot wooden boat was sure looking mighty small! Mighty small, especially in light of the fact with all our gear and the combined weight of Herb and yours truly, THAT small splinter of a boat was our only lifeline

13

on a damned big river! It was then that I realized why I had to show a fish and game captain administering the game warden's physical qualification exams prior to being hired, that I could swim at least a 100 yards without stopping...

Loading up our gear into our 'splinter' sized craft, Herb attached a small outboard motor to the stern of our looking more and more like a lifeline wooden 'boat-let' and out into the madly swirling current we went like a fart in a whirlwind! It was then that I remembered a maxim I had conjured up during my limited experience as a game warden during moments like this that went thusly, "*God loves little children, fools and game wardens.*" I had developed such a saying based on several more than exciting close calls and dangerous adventures I had already experienced as a rookie game warden. Brother, that little maxim sure fit 'like a glove' into our current adventure (no pun intended). Especially that part of the maxim about 'fools and game wardens' since, under the present circumstance, such descriptors were interchangeable under the current conditions for both of us two, soon to be 'ding-bats'.

From our launch point, we two brave souls headed upstream on the Klamath River like we owned the place with not a WHOLE LOT of freeboard. Sitting in the bow of our boat, I had an AMAZING ringside seat! The sounds of fast flowing waters, roaring waterfalls and water ripping through dangerously boulder strewn rapids sounded loudly in my ears as my eyes drew in all the intense and rugged beauty of the area. It soon became apparent to me that God had dumped out all of his remaining rugged geography from His quiver into making those portions of the Klamath River canyons I was now experiencing. Talk about a wild river, the Klamath was an absolute beauty and terrifying monster all at the same time! Fast moving waters, long violent flowing riffles, torrents of white water storming over unseen boulders, steep canyon walls towering hundreds of feet into the sky, thundering back all the river's angry sounds off its basalt sides. The river's beauty and majesty was then followed by long, deep and intensely quiet pools, soon followed by more heart pounding white water heard around the next bend. It wasn't long before I was exalting in the grand experience that was totally absorbing my miserable carcass in its deadly embrace of grandeur. A grandeur that could kill the foolhardy in a moment and then whisk away such evidence of violence like a puff of black powder rifle smoke dissipating into the winds of time.

Moments later, my joy over the rugged beauty surrounding us was interrupted by Herb's voice. "Tiny, observe carefully the terrain around every sand bar that has a quiet pool lying on its lee side. If you see nothing covering the sand bar other than sand, move on with your eyes. However, if you observe leaves and twigs scattered all over the sand bar, point it out to me. That indicates it is a location where the Indians have cleaned their gill nets of debris floating in the water before or after using them. If they leave that debris in the nets, the salmon can see it and swim around the entanglement. The nets have to be regularly cleaned and the best place to do that is on a smooth and clean sandbar adjacent to where they will place the net in the eddy of the river. Also, closely examine the rapids and waterfalls we are experiencing as we move along. Memorize their layouts, especially if we find evidence of someone using a net on a nearby sandbar because we will motor just above that spot, make our camp and, come nightfall, float back down that same stretch of river without the use of our motor or any lights. It is important for you to memorize the dangerous looking water, riffle locations and waterfalls around a possible gill netting site because we will soon be going through them when traversing them at night."

"Remember come nightfall, you will be in the bow with an oar to shove us away from the dangerous obstacles while I am busy rowing to slow us down and keep us centered to the deepest flow of the river's current. We will be doing so without using any lights because if the Indians see us using lights, they will be alerted and it might just blow any case on them we are attempting to make. So, learn the dangerous places on the river through which we are now traveling because you will see them again and in the darkness everything looks differently. Be on your toes because to drag your ass on this part of detail will end us up in the river in the dark of the night and we won't be wearing any life preservers. Those damn things will just get in the way if one is struggling in the river in the dead of night trying to avoid the boulders and waterfalls with his hands. You will need full use of your hands and arms when tossed into the river in the dark and that is why we will not be using any state provided, bulky cork life preservers. Those cheap damn things just get in the way when one is thrashing about in the swift moving waters trying to get back to shore in order to survive, trust me."

I sure as hell didn't remember what I was expecting on that detail never having done one like it in the past. However, you can bet after Herb's 'words to the wise', my crew cut haircut was standing straight up and I NEVER missed any sign or location of rough water after that! Especially when it became known that we would be floating back downstream that evening in the dark without using any lights, motor or life preservers! Herb would be rowing the boat against the current with me in the bow pushing us off the canyon's walls with just a wooden oar to avoid smashing into the unyielding rocky sides of the canyon. Having learned about white water and its hazards while working in Alaska on its big glacier rivers, I knew all about the unseen places of dangerous suction and the chance of being sucked under alongside rocky cliff faces and drowned. Those thoughts included others about the violent beating one would take, especially on one's legs, when being slammed against the canyon walls or the unyielding unseen boulders out in the main stream current of the river!

Later that afternoon, the two of us set up our camp on a small sandy beach upstream from our launch site. After laying out our sleeping bags and building a small campfire, I grabbed the coffee pot and headed for the river to get us some water. As I did, Herb collected more driftwood, built a fire and, once we had a mess of coals, set about cooking our steaks over the open fire on a small spit. In addition, he put several buttered onions and spuds previously wrapped in foil at the edge of the coals to cook. Soon the air filled with delicious cooking smells as I sat there in camp still marveling at my wild and rugged surroundings which I now occupied. All around us two wardens swirled swiftly moving waters, towering canyon walls running up seemingly to the clouds and back again down to the waters' edge. Coupled with those sensory pleasures was a soft breeze wafting down the river's course, common merganser ducks flying back and forth just over the waters' surface, the defiant and warning sounds of white water just below our camp, and the heavenly smell of outdoor cooking filling the air. Man, I was sure glad to be alive and in this dangerous place! Little did I realize at that moment in time the sometimes connection between enjoying the intense beauty of an area and the immediate possibilities of accompanying deep terror when it came to one's life experiences brought on by such places of grandeur...

By nine o'clock that first evening, our world in the Klamath River canyon was pitch black! One could put his hand in front of his face and feel the warmth from his flesh and yet not see the hand it was so dark. There was little light from the moon to aid us in our endeavors because we were in such a deep and narrow canyon. The only sliver of light that I could see was where the smoothness of the water found itself violently ripped apart and delineated by the phosphorescence generated by such swirling rapids or waterfalls. That was scary enough, but the sounds of water being violently thrown around in the darkness long before one got there had such a terrifying

17

and profound effect that it left its deep mark on my soul on what was forth coming just moments away...

I had been raised by my mother, a tough North Dakota farm gal, to meet life's challenges head on with always an 'escape' in mind in case things went 'south'. Thereafter, I always made sure I had a Plan B in case I missed my initial mark. Let me tell all you good readers out there, this was one upcoming challenge and adventure that was not only going to be terrifying but damned exhilarating jammed all into the same instant. There would be no time for a Plan B if spilled into the river's raging waters in the dark of night other than survival Talk about us goofy damn game wardens and all the fixes we could get ourselves into. Would you believe that we did all this for only $526.00 dollars a month!

"Time to go, Tiny," said Herb as he interrupted my thoughts. "That sandbar you spotted a mile or so below our camp with all the leaf litter and debris on it should have an active gill net just below it in that big quiet eddy come dark. The salmon will pull up into that eddy to rest and when they do, they will run into that deadly gill net and that will be the end of their migration. So let's get going because if a net is being used there now, it has had plenty of time to do its deadly work. Grab the rest of your gear that you will need and let's see if we can keep this boat upside-right."

Within moments, we boarded our boat and Herb pushed us off into an adventure I will never forget. I knelt at the ready in the bow with an oar in hand and Herb was to row our boat backwards in the swift clutching current of the river to slow down our forward moving progress as we sped down stream. We were instantly swept out into the fast moving water and flung through that first set of rapids before I was even mentally or physically ready for what awaited me! That first experience of dropping down a gradual but swiftly moving four-foot waterfall and accompanying rapids caught me completely by surprise! When we dropped over that waterfall, my gorgeous 320 pounds of magnificence lifted clear off the floor of the bow of our boat where I was kneeling! At the bottom of that waterfall, I was painfully slammed into the bottom of the boat on my unprotected knees, which reminded me I had a job to do and had better get to it! Instantly, we hurled into the nearby canyon wall at the bottom of a second set of waterfalls with a loud CRUNCH! Thus was my dangerous reward for being unprepared for what I was experiencing.

Quickly regaining my composure and forgetting my stinging knees, I shoved the boat away from the rock wall with the oar with all of my might to avoid swamping or being sucked under by the undertow. As it was, we took on about six inches of water making our boat sluggish and prone to slopping sideways whenever we rocked side to side from the inertia of the swift flowing waters. After almost dumping into that swirling water and resting on a set of stinging knees, I was now all 'ass-holes, eyeballs and false teeth!' The next set of rapids were soon upon us in heart pounding seconds and took us downriver so fast through a mountain of boulders that we almost swamped! After that experience, we had to pull ashore and dump out all the water dangerously sloshing around in the bottom of the boat to avoid swamping.

In that previous heart pounding experience, the rookie big fella in the bow of the boat had quickly learned the Klamath River's lesson for not paying attention on what needed doing in order to survive and now had it down. When we hit the next stretch of white water followed by yet another four foot sloped and fast dropping waterfall, I damn sure knew what to do and do well. Then all of a sudden, the good Lord gave us a long slow drift in smooth water and a chance for me to catch my breath and slow my beating heart. However, my ears could hear what was coming next in the way of danger. At the end of the smooth water was a long set of very fast moving rapids studded with large boulders and then that was followed with one more length of smooth water as if by the Lord's Will to give me time to get my house in order. Who says God does not favor little children, fools and game wardens?

As the roaring sounds of the fast approaching set of rapids increased its crescendo in the dark of the night, so did the sounds of my now speedily racing heart. Damn, let me tell all you readers out there trying to experience through these inadequate words what the dickens we were going through in the waters in the bottom of that canyons at night, how about trying this on for size? Try to anticipate what danger is coming next with just your hearing in total lamp-black darkness, all the while knowing you could be just seconds away from eternity if your decisions and reactions to your current environment, are not correct...

Herb tried to position our fast moving boat into the center of the river where the water was at its deepest point and the current the swiftest. That was also where the river's current was the most violent and dangerous as well. Then **DOWN** we swirled through those rapids like a fart in the whirlwind on a North Dakota prairie during a Type 5 tornado! Kneeling in the bow with my oar, I frantically pushed us from onrushing boulders, thankfully now illuminated slightly by the white water's phosphorescence. Then into the hard basalt canyon wall we slammed at the bottom of those rapids so violently, that it broke off the end of my oar when I tried to lessen the impact! Just as we hit, my shoved out oar, because I anticipated we would hit the canyon wall, snapped off and was shoved back into my gut with such force that it partially lifted me off my knees! But, we made it! Dropping my broken oar into the bottom of the boat, I hastily fumbled around in the darkness for our reserve oar for the next go around with the "River God."

As I did, I kept looking around for the faint outline of our suspect sandbar and as I did, it was with the realization that I still had the heartbeat of a humming bird from our so far wild ride down the river in a postage stamp sized wooden boat... I had to say that was some ride down the mighty Klamath River at night without using any lights in a 12-foot wooden rowboat! The type of experience I will never forget and still get a tinge of excitement in my miserable old carcass over 50 years later as I am writing these words. Can you readers out there imagine what that experience was truly like? All that excitement and danger just to save a few salmon and it all happened in just 12,000 of my heartbeats... Yeah, if you are asking yourselves if I would do that all over again, you damn right and in a heartbeat. That is if I was able and could hold my own with the elements and be able to hold the right hand of God in the process...

Drifting slowly along the edge of the current, the lighter color of a sandbar drifted into view. THEN THERE IT WAS! Sitting below the edge of the sandbar in all its glory was the barely visible white float line of a deadly gill net quietly resting in the eddy. Sure as God made green apples, several of the floats were bobbing up and down signifying the final death throes of a trapped and suffocating salmon!

Realizing the Indians who owned the gill net were more than likely camping up high on the adjacent riverbank and probably sound asleep, Herb and I moved quickly and graveyard silently toward the lower end of the sandbar. Quietly beaching our boat, Herb whispered, "Tiny, you move downstream along the riverbank and hide behind that boulder just below the sandbar. Me, I will quietly tow our boat back upstream and hide it in the brush above the gill net. Then when the Indians come out to tend the net at first light and are out in the water in their boat in the quiet of the eddy, I will start up my outboard motor and head downstream to apprehend those in the boat running the gill net. That outboard motor sound will be your cue to race up to the sandbar and block off their escape route in case they get away from me out in the open water, head

21

for the sandbar and try fleeing on foot. That way, we will have our illegal gill net fishermen trapped from escaping on the water or by land."

Grabbing my flashlight from the rucksack, I headed for my place of hiding behind a nearby boulder. Herb, in the meantime, towed our boat up and out of sight and then the next seven hours of night settled in around us as the river's sounds softly blanketed the area. All night I stood behind my boulder watching in the direction of the sandbar for any signs of movement by those running the gill net and listening for the sound of Herb's outboard motor start-up.

Come the dawn, I could now smell wood smoke from a nearby campfire. Moments later on stiffened legs, I observed the darkened forms of two individuals slowly and silently moving down off the riverbank, through the brush and onto the sandbar. The two men stood on the sandbar for a few moments silently looking all around for anyone who might be watching them. Then, they took a moment and looked long and hard at their gill net float line for any signs of movement that would signify a struggling netted fish hanging in the meshes doing his dance with death. Moments later, they dragged a small wooden boat out from the nearby underbrush, slipped it into the eddy at the edge of the sandbar and quietly paddled out to the end of their gill net float line.

From my place of hiding behind the boulder, I observed the two men tending the net and removing dead salmon from its deadly meshes. Once removed from the mesh of the net, the salmon were unceremoniously flopped into the bottom of their boat. It was then that I heard Herb's outboard motor start up and that was my cue. Leaving my place of hiding from behind the boulder, I trotted quietly up along the still darkened riverbank and out onto the sandbar. I was now between the two men tending the gill net and any landward escape route they might try to use. About then, Herb's boat motored around the end of the sandbar and slid over to the two surprised Indian gill net fishermen.

"State fish and game warden," thundered Herb as he moved alongside the Indians' boat and grabbed hold of its side so they could not escape out into the river. The two Indians, in shock over being surprised running a gill net and now caught in an illegal act, said nary a word. Herb instructed both men to head for shore as he pointed me out in the dawn's early light and then ordered them ashore towards me once again. As the two men rowed ashore, Herb began wrapping up the gill net and placing its rolls and numerous dead salmon into the bottom of our boat. When the two men arrived back at the sandbar where I was standing with their boat, I also identified myself as a game warden. When I identified myself and my official status, that was when the crap hit the fan!

"I don't care who the hell you say you are, you are trespassing on Indian land. You have no authority here. Now get the hell off our land or we will kick your butts!" bellowed out the heavy set Indian standing up in the bow of their boat.

Catching me a little off guard over their instant hostility, I fumbled for a retort and finally managed to keep my 'tang from getting all tungled up'. "Gentlemen, we both are state fish and game wardens and you are running an illegal gill net contrary to the laws of the State of California. That is why we are here this morning," I said with all the authority I could muster in the tone and tenor of my voice.

"I don't care who the hell you say you are, you are trespassing on Indian land. Now get the hell out of my way before I whip the hell out of your big ass and don't think I can't do it. I don't care how damn big you are, I am an ex-Marine and know how to kill people like you with just my bare hands. So get the hell out of my way because I am going to get some of my friends and then we will see just how tough the two of you pieces of trespassing crap really are," my Indian chap continued bellowing out like I was deaf or something. He did

23

so even though I was just standing three feet away from him. It was then that I realized why he was yelling so loudly. He was doing so in order to awaken and alert his partners still sleeping up on the riverbank that the law was at hand!

With those words of warning, my chap stepped out from their boat, tried to shove me aside and storm on by. It was then that I smelled the stale sour smell of tobacco and whiskey on his breath. Just then Herb beached our boat and began walking our way as I reached out to my hastily walking off chap, gently turned him around and headed him back towards Herb before he realized what I had done. That is when I got surprised. My previously bellowing chap 'fluffed up' and slugged me in the face! That poorly thought out move got him decked onto the sandbar in fine style! When I decked the first man and then attempted to get him under control, his partner stepped out from their boat, took his leave of the area and sped off running for their riverbank camp. That got him quickly tackled by one now getting angry as all get out rookie game warden in a fine college defensive football tackle style.

"OOOOFFF," he yelled as he hit the ground with all of my 320 pounds of Germanic Teutonic magnificence and beauty landing on top of him. "Help! Help! Help!" my chap screamed at the top of his lungs. Hell, from all the yelling he was doing you would have thought a grizzly bear was eating him alive. When he began squalling, I heard several other voices up on the riverbank at their campsite beginning to talk loudly back and forth excitedly in a tone and tenor of urgency.

Oh, oh, I thought, s*ounds like our two chaps have some friends up on the riverbank.* With that, I grabbed my chap, bodily hoisted him to his feet and began walking him briskly back towards Herb and the man's partner. As I did, I also kept a wary eye cocked up on the riverbank by the campsite. Shoving my man forward towards Herb and letting my partner control the immediate sandbar situation, I turned my attentions

On that night after almost swamping our boat on a particular vicious set of waterfalls, we rowed shoreward once again and I bailed out about eight inches of water from the bottom of our boat, which I had now named "The Leaking Lena". While I bailed out the boat, Herb noticed a small flicker of light a short ways downstream on our side of the riverbank. Getting back out onto the river with a much lighter boat, down we went through another rough set of rapids and almost overturned once again when my oar slipped off a boulder and we hit it full on sideways! As water flooded into our jammed-against-a-rock boat once again, I quickly shifted my dainty weight and we slid off our boat-grabbing boulder. Thankfully, that bit of hair-raising excitement was followed by a long stretch of the river that was smoother than a 'school marm's thigh'.

Quietly drifting alongside a sandbar makeshift fishing camp, we got a pleasant surprise. That camp turned out to be a group of fishermen let out along the river the day before by a chartered jet boat. From all indications, those fishermen wanted a wild experience and to salmon fish where they wouldn't have any other fishing competition. Hence our finding those fishermen camping in such an isolated spot along the river. As we silently drifted by at the outside edge of the light from their dying campfire and a lone Coleman lantern, we observed five stoutly anchored fishing poles propped up on the sandbar with bells on the ends of their rods. Our chaps were night fishing in inland waters, which in those days was illegal in California. Drifting quietly onto the fishermen's sandbar, Herb and I soon had five fishermen who woke up discovering their worst nightmare of fishing illegally and being apprehended for said violation by two real live game wardens floating the Klamath River at night. After the initial shock of apprehension among our fishermen had dissipated, I looked around their camp while Herb issued citations to our chaps. Lo and behold, guess which two chaps also had over limits of king salmon? Yep, those illegal fish belonged to the two men of the group giving us the most lip about being cited for what they called a puny offense. Soon, we two crazies returned to the river with five citations and eleven seized king salmon in the bottom of our boat!

However, having eleven 20-35 pound king salmon in a 12-foot boat with two badge carriers weighing in at over 250 pounds each was not a sure fire formula for safely floating down the Klamath River in the dark... Realizing that and about to turn around and head back to our camp before we swamped our boat, another campfire flicker of light caught our eyes about 200 yards away. Yes, my readers, observing a small light in the dark of the night from about 200 yards away is a snap. In fact, a single lit candle can be seen from about ten football fields away in the dark of the night with just the naked eye!

Twenty minutes later and two more sets of roaring riffles under our belts, found the two of us once again staked out around the float line of another gill net. Using the same stakeout technique we had employed during the earlier gill net go-around, come daylight, we soon had two different Yurok Indians running the same kind of salmon-killing device. Apprehension went initially almost the same as in our first catch of Indians running a gill net and then turned deadly. While writing up the information on the two lads just caught running the illegal net, all of a sudden we had four heretofore unknown Indians pile off the riverbank from their nearby fish camp and come storming across our sandbar with blood in their eyes. Herb later discovered that all six of the men had pooled their money and had purchased their new gill net now in use. As such, they were not interested in having it or their netted salmon removed by two, to their way of thinking, outnumbered damn trespassing game wardens.

At first, the men listened to what Herb had to say, then not satisfied with his explanation, they got unruly. The whole time

I tried to take a defensive position so I could protect Herb and myself in case someone wanted to fire up a 'river dance.' My concerns were not long in coming. As the men got madder and madder over having white men, to their way of thinking, trespassing on their land and now about to take their gill net because they had been practicing their God given right, things fired up. One lad, who just happened to be the largest of the group and obviously under the influence of alcohol based on how badly he reeked, stomped off into the nearby thicket of brush and broke off a large limb. Coming back, he told Herb that if he didn't return their net, Herb would pay the price. Sensing the increasing danger of that moment, I moved in closer to the man with the big limb. In so doing, I was immediately struck across the right arm, which had been quickly raised in defense when the lad's aggressive intentions became clear. Surprised and then pissed over what had just happened, I saw to it that the chap who had hammered me with the limb got it back in spades! Down the limb-swinger went and moved no more. With that, we now had five fist swinging Yurok Indians! As that turned out, they didn't know how to fight worth sour owl droppings. They came at Herb and me one at a time. Wrong! Every lad who stepped forth with malice in his heart, got dumped with a right cross from the two of us that would have felled a mule. Soon the 'river dance' was over and our six Yurok dudes were lying on the ground in different stages of repose or crawling around holding their heads.

Once Herb finally had everyone's attention again somewhat later, the two men running the gill net lost their net, three king salmon and were informed that they would be filed upon if running gill nets was subsequently decided by the courts to be illegal. If not, they could pick up their net later at the Eureka fish and game office along with their then frozen salmon. Then Herb surprised me again with his following actions. He decided that he would not file on any of the Indians for striking state officers since all the men had been drinking and not right in their minds to his way of thinking. It was amazing the transformation that took place on that sandbar after Herb told the Yuroks that they were to be treated as honorable men and that we would not be filing charges against any of them for assault and battery against officers of the state.

Damned if the six men didn't stagger to their feet still complaining about the loss of their gill net but then thanked Herb and then me for not filing criminal charges against them. They realized, as did Herb, that their actions had been fueled in part by their previous alcohol consumption and they had not been themselves or thinking properly. As it turned out, all of the men had previous criminal records and none of them wanted to appear again in what they considered an unjust white man's court. Especially in front of Warden Hank Marak's tough little female Justice Court Judge in the nearby Willow Creek Judicial District.

After I had checked their fish camp for any weapons to satisfy my safety concerns, Herb and I were once again on our way. Only that time, our little boat had less than ample floatation based on the load of seized salmon and gill net in which we were now carrying. However, somehow we made it back to our camp, retrieved our remaining gear and then even more gingerly made our way back, in daylight I might add, to our parked Jeep and boat trailer at the launching site. From there, back to Eureka we staggered with our four cylinder Jeep which was fully loaded with two rather large chaps, a crap load of king salmon, two gill nets, all our gear and several seized Winchester rifles.

Back in Eureka, we tagged all our evidence and put the salmon into a commercial locker plant for safe keeping. All the other seized property was deposited into our fish and game office's evidence locker. Then Herb went upstairs and informed the captain with the news relative to our enforcement actions. That was when it really got heated back in the office as Herb told the captain what he could do with any more dangerous Klamath River patrols. After that hollering match, the captain found an excuse to head home. I guess he had more liquid courage in his bottles at home than he did in his office lower desk drawer when it came to facing a very mad Herb Christie over the previous nights' events on the Klamath.

As for Herb and me, we were later required to make one final trip onto the Klamath River at night on a gill netting sweep which was subsequently personally ordered by Captain Gray's superior, Inspector Les Lahr. That trip turned deadly when I had a 30-30 rifle thrust into my stomach by an irate Yurok Indian who got the drop on me. When he did in a high state of emotions, demanded back his grandfather's just seized gill net. My talking the man down from his fury over losing his gill net and Herb holding a bead on the man's head with his service revolver from a few feet away, finally convinced the man to back down and not pull the trigger. There goes that *God loves little children, fools and game wardens* thing once again. (To read that story, you readers will have to read that in my National Outdoor Book Award winning book, now in EBOOK format, titled, *Wildlife Wars* in the chapter titled, I Want My Net Back.) Shortly thereafter, the courts settled the issue of gill netting favorably for the Yurok Indians and any such dangerous boating adventures by game wardens became unnecessary.

Looking back on those adventures now, I just quietly sit in my retirement and shake my head. I doubt if any readers out there have ever boated down a mighty, white water river in the dark of night without using any lights, through deep and dark canyons, without using anything other than a set of oars in a 12-foot wooden rowboat. Well, that, a prayer on your lips and for good measure, having your heart up in your throat. Then doing that on Indian lands where one will more than likely be outnumbered in any confrontation and if seriously injured, because of the area's inaccessibility, guaranteed to die right there on the banks of the river along with the salmon you are trying to protect. That is if you don't drown first as you careen off the river's boulders or smash into the steep canyon walls along the swift moving river and get sucked under in the dark of night. However, the king salmon were in need of protection and Herb and I held full houses in our hands full of life's reality cards when gambling against such dangerous odds. You know folks, God truly does love little children, fools and us goofy damn game wardens.

One needs to remember that when a king salmon or any other kind of fish is caught by a gill net, it will hang there and slowly suffocate to death without making a sound. And if someone isn't out there squalling like a smashed cat trying to put an end to such many times illegal lethality then, to my way of thinking, those not doing their wildlife law enforcement jobs are part of the problem! Hence the need for good wildlife officers who will many times gamble with their lives so that others in the world of wildlife who have little or no voice, may live.

As for the Flowers in this adventure, those Klamath River adventures were the unexpected genesis for a future field of rather large blooms. As a young wildlife officer, I was presented with a real life's challenge relative to the world of wildlife that eventually was burned into my soul and stayed with me throughout my 32 year state and federal law enforcement careers. In those dangerous adventure moments in time, I discovered what was required in all reality of anyone who wore the silver or golden badge and the conservation officer greens. That was, if there was to be anything meaningful left wild for those generations yet to come to experience!

Another Flower in the above adventures was the validation of the presence of my two guardian angels. There was no way I did the things I did and came away without injury or serious bodily harm without someone flying 'top cover' for my miserable carcass! During the whole time, although worried when we hit the rocks and almost swamped several times, I NEVER had any worries about my mortality. I just knew for some reason, there was a plan for me and I needed only to worry about the current events and let the rest slide. That 'validation feeling' has never left me. Nuff said...

As for the Tombstones in this story, they are there. As a result of wayward logging practices along the Pacific salmons' inland spawning waters, illegal commercial fishing practices on the ocean, misuse and over use of gill nets by upstream Indian tribes on spawning streams, drought causing low water levels, upstream obstacles like dams, along with associated illegal sport fishing practices and other poor general fishing practices, the five Pacific salmon species are, as these words are written in 2015, in drastic straights! Their population numbers are drastically reduced and some populations' chances of rebounding are in question. That salmon related history is nothing short of a classic representation of the 'world of wildlife' example of man's inhumanity to man. Some may even call it stupidity! The Tombstone applicable to this situation will probably read, "R.I.P.-The World of Wildlife."

Another Tombstone tied to this life's adventure is that relating to my great partner and mentor, Warden Herb Christie. A few years later, Herb drew a hand of "Aces and Eights" in the card game of life and died from cancer of the colon. When we buried him, he weighed only 95 pounds instead of his normally healthy weight of 250 pounds! Take care of Herb, Lord. For when the critters were dying and the fists were flying, Herb was there in Your stead.

Lord, now that I think about it, those very words would look nice on Herb's *Tombstone.*

THE MARK OF A GREAT WOMAN AND A FUTURE WARRIOR'S FIRST PATROL

Carefully reaching for my .44 magnum pistol in the morning's cool predawn, I clamped my fingers around its wooden grips and slowly withdrew it from its holster lying by my side. Moving the handgun slowly towards the head of my sleeping bag in which I lay, I aimed the end of the big magnum's barrel on the head of about a 450-pound curious black bear standing quietly looking at me from no more than four feet away! For the longest time, the huge bruin appeared to be squinting quizzically through his beady dark eyes at what he was seeing lying on the ground. It was obvious to me he was attempting to process if what he was observing was eatable or not. Not satisfied with what his poor eyesight was telling him, the bear began drawing in and blowing out noisy deep 'snootfulls' of air trying to ascertain the meaning through smell of the thing lying motionless in a sleeping bag just feet from the end of his nose.

"GET!" I yelled, as the front sight of the big magnum now settled down on the center of his massive front chest in case he got too curious. I was really hoping that the huge bruin would not charge once I yelled at him because if he did, he was looking at quickly receiving several hot hand loaded 255 grain Keith-Thompson semi-wadcutter bullets sailing out the end of the gun's barrel around 1,200 feet per second! No two ways about it, at that range, there would be bear steak for supper.

WOOOF, was the animal's explosive reply upon hearing a human's voice as it whirled around and ran crashing off into the forest making noises like a freight train coming off its tracks. Within moments, the crashing sounds became fainter and fainter and then finally quit altogether as the bear moved out of my hearing range. Finding any further sleep on the rocky hard ground onto which I had been sleeping doubtful, I rolled out from my sleeping bag, sat up, pulled on and laced up my Redwing boots to face another day. Since I had slept fully clothed and looked like a ragbag, I figured that was just par for the course I was trying to set. I was dressed up like any other cornball outlaw fisherman found on the Klamath River in that neck of the woods and would easily fit in with many of my soon to be encountered illegal salmon and sturgeon snagging fishermen crowd.

Once again, here I was being the subject of dislike by my fish and game captain. He had assigned me to work illegal salmon and sturgeon 'snaggers' in the remote upper reaches of the Klamath River within his north coast patrol district. I was going to be working covertly and alone as a patrol-roving rookie game warden with the nearest law or backup being just a measly 67 miles away! For you non-law enforcement types, a good supervisor does not normally assign rookies to work undercover details by themselves. That is because of a rookie's lack of proven field experience, sketchy legal knowledge and limited common horse sense while operating under fire as a covert operative. To make a long story short, such lone-wolf rookie assignments can lend themselves to one getting into more trouble than a chap covered with honey and staked out over an aroused mound of red ants in the summer heat in the Arizona desert.

I guess the good captain, who strongly disliked wildlife trained college graduates, figured I would be killed by the resident outlaws, eaten by a bear or drown in the river and be out of his hair and eyesight for the rest of his career. In fact, two senior officers in my fish and game squad, Wardens John Finnigan from Arcata and Hank Marak from Willow Creek, upon learning of my single man covert patrol assignment almost at the end of the earth, just clucked their tongues and shook their heads in disbelief. They too often times, were the objects of Captain Gray's ire and fully understood the sheer folly of cautioning him over making such a stupid rookie assignment. However, that did not deter those two senior officers and close friends from bending my ear on what not to do, what to do and how to do it in order to survive.

Being dumber than a box of river rocks, I actually loved the potential challenges and the intense learning opportunities such an off-the-wall assignment stood to offer a rookie in training. Drawing such an assignment was just the occasion I needed to quickly learn the tips of the trade as a wildlife officer. As a point of fact, I later came to understand and appreciate that Captain Gray did me a favor in handing me such assignments. I found that I learned more in six months than most regularly assigned rookie officers would learn in six years by being assigned and working in such wildlife law enforcement crucibles. As far as I was concerned, I was quickly discovering that hunting my fellow man doing to Mother Nature what they shouldn't be doing, was just my cup of tea. Additionally, I had learned early on in my career that I had two guardian angels assigned to me by the "Chief Game Warden in the Sky" for some reason known only to Him, so I did not worry. The bottom line, man has to cross the creek if he plans on getting his feet wet...

The location into which I had been assigned, namely the wilds around the small outback town of Orleans, was historically a hotbed for illegal wildlife taking activity. A hot bed of lawlessness in the world of wildlife because there was, figuratively speaking, 'no law west of the Pecos' in such a remote and untamed area. That lawlessness went double along that portion of the Klamath River when numerous salmon and two species of sturgeon annually migrated within and the nearest regularly assigned game warden resided 67 miles away. Lastly, the region was frequented by lumbermen, out of work loggers, local Indians from two tribes, numerous run of the mill fishermen and hunters, and U.S. Forest Service wildlife outlaws who were stationed in the Orleans Forest Service District.

Rolling up my sleeping bag, I headed for my truck and placed it inside the cab for safekeeping. I was using my

I figured I could physically put the snatch on both men and the illegally snagged evidence fish all in one giant swoop. Ah, it sure is nice being a dumb as a stick rookie, thinking I had my outlaws in the bag.

Walking up behind my now fully engaged chaps, I made sure I was in a position to grab one or both of the men if they decided to run once I identified myself. Running was a trait commonly found among many river outlaws because of the heavy fines associated with such illegal snagging activities. Finally, my snagger beached his king salmon, one weighing about 25 pounds. There in front of God and everybody was his set of monster sized treble hooks imbedded deeply into the fish's back just behind the dorsal fin and above the fish's backbone.

Grabbing my point and shoot camera from the game bag in my hunting jacket (the loose fitting jacket also hid my pistol in its shoulder holster), I quickly took a picture of the man landing a clearly foul-hooked salmon from just a few feet away. I also did so from behind the men as they looked the other way, while totally involved in landing their fish. After taking my evidence pictures, I quickly slipped my camera back into the game bag. Then I stepped in just before the man's partner tried to gaff the foul hooked salmon. As I did, I made sure both men clearly understood that I was a game warden. Following my words of identification, I advised them that they were both in violation of the fish and game laws and NOT to gaff that female king salmon! (To my inexperienced but alert readers, one can tell the sex of salmon up on the spawning grounds by the shape of their heads. For my readers' edification, the female salmon has a normal fish-like looking, sloped head shape and the males will usually have a larger hooked lower jaw. The hooked lower jaw on the males is used to repel other males away from the females or to fight off any kind of egg eating predacious fish once they are on the spawning grounds and have established a 'Redd' or spawning site.)

When those words of identification and instruction left my mouth, you never saw two lads hunch up like a watermelon just struck by a speeding bullet. It was obvious from their surprised actions that they had no clue the law was in country. Leaving the fish in the water to revive after its struggle in fighting against the rod and reel, I identified myself again with my badge, had the men sit down, then requested and collected their driver's licenses. Seeing that the salmon was now recovering from its earlier exertions in fighting the hook and line, I had the other man, the one who had not landed the salmon, carefully unhook and release the snagged fish back into the river. When he did, I took his picture doing so with my camera. (To my inexperienced readers, females of the fast disappearing five Pacific species of salmon are extremely valuable genetically to the overall health of the population as a whole. Therefore, I did not allow it to be gaffed or killed but just released back to the wild so it could procreate.) Knowing the court in which my two chaps would appear, I knew that a picture of the illegal event and my testimony would suffice as the best evidence as opposed to destroying the fish and using its body as an evidentiary item later on in a court of law.

Then the three of us gathered up our gear and walked back to where their vehicle was parked up on the main road. (Remember, I had hidden my vehicle earlier up the road on an old logging spur so they wouldn't know what to look for in the way of the undercover game warden's vehicle. That way they wouldn't be able to announce to the rest of the local outlaw world what my vehicle looked like so if other outlaws ever saw it, they could shy away from any illegality.) Shortly thereafter, my chaps were cited for snagging and the use of illegal terminal gear. Following the issuance of the men's citations, their fishing rods and their illegal terminal gear was seized and held as evidence for later confiscation by the court. Following those actions, the two men left. Waiting to make sure they had left the area for good so they wouldn't warn other fishermen along the upper reaches of the river about my presence or vehicle type, I returned to my truck.

After another Coke, I drove further up the road along the Klamath to another spot holding two vehicles and four what appeared to be Indian fishermen down on a sandbar. My initial judgment was that at least two of the men were attempting to snag a salmon or sturgeon. Hiding my vehicle off the road by a broken down Mack logging truck, I walked back to the area of my four fishermen on the road above the sandbar.

Walking down off the road and over the steep riverbank, I stumbled my way down the rocky footpath to the river below acting like any other fisherman. As I did, I could see the four men watching me very carefully out of the corners of their eyes. Careful not to crowd them where they were fishing, I knelt down a number of yards away from their fishing spot and began rigging up my fishing rod just like any other hopeful fisherman on the river. As I did, I could see that the four men had quit their previous snagging activity and were quietly watching me out of the corners of their eyes as they made work by fussing around with their terminal gear. That effort gave them 'top cover' so they could watch me more closely for any signs of being the law. A few minutes later as I continued rigging up, they appeared to be even more than suspicious of my presence.

It was then, that my Indian lads had quit fishing altogether and were huddled into a loose group deep in quiet discussion over my recent arrival. I could see that they were watching me closely as I started rigging up my own obvious snagging gear. Yes, my readers, I was rigging up obvious snagging gear in which to use as my cover so I would look just like one of the boys. Finally, one of the men detached himself from the group and walked over towards me as the other three men from his party continued messing around with their tackle boxes as if waiting for that member of their party to check me out and then return with what he had learned.

"Got any smokes?" asked an obvious looking Hoopa or Yurok Indian as he approached me where I was kneeling in the sand still in the act of rigging up my fishing tackle. As he did, I saw his eyes dart to the illegal set of huge treble hooks I was attaching to my line and then quickly look back at me like nothing out of the ordinary had just occurred. It was at that moment that I could detect the heavy odor of whiskey on the man's breath. He was also a tad ungainly in his gait and step. In fact, my visitor kind of walked lock-legged like my good captain frequently did in and around the fish and game office when he was into his 'cups.'

"Sure do," I responded to his question about having any smokes. Standing up, I reached into my shirt pocket and took out a five pack of Toscanni cigars. Now to those of you non-smokers out there and those who do but are not aware of that brand of little Italian cigar, LOOK OUT! They look like twisted dog droppings, have a great tobacco smell and possess an unusually potent flavor. When smoked, they have the nicotine kick of an angry Army mule with a short fuse once that chemical dumps into one's blood stream. Opening up the pack, I offered the little man one of those Italian bombshells.

Folks, let me tell you, they taste just like they look. The smoke from one of those little devils can kill mosquitoes deader than a hammer at twenty feet! But, I love them to this day and have two packs of them at my left hand as I write these words some 50 plus years after that event. Those cigars lying close at hand, were given to me by my friend Patrick Bosco, a retired special agent from the U.S. Fish and Wildlife Service, who, like me, loves the damn things.

Reaching out, the man took one, looked closely at the cigar and asked, 'What the hell are these ugly damn things?'

"Those are my favorite brand of cigar. Go ahead and smoke it. Just make sure you are a smoker and used to a nicotine rush when you smoke it," I casually replied like the good Samaritan that I was--- said the 'spider to the fly'....

"Hell, these cigars look like dog turds," he replied as he eyed my offering. "But, I can handle anything that any white man can throw at me," he bragged as he unwrapped my offering and then bummed a light. After lighting up his cigar, he drew deeply and then casually asked, "Goin' fishin'?"

"No, not really," I replied. "The man back at the store in Orleans told me about this snagging thing and I aim to learn. Especially since these treble hooks he sold me are so damn expensive. I would like to be able to snag a sturgeon or a salmon to help pay for what they cost me, plus, have some meat for my freezer."

"Well, if you watch me and my boys, we will show you how it is done. Just remember, if you get a fish on be sure and yell 'fish on'. That way, the rest of us can get our gear out from the water before your fish tangles us all up," he advised. "Oh, if you see anyone who looks like a game warden, stop what you are doing if you are snagging because if they catch you, the fine is pretty damn steep," he continued. With that, off he staggered puffing on my little killer cigar and in the process yelled to his pals, "Go ahead and fish, boys. This guy is as 'right as rain'." *Yeah, I am as 'right as rain,'* I thought with a smile. *Just like the downpour of rain found in a typhoon in the Pacific...*

Within moments, my four chaps were once again snagging for any kind of fish like their lives depended on it. Making sure I observed every man going through their illegal snagging actions at least twice so I could more than satisfy the elements of the crime of illegal snagging, I then stood up and headed back up to the road like I had forgotten something. In so doing, I left my fishing rod and tackle box sitting out in the open on the sandbar indicating that I would return shortly. That gear left behind was my decoy in order to hold my lads on the sandbar in a stand like a buffalo hunter of old would do in a shoot.

The four men did not give me a second glance when I left the area and just kept on with their snagging activities. Once up on the road, I took out my camera and, when the men weren't looking my way, snapped their pictures which would show that all four men were fishing on that day. Then taking out my notebook, I recorded the times I had observed each man's earlier illegal snagging actions. Grabbing another Coke out from my ice chest, I walked back down to my spot on the river and made sure the men saw me drinking the beverage. That way I figured they would assume I had just gone back to my vehicle for a drink and as a result, they would not be suspicious of my brief absence.

Having seen enough illegal activity and not wanting them to foul-hook a fish and lessen its chances of survival, I figured it was time to spring my trap. Setting down my Coke, I casually walked over to my four chaps as they continued concentrating on their snagging activities. They hardly gave me a second look they were so engrossed in what they were doing. Then I quietly positioned myself in such a manner so I could stop any runners of the bunch once I had identified myself. How was that for rookie thinking? One against four, how was that for actual common sense reality in the world of a game warden? No wonder game wardens in real life can be so short lived...

It was then that I noticed a fly in the ointment. Stuck in the sand between the four men, was a quart bottle of Jim Beam whiskey and it was only half full. That could mean trouble if the men, fortified with whiskey and false courage, decided to take me on once my real identity was out in the open. I also noticed my chap who had bummed a cigar from me earlier, was now having trouble standing or talking. Turning to me he said, "What the hell is in this cigar? Damn, my head is swimming and I now feel sick." Those words had barely left his lips when he bent over and puked up a bucketful of slop all over his feet and the sandbar. When he did, his other three friends jumped away from the now obviously very sick man and began laughing at his misery, antics, and discomfort. However, that didn't slow down my chap one bit. My 'cigar man' kept puking until all he could do was dry heave. Leaving his fishing pole at the edge of the water, he staggered off a few feet, fell down onto the sandbar and lay still. It appeared my chap, between the Jim Beam and my little strong killer cigar, had just passed out. Well, that was OK with me. That only left three men snagging fish for me to handle instead of four in case they got angry and decided to get physical with an obvious white man in the process of causing them all kinds of grief soon to come to a head in a court of law.

"Gentlemen," I said. With that statement, the three men turned and faced me. When they did, I was holding up my fish and game badge in my left hand so my gun hand would be free and then said, "State fish and game warden. You men are going to be issued a citation for illegally snagging and the use of illegal terminal gear. Your fishing gear will be seized and now, if you would please, reel up your lines, put your poles down, hand me your driver's licenses or tribal identification cards and sit down."

When those words left my lips, my three men exploded! The basic gist of their fury was that they were Indians and exempt from the white man's regulations on or off the Hoopa Indian Reservation. Plus, I could tell that Jim Beam was now the fourth man standing. After a considerable amount of time discussing their legal problems and my right to be there, they finally proffered their driver's licenses. Keeping a wary eye on the still 'bad mouthing me' chaps, I removed my cite book from the game bag in my hunting jacket and began writing up citations on each man for snagging and the use of illegal terminal gear. The grumbling and calling me every name in the book continued as I finally filled out the seizure tags for their fishing gear soon to be seized. Then all of a sudden, the three men got as quiet as a bunch of mice pissin' on a ball of cotton.

What the hell, I thought. *Why did they get so quiet all of a sudden?* Well, that answer was forthcoming in short order. Talk about a rookie mistake soon to be made there out on the sandbar that fine day. As I was later to learn in my dealing with the Indians of that area, when they were 'grousing' at you, everything was OK. But when they got quiet, LOOK OUT! That meant something serious was 'in the wind and about to happen'.

I had been facing my three chaps all the time and had ignored my passed out chap who was lying down behind me. Realizing something was bad wrong with my now three quiet Indians to my front, I chanced a quick look behind me at my passed out chap to see if he was in more distress. WHAM! Upon turning around, I was struck just below my right eye by my now somewhat revived but still tottering drunken chap. Then he grabbed my shirt as he fell forward and tore off a button as he tried to clumsily wrestle me to the ground. The only person to quickly hit the ground was my ex-cigar smoking, Jim Beam drinking chap! That was when the sandman showed up and my 'swinger' went to sleep.

When my chap hit the ground after I had decked him, my three lads began grumbling at me again. Man, did I ever learn a second valuable lesson that day. Never turn your back on anyone in any enforcement situation. What you can't see will get you killed or injured sooner or later. Thankfully, my drunken fist swinging chap was so screwed up that when he hit me, it didn't have the hoped for effect. It stung but I would live to fight another day. As for my fist-swinger, he had one hell of a closing eye that was getting worse to look at as he now slept quietly on the sandbar alongside the river.

Once chap number four finally joined the living later on, he too was issued citations for snagging and use of illegal terminal gear as well. Then I did what Herb would have done. I advised my three lads that I would not be filing assault and battery charges on their friend because he had been drinking and the booze was causing him to think evilly. However, they were told to let the rest of their community know that to pull any such crap in the future on the big game warden, would only get them the same sound thrashing as had occurred to their friend.

Finished with the lecture and business at hand, I gathered up all their fishing gear, reclaimed my fishing equipment and headed for the road. Getting into my truck, I hurriedly left the scene before the three men could gather up their still sick chap and drag him up to their vehicles. That I did so they would not see what kind of a vehicle the game warden was driving and put out the word on the outlaw trail the type of vehicle they should be on the lookout for in the future.

Realizing I had put a dent into the illegal snagging activities, especially once the word got out about the big game warden being on the river and not wanting to be recognized from the type of vehicle I was driving, I left the area. That way the wildlife outlaws who would now be on the lookout for me would not find me. By leaving that location and making no further contacts that day, that would allow their 'game warden's nearby' concerns to cool off. Following that, I would come roaring back into the area at a later date and grab off another fresh batch of outlaws. Who says a rookie can't rapidly learn his own wildlife law enforcement tricks of the trade as he lumbered along learning the ropes?

Well, I might be able to learn new tricks of the trade when afield but I did not prepare for the one I should have known about when on the home front with the 'love of my life.' Arriving back in Eureka later that day, I unloaded all my seized evidence in the fish and game office's evidence locker, advised the good captain of my successes and headed for my home. Arriving a short time later, I removed my law enforcement gear from my truck and headed into the house. Walking through the front door of my home, I was met by my wife. I got a happy glad you are home hug and a kiss quickly followed by what everyone else in my family has since come to call getting the 'evil eye'.

"What happened to your right cheek below your eye and the button on your shirt?" asked Donna, my wife and the 'Light in my Life' of a few short years at that time in our marriage. Today, some 53 years of marriage later, that "Light" has grown even brighter…

Catching me off guard since I had long since forgotten about being smacked by a drunken Indian, I stammered a bit and then caught myself upright and proper like. "I was chasing a violator through some timber and ran into a low hanging tree limb," I lamely replied. (Author's note: I have since learned I can only successfully lie to my wife on her birthday and Christmas. Then only about what she is getting for presents on those special days. Other than that, I am a sitting duck when it comes to pulling the wool over her eyes.)

For the longest moment, her beautiful blue eyes searched mine for the truth in my answer. Finding none to her way of thinking, she turned saying, "Get washed up. Dinner will be ready shortly and I have baked a fresh blackberry pie for our dessert."

Since she said no more about my bruised cheek and the torn shirt, I figured my little white lie had saved the day. Saved the day because Donna always worried about her fella and the sometime dangerous profession he reveled in. And as such, I tried not to bring home the more lurid details of my profession which would have only worried her further.

Dinner that evening, as always, was a repast fit for a king. Then that meal was followed with a freshly baked, homemade blackberry pie! Man, let me tell all you readers out there, my wife Donna makes the best pies in the world! And what makes them so wonderful are her piecrusts. Donna's homemade piecrusts are so light and fluffy, that when one goes to eat them, they are to die for. In fact, her homemade pies are so good, even God comes down once in a while for a slice… However, being the budding criminal investigator I was fast becoming, I could tell something heavy was still hanging in the air around the dinner table that evening and I just couldn't quite put my finger on it. That was not until the next morning…

The next morning as I loaded my law enforcement gear into my marked patrol car for a 'captain' required overt trip back into the Orleans area, I got surprised. I had just loaded my sleeping bag into the trunk of my patrol car and upon turning around, saw my wife standing on the front step of our home. She was dressed in a roomy sweatshirt, was wearing a set of blue jeans, had her beautiful reddish blond hair all tucked up inside of one of my old cowboy hats so she looked kind of like a man, and WAS CARRYING MY 30 M-1 CARBINE WITH A 30 ROUND, FULLY LOADED BANANA CLIP ATTACHED!

"What the hell do you think you are doing?" I asked in amazement.

"I am going with you," Donna flatly stated.

"Oh, no you aren't!" I said. There was no way I was going to chance taking my wife of a few short years and the love of my life into a hell hole known for its historic violence against peace officers, especially lone game wardens. That area was crawling with mean as a snake Indians, bull headed loggers who usually were as mean as a stepped on owl, out of work grumpy lumbermen, and every other illegal river rat and wildlife outlaw ridge runner known to man. Plus where I was going, there was no radio contact because the country was so ruggedly wild and remote. Additionally, there was no other type of law-dog backup within an hour's high-speed run. In short, that was not a place for someone who was as gentle and as important to me as was my wife.

"Oh, yes I am," she stoutly maintained as she stepped off the porch and made for the front seat of my patrol car. Then she stopped. "If we are going to sleep out in the woods, you need to go and get my sleeping bag," she flatly announced. With those words, she walked over and sat down in the front seat of my patrol car like she owned it and woe be it to anyone who tried to remove her from it or try and change her mind.

By now, I was a flustered as a Rhode Island Red chicken that had just spotted a red-tailed hawk high overhead looking for a chicken dinner. "Honey," I said, "it is just too dangerous for you to go along on this trip. Maybe the next time on a different kind of patrol I can take you along with me." (Author's Note: In those days in California, fish and game officers could take along their wives if the detail wasn't dangerous.)

"I don't care. I am going and that is that," she said as she nestled down into the front passenger seat in my patrol car, somewhat like an abalone stuck tightly to a rock during low tide. Now to all my readers out there who do not know Donna, she can be Norwegian-stubborn at times and this was one of those times.

Later that morning, found Donna and me quietly driving through the town of Orleans and up along the upper reaches of the Klamath River. As I slowly patrolled along the Klamath River, I spotted two chaps who were going through the familiar motions of snagging off in the distance. I quietly stopped the patrol car out of sight and took off down the riverbank to catch and cite my two violators. When I did, I left my wife guarding my patrol car with the carbine while I attended to the fish and game business at hand on the river. (Author's note: Just for my readers' information, occasionally when some of we game warden types worked that area in a marked patrol car, it was not unusual to return to find the tires slashed or the windows or headlights broken out of the vehicle. Hence, my wife, dressed up like a man, stood guard by the vehicle and made sure none of that kind of crap happened. She was a crack rifle shot but, knowing her and her gentle side, she had to be scared beyond all get out the whole time she stood out there all alone.)

I apprehended my two snaggers, wrote them up, seized all their fishing gear and then Donna and I disappeared like a downy duck feather in a high prairie wind into the wilds of the Klamath National Forest. I did this not because I was afraid but had discovered overt hit and run tactics worked well in many outback communities of wildlife outlaws and this was a good one in which to start. Besides, it was starting to get dark and I still had another trick up my sleeve that needed executing.

Back to my little hidden camping spot where I had the earlier run in with the big black bear we went. Then Donna and I feasted on a cold Coke, a chunk of Italian salami and eventually went to bed on the rocky hard ground in our sleeping bags. That was some night for my gentle wife. We had deer moving through our sleeping area at all hours of the night, which kept a very nervous Donna awake because of never being exposed to such elements in such a 'rough as a cob' style before. As frosting on this outdoor 'adventure' we had a striped skunk amble right between the two of us as we lay in our sleeping bags, which got her attention in 'spades'. I doubt that my wife got an ounce of sleep with all of Mother Nature's interruptions that night. The next morning before daylight, we were up and had my typical game warden breakfast of Coke and salami. Then out from my hiding place and back to the Klamath River we went again to see whose day I could ruin as I provided 'top cover' for my migrating salmon and sturgeon.

That day I had plenty of business. I ended up apprehending eight different folks snagging salmon and sturgeon, one out of work logger closed season shooting blue grouse from out of the window of his motor home, and another lad for poaching a deer not 100 yards from where I stood writing tickets to a sturgeon snagger. All throughout, my faithful, scared all to hell little wife persevered and guarded my patrol car. No busted windows or slashed tires on that trip. AND, DONNA DID ALL THAT WHEN SHE WAS 8 MONTHS PREGNANT WITH WHAT WAS TO BE OUR FIRST BORN SON! I would have to say that was the mark of a very loving and great woman. One that I am still married to some 52 years later as these words are written in 2015. By the way, little did he know it but that was my older son Richard's FIRST law enforcement patrol!

Today our son is in the prime of his manhood, stands 6-foot, 7-inches tall and weighs in at a rock solid 275 pounds. As a Flower in this adventure, Rich is currently the Resident Agent in Charge for the U.S. Fish and Wildlife Service over the States of North and South Dakota. As such, Richard himself has created many Tombstones for those who choose to smuggle wildlife, those involved as illegal commercial market hunters, those who commercialize in the illegal sale of wildlife parts and products, those taking endangered species, and those illegally hunting in the national parks or throughout his two states' region of responsibility. In providing such protections, he has created many Flowers in the world of wildlife for those folks yet to come to enjoy.

(Author's note: In fact, Richard, like his dad and younger brother Chris, is an accomplished author. Just recently he and his sidekick, Patrick Bosco, have had a generously illustrated field guide published that will be used by waterfowl hunters nationwide for quick and accurate identification of the ducks, geese and swans of North America. It is the type of field guide easily carried by waterfowl hunters in all kinds of weather and its treated and waterproof pages, no matter the abuse suffered afield, will not be ruined. It's titled, "North American Waterfowl Identification Guide" and is a book for all seasons for waterfowl hunters of all time. Richard and Pat have created a Flower for those waterfowl hunters present and future to enjoy the sport of waterfowl hunting by being able to quickly identify any bird in the air or in the hand. There certainly is no Tombstone in the world of wildlife for that classic bit of handy work! Another Flower is what happens to all the proceeds accrued from the sales of the above book. Those proceeds will all go into the procurement of lands favorable to the overall health of North America's waterfowl populations. That is a classy Flower!)

As for me, another Flower from this adventure was that I continued living and learning the trade of my profession. I learned that when Indians are confronted with a law enforcement situation and are growling away, things are more than likely OK. However, if they grow silent, that probably means that trouble is blowing in the wind and one had better not be a kite.

An additional Flower from this adventure was that Donna, my wife, got a firsthand taste of what many wildlife officers frequently endure. That one trip quickly toughened up a gentle woman, giving her an everlasting and first hand perspective that has served her well in enduring her husband's career at both the state and federal levels. And, we both are still happily married...

Finally, the last Flower garnered from this adventure is this. For all my budding game warden wannabe's out there, let this be a sterling lesson to all of you. If you want to succeed in the world of wildlife as a wildlife officer and perform at your highest levels, **MARRY WELL.** For if you don't, you will not be able to function at the needed 110% level required to avoid injury, death, alcoholism, or divorce, which will follow you and yours as sure as does the darkness of night. Then, THAT will be YOUR Tombstone...

KLAMATH RIVER POTLUCK

Flowers and Tombstones

Pulling into the little store in Orleans during one of my undercover assignments, I unlimbered my tired frame and entered. Just as I did, coming out the front door was the store's owner carrying a 12 gage shotgun and a box of shells. Since I had shopped there several times previously for supplies and illegal snagging gear in my undercover capacity, he casually knew me as a friendly fisherman and a sturgeon snagger.

"Morning, Terry. Whatever you need my wife will give you a hand in finding what you need in the way of supplies. As for me, I hear tell that the band-tailed pigeons are back in the trees where the construction crews are building our new bridge over the Klamath. Since they are there, I can think of no better time than trying my luck with my new shotgun and see if I can't bag a few band-tails for our supper this evening," happily chattered the store owner over the surprise arrival of the great eating wild pigeons in his neck of the woods.

"I didn't know that pigeon season was open," I replied somewhat off-handedly, damn well knowing that pigeon season was not open!

"It ain't. But being that I haven't seen 'hide nor hair' of the local game warden in this area for weeks or hearing of the one working the Klamath undercover for salmon and sturgeon snaggers, I aim to take advantage of having a pigeon shoot without anyone else around to bother me and make it harder to get a bird," he replied. With that and a big grin, out the door he went, loaded up into his old red military jeep and away he drove.

Watching him head out for a moment, I saw which direction he was heading and made a mental note of that. Since this was hopefully my last assigned trip into the Orleans area working covertly, I had planned on grabbing off every outlaw I could before the word got out that a game warden was once again back in country. *Catching the mouthy, illegal fishing equipment selling storeowner taking band-tailed pigeons during the closed season would be a good way to start my patrol,* I thought with a grin. If I was able to catch him, he would have a tale of woe for everyone who would stand still and listen when they came into his store. By telling that story of apprehension numerous times, that, my dear readers, is what one would call a force multiplier. I could just imagine before his story was in its final version, there would be a force of twenty armed men in green running and gunning down the intrepid storekeeper. With another grin, I entered the store, purchased a six-pack of Coke and headed out and down the road in the same direction I had last seen my storeowner heading. Since I was driving my own 1964 Jeep pickup, hardly anyone even gave me a second glance. BIG MISTAKE!

Driving alongside the Klamath River that morning, I checked out several of the most frequented sturgeon fishing and snagging spots. Every likely pull off along the road that day had a vehicle or two parked in it with a fisherman fishing on the river below. Looking down at the river, I could see fishermen at many of those historic fishing and snagging areas. I just figured as I went along looking for outlaw snaggers, that I would also keep my eyes open for my storekeeper, who was last seen heading for a band-tail hunting spot along the river. Depending on any illegal fish and game action encountered, I would go for it and hit the area hard overtly exposing my official presence since this was my last covert assignment in the area. After that, it wouldn't make any difference if the outlaw breed knew if I was in country or not. They would all 'pinch' just the same. Keep in mind, my readers, one can only work covertly just so long before the identity cat is out of the bag. And being larger than most humans, it didn't take long for the word to get out to be on the lookout for the big game warden dressed like every other fisherman. So come 'hell or high water,' today would be the day of reckoning for those choosing to walk on the dark side in the world of wildlife.

For about an hour, I randomly explored the best fishing areas trying to determine where I would start my day and make my official presence known. However, that morning every fisherman I examined through my binoculars seemed to be keeping it on the straight and narrow when it came to obeying the fish and game laws. In short, there was nary a salmon or sturgeon snagger in sight.

Then lo and behold, around the corner on my logging road came a familiar red military Jeep driven by my suspect storekeeper. He was slowly driving down the middle of the road and looking skyward into the trees for resting flocks of band-tailed pigeons. For the longest moment, our two vehicles glided toward each other as the storekeeper kept his eyes skyward looking for unwary pigeons to shoot. Then he realized another vehicle was on the same road and he quickly pulled over so I could pass. Driving up alongside the man, I stopped and said, "How's the pigeon hunt going, Chief?"

"Not too bad. I got three of them pigeons. A couple more and 'Ma' and me will have a fine supper with some left over for tomorrow's lunch," he proudly proclaimed in his Arkansas drawl.

Looking over into his open Jeep, I could see three freshly killed pigeons lying on his passenger side floorboard. Figuring this was as good a time as any to officially make known my 'law dog' presence, I stepped out from my pickup, took out my badge and identified myself. Man, you talk about a surprised storekeeper upon seeing the 'silver star' of my office. Putting my badge back into my shirt pocket, I said, "Hand me your shotgun." For the longest moment, the storekeeper just sat there in his open Jeep in shock over what was happening to him. Then he obliged by handing me his new shotgun which was laying alongside his seat for quick retrieval in case he was able to shoot an unsuspecting pigeon off the branches in a tree while seated in his open Jeep. Jacking open the action of his pump shotgun, I could see he had a live shell in its chamber! In those days in California, it was illegal to have a live round in a rifle or shotgun's chamber and have the firearm in a motor vehicle on a way open to the public. Inwardly grinning over the additional loaded gun violation, I laid his shotgun over the hood of my Jeep for safekeeping. Then I requested the three dead pigeons from his floorboards and he obliged. Shortly thereafter, my storekeeper went down the road with two citations for being in possession of closed season band-tailed pigeons and a loaded gun violation. He also went down the road 'kicking rocks' without his new shotgun since it had been seized as evidence. Weeks later, his settlement with the court came to $250.00 and forfeiture of his brand new, thrice fired shotgun to the State of California to be eventually sold at auction.

Knowing the storekeeper would now be spreading the word about the big game warden in the tan Jeep pickup, I split that immediate area and headed off for another more remote part of the country along the Klamath River. I figured by running off to a different and remote corner of the area, that I could grab off another unsuspecting outlaw or two before they were warned of my presence in that area. Man, was that bit of forward thinking right on the money.

Rounding a turn in the river from up on high on my logging road, I observed two chaps below me at the water's edge. One had a fishing pole in his hands and appeared to be fighting a rather large fish. The other man with him was firmly holding his hands around his partner's waist as if helping to keep him from being dragged off their sandbar and into the river by such a large fish. Quickly pulling off to the side of the road, I grabbed my binoculars and trotted back to where I had first observed my fishermen. Sitting down behind a large Douglas fir tree below the edge of the road so I would not be seen by passing vehicles, I glassed my two suspect fishermen. Sure as God made crickets good German brown trout fishing bait, the

61

lad fighting the fish appeared to have a sturgeon on the other end of his line. My fisherman had about a four foot, heavy duty fishing rod and the reel appeared to be in the Penn 9/0 range. That kind of fishing tackle was typical sturgeon snagging gear for the area used by many other river outlaws. Looking even more closely, I could see his fishing line glistening in the sunlight and it appeared to be very heavy monofilament, maybe in the 80 to 100 pound test class. All those factors, plus the fact that he was slowly being pulled off the sandbar by a yet to be seen large fish, told me that I possibly had a sturgeon fishermen in my field of view.

THEN IT HAPPENED! I observed a huge sturgeon, more than likely a white sturgeon in the 700-800 pound class, broach sideways in the river and create such a drag that it pulled my two fishermen off their sandbar and dangerously up to their waists in the river! The man holding the fishing rod took the cigar he had been smoking out from his mouth and touched its lit end to the monofilament line holding the great fish. PING! went the heavy line as it separated making the sound of a rifle shot and the two fishermen fell over backwards into the water at the edge of their sandbar.

With that, the great fish was gone! However, one thing had not gone unnoticed by the pair of watching eyes from high up on the edge of the logging road. When the great fish had broached, I observed through my binoculars the fishing line holding him snap up out from the water and could plainly see it leading to a set of massive snag hooks firmly imbedded into the sturgeon's heavily scaled back! That sturgeon was clearly snagged and, with those thoughts streaming across my mind, I left my place of hiding and sprinted back to my Jeep. Moments later, I had it pulled off the road and partially hidden in a large copse of Douglas and white fir trees surrounded by a dense growth of sword ferns.

Running back to my hiding spot above the river, I sat down out of sight and began glassing my two chaps along the river once again. They were laughing about being all wet and now were opening and drinking cans of Lucky Lager beer. I could see the men were rigging up the fishing pole on which they had just cut the line with the lit cigar as if preparing for another go at snagging. Soon both men were whipping their fishing rods in the typical jerking motion known to me as snagging. Every time they retrieved their terminal gear from the river at the end of each snagging attempt, I could plainly see they were using excessive weights and larger in size treble hooks than authorized by California's Title 14 fishing regulations. Taking out my notebook, I began recording the men's fishing violations. Then, I got a couple of bonuses. As the men finished drinking their beers, they tossed their empty beer cans out into the river. When they did, they violated Fish and Game Code, Section 5652, which prohibited depositing litter within 100 feet of the high water mark in inland waters.

What was quickly becoming the Klamath River Potluck of bonus cases, continued unabated. One of the men walked over to a small inlet of water jutting into the sandbar onto which they occupied and took two more beers out from the water where they had been cooling. When he did, I saw the movement of a large tail break the water's surface in that small shallow inlet. Really scrooching into my binoculars now and looking at the place where I had just seen the tail movement, I got another surprise. Lying there in the shallow water of the inlet were two small sturgeon! I noticed where my snaggers had driven a stake into the sandbar at the edge of the inlet with a rope leading from it and into the water. It now became apparent that my chaps had caught the two smaller sturgeon earlier in the day and were keeping them alive and fresh in the small inlet or water running into their sandbar.

Realizing I had enough evidence on my two chaps of their 'wrong doing' and not wanting them to injure any more fish, I began figuring out how I was going to get down to where they were snagging without being seen. Because true to the code of the outlaw trail and their bag of tricks, once they saw me heading towards them they would try to get rid of their soon to be evidence short sturgeon. Since the best evidence in a court of law is the real or actual evidence, I needed to be sneaky and be upon them before they could chuck my needed courtroom evidence. Scouting out my options, I discovered a way in which I could surreptitiously crawl down the bank by some brush and boulders and then with a short sprint when they were looking the other way, I, like the R.C.M.P., would have my two men.

Well, as was usual in the world of wildlife law enforcement, fate found a chink in my armor. Getting half way down in my sneak towards my two chaps, I came upon a dense stand of poison oak brush that I had not seen earlier! That was all I needed being heavily allergic to the damn stuff and all. However, I was far enough along in my approach that I couldn't go back without possibly alerting my chaps as to my presence. And I damn sure was not letting these chaps go without receiving a citation for their list of violations. I did the best I could under the circumstances by sneaking through the poisonous mess and hoped for the best. As a result of my poor sneaking ability through the poison oak, I was later to discover, my sneak-plan through the poison oak did not work for sour owl droppings. I came down with a screaming case of poison oak as did my poor little wife when she later washed my clothing. I guess catching those two men and going through what I did had to be like taking one for the "Gipper."

Then the "Game Warden God" smiled upon me. Somewhat later one of my lads snagged another large sturgeon and before long, both men were working together battling another river monster. That was my cue. With both men distracted with their large fish and the one hanging onto the other by his waist so the man with the rod could not be pulled into the Klamath, I emerged out from my place of hiding and trotted across the sandbar towards the two fish-fighting men. Once in position where I could control the situation and make sure they didn't toss any evidence back into the river, I knelt down in plain sight on their sandbar behind them and quietly waited.

As it turned out, the men had another river giant on the end of their line and soon both chaps were dragged off the sandbar and into the river up to their waists. Like before, the cigar had to be applied to the heavy monofilament fishing line to separate it from the fish so that the men would not be dragged out any deeper into the swiftly flowing river. As the men emerged from the river laughing and swearing all at the same time, they both looked right at me kneeling on the sandbar a few scant yards distant and did not see me. A situation that is typical many times when the wildlife outlaws are not expecting you and many times will not register seeing you right away even though they are looking right at you. However several steps later as they continued walking back towards me, talking all the way, the light finally shone on the 'manure pile behind the barn.'

"Who the hell are you?" shouted the one who had just lost the fish as he jumped back in amazement over finally seeing me kneeling there nearby on their sandbar.

"State fish and game warden," I quietly replied as I rose up and parted my hunting jacket so the men could see the silver star of my office on the left breast of my uniform shirt.

Then the sandbar blew up! The chap who had just lost the fish whipped around and sprinted for the edge of the river. Thinking he was going to throw his fishing pole into the fast moving river, I took off after him like a bat out of hell. Boy, did I ever get surprised. My lad with the fish pole ran right into the fast moving river full bore and began swimming for all he was worth for the far bank, fishing pole and all! Sliding to a stop at the river's edge, I just watched my outlaw desperately battling the swift current of the river and getting violently swept downstream towards a mess of dangerous looking boulder strewn riffles. Then moments later, into the riffles he was quickly swept and now found himself swimming for his life. In a moment of dangerous swiftly moving current and on rushing boulders, my chap dropped his fishing pole into the fast moving waters to be lost forever. Since I wasn't going to take a stupid chance like that in the river, I tried running downstream on the bank as far as I could while keeping my swimmer in view. That I did, figuring my swimmer would soon come to shore downstream on my side of the river and I would have him cold for illegally snagging sturgeon.

Forty yards downstream, I was brought up shortly by a monster rocky outcropping jutting far out into the river and had to stop my chase. I finally saw my swimmer make it out from the river onto the far side, crawl up the bank, and then hobble off into the dense timber of the Marble Mountain Wilderness Area with an obviously injured right leg. That was an area of no roads and one in which my chap was going to have to later swim the river once again to get to the side he had previously occupied so he could walk back to the town of Orleans and civilization with his badly injured leg. I never saw that lad again. I could only just imagine what had caused him to do such a dangerous thing as swimming that river, but out of desperation, he sure as hell did and without a second's worth of hesitation.

Realizing I still had another chap behind me on my side of the river, I turned just in time to see my man sprinting for the safety of the hillside leading back up to the road. Since he was heading for his vehicle to make his getaway, I cut across his escape route and after running through another dense patch of poison oak in my hurry to apprehend my chap, finally caught him. With that chap in hand, we returned to their sandbar along the river.

There I checked out my two live sturgeon still tied to a rope in the little watered inlet in the sandbar. Both sturgeon were green sturgeon and under the required minimum size limit of four feet. Careful with the two fish, I photographed the pair and then gently unhooked the rope that had been passed through their mouths and out through their gill plates so I wouldn't damage their fragile gills. Talk about two happy sturgeon once they were released. When I released them back into the wild, I would swear they had grins from stem to stern. And, that is hard for that species of a fish to do since it has a rounded sucker like mouth...

Then the paperwork began since my captured lad would not divulge the name of his now long gone, goofy river-swimming partner. All he would say was there was a warrant of some kind out for the arrest of his friend and he had declared earlier that he would never return to incarceration. So, he took a swim and now was in the process of making a long walk to somewhere through a road less wilderness area with nothing more than what he carried on his back. And of note, I noticed that he was only wearing one tennis shoe when he had emerged from the Klamath River after making good his escape. The other shoe was long gone in the unforgiving river just like his fishing pole.

My sole remaining snagger was cited for snagging, using illegal terminal fishing gear, possession of two undersized sturgeon and littering (remember the tossed beer cans). In those days, such filings garnered at least $1,000.00 in fines for any such miscreant rendered by the tough little female judge sitting in that judicial district. In the process, I had seized his fishing pole and his Penn 9/0 reel along with his illegal treble hooks. All those court ordered forfeited items went to the State of California to be auctioned off at a future date.

Meanwhile back at the ranch, I was now paying the price for running through the poison oak patches. Having worked up a sweat in my chase of the fleeing second snagger, I was now beginning to itch like crazy after my two unfortunate sessions with 'my friends', the two poison oak patches. Trying to decide what to do, I finally arrived at what I thought was a credible solution. Finding a deserted spot along the river, I stripped down and took a swim to get rid of my sweat and any poison oak oils that might be still working me over. I also hand washed out all my clothing. I think all that did was spread the oils from those plants all over my gorgeous body with predictable results.

Having worn out my welcome with the local outlaw populace and having enough of the Klamath River and its follies, I figured I would head for home. However, that was not to be. Driving out along a backcountry dirt road heading toward Orleans, I kept running across freshly spent shotgun shells lying on the road's surface. (Author's Note: telling freshly fired shells from old ones is simple. Just pick them up and smell them for freshly burned powder smells.) Coming around a turn in the road moments later, I happened upon another suspicious looking chap. Only this time, the lad had his shotgun barrel sticking out his driver's side window as he slowly road-hunted along. Moments later, one surprised chap got to meet yours truly up close and personal like. That chap was subsequently cited for possession of several closed season blue grouse (also called Fool Hens because of their general lack of fear of humans since they hardly ever see a human because they live in such a backcountry wilderness environment) and possession of a loaded shotgun in a motor vehicle on a way open to the public. As was the standard course of business, that chap had his illegal birds and shotgun seized. I discovered weeks later that little shooting trip cost the man $250.00 in fines and loss of his shotgun to the State of California.

Then I finally headed for home, itching all the way I might add. However, I could see the Flowers derived from this trip in the fact that I was able to release two previously snagged young green sturgeon back into the wild from whence they came. Being as long lived as they are, unless they ran across other snaggers, they may still be alive and procreating even as these words were written some 50 plus years later.

There were Tombstones from this adventure to report as well. When I was a young warden in the north coast fish and game squad, green and white sturgeon commonly ran in **nine** of the major river systems in northwestern California. I am now told by my contacts back in California as these words are written in 2015, that because of a number of natural factors and the historical illegal taking of those great fish by snagging and illegal nets, that only **two** north coast rivers now commonly have the mighty migrating sturgeon naturally occurring within! A species of fish that has existed basically unchanged for the last 65,000,000 million years and, because of man's inhumanity to man, are now basically eradicated from many of their natural and historical waterways in the California north coast river systems.

I have often wondered what those who are yet to come will say about the humanity that inhabited this place before their arrival and how they treated the natural resources of the land. Natural resources that many of those yet to come will never again see in the wild but only in zoos or zoological gardens.

You can damn well bet that those folks yet to come will be sorrowfully seeing many plots of world of wildlife Tombstones instead of fields of Flowers because of that lack of foresight and care of the natural resources of the land on the part of those who came before them.

AN UNDERCOVER DETAIL TURNS DEADLY

Slipping into the Eureka Fish and Game Office early one morning, I deposited a slew of closed case citations with our secretary. Then I hustled my tail end down the hall to the evidence room and left an armful of seized fishing rods taken from salmon snaggers, along with two rifles removed from the hands of a couple of deer spotlighters. Knowing the love my fish and game captain held for me, I started to scoot out the office door and return to the field and more salmon stream fishing enforcement. However, my scoot was a tad slow that morning when it came to 'picking um up and laying um down.'

"Mister, you get your tail end into my office and make it snappy," bellowed out my captain with a somewhat slurred tone and tenor of voice. Turning, I slowly walked back towards my captain's office wondering what I had done wrong in his eyes this time. Standing at attention in the doorway to his office, I waited until my good captain finished the serious job of cleaning his fingernails before he officially acknowledged my living presence.

"Get your butt in here. I have another undercover detail for you," bellowed out the good captain in his slurred, alcohol laced speech. As I entered his warm office, I could smell the sickly sweet smell of cheap gin hanging heavily in the air. *Damn,* I thought. *It isn't even nine o'clock in the morning and the good captain is already into his cups.*

"Yes, Sir, Captain. What do you want me to do?" I asked.

"Since you didn't screw up your Orleans undercover detail even though you are a rookie, and somehow managed to capture a nest of those salmon and sturgeon snagging rascals, I have another assignment for you. Bill Williams, the Klamath warden, has a clan of outlaws that are rumored to be gill netting salmon by the ton and selling them under the table to some of the local smoke houses and to fishermen who are not having any luck in catching their own salmon. Bill called in this morning and requested I send up an officer to work undercover and see if that officer can't break up this illegal salmon netting and selling ring. Since you are my roving land warden, you get the assignment. Try not to screw it up or I will have your ass," he advised with emphases on the threat at the end of his warning sentence.

"Yes, Sir, Captain. When do you want me to leave?" I asked.

"Yesterday would be OK with me if I had my druthers," he slurred once again.

"Yes Sir. I will get on it right away," I said, glad to be finished with the business at hand with my drunken superior officer.

With that, I scooted out the door, went into the warden's ready room and called Warden Bill Williams in the town of Klamath. When Bill answered the phone, I greeted him and advised him over the recent turn of events that had just transpired in the captain's office. Bill just grunted over hearing I was the one assigned the undercover detail in his district and then I heard him swear softly under his breath over the phone line.

"I sense some concern in your voice, Bill. What is it?" I asked.

"Terry, you have been given a dangerous assignment to my way of thinking and not one for a rookie. The folks you will be going against are from the local Oscar clan and they are as mean as a bunch of car-run-over snakes. They are part Indian and the meanest part of their clan is the old man, Herman Oscar. The old man and leader of the group, weighs well over 200 pounds and has a violent temper and a criminal record as long as my arm. He has two sons, Albert and Devon, who aren't much smaller than their old man and, to my way of thinking, are a damn site crazier and meaner. If they ever get you into a fight, and they don't fight fair, they will leave you in such a condition you will wish you were dead! That is why I am concerned that Walt (the captain) didn't send a more experienced officer or at least two of you fellas so you would have some degree of protection in case you are identified as a fish and game officer," quietly uttered Bill.

"Oh well, that is our gifted captain for you," continued Bill. "No damn common sense when it comes to officer safety. O.K., here is the problem. These three Oscar clan outlaws congregate at Pete's Sump, which is a local rundown bar and grill in the town of Klamath. The word I am getting is that Pete Oders, the owner of Pete's Sump, is acting as an under the table illegal fish salesman for the Oscar clan. Pete listens to all the fishermen who come in to drink and if they have tales of woe about not catching any salmon, Pete befriends them and offers to provide some fish to them from some of his friends, for a price of course. If the out-of-luck fishermen are interested in buying some salmon under the table, Pete calls Herman Oscar and a transfer of fish and money is arranged. The other word is that the Oscar clan is selling to willing smoke house buyers in the area as well. The old man and his sons are running a gill net somewhere on the river and damned if I can locate it. I have worked all the way from the mouth of the Klamath River upstream into the canyon areas and have yet to find that net. But it is out there somewhere and I will keep looking as long as my carcass can hold up and allows me to continue looking."

"In the meantime, I need you to pose as a wealthy disgruntled fisherman on vacation and have you frequent Pete's bar and grill. Maybe you can befriend him and after some drinking time, get him to call Herman and arrange for a purchase of salmon. Being that the sale of these river salmon is illegal, we will have those chaps where we want them and can bust their chops. But I have to warn you. You will be on your own so be careful. If those bastards ever get wind that you are a game warden working undercover, they will stomp you within an inch of your life. Now I know you are a big old dude and after your successes on the Orleans crowd of salmon and sturgeon snagging outlaws, you might be feeling pretty damn good about yourself. Don't let that go to your head. These three are very clever wildlife outlaws. All of them have serious criminal records that go back years and the old man is extremely careful and smart, if not just damn dangerous. If he ever suspects you are the law, he and his two sons will pay you a visit. When they do under those circumstances, they will see to it that you will remember it for one hell of a long time. That is if you survive the ordeal and they don't kill you first!

Feeling I had what I needed in the way of the background information surrounding the problem, I gathered up the appropriate salmon fishing gear from the confiscated property room in the fish and game office. Then I got permission from Captain Gray to use my own personal Jeep pickup because I felt the Klamath River outlaws, having been worked before by our squad's fish and game officers, would have recognized any state owned, commonly used undercover vehicles. By using my own vehicle, I would not be inadvertently discovered before I had gathered enough evidence for an arrest and subsequent prosecution. At least those were my rookie thoughts... Then I headed for home in order to get geared up and commence working on my newest assigned undercover detail.

Kissing my bride and telling her little of the upcoming assignment so she would not worry, off I went. In fact, I never did discuss this operation with her until the evening of June 5, 2015 when I got the idea to write about this particular adventure in my newest book. My wife said nothing about what happened as I explained the basics of the story to her but I got the feeling she was glad I was now retired and out of the line of fire.

Heading north on State Highway 101 from Eureka, soon found me in the small town of Klamath. There I rented a seedy, mildew smelling motel room characteristic of those found in the always damp temperate rain forest area of northwestern California. Following that, I headed out to see what I could do about Bill's little illegal salmon netting and selling ring. First, I headed by Pete's Sump, the local bar and grill allegedly frequented by the Oscar clan, to get familiar with its location and overall layout. Following that, it was out to the Klamath River to look the part of a fisherman by being seen along the river and getting familiar with its terrain and fishing successes. For the rest of that day, I pretended to be a salmon fisherman, all the while gathering information on other illegal fishing activities occurring in my area so I could report them to Bill and have him work those areas of discovery the following day in an overt capacity.

Then come nightfall, I headed for Pete's. Walking in, I hardly got a parting look from the gathered crowd of locals and other fishermen or whom I suspected was Pete himself. The bar was full of loggers and it was noisy and full of cigarette smoke. So acting like everyone else, I sidled up to the bar and ordered a pitcher of beer. In so doing, I hoped to make an unusual impression on the barkeep, one in which he would remember me when I returned by. My goofy plan worked 'slicker than cow slobbers'.

"How many glasses do you need? The barkeep asked as he placed my just ordered pitcher of beer before me on the bar and looked all around for any other drinking buddies I might have brought along in attendance.

"None," I quietly replied. "Don't need any."

"How the hell you 'gonna' drink any beer?" asked the barkeep over my refusal for any glasses.

"Just you watch me," I said as I hefted up the pitcher of beer and began drinking straight away from the pitcher in order to make an impression on Pete of a large man with a powerful thirst for a number of cold beers.

"Damn," said Pete. "I like you already. Just what one doesn't see much of anymore. A one-fisted drinker who knows how to drink a beer!" he said with a big grin showing a mouthful of chewing tobacco stained teeth. With that he turned, walked to the far end of the bar and then returned shortly thereafter with a large bowl of unshelled peanuts for me to eat. "Anyone who has a powerful thirst like you has got to have some peanuts to go along with it," he said with a big grin. "Name's Pete. And yours?" he asked, as he extended his hand for me to shake.

"Name's Terry," I responded.

(Now to all my quick budding law enforcement readers out there, I can already see the looks of puzzlement and disbelief splashed clear across your faces. If I was working on such a dangerous undercover assignment, why did I use my real name? Simple. Keep it simple when working a simple undercover investigation. One is less likely to get tripped up later on over what was and has been said previously if one keeps it simple and truthful. Truthful like using what one is familiar with like one's own name and life history. So, that is what I did. Since I lived far away, I wasn't too concerned that I would run across anyone I knew there in Klamath or along the lower portion of the river. Bottom line, I was a rookie officer who was less known in the wildlife outlaw circles in the Klamath area compared to my home base of operations in the Eureka area. So, I chanced it and kept it simple.)

"Catching any salmon?" casually asked Pete during one of his business lulls in visiting with me as a barkeep.

"Naw," I replied. "But, I have only been here for part of a day and I have a few more days left on this fishing trip. So, I expect I will catch a fish or two before I have to go back to work. Or at least I had better catch a few. I am putting on a big fish fry for about 20 of my closest friends back home. So, a mess of fresh run king salmon would go a long way toward filling that bill at my planned dinner for family and friends," I innocently laid out for him to hear.

(Again for my clever readers who are students of law enforcement, do you see what I am doing? I am not asking to purchase any illegal fish outright. To do so would be entrapment and would get one thrown out of court when it came to any Fourth Amendment to the Constitution tainted evidence used in a court of law. I am simply just letting the barkeep know, one who is suspected of illegally running and selling fish for the Oscar clan, that I am a fisherman that has a **NEED** for some fresh run salmon for a dinner. In other words, an open invite for him to assist me in my endeavors if he, of his own free God given will, wishes to help. No entrapment there so I can safely proceed along my line of 'attack'.)

Pete said nothing other than the fish were running heavy in the river and with a little luck, I should be able to catch a king salmon or two. Then he ambled off to service other customers and I sat there nursing my beer. However, when Pete was busy at the far end of the bar and not looking my way, I quietly walked over to the nearest table of noisy, two-thirds drunken loggers and, without being asked, filled up their mostly empty glasses of beer for which they greatly appreciated. Then I hustled my tail end back to the bar as if I had been there all along. Shortly thereafter when Pete worked his way back to me along the now really crowded and noisy bar, I ordered up another pitcher of beer as if I had polished off that first pitcher all by myself. Then I ordered a hamburger and a mess of fries for my dinner. Pete was all too happy to refill my pitcher and soon my dinner had arrived. Finishing my dinner, I thanked Pete and left him a $5.00 tip, which was big money in those days. To my way of thinking, my trap was laid and now it was up to Pete to step onto the 'pan'.

Back at my motel room, I called Bill and reported on my progress. He was pleased with that progress, especially with Pete the bar tender and requested that I keep up my interactions with him. Bill figured if I could get by Pete and allay his suspicions, I would have a good chance in getting into the Oscar clan and eventually buying some illegal fish. With that, I ended the call and hit the rack. The next morning at daybreak,

I was on the river making like a real live salmon fisherman and, in the process, releasing back into the wild every fish I caught.

That evening, it was back to Pete's Bar for a second go-around. Walking in, he looked up at me as I entered and then came right over to where I sat down. "Want the same as last night?" Pete asked with a big grin on his face.

'You got that right," I said. "And a bowl of those peanuts would be a good way to start my evening," I continued with a big ole dumb looking 'gumby-like' grin.

"Comin' right up," he sang out as he headed for the pitchers and began filling one up with beer. Moments later my pitcher of beer arrived along with a bowl of peanuts slid down the bar. Handing me the beer, Pete said, "Thanks for the tip last night. Not many of my clientele think of doing that or are too poor or out of work to consider doing such a thing. So, thank you!" "Don't mention it," said the 'spider to the fly', like a five-dollar bill was nothing.

Hell, it really was big money. In those days, a five-dollar bill would fill up one's vehicle with gasoline or buy six pounds of T-bone steaks! After all, it was just the fish and game department's money and well spent I might add if the way Pete stumbled over my needs was any indication of early on success on my part.

"Catch any fish today?" Pete casually asked.

"Naw. Lost a big one that managed to break my line but that was about it. But there is tomorrow and I had better start catching or my butt will be grass and my wife a lawn mower if I don't catch enough for our fish fry coming up," I said as I took another long draw on my pitcher of beer like Joe Casual.

(I would hope that some of my smarter readers see where I am going with this. Note that I have still not asked to purchase any fish. As I said earlier, if I did and then hammered my seller in a court of law, that would be entrapment. I am just letting Pete know that I have a REAL need for some salmon for an important upcoming dinner. Especially in light of the now known fact that I am a crappy fisherman and on a short leash for time in which to catch some salmon. If Pete were to respond to that with an offer to sell me some fish under the table and did so, then I would have him by his 'last part over the fence'. In short, he has to make the offer and then I will just let his greed and ego run what is about to happen next.)

"Well, let's hope you have some better luck tomorrow," he said. "Want a hamburger and some fries like last night for your dinner?"

"Yep. That would be fine and maybe a little of bit of Tabasco sauce would be nice to liven up that hamburger and my fries," I said with a grin. (Sharks have grins, don't they?)

"You got it, Terry," he said as he yelled in my order to his short order cook through the opening in the wall between his bar and the kitchen in back.

When I left for the night, I left another five-dollar bill as a tip. Once again, I reported to Bill with my evening's progress. That kind of reporting on an undercover assignment was standard operating procedure since we did not have a first line field supervisor on site. Being that Bill was the senior officer present and the district warden, protocol dictated that he be kept in the loop at all times. I also told Bill that I figured the following evening, I would make a play to see if Pete would sell me a salmon since I had not caught any as of yet. Bill reminded me regarding the issues surrounding entrapment and, since I had finished number one at the recent fish and game academy out of 80 students academically and number two as the second best pistol shot in that group, I had to grin. There was no way I was going to mess up my second major undercover assignment by not adhering to the proper legal principles and procedures when it came to making a legitimate buy of an illegal item.

The next evening after an uneventful day fishing (of course), I headed for Pete's bar. Walking in, I headed for the bathroom first to see a man about a horse. Coming out from the restroom, I saw Pete waving me over to the far end of his bar. Walking over to the barkeep, I took an empty stool fronted by an already present full pitcher of beer and a bowl of peanuts. I just had to inwardly grin. It was obvious that I was making headway and had made just the right kind of an impression on Pete.

"Have any luck today?" Pete casually asked, as he wiped off the bar to my front.

"Lost one right at the edge of the bank and had two nice ones break off. But other than that, drew another goose egg. But there is tomorrow morning and then I have to leave by noon because I have to meet with a couple of investment clients," I casually said after taking a long draw on the pitcher of beer.

"I will tell you what. Maybe I can help. I know you have that fish dinner planned when you get home but if you don't catch a really big one, stop by my place. I might be able to get you a salmon or two for your dinner so your wife won't be so disappointed," Pete volunteered with a big old friendly grin. I just smiled inwardly over Pete's words as I thought that greed is a wonderfully magic thing in the world of wildlife. Especially if one is a hunter of humans and finds an outlaw close within his grasp doing to Mother Nature what he shouldn't be doing. However, my dear readers, greed can work both ways if one is not careful. That is why law enforcement officers have such a short leash...

"Naw. That won't be necessary, Pete. I don't want to take food away from your family," I said, once again trying to be Joe Casual and look genuinely concerned over his own personal family needs over mine. That I did, full well knowing as to where this one was eventually going, especially if the case ever went to trial and what my 'concerns' looked like in the eyes of a jury when they considered the issues of entrapment.

"No, that isn't the case. I have several friends who are really good fishermen and I am pretty sure that I can tap them for a fish or two," he replied with a big helpful looking grin.

"Naw, that is OK," I replied once again said the 'spider to the fly'... "When I get back home, I can purchase several salmon at Lazio's." (Lazio's was a well-known commercial fish market and restaurant located along the docks of Humboldt Bay in Eureka.)

(Can you readers see what I am doing and where I am going with this? I am making sure that when this case went to trial and because of the serious nature of the violation, the judge and jury could see that I never suggested buying any fish that were illegal. And, that I even went the extra mile suggesting I could always buy a legal fish from a commercial fish processing house back in Eureka over accepting any deal Pete might want to make. That is called in my lexicon, 'closing the ring'!)

"No, I insist! I can get you all the fresh fish you will need for your dinner and at a price that is less than you would be paying at a damn commercial fish house. Plus, my fish would be a hell of a lot fresher," insisted Pete as he tried to really be helpful since I had yet to land any salmon. Plus, I was a friend now, especially with my nightly five dollar tips...

"Are you sure? I don't want to get anyone in trouble since selling salmon is illegal if you are not a commercial fisherman," I replied.

(Once again, my readers, see what I am doing? I am in the process of establishing the fact that Pete knew it was illegal to sell such river caught fish and yet he did so anyway. A subject's knowledge of the law he is breaking in any criminal matter is always helpful, especially in the eyes of some of the goofy damn juries we run across and seat in today's trials.)

"Not to worry. Tell me how many fish you will need and I will have them here out back behind the bar for you tomorrow by ten in the morning. That way, you don't have to worry about catching any fish. You can just sleep in late in the morning. And, the fish I will have here for you will be day old fresh. In fact, most will still have sea lice on them," he bragged connoting fresh-out-from-the-ocean fish.

"Well, just as long as it doesn't get anyone in trouble, I could use about 60 pounds of fresh salmon if that is possible because of the size of my party," I limply and humbly replied.

"Got you covered, Boss," replied Pete as he lit up like a Christmas tree seeing that he had helped out a friend and had made a sizeable sale and profit for himself in the process as well.

Later that evening when back at the motel, I advised Bill of my success in being offered illegal salmon for purchase the next day. Boy, was he ever tickled. I told him I had $300 dollars in state furnished buy money and that should be enough to conduct a transaction for the 60 pounds of fresh run sport salmon I offered to purchase. Again, Bill cautioned me that every night I needed to be taking down notes on everything that had been said or done. Since that was my standard operating practice anyway while working undercover assignments, there was no harm and no foul.

The next morning I went down and purchased three of the largest ice chests I could buy at the local hardware store. Promptly at ten in the morning, I went to Pete's and he had me drive around and park behind the bar. Then he got on the outside public telephone and talked to someone about bringing me the fish. After hanging up, he walked over to me and we went inside the bar. In the quiet of the empty bar, Pete told me his contacts were on their way and they would be bringing me the fish I needed. Then he offered me a drink on the house and I accepted. (Remember, folks, when working undercover, one must look the part and when in Rome, do as the Romans do. So, I drank on duty which was acceptable. That was providing it was not to excess while trying to look the part.)

Twenty minutes later, the front door to the bar burst open and in walked three rather stout looking chaps. Pete waved the men over to where we had been drinking a beer and introduced to me one Herman Oscar, a Devon Oscar and one named Albert. *Hot dog!* I thought. Those three men were the ones that Bill had intelligence on as to the ones illegally selling river caught or illegally gill-netted king salmon. Now if I could just hold everything together during that first meeting between the illegal sellers and what appeared to them to be just an innocent, down on his luck salmon fisherman in need.

At first, the three men were a little standoffish and closed mouthed. But when they offered the fish to me at a dollar a pound, which was more than normally charged, and I dug out my $300 dollars without question, they lightened and loosened right up. Soon all of us were chattering away like a mess of gray squirrels over a cache of acorns as we transferred salmon from the trunk of Herman Oscar's Buick automobile into my three ice chests. In fact, instead of buying just 60 pounds of illegal fish, I saw they had more in the trunk of their car and upped my purchase to around 100 pounds of fish.

That really surprised the men and they were all too happy to unload the extra fish into my ice chests and so they did with Pete's knowing physical help and knowledge of course.

Then it was into the bar again once all the salmon had been transferred and I bought everyone a round of drinks and lunch since it was about noontime. Now, we were all good friends. That was except for old man Herman. He was still a little cool towards me and kept looking at me kind of like a robin does a worm. I was hoping I had not run across him on some other sort of wildlife law enforcement detail I had previously participated in.

Finally he popped a question that I was not really prepared for. "Don't I know you from somewhere?" asked Herman slowly, as he continued to eye me suspiciously.

For a moment, I almost froze not expecting to being skewered like that with such a pointed question. Then my survival instincts kicked in, especially in light of what Bill had advised about what would happen to me if they ever discovered who I was. So, away I went with my song and dance hoping it would be good enough in allowing me to escape the pointed question.

"I don't think so," I slowly said, looking my questioner straight into his coal black accusing eyes acting as if I was trying to remember Herman's face. "Not unless you are into banking, stocks and bonds and we met that way somewhere," I continued, full well knowing Herman was not of that cut of the cloth or flavor of life to be into stocks and bonds.

"No, maybe I was just thinking about someone else. Course, maybe I was just a-funnin' with you," said Herman, as his face broke out into the first smile he had registered on his old puss all morning.

Funnin' hell! His shot across my bow regarding his question of knowing me almost took all the wind out from my sails! Thank heavens my two guardian angels rose to the occasion and provided me the verbal ammo needed to shoot back a damn fine answer if I do say so myself.

Not knowing what my captain wanted done as for the rest of the case, before I departed I left a door open. I let the Oscar clan know that my brother-in-law was interested in opening up a smoke house and if he was interested, could the three men supply enough fish if he were to offer to purchase up to 500 pound lots at the great price they had quoted me (the price quoted me was .50 cents below the going market price)?

Brother, when I mentioned 500 pound lots, you should have seen the eyes light up on the three salmon poachers' faces. All I could see written across their faces was greed and ego. Then Herman said, "If you give us a couple of days-notice, just as long as the salmon are running, we can supply five hundred pound lots of fresh run king salmon to your brother-in-law throughout the rest of the summer months." Man, with those words regarding future salmon sales, was I ever tickled! I was in 'Like Flynn', to coin a popular phrase of the day. (Author's Note: Errol Flynn was a popular movie actor and alleged notorious lover in those days.) After I paid for a few more drinks and all of our lunches, we all left the bar and went our separate ways. It now appeared that I had made my case and was more than pleased over being able to catch a number of outlaws who really needed catching.

Before I headed for home, I quietly met Bill at his home and off loaded all my fish so he could place them in his evidence locker since his local court would be handling the matter. Bill then advised he was going to call Walt (our captain) and let him know I was in and that he would recommend to the captain that he not speak of this covert operation to anyone else in the squad because of the danger I was facing alone and in the outback with the three main outlaws of the investigation. I thought that was a good idea and concurred. Then, I headed for home for some much needed down time.

The next week I was right back in the town of Klamath. That first evening at Pete's bar, I met with Herman, Devon and Albert. Once again, I stood for the drinks and supper like my character as a rich guy would ordinarily do under the circumstances, as the four of us conducted business regarding additional salmon purchases for my freezer and my imaginary brother-in-law's mail order smoked fish venture. I had called Herman earlier in the week with a request for a case load lot and he indicated they were catching the hell out of the fish and that he could meet my order. Later that evening after the business and drinking was done, that time found Bill and me off loading 400 pounds of illegally taken and sold king and silver salmon into his truck so he could transport the fish to his commercial evidence lockers in Crescent City.

Additionally, I had made arrangements with Herman and his sons for another load of illegal salmon to be picked up the following week, only the next pickup was to be at Herman's home near the small town of Klamath Glen. That change in pickup plans bothered me just a bit because for the first time, I would be all alone with a wad of cash in my pocket and in the presence of three rather stout looking and dangerous renegade Indian lads with a reputation to boot. But, the captain and the county attorney wanted one more buy to 'cement the case' as they called it and, since I worked for the state, I was solidly in the mix of events to come. Little did I realize there would be no more 'funnin'' this next time around... But, I was young, immortal, had two guardian angels and this being my second major successful undercover case in the squad in just a matter of weeks, I was flying high. However, I didn't realize that God always has a way of getting the attention of those of us badge carriers who are getting a 'bad case of the big head'...

Driving into Klamath Glen on my following salmon pick up date, I eventually located Herman's ramshackle home and parked my Jeep in his driveway. Hearing me drive up on his graveled driveway, Herman exited his home and warmly welcomed me. He then had me drive around back and the two of us loaded up about 400 pounds of freshly gill netted king and silver salmon into my mess of ice chests. Once again to my non-salmon fishing fishermen, salmon who have been gill netted will have dark net mesh marks around the front portions of their bodies where the mesh rubbed off their scales as they fought to escape exposing the dark skin underneath. I was then invited into his home for a drink and the exchange of the buy money.

Sitting around the kitchen table, I paid Herman in twenty dollar bills, all with non-consecutive serial numbers like he always demanded and then looking around, off handedly asked where his boys were. Herman indicated they were off patching up one of their gill nets that had been torn by a floating log and wouldn't be home until later. With money in hand for the illegal fish, Herman walked over to the kitchen cabinets, got out a bottle of 101 proof Wild Turkey whiskey, a couple of glasses and sat back down at the table. Without any further conversation, he poured himself a three-fingered drink and then sat the bottle back down on his side of the table without pouring me one as well...

That was strange, I thought. He knew I would drink whiskey. But, he had poured himself a drink and had ignored me. *Damn, what poor manners,* I thought. Then out of the blue, Herman looked behind me and loudly said, "Maria, come here!" Moments later, I could hear some shuffling of feet and a door into the small kitchen opened up and out stepped a young girl, maybe all of 13 or 14. She had her hands clasped in front of her stomach and had a look of intense terror splashed clear across her face! I looked over at Herman with what had to be a questioning look of 'what is going on?' written all across my face.

Then Herman fixed his eyes on mine with an eagle like stare and said, "Terry, for the longest time now, my Indian Spirits within me have questioned me as to who you were. They have told me to be careful around this 'white man' and I don't know why. Then I began to wonder if you might be a game warden working undercover, trying to catch me and my boys illegally selling our gill-netted salmon."

With those words and the look he was now giving me, my heart skipped a beat or two!

I then just started to deny what he was suggesting when, with a wave of his hand, he shut me up. "Here is what we are going to do," he said without his dark eyes ever leaving mine. "Maria is my only daughter. As you can see, she is already a woman. **I want you to have sex with her!** If you refuse, that will tell me the Spirits were right and that you are a forked-tongue white man and more than likely, a much hated game warden. If you don't refuse and have illegal child-sex with her, that will tell me the Spirits were wrong and that we can continue doing business with the salmon because you speak with a 'straight tongue'."

Then at that very moment, Herman quickly removed a Colt .45 A.C.P. from under a newspaper from a seat next to him on his side of the table and laid it in front of himself across from me. "Now, you go and have sex with her in her bedroom and I will know you are a good and trusted white man and will continue allowing you as one of my business partners. Because if you have illegal sex with her, that will tell me you are not a law enforcement officer and just as much of an outlaw as I am. But if you don't, that will tell me you are a cop and don't want to break the law by having sex illegally with a juvenile. That denial happens and your people will never find your body!" Then he just intensely stared at me like a diamond back rattlesnake about ready to strike. I tried looking back at him in the same manner he was looking at me but had the feeling that he was looking right into my very soul for the answers he sought.

Trying to break the intensity of that moment and get my head on straight as to what I could do to extract myself from this now turned deadly situation, I looked over at Maria. Her face was contorted in terror over being forced into a sexual act with a total stranger. I stood 6-feet 4-inches tall and she couldn't have been more than a little over five feet in height. I weighed in at 300 pounds and she couldn't have weighed any more than 95 pounds. I could just imagine what was going through her terrified mind if the two of us were to have sex. If this monster sized white man tried to have sex with her as her father was demanding, she must have figured that forced sexual act would probably ruin her physically for life and destroy any chances that she would ever have of having any of her own children because of the bodily damage she could possibly sustain in such a union.

Then my guardian angels kicked in and I would swear, I could hear the sound of a Calvary bugle being blown. With the thought of the situation I found myself in, my madly scrambling mind began formulating a plan now that the Calvary 'had arrived'. An idea that if it didn't work, I was a dead man because there was no way I could reach across that table and grab that gun before Herman laid his big paws on it. And, the semi-automatic .45 caliber handgun laying on the table in front of Herman, was already cocked! I even thought of quickly over turning the table like I had seen done in cowboy movies and making a play for Herman's gun before he could. However, I quickly nixed that idea because if I wasn't successful, I would soon be dead. I then turned to my training for the idea now running around in the back of my mind. I had been taught at the fish and game academy in one of my classes that your mouth can get one into trouble as well as getting you out of trouble. I always had a great gift for gab so I ran down that avenue of potential escape with my heart up in my throat.

'Gathering up my skirts', I began speaking and when I did, I realized I had better steady and carefully measure my words. If I didn't, like Herman had said, they would never find me or what was left of me. "Herman, I would be honored and love to have sex with your daughter. She is beautiful and you are right, although very young in years, she is already a woman. Just hear me out though because I can't have sex with her. When I was in Viet Nam with the first group of Special Forces Advisors that went in to help the Vietnamese Army fight the Viet Cong, I, like others when we had time off, went into Saigon to forget about the war. One of those times when in Saigon, I was with a Vietnamese woman and came away with an incurable sexually transmitted disease. Military doctors have told me there is no cure and if I ever have sex with a woman, that infectious and parasitic disease I now have, will be transmitted to her and will sterilize her forever by destroying her ovaries and leaving massive scar tissue in the process. That is why since I returned from Viet Nam, my wife and I have never had sex and as a result of my indiscretions in Vietnam, we have no children. I am just thankful that my wife kept me after she learned of those revelations. So if you force me to have sex with your daughter, she will be sterilized forever and be unable to have any children of her own. And that means you will have no grandchildren from her, your one and only daughter. So, you think what you want of me but I refuse to destroy your only daughter's life like I have mine." With those words, I sat back and tried to come up with a Plan C if Herman did not believe my Plan B Vietnamese story. For the longest moment, Herman just sat there stone faced over my words. Then he exploded, reached for that cocked .45 semi-automatic, let out a loud laugh sounding like one more of relief than joy, then let the cocked hammer down on his pistol...

It was then that I detected a complete change in Herman's presence. His eyes softened from the earlier hardened look with moisture and then misted over slightly. He then said slowly in carefully measured words, "You are right. She is my only daughter and because of the death of my wife, I will have no more. I want to have grandchildren. And since my boys are showing no interest in getting married and no one is showing any kind of interest in them, she is my only real chance to be a grandfather in the near future. And, I want to be a grandfather in the tradition of my people."

With those words, Herman picked up the forty-five, slid it into his coat pocket and then yelled, "Boys! Come here!"

At that very moment, Devan and Albert burst forth from an adjoining bedroom carrying aluminum baseball bats! Then it dawned on me. They had been there all along listening and ready for their dad's command to storm into the kitchen and using the ball bats, beat me to a pulp. Do so because the old man had determined that I was a threat. "Put those bats down, Boys. We have a friend in our midst and now grab two more glasses so we can have a drink and celebrate the sale of this last batch of fish," said a now broadly smiling Herman.

Let me tell all you readers out there, that 101 proof Wild Turkey whiskey went down my throat like water after that seminal moment in time... And to be quite frank, I probably shouldn't have driven home that afternoon but I did. I had my load of evidence fish and what was needed to fully prosecute the Oscar clan for the damage they were doing to the salmon fisheries resources in the Klamath River. Especially after hearing about how many salmon they had gill netted that season after the whiskey had loosened up their tongues. How about over two tons of king salmon, illegally netted and sold according to Herman? And that didn't take into account any of the silver salmon they had also caught and sold that summer either!

After completing all my case reports and presenting them to the county attorney, a meeting was held to go over the facts of the case. And because the case of sale of river caught salmon was so serious, the attorney trying the case really grilled me as to what had been said and when the exact moment came in initiating and consummating the sale. Particularly when it came to the rules governing entrapment. Finally satisfied legally and ready to drop the hammer on the Oscar clan, God did it for us...

As was later explained to me by Bill, the Klamath warden, the Oscar clan moved their illegal gill netting operation from the lower reaches of the Klamath River after the bulk of the salmon run had migrated upstream into the Trinity River on the Hoopa Reservation. This they did in order to catch the last of the migrant salmon from that watershed. That plus, they wanted to cover their tracks by mixing in their illegal operation in among the legal Indian gill netting that was going on throughout the Hoopa Reservation.

One morning early while transporting a load of their illegal salmon on Highway 96 on the Hoopa Indian Reservation, they were hit head on by a drunken Hoopa Indian driving at a high rate of speed. The Oscar clan was wiped out to a man as was the driver in the car that hit them head on! I guess God had His say when it came to punishing those illegally netting and selling so many of His creatures. As for Pete's involvement, Bill later filed on him for his role in the illegal sales operation and he forfeited $450.00 dollars for his level of involvement in that sordid matter. For obvious reasons, I never had another drink in Pete's bar after that.

Thus ended my second covert effort working undercover for the California Department of Fish and Game as a rookie. As for Herman's daughter, I hope she married well and had several children. I also hope those kids did not turn out like their grandfather or their uncles.

As is usual in all of my adventure stories, there are Flowers. First and foremost, even as an inexperienced rookie, I was rapidly learning the wildlife law enforcement trade. And in so doing, picking up tips of the trade along the way that would serve me well throughout the next 32 years during my state and federal law enforcement careers.

Another Flower was starting down the road in the covert process towards putting three pretty dangerous and arrogant gill-netting outlaws out of business. That was the one Flower I was most proud of. I have often wondered if by increasing the size load lots of salmon ordered by me to satisfy the county attorney's legal threshold for a major salmon selling case, ultimately had anything to do with their demise? That and a Heaven sent assist via a head on car wreck which became the progenitor in sending my lads on their way. That deadly incident allowed untold hundreds of king and silver salmon to escape the gill nets of those three killers and move forward with their spawning migrations. That thinking on my part of starting those three wildlife outlaws on their ways to an ill-fated demise may sound a little weird, **but in God we trust, all others pay in cash...**

As for Tombstones, they littered the way. Three Tombstones were planted in the ground for my three gill-netting outlaws on the Hoopa Indian Reservation after they were hit head on by a drunken driver. Who says there isn't such a thing as a Salmon God?

Another Tombstone relates to the two plus tons of migrating salmon that the three men removed illegally from the environment. Remember, half were females statistically and the other half were males. Multiply that one ton of females who would have laid about 3,000 eggs per spawning fish and one can see the very real impact that took place in the losses of those salmon from their overall population and their field of genetics. A heritage that once lost is forever gone...

Another Tombstone to this story occurred many years later. Because salmon populations on the Klamath River had sunken to such lows, in part due to the use of Indian run gill nets on the salmon spawning grounds, the Secretary of the Interior closed that river in 1978 to all Indian gill net fishing. And out of that river closure enforced by special agents of the Fish and Wildlife Service of which I was at that time a member, that Tombstone somewhat later became a Flower. With that closure came a resurgence and increases of the salmon spawning numbers on that river system. That resurgence ran from two to five fold increases in numbers of salmon spawning in that river system over the next several years! A spawning numbers increase that was a direct result of the successful river closure in 1978. That plain and simply was a win for the American people and the Native Americans along those river systems in the heritage department.

Another Tombstone was that of Klamath Warden, Bill Williams. He later died from cancer of the pericardial sac which surrounds the heart. Bill was a good man and worked up till his last three days of life trying to enforce the wildlife laws of the land so others yet to come could enjoy them. I have to think that Bill knew he was dying and like the salmon he was trying to protect, knew he would also die after his 'migration' was over. And true to form, Bill died shortly after the salmon migration in the mighty Klamath River had ended. May you rest in peace, my friend, and thank you for your service to our nation and for taking a rookie under your wing and teaching him how to fly.

Flowers and Tombstones

Chapter Two: "The Rainbow"

DILL PICKLES AND SODA CRACKERS

One of my secondary duties as a roving game warden within three adjacent wildlife law enforcement districts in the North Coast Fish and Game Squad was that of also being assigned as a boarding officer on The Rainbow. The Rainbow was a 32-foot patrol vessel powered by twin inboard engines and possessing marine operational capabilities for use off the California coast. Those associated duties included patrolling the marine environment off the north coast of California, checking fish and crab processing houses and making sure commercial fishermen of all makes and models operated within their proscribed fishing regulations. The Rainbow was usually crewed by a lieutenant and one game warden boarding officer while operating in that sometimes dangerous Pacific Ocean marine environment. Dangerous because of having to operate many times in 30-50 foot seas, maneuvering through dense fog banks while within shipping

95

lanes and surviving sometimes off shore north coast weather conditions that bordered on the ugly.

Operationally, the fish and game patrol boat was used to put the boarding officer aboard any suspect commercial fishing boat at sea so it could be checked for compliance with the state's commercial fishing regulations. If any commercial fishermen were found operating outside the law, citations were issued or arrests made and the ship and its illegal cargo seized, brought to shore and held as evidence to be used in a court of law.

As for the opinion of the commercial fishermen monitored by The Rainbow and her crew enforcing the commercial fishing regulations, well, let us just say that we were understandably considered to be a pain in the ass. A pain in the ass because a goodly number of the commercial fishermen encountered were out to catch everything they could, legally or illegally, in order to fiscally feather their nests. This mind set is not uncommon among the competitive commercial fishermen types around the world when one's life style is at stake, operational costs are seemingly higher than a dog's back in a cat fight and one's personal ethics many times are in question. Suffice to say, we on The Rainbow had a somewhat adversarial relationship and role with a number of commercial fishermen off the north coast of California in the late 1960s when I helped crew that patrol boat as a backup boarding officer.

In those days, commercial fishing off the north coast of Northern California in our assigned fish and game patrol district involved those activities centered mostly around king and silver salmon, Dungeness crab, halibut, and the drag boat fishermen fishing for various species of bottom fish. During those halcyon days, the commercial fishing fleet berthed in the Port of Eureka numbered about 300 boats! Also located along the docks of Eureka were a number of commercial fish and crab processing houses. Suffice to say, commercial fishing was a BIG business when I was stationed there as a fish and game warden.

However, that is where this fairy tale ended. I loved the sea for the mystery it projected, and the inherent dangers and challenges it constantly presented officers of my ilk. But, I did my level best to stay the hell off it other than to walk the beaches and work the bays checking numerous clam fishermen found clamming during a low tide or the waterfowl hunters found and checked during the fall and winter hunting seasons.

Why you ask? Simple. I got seasick as hell every time I got on a boat in the marine environment, whether I lost the horizon or not. Hell, I always found myself starting to get seasick once I even got near a marina! However as part of my assigned duties, I still had to check the off shore deep sea salmon fishermen when the runs were on going in my three ocean-bordering assigned land districts. Those duties included checking hundreds of salmon sport fishermen fishing in the Pacific Ocean just off the north coast town of Trinidad. Unfortunately, that entailed working alone in the ocean in an 18-foot patrol boat with a thirty horse outboard. The result was that I got totally seasick every time I ventured forth on a marine enforcement patrol checking my many offshore sport salmon fishermen. Let me tell all you folks out there reading these lines, finding 300 sport fishing boats just off the coast of Trinidad when the salmon were migrating heavily was not uncommon. Do any of you realize just how long it takes a seasick mariner to watch over or check that many sport fishing boats? Well let me tell you, it is long enough to puke up everything except your shoes if you were a wimp like me when it came to experiencing bouts of seasickness while on those patrols!

Once the good captain who 'loved me dearly' found out about my many bouts of seasickness while on my numerous marine patrols in a small boat, he promptly assigned my miserable carcass to sea duty aboard our resident ocean going patrol boat, The Rainbow! Because my captain had a mess of crooked buddies in the commercial fishing trade, it didn't take long for the word to get out around the docks and within the commercial fishing fleet that the new game warden, one the size of a 'woodland gorilla', was a seasick prone 'chimp' when it came to sea duty. A rather large wimp, but a wimp just the same, who could broadcast puke with the best of them upon the onset of seasickness.

   With that new found reputation proceeding me, I decided I would not be a quitter and let the captain get the best of me. I just figured I would puke my way through every sea detail I drew and learn the best that I could from that marine enforcement experience. Dang, Folks, I used to get so sick that coming back from a law enforcement patrol at sea in my small boat, I would just numbly sit on the seat and dry heave over the side since I had already puked up my liver and gizzard hours earlier! Once back on land, it would take me three full days to get over the uneasiness caused by such an inner ear malady, especially every time I made any kind of a quick physical move on land. Hell, the residual seasickness was so bad that I had to be careful once back on land even when I took a long drink of water for fear of losing my innards all over again... Worse for my physicality was when I would be chasing deer poachers late at night in my patrol car after a day's bout of sea duty. That type of field work could occasionally cause me to lose it if I swung a turn too fast in my pursuit of a night shooting outlaw during a high speed chase! Sometimes in so doing, I would hammer into a turn at high speed and then find myself starting to get a queasy feeling all over again! Let me tell you, there is nothing worse than chasing down a deer poacher at night in a high speed chase and then when you have him stopped, get out and puke in front of him. What a wimp! But as all my readers have come to know, I was a most beautiful wimp...

One afternoon I received a call over the fish and game radio from Lt. Ken Brown. Ken was The Rainbow's skipper and was requesting my assistance on the patrol boat the following day because the normally assigned boarding officer, one Warden Chuck Monroe, was sick and unable to report for sea duty. That turned out to be one of my numerous epic patrols on The Rainbow. Because of that upcoming assignment's long proposed duration at sea patrol, I looked forward to it with dread because of my known penchant and proclivity for seasickness. However, I also did so with anticipation because it was a great opportunity to learn another aspect of my new profession because I had yet to work commercial fishermen at sea from the bigger and faster patrol boat. Let me tell all you readers out there, it was another whole new world of wildlife law enforcement once at sea in the blue water among the many commercial fishing outlaw cutthroats of those days. As I was soon to conclude after experiencing commercial fishermen up close and personal like and witnessing a number of them and their lack of conservation ethics, whoever said the age of the seagoing pirate was dead was a damn liar...

Realizing the physical dilemma that I was soon to encounter, I called on what I considered a learned friend and trusted fellow officer, one Warden Hank Marak from the nearby town of Willow Creek. Hank was also one of the much loved officers under the glare of the illustrious Captain Gray. Hank had been a good friend and mentor to me on a few details and we soon became a Band of Brothers. As a result, we continued teaming up on a number of dangerous and problematic assignments on his Hoopa Indian Reservation and I had learned a plethora of valuable survival lessons from him. Somewhere in the back of my mind, I remembered that he had earlier indicated a history of his service in the Army in Europe during the Korean War. *If that was the case, surely he would be a worldly man relative to seasickness, having crossed the stormy Atlantic during his trip to Europe. With that, he would surely more than likely have a solution to my seasickness problems having experienced the story north Atlantic,* I hopefully thought.

Sure as God made grasshoppers great fish bait for German brown trout, a subsequent phone call to Hank produced the hoped for solution to my seasickness problems. During that phone call, Hank told me to eat all the sour dill pickles and soda crackers I could possibly hold prior to going to sea. He further advised that meal should include consuming at least a gallon of the prescribed filling! Hank said that some of his naval friends had told him that during the advent of rough seas off the coast of Korea during the war, the ship's cooks recommended that pickles and soda crackers diet to everyone with weak stomachs to preclude seasickness so that they could remain battle ready. I had never heard such a thing but you could darn well guess I never missed a word of his helpful advice. Hell, I soon came to realize when it came to having a bout with seasickness, even a drowning man trying to avoid such an issue will gladly reach for a sharpened spear thrown directly at him.

Later back home, I ate sour dill pickles and soda crackers in preparation for my upcoming sea duty until I could barely wiggle. Being 6-foot 4-inches tall, weighing in at a beautiful 320 lovely pounds, plus having a comparably sized 'boiler', that was a wooden barrel full of pickles and a Tibetan K-2 mountain sized pile of soda crackers consumed! And by God, the next morning when I bailed out of bed, I felt like a million bucks! No mental pre-seasickness queasiness as I had always experienced in anticipation of conducting previous marine patrols off Trinidad Head in a small boat were happily anywhere to be found! Boy Howdy, those good feelings meant to me that going to sea on The Rainbow was going to be a snap. To my way of thinking, I had this seasickness thing on a 'downhill pull with a ten span of hardworking mules in the traces'.

The following morning at 0400 hours, after more pickles and soda crackers for breakfast, I was front and center at the marina where our patrol boat was docked. There Lieutenant Ken Brown briefed me on boat safety, taught me how to calibrate our radar, pump the bilges, what to inspect and look for on our engines in the way of potential problems, how to check the engine's lubricants, locations of our on board fire-fighting equipment, and briefed me on his immediate plan of operation for the day.

Then he had me start the engines, check the gages to make sure they read in the normal operating ranges and give him the all clear sign, as he stood there observing my actions. When everything was a go mechanically and operationally, Ken took the helm. I cast off our bow and stern lines as Ken then slowly moved us out from our mooring slip and into the main channel of Humboldt Bay. As The Rainbow picked up speed, so far so good when it came to my 'feeling good' department. I couldn't believe it, I now felt great and didn't feel queasy at all as our patrol boat rocked along. Hell, in a like patrol situation off Trinidad in my smaller patrol boat, my insides would already be rolling by the time I was backing down the boat trailer for launch. My insides would be rolling even further by the time I took the boat off the trailer in the old days. Man, I could have kissed Hank for giving me what I considered lifesaving advice on how to squelch my bouts of seasickness. Ken knew of my declared penchant for getting seasick and looking over at me, asked, "How you doing, 'Tiny'?"

I really admired Ken. He had a great reputation for operational worthiness at sea, an outstanding work ethic and a world of humanity when it came to his crew. Ken was a damn good skipper as I was soon to appreciate, a really good guy and an outstanding fish and game officer. The ocean going critters were lucky to have such a voice of defense in Warden Lt. Ken Brown.

In response to his considerate and thoughtful question regarding my wellbeing, I replied, "Pretty damn good, Skipper." In my reply to Ken, there was happiness in my voice and a song in my heart over my wellness. Those words might sound a little bit corny to all you readers out there but just get seasick once and you will come to appreciate the sincerity of what and how I speak about the subject.

With a smile of what had to be relief on Ken's face over his boarding officer's internal well-being, he thrust the throttles forward and soon we were up on step and smoothly gliding up and down the huge Pacific Ocean swells routinely found at the mouth of the Humboldt Bay channel. Moments later, we cleared the channel out into the swells of the Pacific Ocean and headed north to an area where Ken knew a number of the crab boats would be operating after overhearing the loose CB radio talk from the commercial fishermen the day before.

Talk about excited! I had the wind in my face, could feel the rhythmic throbbing of the twin engines through my feet as they powerfully thrust us forward, could feel the sea spray on my face, and was very happy about this opportunity to learn about another facet of wildlife law enforcement that heretofore was foreign to me. Man, let me tell you, it was great to be alive and I wasn't seasick!

For the next hour, The Rainbow thundered northward towards the Dungeness crab fishing grounds as if 'it' couldn't wait to mix it up with some of the less than honest commercial fishermen. Me? I was in the same boat (no pun intended). I felt great and knowing the danger I would first time experience jumping from the front deck of our smaller patrol boat onto the decks of the larger boats in the commercial fishing fleet, I was up 'on step' as well. Little did I realize at the time that fate was fast catching up with me on its 'dark horse of destiny'... When it did, my enthusiasm for jumping from bobbing boat to pitching and yawing ship at sea to enforce the commercial fishing regulations would soon be tempered as I fought through a familiar demon. That was especially so when it came re-boarding my own vessel on the high seas after conducting an inspection on a fishing vessel. That meant jumping from a higher decked commercial fishing vessel, down four to six feet, to a lower hulled bobbing and pitching smaller patrol boat. When that was dangerously done, found myself not having anything to grab hold of when I landed on the smaller deck of our patrol boat! Plainly and simply, in order to land safely, I had to land like a gymnast sticking a landing after doing the vault in the Olympics. One miscalculation and I would be in the icy cold ocean waters trying to survive from being crushed between the hulls of two close at hand vessels. Bottom line, I had better have the luck of the Irish when I re-boarded The Rainbow or else!

Right at daylight, several vessels of the Eureka based crab fleet came into view on the horizon as they ran their strings of crab pots. With our far off arrival, Ken stopped our patrol boat and we just sat there quietly bobbing in the waves like another smaller fishing boat. Ken's plans were to sit off from the fleet where they did not recognize who we were and glass their activities with our spotting scopes and binoculars. His battle plan was not to just barge into the fleet and try to randomly catch someone breaking the law but observe the crab fishermen from a distance and then have our suspects in a known violation before we made our approach.

Now in those days, California did not allow the commercial crab fishermen to take female Dungeness crabs or what were called short crabs. Those crabs taken had to be males only plus a certain measured distance between points across the carapace before they were legal to keep. Females were the brood stock and in order to keep the crab population healthy, regulations required the fishermen to return the females unharmed immediately back into the sea. Since it was easy to tell a male from a female crab externally, automatic release was an easy common sense given. Also, the short crabs were next year's crop and returning them safely back to the sea was a no brainer because size could quickly be ascertained with a hand held measuring device. Thusly, by sitting off at a distance and watching our crab fishermen as they pulled their crab pots, we could easily zero in on anyone who was not throwing the females or short crabs overboard. That would be simply evidenced by the fishermen's illegal overt actions if they kept everything they removed from their crab pots and threw nothing back into the ocean's waters.

If a crab fisherman was spotted keeping every crab they were pulling from their crab pots, Ken's plan was to wait a bit until the fisherman had a mess of illegal critters on board and then zoom up onto the offending boat before the crew could toss the crabs and our evidence of wrongdoing overboard. With that, an apprehension of the violator would soon be in order. That plan sounded simple enough to me. But what the hell did I know, being a rookie and all when it came to working the many times ingenious commercial fishermen on the high seas? However, I was one rookie who was soon to learn the tips of the trade among violating commercial fishermen or, I would soon take a 'drink' out from 60 fathoms of the ocean...

As we sat there that morning and watched several of our crab-fishing quarry, Ken went over the proper boarding procedures again with me when it came to safely jumping from ship to ship. After watching for about an hour, we finally had zeroed in on one boat's crew that never tossed a single crab overboard as they emptied their numerous crab pots! There was no way those commercial fishermen were only catching just male and all legally sized crabs to our way of thinking! Statistically, biologically, and realistically speaking, that was all but impossible to be only catching legal crabs in such a random commercial fishing operation. Bottom line, those crab fishermen could take the illegal crabs and sell them under the table or take them home for their use or for their neighbors and friends to enjoy. Or more insidiously, they could sell the illegal catch under the table to an outlaw crab processing facility to have the meat removed and sold as bulk crab meat. Once that process had occurred, there was no way to tell a legal crab from one that was illegal, thereby thwarting the law of the land and environmental common sense.

No matter how one looked at it, taking illegal crabs was a wasteful practice designed to make the resource, with all the fishing pressure it was under, eventually go the way of the buffalo. The icing on our cake came shortly thereafter when we could see members of the suspect crew taking several boxes of crabs below deck as if trying to hide a portion of their catch where it would be out of sight and out of mind. This they did while they presumably kept the legally possessed crabs in their crab boxes up on deck in case of any forthcoming inspection from the fish and game department.

Having seen and recorded enough for our records needed in a court of law to procure a prosecution, Ken fired up our engines and soon we were moving in on our crab boat of choice like the devil was on our tail. Man it was a great feeling! We were skimming over the waves at what had to be at least thirty miles per hour! The Rainbow would hammer up the steep side of a large oncoming swell and then we would just surf down the backside of that wave like a bat out of hell. The hull design of our boat was such that when slamming down into the trough of each swell, the onrushing water would come right up to the very lip of the boat's deck. Then the boat would recover, quickly lift itself up and slip into the advancing edge of the next oncoming wave. When that happened, we would repeat the whole surfing process all over again on the backside of the next wave. Talk about exhilarating, man, I was pumped and loving the hell out of every exciting moment in time! The hunt was on and I was not seasick. Good ole Hank Marak for sharing with me his 'sure fire' pickles and soda crackers recipe for countering my seasickness. That food formula was working like a 'champ' and I couldn't wait for my first illegal commercial fishing contact and apprehension at sea.

Speeding up to our suspect crab fisherman, I noticed their boat was named, "The Alaskan." I knew it was one of our local boats of constant interest because of its past illegal discretions regarding the commercial fish and game regulations and her notorious, short-tempered Italian captain. In fact, I knew from overhearing other warden's conversations that the boat's captain, Guido Gilbertini, and the rest of the Italian members of his lifelong crew, were known commercial fish and game outlaws. Local outlaws who were known for taking short salmon, short and female crabs and for taking every other illegal commercial fishing opportunity that arose from which they could make a dollar.

Approaching from The Alaskan's starboard side as if we were going to form a "T" with our vessel to theirs, Ken hailed them over our loudspeaker as we made our final approach. For the longest time, The Alaskan kept moving on like it was heading for its next set of crab pots and was deliberately ignoring our signal to stop and prepare for a fish and game inspection. I heard Ken swear under his breath as he adjusted the throttles and steering on his approach, in order to reposition our boat one more time so I could safely board the suspect boat.

Again Ken hailed The Alaskan and not a single crew member acknowledged out request to heave to and make ready to be boarded. Hell, they didn't even look up from their activities on deck or acknowledge that we were even there. Then Ken got pissed over being ignored after he had tried hailing the suspect vessel and turned on our siren. It was then that Captain Guido Gilbertini, casually left the wheel house and walked over to the rail of his ship like he had just seen us. Acting like the hind-end he was reputed to be, Gilbertini shouted back at us as his boat continued on its present course. He basically told us to wait until they had pulled the last of their string of crab pots. As Guido was shouting back at our boat, I saw one crew member casually move below the deck of The Alaskan like he was heading to the toilet. However, my budding fish and game warden suspicions said that lad was heading below decks in order to hide something he did not want us to see. I thought to myself, *If that move was made to hide a mess of illegal crabs from the searching eyes of "The Great Grotz", that would be me all you land lubber), they were in for a big surprise.* Little did I realize at the time, that world of wildlife law enforcement surprises cut both ways like a sharpened, double edged knife if one is not at the top of his game...

"Pull over and prepare for boarding and inspection of your catch and commercial fishing licenses. If you don't, you will be cited for Section 2012 of the Fish and Game Code for Failure to Show," said Ken over the loud speaker. Moments later, I could hear The Alaskan's outside radio speaker tuned into the crab fleet's frequency crackling with many voices from other crab fleet skippers. They had heard our siren off in the distance and observing us, a suspicious looking boat trying to board The Alaskan, were now warning their other brethren. Within moments, they let the rest of the fleet who were over the horizon know that the fish and game were in their midst. *Typical commercial fishermen attitudes from the north coast fishing fleet,* I thought. *Here we are trying to preserve the health of the crab population and the fishermen's way of life, as they stick it to us and ultimately themselves,* I thought disgustedly. Their 'hurray for me and screw you' attitude appeared to be the overall general feeling of the nearby fleet that fine day. That was if their ship-to-ship communications now being heard over The Alaskan's outside speaker and ours meant anything to the casual listener.

Once again, Ken tried to position The Rainbow alongside The Alaskan and form a T so I could safely board. I realized Guido had only slowed and not stopped his engines and their forward progress. He continued slowly yet coyly creeping forward and every time we tried to close so I could board from the starboard side, he would alter his vessel's course a tad more to port like he was just maintaining his steerage in the face of the oncoming swells. Every time he maneuvered his vessel in such a manner, it required Ken to start over and re-set our approach. It became obvious to Ken and me that Guido was just stalling for some reason or just being a hind-end because he historically had no use for the fish and game department. I wondered if his stalling was because of the crewmember that had quietly dropped below decks earlier once they became aware of our official and nearby soon to be inspection presence?

Shortly thereafter, the earlier disappearing crewmember came back up on deck and said something to Guido and with that, the captain finally quit playing his little game as we began moving alongside. Then Guido said something to that crewmember and he immediately grabbed up a nearby hose and began hosing down the deck of their iron-decked vessel with seawater.

Ken turned to me and said, "Watch your step when you jump onto the deck of their boat. They are hosing down the deck to make it even slicker for you when you land on their boat. Be careful you don't skid across their slick deck and smash into something and hurt yourself or slip across their deck and fall overboard on the far side."

With those words of caution ringing in my ears and somewhat pissed that Guido would do such a thing, I exited our cabin and walked alongside the narrow walkway by our wheelhouse to the small front deck area. Moments later, I was more than ready standing on the bow of our patrol boat as Ken cautiously slowed even further as we made our final approach to the side of The Alaskan. Ken hailed them again on our radio and advised them to lay to and prepare to be boarded. By now, the entire crab boat's crew was gathered at the rail and intently watching us as we made our final approach. A few moments later, Ken expertly maneuvered our boat as it approached the crab boat so that we formed a perfect T. That maneuver placed our boat no more than a foot off the side of their crab boat so we wouldn't strike each other as we bobbed up and down in the swells.

Standing on the heavily painted and sanded bow of our boat for the traction such grit offered the boarding officer and hanging onto a four-foot-long nylon rope attached to our bow to aid in steadying me as we bobbed up and down, I waited for the right opportunity to safely jump. I knew that if I jumped incorrectly trying to board another pitching and bobbing boat whose deck was higher than ours, my reward would be a cold Pacific Ocean bath in 60 fathoms of saltwater. That would be the 'best' part of a boarding screw up. Jumping incorrectly while alongside another heaving up and down vessel meant I could plunge down between two very close moving hulls and possibly be injured or crushed between them. Understanding that set of consequences, I tried to carefully judge when I would leap from our lower hulled boat onto their higher sided crab boat. I realized I would have to make a more than exaggerated leap to safely land mid-ships the vessel to be boarded. If not, I could lose my balance and fall over backwards into the ocean or drop down between the two vessels with disastrous results if I wasn't careful! With that, I looked over at the cold Pacific and watched the oncoming swells for the right moment to board. When I did, I lost the horizon by paying such deep attention to the movement of the swells and the pitching vessels.

That was when fate, which had been lurking between the internal intestinal swells caught up with me. Standing there on the bow of our boat, pitching wildly up and down with no horizon in view, I began to get queasy! Not a lot mind you, but it was there in my hinterland just the same. Trying to throw that sickening thought from my mind, when our two vessels were just feet apart, I checked the next on coming swell and, at the hoped for correct moment, jumped. However at the last second, The Alaskan caught a larger unseen swell than I had anticipated and as I sailed upward in my leap, my feet caught on the lip of the hull of their boat rising to meet that on coming wall of water. With that, I took a header onto their deck face first with a discernable and painful whump like a spilled sack of loose potatoes!

"Clumsy son-of-a-bitch, ain't he?" said Guido with a big grin as I lay there for a moment stunned and trying to get my physical bearings after the hard landing. "I hope this gorilla sized son-of-a-bitch doesn't destroy my boat," Guido grumbled. "Pick yourself up, you puke, and get done what you have to do. We have work to do and I don't have any time for you fish and game parasites," he continued as he spit a big spew of tobacco juice onto the deck near where I laid.

Rising up to my knees, I tried to stand on the now heavily pitching and rolling crab boat since it was not now under steerage, only to lose my balance and fall back onto my rump. Quickly getting to my feet, I carefully wiped the tobacco spittle off the arm of my uniform shirt that had splattered on me as I lay there on the deck that first go-around. You know, Folks, it is not nice to piss off Mother Nature or one of her minions. That goes double in the 'piss off department' when it comes to one now getting seasick, Teutonic son-of-a-bitch with the last name of Grosz.

By now, with the overwhelmingly strong stench of diesel smoke flooding into my nostrils from the nearby overhead stacks of their boat's engines, I was really starting to get queasy as hell! Holding back my new urge to puke, I asked to check the fishing licenses on all the members of the crab boat. It became very apparent that all the crew was not impressed with my grace or sea legs and took their time in producing their commercial fishing licenses just to add to my misery. By then, standing just below the exhaust stacks of their boat and breathing in those fumes from unburnt diesel fuel, I had to be turning green. I then realized that my legs were turning to rubber, my guts were looking to jump out of my throat and I was now sweating like a Methodist preacher at election time. For those folks who have not experienced the classic signs of starting to get seasick, trust me. Those were the classic signs and I was on my way to dying big time on that crab boat as I tried holding everything down and not looking like the sea going wimp that I was.

Finally all the crab fishermen's licenses checked out and then I had to examine their catch up on the forward portion of the deck to make sure the crabs they had kept were not females or undersized. Try that sometime when you are about to puke as you stand over a ton of crabs with a measuring device checking out the catch for correct width and all the time looking down into a crab box. Try that sometime, while standing on a pitching and yawing vessel blanketed with the smell of unburned diesel fuel and rotting sea creatures from days past harvests and you have a tendency for seasickness.

By now, Guido could tell from the obvious looks on my face and my demeanor that I was one sick puppy and just a small step away from puking all over the place. Seeing that, he went into his wheelhouse, opened up his lunch sack, retrieved an Italian salami sandwich, exited and offered it to me. "Here, Gorilla. Take a bite of this. It will help you in holding down what is ailing you and your obvious lack of sea legs," he said with a devious, all knowing grin. I was sure he had heard my fish and game captain's words around the commercial fishing crowd that I was a wimp when it came to sea duty. Offering the sandwich to me, he jabbed it straight under my nose and I was now smelling not only the boat's exhaust fumes but the strong smell of garlic from the salami in the sandwich!

Turning away and being pissed over the fact Guido, (1) had made us change our boarding procedures several times because he was an ornery cuss, (2) me having to leap over a higher rail when boarding and falling flat on my face on a deliberately hosed down slick deck, (3) being embarrassed over such a clumsily event, (4) made to intentionally stand directly under the exhaust stacks while checking their slow to be produced fishing licenses, (5) having his tobacco spittle being splashed on my clean shirt and (6) now having a stinking sandwich thrust deliberately under my nose, I allowed my Germanic temperament and mischievousness to 'rule the waves' (no pun intended). The way I figured it, Guido's deed of 'pissing' on me was now going to come back to haunt him in spades if I had my say.

"Your licenses check out as does your crab catch on deck from what I can see. Now, I will be going below deck to check out the rest of your vessel to make sure you are not hiding any illegally taken crabs," I said as I could tell puking up my gizzard was soon going to be an option and a gut-wrenching fact. With those words of my inspection intentions, Guido exploded! Instantly he began calling me every name in the book and advising me that he would tell his friend, Captain Gray, my boss, on just how unprofessional I was. Especially since to Guido's way of thinking I was stopping them from their God given right to crab and the monetary benefits from such activities that added to their livelihoods.

Letting those words slide off my being, I headed below deck in the same direction I had earlier observed one of his deck hands doing. With that, I turned on the slippery and heaving deck and almost fell as I went below. Big mistake!

Once below deck, the diesel smells were more intense and the stench of rotting crab juice from previous trips slammed into my nostrils like a thrown shot put. As a result, I found myself almost losing all those wonderful pickles and crackers I had earlier hogged down because of all those intense smells. Then I felt Guido's boat beginning to move forward and off he went on his way to check his next crab pot. *Great,* I thought. *Now I will have even more movement up, down and sideways to add to my discomfort while down here in the stinking hold of this vessel.*

But, wimp or not, I continued my search in the confined, below deck stinking spaces until I had located my suspected large wooden fish box clear full of illegal short and female crabs. From the looks of it, there were probably 250 pounds of the illegal critters all thrashing around in their crab box! Thank heavens, I still had the presence of mind to fill out and stick state fish and game seized evidence tags on the boxes of illegal crabs as I pitched and yawed below deck further churning up my insides.

Still excited over my first commercial fishing case, I almost forgot the rather serious issue of my seasickness for a moment. Almost... Remembering the previous issues on how we had been treated when we had originally approached Guido's vessel, my spill on his purposely wetted deck, the sleeve of my shirt covered with a splatter of Guido's tobacco spit, being purposely maneuvered directly under his stinking diesel stacks while checking their fishing licenses and then having a smelly salami sandwich thrust under my nose, totally struck home and now those slights all came home to roost.

About then my insides advised it was time to come up for air... Starting to head for the topside so I could get rid overboard of what was ailing me, I abruptly stopped in my tracks. I figured since Guido had been such a hind-end in making my job harder if not more dangerous, I was now prepared to reward his bad behavior with some of my own.

That thought running freely through my mind set off my now very intense desire to puke. Without a moment's hesitation, up spewed a gallon of dill pickles and a crate of soda crackers. Talk about broadcast puking! I blew a three foot stream of goo all over the insides of the hold of their ship. Suffice to say, it had to be a nine or a ten in the pretty department! Then the sickening sweet smell of fresh vomit and unburned aerosol diesel fumes slammed into my nostrils. Simultaneously, The Alaskan gave a lurch as it hit a large swell incorrectly, slamming me off balance and sideways. When it did, I hit a bulkhead and then puked up another gallon of pickles and crackers directly into their vessel's small galley. Man, my 'soup' splattered all over and into the grates of their little gas stove, covered their small table and blew across the galley floor like a fresh breath of wind moving across the tops of the grasses on the prairie before a storm. In short, my mess was more than equal to Captain Guido's acts as a hind-end towards me after I had boarded his ship.

Now deathly seasick since I had unleashed the lions from hell inside me, I continued puking oodles of partially digested pickles and soda crackers all over their fish boxes of legal crab stored below decks. Those legal crabs would have to be later picked over by the poor chaps working in the crab-processing house and I could just imagine what they would have to say. Brother, I hadn't realized I had eaten so many pickles and crackers... But sure as all get out, I had a full boiler and now Guido and his boat were the recipients of my boiler full of partially digested misery.

Staggering back topside feeling better after puking up two gallons of pickles and cracker soup and feeling somewhat avenged, I informed Guido that he and his crew were in possession of several hundred pounds of short and female crabs. As such, he was directed to follow us back to Eureka where those illegal crabs would be unloaded and held as evidence. I also advised that if he or any member of his crew tried to off load any of that evidence overboard while on the way to the docks, they would be additionally charged with 2012 of the Fish and Game Code for Failure To Show and destruction of state's evidence. Being prosecuted for those violations as commercial fishermen could very well cost him them their fishing licenses and I could see those facts being now registered in Guido's eyes!

With those words of warning, Guido blew his stack! I really didn't realize how low brow my lineage was until Guido spelled it out for me with his ranting and raving. I was called a parasitic state gorilla and not worthy of suckling from my mother's breasts. Then it got even worse as I waited for Ken to come alongside with our patrol boat so I could board.

That was when it got dicey. I was still sicker than a gut shot dog, had a terrible case of rubber legs instead of the needed and required strong sea legs and, at that point, didn't really care if I died or drowned trying to get back on board my own vessel. Ken expertly brought The Rainbow carefully amidships and, looking down at the heaving and yawing bow, I realized what a small space I had to land on in order not to take a dip into the ocean. The more I stood there looking, the sicker I got and the smaller that spot onto which I was to land continued diminishing in size. Ken, realizing I was hesitating because of my seasickness, brought the patrol boat right up to the edge of The Alaskan and with that, I jumped! My landing showed that this gorilla needed to be back into his jungle swinging from vines instead of jumping from ship to ship. But suffice to say, I got an A in the avoiding getting wet department and an F in the grace department with my landing…

Making a long story short, we tailed The Alaskan back into the Port of Eureka and hosed off the boxes full of vomit once we got them up onto the docks. We offloaded our seized evidence and conducted an exact inventory, recorded the same, and photographed the evidence. Ken made a quick phone call

115

to the county attorney for permission to dump the live crabs because he felt there was no use in destroying the crab resource since we had already documented the same with our cameras. Keeping only the dead crabs, we returned the rest of the live ones back into the waters of Humboldt Bay with the permission of the county attorney. We did that by just dropping the live crabs off the dock and into the channel's waters.

In the meantime standing on the docks, Guido continued calling me every name in the book except a white man and the words of a damn fish and game gorilla were high on his list of expletives. He became especially 'complimentary' when he subsequently discovered the hold of his vessel smelling strongly of rotten crab juice, diesel fuel, vomit and a literal barrel full of digested and partially digested dill pickles and crackers...

Having enough sea adventure for the day and still being deathly seasick (I had lain on the stern of The Rainbow all the way back to Eureka going through numerous bouts of dry heaving), Ken moored our patrol boat back at the marina and we disembarked. Ken reported to Captain Gray about our success in catching a local outlaw who needed catching and I went home trying to recover.

The next day, I got on the phone and called my true friend and one of my mentors, Warden Hank Marak. You can bet your bottom dollar he got an earful about his suggestion of dill pickles and soda crackers as a medicinal for my motion sickness! However, true to form and the inexperience of youth, I didn't learn from my dill pickles and soda crackers lesson...

Sometime later I was assigned to The Rainbow for an extended assignment during a spat of really foul weather at sea. Concerned over my plague of seasickness, I turned to my veteran warden and dear friend, Hank Marak, once again for some more fatherly advice. You would have thought that Hank, after the hind-end chewing I gave him over his first seasickness food suggestion, would have only shared his deepest family seasick secret recipe with me for my next marine patrol. In fact, you would have thought I would have learned as well. But, it didn't happen!

On that next occasion in which I sought out his wealth of knowledge and well-meaning guidance, Hank recommended I eat all the chili I could hold and the secret in such a technique was to spice it up as hot as I could stand it with extra hot sauce. If I did that, Hank said that would surely do the trick. In fact, he validated that suggestion with the story of how some of his Navy shipboard cook friends, in the face of an oncoming typhoon at sea, would feed all the sailors such spicy hot grub so they could combat the seasickness associated with such a violent weather event and remain battle ready.

(For all my readers out there, you will have to read in my National Outdoor Book Award winning book titled, *Wildlife Wars,* in a chapter titled, Chili for Breakfast, as to how I fared using Hank's newest suggestion. If you do read that story, make sure you are sitting down so you don't hurt yourself falling over laughing.)

As for the Flowers in this story, here they are. One Flower in particular was that I continued learning about the various facets of my profession relative to marine patrols. I was fortunate to experience not only having a fine skipper to teach me the right way of doing law enforcement at sea but also learned an ocean full of knowledge about marine species, weather at sea, how to read the seas, and operating a twin screw, 32-foot vessel. I learned about a new set of laws pertaining to the marine environment and a gained world of knowledge about working a totally new facet of human induced law enforcement problems. That Flower of knowledge about the greed of man over any other form of common sense and the understanding of what was to come if one abused the natural resource, was more than driven home to me on those marine patrol experiences in spades.

Flowers and Tombstones

As a follow up to the above, think about what has happened to some Pacific marine species after the greedy and thoughtless minds and hands of man have left their mark. I can remember when Dungeness crabs sold for 19 cents per pound and wild king and silver salmon went for 50 cents per pound. Because of their reduced availability in today's markets, $13.00 dollars per pound for Dungeness crab is the price in Colorado in today's market place and over $14.00 per pound for wild caught Frazier River sockeye salmon is now not uncommon. Being a student of history and having worked with the shortsighted commercial fishermen in the 1960's, I can see the correlation between the thinking sameness of that facet of our humanity and that of the buffalo hunters of old. Need I say anymore?

There are several Tombstones associated with this story as well. No longer does the Dungeness crab and Pacific salmon fleet in Eureka number about 300 plus fishing vessels. For the most part as these words are written in 2015, the fishing fleet has mostly gone elsewhere because the above resources have been drastically reduced or, in the case of the Pacific salmon species, severely depleted. There were plenty of Tombstones to go around in those arenas for those species, especially when it came to humankind using their God-given common sense.., or not! Gee, I wonder if Guido and others of his kind who took illegal shorts and females in great numbers every time they had the chance, had anything to do with such a drastic change in the overall crab populations?

The last Tombstone is for my friend, Warden Lt. Ken Brown. What a hell of a good man! Bright, dedicated, smart as a whip, resource oriented, a real man, and great human being. He always cared for people, especially his crewmates, and the Rule of Law. His caring went doubly so for those of us who rode with him in the patrol boat and were seasick prone. I will never forget the steps he went to while operating the boat to keep it from pitching and yawing so much when I rode with him. I didn't ask him to do that. He was just an understanding human being and did so in order to make my life bearable.

Ken made fish and game Captain in his later years and carried on his good work in and for those in the world of wildlife and those folks yet to come. He later contracted cancer and died a horrible death before his works were finished.

Lord, when the fists and bullets were flying and Warden Ken Brown was on 50- foot Pacific Ocean swells with a 32-foot patrol boat, You were there for him. And, when Your critters were dying, Ken Brown was there for You, Lord! Those would be nice words to place on Ken's Tombstone if You were of a mind...

THE LURE OF THE PACIFIC BLACK BRANT

Early one morning during California's Pacific black brant hunting season in February, I was quietly sitting high up on the bluffs overlooking South Humboldt Bay. It was a typical north coast morning with drizzling rains moving through the area trailed by wisps of fog drifting about. To the west out over the Pacific Ocean hung a dense fog bank running north and south along the California coast until it drifted out of my field of view in both directions.

Below where I sat, I could hear the familiar popping sounds of the brant hunters' shotguns muted by the sounds of the nearby pounding surf as they pass shot the low flying black brant sea geese moving off the ocean, over the sandy spit into nearby South Humboldt Bay. Once there, the little species of sea goose would feed on its favorite food among the bay's numerous eelgrass beds. When fed-up, the geese would quietly pause and rest on the bay's waters from the rigors of their northward migrations to their breeding grounds in the high Arctic. However, as the great eating and culinary delight little black brant overflew the south spit or rested on the bay, they were hotly pursued by the area's local sportsmen. Sitting on the bluffs that fine morning was a game warden who just as aggressively pursued the local hunters, especially those with an outlaw bent, as much as they did the elusive little brant.

Just as I was getting ready to descend from the bluffs and onto the beach pass shooting area in order to check the hunters, a soft sound came through my open window that stopped me in my morning's endeavors. In the recesses of my game warden's mind, I would have sworn I heard the soft 'crumping' sounds a shotgun would make far out to sea. *What the heck was that all about*? I thought. *Did I just hear someone shooting a shotgun far out to sea and, if so, at what?* Exiting my patrol vehicle, I quietly stood there in the morning's coolness and listened. Not another like sound greeted my ears for the longest time. Tiring of waiting for a possible phantom sound to reoccur, I gathered up my skirts and prepared to head off the bluffs and move down into my pass shooting brant hunters scattered about below on the South Spit.

BOOM, BOOM, BOOM, BOOM, went four quick shots from a single shotgun that I had now deduced WAS being fired from far out in the ocean! Grabbing my binoculars from the front seat of my patrol car, I scanned the length of the fog bank's westward line trying to echolocate in on my mystery shooter out on the ocean. Nothing greeted my eyes except a single small fishing vessel anchored out in the ocean at the edge of the distant fog bank in the area of the sounds of the shooting.

My 7X50 binoculars just didn't give me enough fishing boat definition at that distance so I went to Plan B. Grabbing my sixty power spotting scope from the seat of my patrol car and steadying it on the hood of my vehicle, I zeroed it onto my suspect fishing vessel. I figured if that was where the mystery shooting had come from, they must have been illegally shooting gulls that were interfering with their fishing in some manner. The kind of illegal shooting of gulls was commonly practiced by many commercial fishermen in that day and age when out to sea. Notice that I didn't call them 'sea gulls' because there is no such a critter. (For my readers' edification, there are black-backed gulls, herring gulls, and the like but no generic maritime bird called a 'sea gull'.)

In the morning's cool air, looking through my spotting scope, I could clearly see two lads on the stern of a fishing boat and both men appeared to be deep sea fishing with rod and reel. That was it! No one was shooting any gulls off the stern of their vessel nor were there any such birds in the air around the vessel. Then I carefully glassed off their stern of that vessel to see if I observed any dead gulls floating in the wake of their boat. No such luck there either. Keeping the 'big eye' on my suspects, I saw nothing else of interest. After a few more minutes of fruitless observation, I put away my spotting scope and prepared again to descend from the bluffs and onto the South Spit brant pass shooting area below with its many sportsmen.

BOOM, BOOM, BOOM, went three more quick shots from the ocean and nearly as I could tell, adjacent to the fishing vessel located at the edge of the fog bank! That time I knew my mind nor my ears were playing tricks on my miserable carcass and out came the spotting scope again. That time I was a little more patient and soon rewarded for having such a heavy dose of curiosity.

At first, I couldn't believe what my eyes were now showing me through the spotting scope. Between the ocean's long swells. I had just spotted a sliver of a low-hulled boat emerging from out of the nearby fog bank approaching the anchored fishing vessel. As it approached the fishing boat, the vessel's two fishermen reeled up their fishing lines, laid down their fishing poles and walked over to the side of their boat from whence the low hulled boat was fast approaching. It was then that I realized the low-hulled boat was none other than a 'scull boat'.

(To all my readers out there, a scull boat is a very low-hulled structure of a boat that is propelled by normal rowing oars or a sculling oar positioned out behind the vessel's stern. The shooter lies down inside the low hull and, once his quarry is located, begins sculling or moving slowly towards the swimming migratory waterfowl objects of his interest. Once the sculler is within shotgun range, he quickly rises up and shoots his unsuspecting nearby swimming quarry. It historically has been a very successful shooting platform because of its stealthy, low-hulled approach almost unseen by the critters because it rides so low in the water.)

Man, I could hardly believe my eyes! That type of boat with its low freeboard hull design was usually only used in calmer waters like a lake, river, bay or estuary. Sure as hell not on any potentially rough watered ocean! However, there it was just as sure as God made cow slobbers slicker than all get out. What happened next gave me an almost unbelieving case of the BIG EYE! The man operating the scull boat began tossing up into the fishing vessel (or mother boat) dead black brant. By the time I got hold of my senses and my law enforcement brain caught up with those senses, I began counting. Within a matter of moments, I had observed the scull boat operator throwing 22 dead brant up onto the deck of the fishing vessel. Since the daily bag limit was only three brant per person per day, my lad had a HUGE over limit problem! The two men on board the vessel then picked the birds up and began tossing them into an open fish box located amidships of the 'mother ship'.

Following that moment in time, my astonished eyes got an even bigger surprise. Out from the fog bank emerged another scull boat! By the time that boat's shooter had finished unloading his dead birds, he had tossed 31 dead brant up onto the deck of the fishing vessel as well! Then as the scull-boat operators carefully exited their boats and jumped up into the still anchored fishing boat, the damn fog bank began rolling over them. Within moments, my two illegal brant shooters and their protective mother vessel were misted over within the cover of the fog bank and soon lost from sight. However, in my last moments of observation, I saw the two scull boats lifted up out from the ocean and placed onto the deck of the fishing vessel. Then the fishing boat operator pulled up his anchor and began sailing northward into the deeper gloom of the fog bank and out from my sight.

Damn, I was more than perplexed because of the moving fog bank hiding my outlaws' craft and my amazement at what I had just observed. Hell, I was so spell bound over what I had never seen before, namely scull boats being hunted from out on the ocean, that I didn't even get the name from the stern of the fishing vessel. Talk about a damn dummy rookie trick. That whole episode sure took the cake! Even worse, I couldn't personally identify the two scull boat shooters in my 60 power spotting scope. (Note: I didn't call them hunters because of their lack of obeying the law when they had obviously taken and possessed huge over limits of brant as observed by me.) Then my frustration really set in. Here I had two shooters with huge over limits of brant, a state and federal wildlife violation, and I couldn't even bring them to justice. I didn't know the name of their mother ship so I couldn't cold track a subsequent investigation back to the vessel's owners or operators and, through interrogations, procure the names of my outlaw brant shooters for later prosecution. Hell, I was as high and dry as a mud turtle in the Arizona desert when it came to solving this mystery…

Then the seriousness of that moment really hit me right between the eyes. The brant were currently in their northward migration to their Arctic breeding grounds. That meant they were already paired up since they mated for life. That being the case, anyone killing them now would be breaking up the pair bonds of the two birds. That meant the remaining bird of the pair had to use up a lot of its vital energy in going through the ritual of pair bonding once again. When that happened, by using up all that energy in the courting process, vital fat reserves were then used up and the clutch size of the new nesting pair would probably be smaller and laid later in the summer. The clutches would be smaller because the length of the nesting season and the incubation period of opportunity in the high Arctic would be reduced because of the time taken out during their start-over earlier courtship rituals.

Normally something like that can be overcome by many populations but not so much in the high Arctic nesting brant species. The black brant's population numbers in that day and age in 1966 were already historically low. Any such unusual mortality suffered by that species, like over killing on their migration route on the ocean, would have had a very deleterious effect on the overall health of that animal's population. Hence, I had to find a way to shut down those brant killing sons of a gun before they made a real dent in the brant's numbers. In short, what my shooters were doing was setting themselves up in an ambush pattern within the brant migration corridors out on the ocean. The brant, not expecting such a deadly obstacle, would unknowingly fly into easy gunning range on a historically quiet and safe ocean migration corridor. To my way of thinking, such a gunning operation was paramount to disaster.

Knowing a fishing vessel that size more than likely would normally be docked in the Humboldt Bay area somewhere, I headed for the South Spit's jetty and the only entrance into the harbor. I did so because I could closely examine any vessel passing into Humboldt Bay from that location. If I spotted a vessel with two scull boats on board going through the channel during my stakeout, guess who would be waiting at the marina or commercial boat docks for my two shooters and their boat crew to dock? I sat there all the rest of that day looking over every vessel that entered the harbor and never saw my suspect vessel. Where they went I did not know but now, by damn, I had my German Teutonic dander up. For all of you non-believers out there, it is not nice to mess with Mother Nature or any of her minions. Especially one who now had the bit in his teeth after getting his butt figuratively kicked by the illegal brant shooters earlier out on the ocean. Plus, the little Pacific black brant was one of my favorite species within the world of waterfowl. To my way of thinking, the glove of challenge had been tossed at my feet and come hell or high water, I had picked it up and was going to do something with it. When I did, you could bet your bottom dollar it would be picked up not to warm my hands!

Then it hit me! The only way I could get my man was if my shooters returned and repeated their little illegal over bagging trick out on the ocean. That meant that if I wanted to be like the R.C.M.P. and get my man, I would have to go to sea and apprehend those shooters in their little illegal killing act while out on the ocean blue. To all my readers out there who have just finished reading the first story in this chapter, you know what that meant. Yep, I was going to have to get hold of Lt. Ken Brown, take The Rainbow to sea and try to catch these brant shooting varmints red-handed. That also meant upchucking my way to and from the capture point. With another seasick trip on The Rainbow at sea facing my miserable carcass, I began wondering what the hell I had done to have offended God so much?

The next day I met with Ken and advised him of what I had earlier observed. Together we came up with a capture plan. We would wait until we had another like calendar day with the ever-present fog bank and then venture forth with the patrol boat. (For my readers' edification, many times wildlife outlaws who are successful on a certain day, under the same weather conditions and not having been molested by the law, will return under those same set of circumstances because of their first time successes and in so doing, will repeat their killing actions.) With that maxim in mind, Ken and yours truly were trying to line up the stars so to speak on our plan of attack. Since the brant migration and hunting season was in full swing and the birds tended to migrate just over the ocean wave tops a safe distance from land, that is where we decided we would set up shop. Then we would wait. By going out to sea during the same kind of foggy weather event, a like day on Saturday when the initial shoot had occurred and hide in the fog, we could hopefully surprise and capture our violators. With that, our trap had been planned and I headed off to see my doctor to see if he could recommend a sure fire medicine that would help alleviate my damn seasickness. No more was I going to trust Warden Hank Marak with any of his home remedies when it came to controlling my bouts of seasickness when at sea.

For the next three outings with The Rainbow during like weather events when our lads had been originally observed scull boating at sea, we drew big fat zeroes. On those occasions at sea, I was going to be as good physically as I could be. My doctor had prescribed several types of seasickness medicines like Bonine and I was loaded up to the gills on that medication. One of those medicines so utilized 'killed' my brain and the other killed my guts. At least that was what I was told would happen by my doctor. However, after an hour of bobbing in the ocean off the edge of the perennial west coast fog bank, I had managed to puke up everything inside me including my shoes, gizzard and expensive medicines! But no brant shooters capture-luck for the physical and mental discomfort I suffered during those outings was forthcoming.

Come the fourth outing and the last weekend of the brant hunting season, Ken and what was left of my miserable seasick carcass were quietly bobbing in the fog just a mile or so off the mouth of Humboldt Bay where I had originally observed my brant shooting lads. I was quietly watching the radar as Ken stood watch on the stern of The Rainbow and listened for any sounds of shooting as we silently bobbed up and down. Can any of you imagine what it is like under the radar hood watching the gizmo go round and round while you are pitching and yawing at sea? And in so doing, being the chap that is somewhat inclined towards getting seasick even when you take an abrupt drink of water from a glass? Yeah, that was a real wonderful experience for me to say the least. Feeling the urge to heave again, I yelled at Ken to come and spell me from my radar duties so I could go and puke overboard once again. Standing on the bobbing up and down stern (damn, I am getting seasick just writing this story), I fed the Dungeness crabs the remains of my liver and a gizzard.

Standing back up after leaning over the rail, I heard the distinct sounds of three shots fired on the ocean way south of our position! Talk about excited! When I had been watching the radar, I had observed numerous other boats moving about in the fog but nothing that really interested me as possibly the shooters. Standing there on the stern of The Rainbow, I broke out into a rather seasick smile. That shooting just heard had to be coming from my scull boating brant shooters!

Turning, I saw that Ken had also heard the shooting off in the distance and was in the process of pumping our vessel's bilges for the run that was to come. Moments later, I heard the familiar rumble of The Rainbow's powerful twin engines stumbling to life and could feel our craft beginning to turn to the south. Now that we were slowly moving again, I felt a lot of my queasiness beginning to subside. No, my impatient readers, we didn't roar forth in the fog after our shooters. Remember that our shooters were in tiny scull boats that rode so lowly in the water that our radar would not pick them up on the screen. Can any of you think what it would be like to be in such a dinky vessel and then be rammed by a 32-foot patrol boat moving along about 25 knots? I rest my case as to that impulse on your parts to make us get our hind ends into gear and go after our shooters.

Following that, we would idle south for a ways, then stop, kill our engines and listen. Each time we stopped, we could hear more shooting to our south and by then, Ken had located on the radar which boat or mother ship he figured to be that of our culprits. In the meantime, I stood on the bow in the cooling dampness of the fog and just let the moisture thankfully collect on my face. That coolness and wet sure went a long way towards making me feel better as did any forward motion we had. Then throw into those elements the excitement of the chase and we had the icing on the cake. As we motored along in spurts, I observed hundreds of northward migrating streams of brant skimming just over the tops of the swells off our bow and could hear their soft, plaintive calls of Cr-r-r-ruk. God, it was great to be alive and finally on the hunt, even if I still didn't feel worth a damn.

For the next forty minutes or so, we slowly crept our way southward towards the sounds of constant shooting as those sounds became louder and clearer. Finally, Ken stopped, fearing if he proceeded any further he may hit and swamp any scull boat he came upon in the dense fog. However, the shooting persisted and it was obvious that our scull boaters were blasting away at the streams of low flying little brant like there was no tomorrow. And for some of those little critters, there would not be any tomorrow...

Man, that little sea goose was so vulnerable. It was no larger than a mallard duck and was pretty easy to kill or maim. *Finally getting my hands on those dedicated killers will suit me just fine*, I thought. *Especially if they were to have big over limits in their possession.* I was sure they would if the dense streams of migrating brant flying by our craft and the frequency of their shooting spoke to that end.

About then the shooting abruptly stopped and both Ken and I were glued to our radar set to see what might be happening. Ken figured the vessel we had been watching and slowly approaching was now in the process of loading up two smaller craft on board. Taking that as our cue, Ken began idling once again slowly towards what we suspected was our fog-shrouded shooters' mother boat's location. About five minutes later, a dark shape emerged out from the dense fog which moments later became identifiable as our suspect fishing boat catering to our ocean-going brant shooters.

As we emerged from the fog, we observed what appeared to be two shooters getting out from their scull boats and stepping up onto the mother ship's deck. About then they saw our approaching vessel as they began pulling their scull boats out from the ocean. Emerging totally from the fog bank out into the light of day a few moments later, we observed four men standing on the deck of their vessel looking hard at the oncoming patrol vessel. They had looks of dread and surprise all at the same time splashed across their faces. Sticking up out from the stern deck of our suspect vessel were the shapes of the bows of two scull boats and, man, did that ever warm the cockles of my heart. As I said earlier, just like the R.C.M.P., we finally had our men!

"Heave to! State Fish and Game Wardens," I shouted from my bow position on The Rainbow as Ken maneuvered us alongside their vessel moments later. "Attention! State fish and game wardens. Heave to and prepare to be boarded for inspection," I yelled again so there would be no misunderstanding of the reason for our vessel's nearness and direct approach.

You talk about four surprised chaps. They had nothing but amazement splashed clear across their faces. Just imagine that, my readers. Having the illegal brant shoot of a lifetime out in the middle of the ocean in open violation of the fish and game laws and then all of a sudden, being hailed by those enforcing the very law you, the shooters, were breaking. That sure as hell would put a crimp in anyone's style and a smile on any badge carrier's face.

Even more amazement followed as the locally well-known fish and game patrol boat unloaded a gorilla-sized human being onto the stern of the suspect shooters' mother vessel. When that gorilla-sized chap landed on the deck of their boat, it was alongside a huge pile of freshly killed brant. The only other thing that I observed that was even slicker than cow slobbers with our actions, were the four unbelieving looks on the faces on our totally amazed violators. Ken backed The Rainbow off a few feet as I identified myself again and began collecting drivers' licenses from our four suspects. Brother, talk about glum faces, especially when I counted out 63 dead brant! Suffice to say, having 57 brant over the limit is not a real good position to be in. That would be even more so, if the game warden was standing right there examining the whole mess of shooters, a mound of dead birds and the shooters' two boat-driving accomplices.

Two hours later, we had escorted our brant shooters and their two boat partners in crime back to the docks in Eureka. There citations were issued to all four men. To our actual shooters, citations were issued for being in co-possession of 57 brant over the limit. They were not cited for a taking' violation because neither Ken nor yours truly observed either of them shooting the brant. We knew they had been the ones killing the birds but since we had not observed such illegal actions, under the law, we could not file those 'taking' charges against our shooters.

Since the boat operators denied any taking activities and neither possessed a valid hunting license nor were seen shooting, they were cited for Aiding and Abetting in the possession of brant over limits. As I later discovered through individual interrogations, they had knowingly rented their boat out to our two shooters for such an illegal brant-shooting escapade at sea. The boat operators also admitted that they knew they would more than likely be transporting over limits of black brant back to the docks. With those admissions, citations were hung on the boat owners and operators as well. As an added bonus, both of the men who had been in the scull boats and doing all the shooting, had been using unplugged shotguns and were cited accordingly.

Then as an afterthought, Ken ordered both scull boats seized and they were placed on the dock as was the pile of dead brant and two seized shotguns. When that occurred, talk about howling from the scull boat owners. Both scull boats were richly handmade from cedar and were works of art from days long past and part of the history of the north coast scull boating fraternity. A rich and historic loss on the parts of the two owners would be an understatement if they were later forfeited to the government.

Two weeks later, our four men stood before the mast and pled guilty to the charges laid against them in the Eureka Municipal Court. The scull boat shooters were fined $650.00 each for their two violations and their shotguns were forfeited to the State of California. The two commercial boat operators in crime were fined $500.00 each for their bit in aiding and abetting in the illegal taking and possession of the black brant. The judge also ordered the two scull boats forfeited to the State of California because of what he considered the seriousness and deliberate intent to commit such a blatant fish and game violation. Talk about howling from the two scull boat operators when they were advised their scull boats were no more. You would have thought we had just eaten their firstborn. That howling was soon stopped by the judge when he asked the two scull boat owners if they each would have preferred to serve 30 days in jail for their offenses along with his other judicial renderings. It was amazing how those words from the judge regarding an additional 30-day sentence in the pokey silenced any further clamoring about losing a couple of wooden boats.

As that case turned out, it was memorable. It all started with a great set of God given game warden's ears hearing something out of the ordinary occurring far out on the ocean coming from the edge of a sound-deadening fog bank. A sound heard from out of the ordinary that, when investigated, led to the Flowers in this story. Especially when that led to two very dedicated and devious wildlife killers being apprehended red-handed in a major waterfowl over limit violation in which they were doing serious damage to the black brant breeding resource. In fact, that was the largest black brant over limit case I ever made in my state or federal career as a wildlife officer! I would say that represented at least a Field of Flowers to my way of thinking.

Now come the Tombstones. There were 63 brant illegally killed on the day of the apprehension. Of that number, half would statistically be males and the other half females. Had they lived, those females would have produced 4-8 young each. Multiply 32 times or half of that clutch size with a minimum of four young of the year produced and you get 128 young of the year. Had those 63 brant not been taken, they would have more than likely produced at least 128 young of the year. That might not sound like much but to a species population that is struggling to maintain its healthy numbers, that is a scull boat full! Then multiply that number by 4-8, had they all lived, for the breeding season the year following. There was also another very important unknown associated with this illegal happening. How many breeding pairs were broken up in that gross illegal shoot where only one member of the pair had been taken? With the breakup of those breeding pairs, there will be additional loss as those remaining birds are forced to go through the mating ritual all over again. In that process, those birds would be burning up vital fat reserves and time needed for breeding, egg laying, incubation, rearing and then their return migration before the high Arctic closes in with the ravages of winter once again. Then how many were crippled and managed to escape during these illegal shoots only to later die out on the ocean? And more than likely, those that crippled off, were in turn later eaten by seals or sea lions. With those potential losses in mind, how many birds out of a struggling population do you readers out there figure we additionally lost?

Another Tombstone related to this adventure was the fact that I was unable to prosecute my lads for the first over limit violations I had initially observed while sitting up on the bluff overlooking the ocean . I truly could not definitively identify my first set of lads as being those Ken and I apprehended weeks later. I knew they were the same lads based on their method and location of operation and my lads knew it as well. However, without definitive proof such as me being able to testify as to that level of proof in a court of law, all I had was a whiff in the wind. That was especially so when they were interviewed and, realizing their peril if they said anything more about the earlier trip, all four men clammed up. They were initially just too far away and, with the fog rolling in, at too great a distance for me to make a positive identification. So, I had to walk away from any subsequent prosecutions for that original over limit violation seen from the bluff that first go around. You know, the instance involving the 53 brant flopped up onto the deck of their mother ship in the original observation. As I have said many times in my previous writings, sometimes you eat the bear and sometimes he eats you.

You can quickly see that one's illegal or unintended actions in the world of wildlife can fill a graveyard full with one hell of a stand of Tombstones. Imagine being able to propel yourself back 65,000,000 million years in time. As you land on earth during that period, you find that you have landed on a butterfly and killed it. Imagine, if you can, the long-term possible ramifications of just killing that one butterfly 65,000,000 million years ago. Had that butterfly lived, it may have been eaten by a bigger insect, which in turn was eaten by a lizard whose eggs were later eaten by maybe the 'genesis critter' of a human being. That 'genesis critter' was saved from starving by eating those eggs which saved its life and in the end, its genetics for all time, eventually led to YOU! I know that example sounds a bit farfetched and does not truly equate to a few black brant removed from a flock of breeding birds. But, we are talking about a total of 119 black brant killed in these two instances. Who knows what those loss ramifications will equate to 65,000,000 million years from now? Nuff said for now!

In the middle 1960's when I was a college student at Humboldt State College in the town of Arcata, nearby South Humboldt Bay was home to about 50,000 Pacific black brant. Black brant who were resting from their northward migrations on their way to the high Arctic. As these words are written in 2015, I am told by local residents living in that area that there are but a fraction of those numbers in Humboldt Bay today during their northward migration to the Arctic nesting grounds. Once again, a Field of Tombstones instead of a Field of Flowers is the end result, in part, of our overshooting along their migration route... It sure didn't take 65,000,000 million years to already be showing the deleterious effects of over harvest of a species during its northward migration from Mexico all the way up the western seaboard of California, Oregon, Washington, Canada and Alaska. Gosh, there goes that damn butterfly thing again from 65,000,000 years ago...

CATCHING A THIEF TO SAVE A SALMON

Sitting at my home in Eureka one evening reading the National Rifle Association's monthly magazine, I all of a sudden became aware of the almost physical presence of my two guardian angels moving around inside me. Guardian angels who were beginning to flutter around inside me like there was no tomorrow and I had damn well better be on my toes for what was yet to come. Having learned early on in life that when those Heaven sent messages became internally apparent that meant something was wrong in the hen house, be it danger heading my way or some other kind of world of wildlife problem. Being a wildlife conservation officer used to working long hours and alone because of the limited numbers of my counterparts, I had learned early on to take serious notice of such frantic guardian angel events in order to avoid a wreck and enable me to come home at the end of each day.

Now before I continue this story, I feel an explanation is necessary, especially to all you readers out there. To those of us who are fortunate enough to have guardian angels like many others in the field of law enforcement or to those who are just blessed, guardian angels are a force to be listened to and reckoned with! The key is not only to have such blessings of forewarning but be able to understand what such events translate into and take the appropriate actions. In my case, I had two guardian angels because I was twice as big as the average "Yogi Bear" and needed greater protections because I possessed such a magnificent carcass... Well, that and I always seemed to be getting in over my head more times than not in the field of wildlife law enforcement.

Laying down my magazine, I quietly took note in my mind's eye of what was now going on inside me and the ramifications of what could possibly be going on around me in the world of wildlife that would cause my angels such concern. Sport and commercial salmon seasons were in full swing in the rivers and on the ocean along the west coast. I had the usual numbers of out of work lumbermen illegally taking deer and elk during the closed season in the surrounding temperate rain forest and during the lowest of my ocean tides, I had my outlaw clam diggers. Other than that, things were quiet on the western front. I then noticed that my wife, Donna, had put down her sewing and was quietly watching me. She had sensed a physical change come over me and was wondering, knowing me as well as she did, what law enforcement action-thoughts were stirring within my miserable carcass. Action thoughts that more than likely, would be leading to having her husband 'hit the decks a-running and spin the guns' around in order to 'head 'em up and move 'em out'.

"Honey," I said, "I think I need to be out and about. My sixth sense is telling me something bad is in the works and I need to go and have a look-see."

"Are you going out to work deer poachers alone again?" she asked. "Because if you are, why don't you take our neighbor along with you this time. He has been hoping to go out with you on a patrol and it being Friday night, this would be a good time to take him since he does not have to work tomorrow at the power plant."

That was typical Donna. She was always the one to worry about my well-being when out on patrol by myself. Especially when it came to having her fella working alone at night chasing armed poachers who were many times fortified with "John Barleycorn" and in numbers greater than any single fish and game officer chasing them at the time. Such classes of outlaw chaps were often times with an illegal critter in their possession and inclined to do stupid things when confronted by an officer of the law. That was just one of the many reasons why I loved Donna so dearly. Not only for her concerns about my well-being but she always seemed to sense when my soul, like the wind who never knew its place, was becoming ever restless.

"Yeah, I suppose I can grab off Bob and see if he wants to spend some time this evening chasing outlaws," I quietly replied to ease her concerns. To be frank, having Bob, a non-law enforcement type who knew nothing of the dangers in the

Humboldt County outback, could quickly find himself being no more help than just being another target if and when the shooting started or the crap hit the fan.

An hour later, Bob and I were quietly sitting hidden in among numerous other parked vehicles at the commercial fishing fleet boat dock in Eureka. The harbor was 'jug' full of commercial salmon fishing vessels and, even at that time of the evening, was a beehive of activity. Boats were arriving and departing; crews were arriving and leaving; materials were being loaded and off loaded; and maintenance work in general on the vessels was the word of the day under the glare of numerous overhead lights.

Why my presence at the commercial fishing docks you might be asking yourselves? Well, as I said earlier, commercial salmon fishing season was in full swing and so were the opportunities for greed-based illegality to rear its ugly head in and among the docked vessels. When I had decided to give the active boat docks a look-see, my guardian angels, realizing I had made the right enforcement based decision, backed off fluttering around inside me and began quietly preening their feathers so to speak.

I had worked with the salmon species while stationed one summer in Alaska gaining job experience for my career in the world of wildlife once I graduated from college. In that summer's work, I had learned a lot about the five species of Pacific salmon and their life histories. Because of those endeavors, I had come to REALLY respect the salmon species and their quest for life and procreation. I had also come to the realization that without proper wildlife law enforcement protections, there were those who would take more than their fair share and the salmon resource would be poorer for it. Hence, my little stakeout in the Eureka parking lot that evening looking for those who liked to play loose with the laws of the land and the "Rules of Engagement."

Bob and I sat there out of sight in my patrol car with all that commercial fishing related dock activity swirling around us until around midnight. Not much of anything happened that piqued my interest so we were just getting ready to leave since it was so quiet. That was when my two guardian angels began stirring again and they were now all a-twitter! Knowing how to read such ethereal signs having been there before, I perked up my senses, grabbed my binoculars, and began watching the boat dock's coming and going activity ever more closely.

I had no more than focused my binoculars on the ramp leading off from the main boat docks to the parking lot, when I observed two men hurriedly staggering down the boat dock's main ramp. They were struggling with a large fish box and were obviously carrying a heavy load. As they got closer to the parking lot, I could see under the lights over the docks that the fish box was loaded with what appeared to be freshly caught salmon! Now in those days in order to be legal, any commercially caught king salmon had to measure at least 26 inches in total length and any silver salmon at least 25 inches in total length. And the Fish and Game Code specified, "That no species could be brought ashore where size and species restrictions were in place, in such a condition that size and species could not be determined."

Since numerous commercial salmon fishermen were not outside the possibility of sneaking ashore headless short salmon they had illegally taken earlier in the day, I perked up my senses. It just seemed strange that my now suspect fishermen would be bringing a huge box of salmon ashore at that time of the night instead of selling them at the local fish processing houses during daylight hours. That would be especially so if the box full of salmon now being carried off the dock was of the legally proscribed lengths. I then realized that my fluttering 6th senses were telling me this was the reason for me being there that evening and to get my tail-end in gear!

Now before any of you readers fly off the deep end thinking I have been nipping at the bottle, you "Hold her, Newt, she is rearing for the barn." I had been in dozens of like situations when my guardian angels lit up my insides with their worried activity. So much so, that I had learned to pay attention to what they had to say.

(If you readers still doubt my words, read any of my 12, at last count in 2015, true-life wildlife law enforcement adventure books whose genesis is based on my state and federal 32-year career. If you do, you will see that 6th sense theme and the results of paying attention to such ethereal concerns portrayed and documented throughout. You will also see the results of such 6th senses being played out and the resultant outcomes from many such ventures.)

Waiting until my two struggling fishermen with the weight of the loaded fish box got to the end of the ramp leading into the parking lot, I quietly stepped forth from my vehicle and briskly walked their way in full uniform. As I did, my neighbor Bob Moore slowly trailed behind me. Walking up to the two surprised men, I said, "Good morning. State fish and game warden. I would like to check your fish and commercial fishing licenses if I may." When I did, I recognized one of the commercial fishermen as Jacob Dunham. Jacob being a local commercial fisherman whom I had checked several times while working off The Rainbow on one of my many marine patrols.

That was when my world blew up! The two fishermen dropped the box full of fish and the one nearest the dock's ramp, exploded and sprinted for the safety found in hiding among the 300 plus docked fishing vessels! After the other man had dropped his end of the box, that chap took off at a dead run for the parking lot! Surprised at the men's two separate explosive actions, I took a quick look at the box of dropped salmon. They all appeared to be headless illegal short salmon that more than likely were taken commercially. Realizing I had a serious commercial fishing violation, I yelled at Bob to guard the box of salmon. I then took off for my man running into the parking lot. However, by that time I managed to reach the bulk of the parked cars in the parking lot, I was too late.

In short, my runner, one Jacob Dunham, had gotten into his vehicle and was starting to speed away. Running to my patrol car and bailing in, I immediately gave chase. Roaring out from the parking lot in my patrol car, I caught and stopped Jacob by the time he reached the stop sign at the First Street intersection. Pulling him over with my red light and siren, I walked up to his car and ordered him out from his vehicle. As I waited for him to disembark, I told him he was under arrest for possessing short salmon. It was then that Jacob refused to obey my order to get out from his car and began driving off. That is when the wheels came off his wagon. Using a martial arts move, I withdrew his miserable carcass at a high rate of speed through his open front door window! Following that, he was slammed unceremoniously onto the pavement and had a set of stainless steel Smith and Wesson bracelets placed upon his wrists post haste! Following his physical arrest, Jacob was advised of his rights, told why he was under arrest again and then seated into the backseat of my patrol car for eventual transport to the boat docks and then to jail in Eureka.

Returning to the boat docks moments later with my prisoner, I drove up to Bob, who was still nervously guarding the fish box full of headless short salmon. Bob, unused to such activity, was trembling like a dog passing peach pits to say the least. Suffice to say, Bob was pretty damn happy to see me. The two of us then unloaded the fish box of 45 headless short salmon and placed them into the trunk of my patrol car. Following that, Jacob was booked in the Eureka Sheriff's

Office lockup. As for the evidence fish, they were placed in a commercial locker plant for preservation.

To make a long story short, I never did find the other runner in among that fleet of fishing vessels. At least not then did I locate his miserable carcass... Jacob, on the other hand, was subsequently prosecuted in state court for possessing 45 short salmon and fined $500.00 dollars but was allowed to keep his commercial fishing license. The 45 salmon were donated to a Catholic Church group who had a program whereby they were feeding the homeless found in the city of Eureka.

The results of that evening and the clear-cut realization that the flag needed to be shown more often than not among the commercial fishing fleet, I got an idea. I would volunteer for additional sea duty aboard The Rainbow if Lt. Ken Brown thought it necessary to initiate extra patrols checking the commercial salmon fishermen. Remember, my readers, I had developed a real interest in protecting the salmon species after my summer working in Alaska. My seasickness be damned, especially if I could just provide a little more protection to such a valuable species of fish. As it turned out, Warden Chuck Monroe, the normally assigned boarding officer, was leaving on his annual vacation and I was to be his replacement. The operation to provide more protection to such a valuable species in the salmon wars was now on!

For the next two weeks, I ate a million dollars-worth of Bonine and Merrazine seasickness pills and Ken and I made it a habit of letting the commercial salmon fishing fleet know that the fish and game department ruled the waves and not the number of greedy salmon outlaws among their many times questionable ranks. Man, let me tell you. Anyone who wants to lose weight over being seasick all the time ought to try and give marine duty a run for its money. At the end of those two weeks, I had lost 19 pounds! Of course, the Dungeness crabs ate well, if you readers get my drift (no pun intended).

During that marine work period, rain, hog, dog or frog, 30-foot swells or not, Ken and I made our presence known among the salmon fishing fleet. Between bouts of heaving up everything but my shoes, I must have boarded at least six to ten fishing boats daily. We only tried to board just those vessels that looked dirty in some sense of the word. Suffice to say, we more than paid for the gas and oil in the fines collected department over that seminal period of time.

The commercial salmon fishermen of the day off the north coast of California were running what were called 'down-riggers.' Those were nothing more than power driven mechanical fishing devices. That mechanical fishing apparatus would consist of hooks and line strung through a metal arm and pulley system hanging over the sides of the fishing vessel with the end of the spool of many fathoms of line attached to a drum powered by a mechanically driven winch. The hooks were then baited and eventually let over the side of the boat when a school of salmon was discovered nearby. Attached to that line, were various heavy lead weights depending on the depth fished and then the whole works was dropped overboard. The whole kit and caboodle would then be trolled behind the fishing boat until a salmon would strike the bait and be hooked. With a fish on, the deck hand would activate the power winch and the salmon would be bodily hauled up to the side of the fishing vessel. If the fish was determined to be of legal length, it was brought on board. However, if the deck hand thought the fish was not the legal length required by the fish and game regulations, it would be released back to the ocean.

Therein came the rub for Lt. Brown and me. Many commercial fishermen would properly release the fish. However, the ones I called the knot heads, upon visual determination that the fish was too short to legally keep, would slam the salmon against the side of their vessel until the hook was torn out from the side of its mouth! In so doing, many times the salmon would have a portion of its lower jaw badly ripped apart, deformed or severely damaged. This action was done in the interest of saving time so the line could be quickly baited and set to fishing once again. The main reasoning for their slamming action was that salmon traveled in schools. In order to catch as many as they could before the school moved on, one whanged the short salmon alongside the boat for a quick release after being hooked, so the hook could be baited and fishing could quickly resume.

Real conservationist some of those lads to say the least... And those were just some of the "F Troop" commercial fishing chaps that Ken and I targeted. If they were going to be hind-ends in the name of working as fast as they could to board and smash-release the fish, then we saw to it that some of the worst offenders were routinely stopped, boarded and checked. As expected, many times that flavor of chap so boarded was also cited for various other violations that he or his crew had committed.

(For You readers' edification, slamming a salmon alongside your vessel until the hook was torn loose was a standard release practice by many commercial fishermen in those days and was entirely legal. However, many times severe damage was done and in many cases, the salmon could no longer forage efficiently because of its destroyed lower jaw.)

Gee, I wonder if some of the above lazy actions on the part of the deck hands to quickly rid themselves of a short fish so they could get that line back to fishing might have led, in part, to the serious reduction of our Pacific coast species of salmon as of this day and age in 2015?

One day while out on another of my famous seasick marine patrols, I discovered there really was a "Salmon God". Ken and I were sitting off a distance from a group of commercial fishing vessels watching them through our binoculars or spotting scopes as we always did looking for any obvious signs of fish and game violations. There was one smaller commercial salmon fishing boat that caught Ken's eye. Without removing his binoculars so he wouldn't lose the action he was watching, Ken directed my attention to look at the same vessel. The deck hand on that vessel was not slamming the salmon alongside when he reeled up a fish but was gently dip netting and swinging the fish aboard. What he was doing was unusual and more like a sport fisherman would be doing than some of the run of the mill commercial fishermen.

"Hell, Kenny. There is nothing wrong with the way he is treating those hooked salmon," I said as I watched our two fishermen on Ken's suspect fishing vessel. That fish of our interest was then routinely unhooked and tossed into a fish box. That empty hook was then baited and once again dropped overboard. Moments later, another fish was hooked on another down-rigger and brought onboard just like the last fish. Following that action, there was a third fish boated almost immediately on another down- rigger. It then became obvious to us that the fishing boat was over a large school of salmon. Losing interest over what I considered good fishing practices, I swung my binoculars over to the boat I had been watching earlier. One in which was horribly mistreating any short salmon caught on their down-riggers with their usual side-smashing technique.

"Tiny, you still watching the boat I asked you to?" Ken asked.

"No, Skipper. I switched back to the one I was watching earlier because I could not see anything wrong with the one you were watching," I replied.

"Better watch them again," he slowly advised like he had an issue floating around in his mind that would soon need addressing.

Swinging my glasses back to the boat Ken was watching, I saw the deck hand land another fish. Then I got a nudge from my guardian angels. *That last fish looked suspiciously shorter than the law allowed* spun crazily through my mind as I saw the deck hand throw that fish into their fish box.

It was then that a major surprise manifested itself. The skipper of the suspect boat stepped out from his wheelhouse and said something to his deck hand. Turning, the skipper entered his wheelhouse and changed the direction his boat was heading. That was when I about fell overboard. The suspect boat's skipper was none other than my previously convicted commercial fishing friend for possessing short salmon at the Eureka commercial boat docks, namely one Jacob Dunham!

"Ken, that skipper is the commercial fisherman I caught the other night at the docks with the box of short salmon. You know, the one who ran on me and I had to run him down with my patrol car and forcibly remove him from his vehicle!" I shouted in amazement.

"Well, he may be at it again. I will swear that a number of those fish that his deck hand brought on board were short salmon. I may be wrong because of the distance I am looking at him and the heat wave distortion over the water messing with my binoculars but I don't think so. I think that chap is keeping everything he is catching and that is not possible. There are always jack salmon in those schools who are too short to meet the commercial fishing size requirements. But, out of the last nine fish I saw him catch, he kept every one of them," he quietly advised.

With that kind of 'bait on the hook' (no pun intended), the two of us closely watched our suspect fishermen and recorded our observations as they occurred. Soon we had recorded the landing of 23 fish and not a single salmon was released back into the ocean! Then Ken and I figured out what was happening. Those salmon caught that appeared to be undersized were placed into one fish box, and those salmon that appeared to be of legal size went into a separate fish box.

"So that is it!" I exclaimed out loud. "That damn fool is keeping the shorts in one box and the legal ones in another. If

I was a betting man, I suspect that box full of short salmon will be illegally brought off their boat sometime later at night or early in the morning and taken home, just like Jacob did earlier when I caught him."

Then we got the break that told me there really was a Salmon God. Jacob left his wheelhouse and walked back to his deck hands. Once there, he held a short conversation with the members of his crew. Then the two men lifted up the fish box containing what Ken and I figured were full of the short salmon and took it below deck.

"Perfect," said Ken. "Now when we approach, it won't be so easy for them to toss the short salmon overboard once they suspect or recognize who we are. They will have to keep their illegal fish below deck in the hopes we won't go below and check for other violations. That kind of thinking may just manifest itself in this set of circumstances because of your reputation for being so seasick all the time. Who knows, maybe they will just chance it that you won't look below decks because of your seasickness and just leave the shorts to remain undiscovered where they are currently stashed. If that is the case, we will have them and you will have Jacob once again for the same violation within a short period of time. Maybe then our judge will revoke his commercial fishing license and we will have him solid," he continued with a smile on his face. You talk about a smile. My smile was like that of the Cheshire cat in a Walt Disney movie over the possibility of a soon to be double catch on a well deserving wildlife outlaw.

"Here is my plan. We will slowly drift a little further away from our friend and then I will head north away from him. That way if he is at all suspicious, he will see us leaving and maybe not give us another look. Once we get up on step and are running at our top speed, I will make an abrupt 90 degree turn and steam directly at him. As we get closer, you run up onto our bow deck and get ready to board. But don't go out on deck until I tell you. Otherwise he will recognize fish and game's gorilla and maybe make an effort to run or at least try to somehow toss the soon to be evidence fish overboard," he concluded.

By then The Rainbow was up on step and the engines were maxed out at a safe RPM. Ken trimmed the throttles, swung the boat into a sharp turn and headed directly toward our quarry. Watching through my binoculars, I could see that for the longest time Jacob did not pay an ounce of attention to the boat rapidly bearing down upon him. Then suddenly, Jacob realized that there was a boat running right at his amidships! Stepping out from his wheelhouse, Jacob tried to wave us off from his pre-planned trolling course. When we didn't alter our course of approach, we could tell he was getting pissed at whomever was operating the boat fast bearing down upon him in such a manner as he tried to fish.

Moments later, we could see that he recognized the boat bearing down on him as that being from the fish and game marine arm and then he ran to the stern of his vessel. Jacob and his deck hand began throwing just recently caught short salmon into the ocean from another short fish box. The one that they had begun using to replace the fish box they had taken earlier below decks. However, it was too late because we were soon upon them.

"Get up on our bow, Tiny, and prepare to board that son-of-a-bitch before he tosses anymore short salmon," Ken yelled over the sounds of our racing engines!

Carefully moving along our narrow catwalk alongside our wheelhouse, I safely got to the bow, grabbed the rope used to help steady a boarding officer and hung on for dear life! By now, I could see pure 'hells-a-poppin'' on the deck of Jacob's vessel as short salmon literally flew overboard from the stern of their craft! Seconds later, it was all over. It was then that Ken expertly placed The Rainbow alongside Dunham's slow moving trolling vessel and I jumped without hesitation onto the lower deck of our suspect's fishing boat.

"Afternoon, Jacob. You know who I am but just to do it right, I am a state fish and game warden. I am here to check the commercial fishing licenses of you and your deck hands and to check your catch. Any problem?" I asked with a knowing grin in my heart. (By the way, for you non-believers, my guardian angels, aroused earlier, had both since settled down and were happily preening all their primary flight feathers.)

"Go ahead and do what you have to do and then get your fat butt off my boat, you big bastard. And make haste about it. You are ruining my livelihood by slowing me down and if you don't make it quick, I will call and tell Captain Gray what a pain in the ass you were," grumbled Dunham.

With that, I professionally checked their quickly proffered commercial fishing licenses and took a gander at their box of keeper salmon. It was apparent that the salmon they had in that separate box were all keepers or within the required commercial lengths for king and silver salmon.

"Why were you and your deck hands throwing over those other fish as we approached?" I asked, full well knowing they had to be short salmon and were now long gone and could not be used as evidence of a violation.

"They was just bottom fish we had caught by mistake," said Jacob with a 'kiss my last part over the fence' smirk on his face. He was smirking because he knew we were without any evidence to the contrary and as such, unable to file any charges against him regarding a short salmon violation.

"O.K.," I said. "I guess that is it." Then just for giggles, I made a move like I was going to board the patrol boat and then turned as if I had an afterthought. "Say, Jacob. Do you have any other fish on board other than those legal ones in the salmon boxes?" I asked.

"You see all the salmon that we have. Now get your lazy ass off my boat so we can get back to our fishing," he growled.

"Then you won't mind if I check that box of fish you took below decks some time back, will you?" I said with a knowing grin.

For a moment you could tell that Jacob figured he had it made and we would soon be out of his hair. Then it dawned on him with my question that fish and game's gorilla had a lock on his last part over the fence. "You keep the hell away from my wheel house and from below deck unless you have a warrant!" Jacob bellowed, as the veins on his neck stood out in fine style! However, the tone and tenor in his voice betrayed deep worry over my 'below decks' question.

"Won't need a warrant, Jacob," I advised. "Both of us officers saw you and your deck hand catch a number of what appeared to be short salmon, load them into a fish box and then take them below decks. And now, that is just where I am heading to check it out. If you try to interfere with a California State Peace Officer in the performance of his duties, you will be arrested on the spot and you can try on my handcuffs to see if they fit any better than they did the first time I apprehended you for being in possession of short salmon."

With consternation splashed all over Jacob's face, I took my leave and went below decks. Sure as raw peanuts make good Douglas squirrel food, there laid a number of short silver and king salmon in an iced down fish box! Moments later after making a count, 31 short salmon to be exact, I just had to grin that Cheshire cat grin again. Moving back up onto Jacob's deck, I beckoned for Ken to move the patrol boat closer. When he did, I announced to him that there were 31 short silver and king salmon below decks. Ken got a big grin on his face and then told me to inform Jacob that he was under arrest for possession of short salmon and those and his boat was now seized by the State of California. Ken further instructed me to tell Jacob to head for the Eureka docks and that he would follow in the patrol boat. Lastly, I was instructed to stay on Jacob's boat until we got back to the docks to make sure our evidence was not tampered with or somehow quietly dumped overboard.

Those instructions were passed on to Jacob who grudgingly complied. A couple hours later, Ken and I were off loading 31 short silver and king salmon into the waiting arms of the Arcata Fish and Game Warden, John Finnigan. A warden whom Ken had called on our patrol boat radio and asked for his assistance at the docks once we arrived. You can bet there were a number of big eyed commercial fishermen standing around clucking their tongues because the often despised 'fish and game' had run to ground and captured one of their own. As we unloaded the short salmon from Jacob's boat into another fish box up on the Eureka commercial docks, I heard a passing fisherman watching us unloading all the short salmon saying to his friend referring to me, "Damn, you were right. Fish and game's 'gorilla' is really is big enough to eat hay and pull a wagon."

Several weeks later, Jacob appeared in front of the same judge for the same violation committed just a few weeks earlier. That time maximum fines were imposed on Jacob and his deck hands and their commercial fishing licenses were suspended by the court for sixty days. That eliminated Jacob from any further salmon fishing the rest of that season off the coast of California.

Once again, Flowers all around! Jacob, who was a real wildlife outlaw, and his aid de camp deck hands Jim Laughten and Paul Joiner had their short salmon thieving streak broken, large fines extracted for their errors in judgement and temporarily lost their commercial fishing license privileges. In that apprehension of three well known outlaws and their successful prosecutions, there were more Flowers spread around the Eureka docks for all the other potential outlaw commercial fishermen watching fish and game seizing a mess of short salmon to smell in the process. Hopefully in so doing, they would pay more attention to the fish and game regulations or potentially suffer the same fate as did Dunham and his crew. Additionally, I recognized Jim Laughten as the chap who had run back into the docked commercial fishing fleet when I had first captured Jacob. However, there wasn't much I could do legally at that juncture regarding Jim and that first short salmon violation so I let it drop. But once again, who says there isn't a Salmon God? With that and the news of the capture of Dunham and his crew swirling around the commercial fishing community, it only stood to reason that many of the other outlaws 'stepped a little higher' when they broke the law around The Rainbow and its 'gorilla'! Remember what I wrote about earlier regarding the black brant's life history and its statistical losses? Well, those short salmon were in the same boat (no pun intended). Statistically, half those seized salmon were males and half were females. Had they lived and spawned, the females would have laid about 2-3,000 eggs each. So, the loss was 15 times 2-3,000 lost eggs that could have added to the overall wild salmon population down the line after spawning had taken place... Well, you readers get the message in the form of more Tombstones, present and future, regarding that matter.

Flowers and Tombstones

Chapter Three: King Salmon Escapades on the Eel River

MOTHER NATURE'S LESSON

When hired on as a State Fish and Game Warden by the California Department of Fish and Game in 1966 right after graduating from college, my first duty station assignment was in northwestern California in the coastal town of Eureka. My duty assignment as a roving game warden was to work in three adjacent game wardens' districts and as a secondary or replacement boarding officer on our marine patrol boat named "The Rainbow". In short, when any of the other three land district game wardens were off duty for whatever reason, I automatically moved into their assigned patrol districts and worked those days the resident officer was absent. When the marine patrol boarding officer was off for whatever reason, I filled in for him during those periods of time as well. In short, I was going to be one busy son-of-a-gun in holding down that line of assignments but came to love the work with all my heart and soul!

As I was soon to discover, that kind of a roving law enforcement assignment was a Heaven sent jewel. That type of work assignment easily gave me a leg up in quickly learning the game wardens' tips of the trade in short order and did so with a very steep learning curve. Every day I found myself exposed to a new geographic area with all its specifically inherent wildlife related law enforcement problems. I would have to say that because of the soon to discover high learning curve associated with such a varied job related set of experiences, my knowledge level of the practices and principals of wildlife law enforcement skyrocketed! To be frank, I probably learned more in six months in that roving position than did most other rookie game wardens in six years just being assigned to a single officer duty station.

One of those memorable learning curve adventures was soon to manifest itself in the Fortuna Game Warden's District. That particular warden's district was located just south of Eureka and was 'crewed' by one Warden Herb Christie. You readers had a chance to meet Herb earlier in the first chapter of this book so I need not say anything further about the man except, May God rest his soul.

During the summer months when this adventure took place, the mighty king salmon, some up to 60 pounds in weight, and the smaller sleeker silver salmon, were in full migration moving up all of California's north coast river systems to the spawning grounds of their genesis. With that migration miracle of nature in full bloom, the good, the bad, and the ugly fishermen types were lining the river banks in their efforts, hopes and dreams, to land a trophy salmon or an excellent eating fish for dinner. Found lurking along those same heavily recreationally utilized waterways were small numbers of us many times hated "Tule-Creepers" trying to keep the peace in the world of wildlife. So named Tule-Creepers by many of the areas resident wildlife outlaws or poachers, because of our innate secretive abilities to quietly and with the stealth of a snake moving across a wet lawn, move around in the land's covering vegetation like a long-tailed weasel after a deer mouse. You see, my readers, any time you mix humans and just about any species of wildlife, you will have wildlife law enforcement related problems. Problems such as over limits, illegal take, unlawful possession, closed season taking, illegal methods of take and the like being committed by the numerous local wildlife outlaws utilizing those within the world of wildlife. That went doubly so for those wildlife outlaws living in northern California's remote, wildlife laden Humboldt County, when they 'hit their step' in the criminal violation department. Good game wardens, those who make a serious living hunting humans walking on the dark side in the world of wildlife, will find themselves figuratively speaking, always moving to the 'sound of the guns.' They move to the sounds of the guns or any areas rich in wildlife resources all populated by vast numbers of humankind trying to take such wildlife resources, both legally and illegally. Suffice to say, not much moss grew under the feet of the Tule Creepers in Humboldt County because of so much movement toward the sounds of the gun!

Knowing the following two days were Herb Christie's days off and his being one of the districts I was expected to cover under such circumstances, I rolled. Exiting my home at four in the morning, I headed south in my patrol car to the town of Fortuna. My ultimate overall destination was to covertly patrol a number of historically famous salmon fishing locations along the nearby mighty Eel River. Driving a few miles south of Fortuna to those historically heavily fished Eel River locations, ones that I had fished many times previously as an attending wildlife student from nearby Humboldt State College, I set up shop. The area of choice that morning was one in which I had not only successfully fished many times previously but one in which I had observed much in the way of illegal wildlife related chicanery by wildlife outlaws fishing along that stretch of the river. I had witnessed during those earlier days the out-right taking of huge over limits of salmon, the secretive and hard to catch fishermen 'double-tripping', the snagging of salmon and even selling freshly caught salmon to other unsuccessful fishermen right along the river itself. Hence my selection of that location to begin my morning's duties as a "Sword for Mother Nature".

For you folks, 'double-tripping' was nothing more than that. It involved catching a limit of salmon, leaving the area to dispose of said fish and then returning that same day to catch another limit. That is a violation of the fish and game regulations and one type of case that is extremely difficult to make unless one is right there to witness both sides of the activity and catch the culprit red-handed on his or her second go-around. As it just so happened that fine day so long ago, that type of case would soon be thrust upon me in all of its glory and difficulty.

Parking my patrol car in an out of the way place, I grabbed my binoculars and began sneaking down towards my chosen fishing spot on the Eel River. The place I had picked for my on foot stake out was one heavily utilized by salmon fishermen because of its historical good fishing riverbed geography. That stretch of the Eel River was full of great riffles, plus a number of deep, long and slow moving pools where migrating salmon could pause and rest from their strenuous upstream migration efforts. In short, perfect salmon fishing geography and a tremendous lure and attraction to any Nimrod with a fishing pole and a hunger for great salmon fishing activity. All I needed now was any kind of an unthinking chap with an opportunity and an inclination to illegally mess with Mother Nature and in so doing, make my day. When he or she (yes, I

Terry Grosz

did find female outlaws in my day) did in fact mess with Mother Nature illegally, I would be off and running like a slobbering dog after a speeding rabbit. Damn, it was sure nice being a rookie and thinking how easily the outlaws would drop into my lap like rotten apples falling off a tree in the winter time, once I decided to spring my trap. Ah, my youth and inexperience as always, was springing forth, eternally...

Burying myself into a dense stand of brush a short distance from the river to avoid discovery, I laid back like a big old garden spider in wait. However, as all of my readers out there have come to know me, when I lurked in the bushes, it was as a beautiful spider, not an ugly duckling...

Soon I could see headlights moving into the several river-adjacent parking areas in the predawn darkness. With my binoculars, I observed groups of fishermen and numerous singles walking down to their favorite spots along the Eel. Soon, I had 16 fishermen strung up and down the Eel whipping the waters to a froth as some used artificial lures and others 'drift-fished roe.'

To all my readers out there, 'roe' are immature fish eggs still in their egg sac, removed from female salmon previously caught and are highly prized as potential fish bait by skilled fishermen. With many good fishermen, the roe is often cured with borax and brown sugar, cut into small dense clusters once it has cured and is then fished by casting out the small roe egg cluster and drift-fished as it bounces along the river's bottom. If no migrating salmon strike the drifting cluster of fish eggs, it is retrieved, recast out and drifted just off the bottom until it is taken by a fish or retrieved once again. To those who know how to fish in such a manner, it is a deadly successfully way to fish for salmon.

(Author's Note: I went to college with a good friend and tremendously successful fisherman named Bruce Fulmer. Bruce had such a touch when it came to drift-fishing with a cluster of roe that he seldom came home without a salmon or two. He was so good that he could almost 'talk' the bait into a salmon's mouth. He had such a gentle touch with his fishing pole, that he even knew when a salmon had gently just soft-mouthed the bait. Bruce would set the hook and excepting a mechanical or equipment failure, a flopping salmon would soon be his. He was that good! Bruce continues to be an outstanding legal fisherman and friend to this very day in 2015, some 50 plus years later and is still successfully catching fish.)

However, get an outlaw who knew how to fish with roe as well as Bruce, who was not a fish and game outlaw, and you had a problem. Once a salmon leaves their saltwater environment for that of a freshwater river system, their physiology completely changes. They stop eating and begin slowly dying as their system begins consuming the nutrients from their bodies as they migrate upstream to their historical spawning grounds. However, they remember what it is like to feed and if confronted with an appealing gob of roe deftly drifting by their noses, they will reach out and gum the bait even though the salmon cannot eat or digest it. That is when a good drift-fisherman will detect the speed of drift change in the roe's movement along the river bottom and set the hook. When the salmon are in the river, many a fisherman who is skilled in this form of fishing will bear watching for obvious over the limit concerns.

For about an hour, I watched my fishing clientele from my brush patch and did not observe anything out of the ordinary. Then my scrutiny shifted to a tall skinny drink of water looking like he could have used several good meals, a haircut and a damn good bath. He had already landed two silver salmon drift-fishing roe. It then appeared that he had run out of roe and was now in the process of switching out from that form of bait fishing to use of an artificial lure. Watching him closely with my binoculars, I could see that he was already using questionable methods in his fishing retrieval tactics with his artificial lure. Just as sure as God makes green apples, my skinny lad was almost going through illegal snagging methods to catch a fish. Almost, in my judgement, but not quite enough of the patented snagging action to meet the local cantankerous old judge's requirements pertaining to any such related charges.

Because everyone else was appearing to remain legal in their endeavors, I applied my full attention to that chap with the two salmon and the possible illegal snagging use of his artificial lure. Since the daily bag limit for salmon was only three per person per day in those days, he had one fish to go and that was it. I just held in my hidden position to determine what the outcome of my fisherman's eventual actions and intent would be.

About 20 minutes later, my skinny fisherman hooked and landed another small jack silver salmon (a small immature male salmon). With that, he picked up his three fish on a stringer and walked back to the parking lot, disappearing in among the vehicles. Figuring him to be all through for the day and not deserving of any further attention, I switched my binoculars onto another chap who had just successfully landed his second salmon. I kept my glasses trained on that chap until I was surprised at what occurred next.

Into the field of view in my binoculars suddenly appeared my skinny looking chap. You know, the one with a legal limit of salmon already back at his vehicle. Without a look backward or all around, my chap went back to his original spot on the Eel, wound up and cast out his artificial lure into the waters once again and began salmon fishing. He already had a legal limit and now here he was trying to load up on any other salmon happening his way.

Suffice to say, that bit of activity got him this game warden's brass ring. My attention shifted from the other fishermen along the river and solely onto him and his now possible illegal fishing actions. No, I could not yet arrest the chap for fishing again after he already had a limit of salmon. Yes, I figured my chap was after more salmon but until he caught another salmon placing him over the daily bag limit, I had to let him fish. After all, the Eel contained trout, which he could now legally fish for and catch. However, my guardian angels were telling me to hold the line because my suspect chap was going to be doing to Mother Nature what he shouldn't be doing and in short order.

For the longest time, my suspect fisherman had no luck in latching onto another salmon, which if successfully landed and kept, would place him one over the limit and garner him a visit from the world's most beautiful game warden. Then in direct violation of the fish and game laws and the dictates of Mother Nature, my lad hooked another salmon. That time it wasn't a small silver salmon but a big king salmon from the looks of the way it stripped out his line from his reel and doggedly fought. That salmon was so large and aggressive, that it took my fisherman-game hog about twenty minutes to land. As he fought the large fish, I began realizing that something was dead wrong. The way the fish was fighting and the length of time it was taking to land the fish, I figured that it was foul-hooked (snagged). To me, it was taking longer than the usual battle would in landing the fish compared to one lawfully hooked in the mouth.

Finally, the big fish tired and was dragged backwards towards the shore. As I had suspected, the big fish was foul-hooked in its tail section of the body near the adipose fin and that is why my lad had such difficulty in landing the critter. Dragging the fish onto the gravel bar at the edge of the river, my chap surprised me with his next move. My fisherman suspect immediately noticed that he had foul hooked his fish. Realizing that was illegal and by all rights the fish had to be released, he made a furtive move that quickly caught my eye. In front of other nearby fishermen, he ran to his still flopping fish on the river's graveled edge, jerked it up onto land and quickly removed the lure's hooks from the fish's tail section to avoid any undue attention. Then my lad took his lure and stuck it into the mouth of the fish as if it was legally hooked. Looking all around to make sure no one was offended by his illegal action, he dragged his prize further up onto the shore and away from the river.

With that move and his earlier illegal action, I went into motion from my place of hiding. Now out in the open and in full uniform, I hustled my beautiful carcass towards my chap in such a manner that everyone fishing on the river realized my targeted fisherman with the foul hooked fish was my man of the hour. In the meantime, my lad knocked his big king salmon on the head killing his illegal prize before I could get there and release the fish back into the river! However, my chap was about to get another prize in the form of a game warden speeding his way with a grin on his puss and a citation book in hand.

"Look out! Game warden on the river," shouted one of the other fishermen when he observed me trotting towards my chap and his still flopping illegal salmon.

With that, heads turned almost in unison from all the other fishermen to look at me as I continued rumbling across the riverbank towards my illegal fisherman like one of General Patton's tanks during the Battle of the Bulge during the Second World War. Hearing those 'Game warden on the river' words of warning, my skinny fisherman turned and, seeing me churning towards him on a collision course, grabbed up his fishing rod and began sprinting for the dense stand of brush lining the Eel River's nearby banks.

Why that son-of-a-gun, I thought. *He can't outrun me.* In junior college, I consistently ran an eleven second flat 100-yard dash wearing a football uniform when I weighed in at a lovely 265 pounds. I never lost a chase in college football as a defensive tackle and I wasn't about to lose one now going after a river-rat! I was a little heavier in that day and age as a game warden but I damn sure was still a speedy runner and would run him down and then the proverbial "Hammer of Thor" would drop on my chap like a ton of bricks.

Hitting my stride in pursuit of my outlaw, I was soon up on step and flying. To my way of thinking, fleeing from the game warden, one of Mother Nature's minions, was a no-no. But by damn, that skinny lad that could have used a meal or two, could really pick them up and lay them down. That was especially so when he could feel the ground shaking under his feet from the thundering footsteps of the rather large sized game warden closely pursuing his miserable fleeing carcass.

By now, my fleeing lad had made the nearby brush line and disappeared into the green gloom of the Redwood forest like that human 'wisp of the wind' from many years past in merry old England named Robin Hood. That disappearing act was OK with me though. I knew exactly where he had entered the forested glen and now it was just a matter of time before my skinny 'merry old Robin bit the dust'. From the sounds of the crashing brush just ahead of me, I knew I was gaining ground on his skinny hind end as we two chaps tore through the brush and understory like a couple of maddened bulls. I quickly discovered that I was really gaining on my chap because his skinny body was glancing off the different vegetative obstacles and numerous grabbing tree limbs. Weighing as much as I did, I just plowed through the same forest-grabbing obstacles like a bull bison in rut or like Grant took Richmond. My runner would soon be mine and then he would be in for a real 'come to Jesus meeting' for catching to many salmon once I got my hands on his miserable fleeing carcass.

It was then that Mother Nature, unhappy with my progress in catching the one who had dipped one time to many into Her salmon natural resources cupboard, lined up one of her surprises of nature. My chap was just 30 feet or less ahead of me and I was gaining on him like a fast moving freight train moving through a railroad crossing. My skinny chap was showing signs of getting fatigued and all that did was spur me on to an even greater effort. *He is now mine,* I thought and an old-fashioned college tackle was soon to become the word of the day in that fleeing chap's list of life's experiences.

Then Mother Nature, as earlier indicated, provided her surprise intervention on the side of the high stepping Tule-Creeper and the fast moving 'skinny' one. My skinny chap then blew through a dense stand of brush, whipping the branches every way but loose as he steamed along. It was at that moment in time, when he busted in the run through the brush and then discarded his now broken all to hell fishing rod. Approaching an old storm-downed, second growth redwood tree, my skinny sprinter, now running for what he must have figured was for his life, attempted to high vault the log obstacle. In so doing, he almost cleared the downed log. However, it was then that he caught his pant leg on a small dead limb and took a violent header over the log, crashing out of sight on the other side in a tremendous explosion of leaf litter, flying twigs and yellow banana slugs! Milliseconds later, I observed a beautifully colored 'spray' of 'something' on the other side of the log rising high into the air. When that 'spray' hit the air striking the rays of sunlight filtering through the tree tops, its droplets formed the prettiest rainbow you ever saw! *Nothing like the beauty of a rainbow in a darkly forested glen when the Sheriff's Man is about to apprehend a salmon-killin' Robin Hood,* I thought.

However, that is where the beauty in the forest ended. With the rainbow's colorful spew, my guy leaped high up into the air and, somehow defying gravity, came flying back at me after just moments before steaming forward at a dead run. *This is O.K. with me,* I thought, as I blasted into his skinny carcass with a perfect 'ten' flying tackle with my 'umpteen' pounds of absolute Teutonic magnificence.

"Auuuggghhh!" I immediately bellowed. My now smashed 'flat as a sail rabbit' runner, the one and same who had pissed off Mother Nature with his illegal taking of one of her salmon, found himself getting 'pissed' on in turn by one of Mother Nature's black and white coated minions! Grabbing up my now blown up quarry from a perfectly executed flying tackle, I quickly realized what had happened. My fleeing chap had fallen while running at full bore onto a Mother Nature's perfectly positioned surprised striped skunk! One that she had placed there purposely on the other side of the downed log for the skinny one's benefit. When my skinny runner had slammed running full bore onto the skunk's quiet little bug hunting world, he had flattened out Mother Nature's black and white chap like a tortilla! The skunk had then defended itself with his gifted form of retaliation. Hence, the cloud of spray that I had observed earlier, creating the rainbows of color in our little forested glen. In tackling my quarry, I had gathered unto myself more than a 'smidgeon' of that critters essence! Additionally, Mother Nature had shared with me a liberal dose of her impatience with me over having to run my chap so far before I caught him…

Once I realized what had happened, I dropped my once fleeing quarry and jumped back so my beautiful carcass would not also garner a squirt of Mother Nature's essence of 'wood-pussy'. But, I was too late. When I had wrapped my arms around my chap upon tackling him, I got nature's perfume on my arms and the front of my uniform shirt in spades. ZUH! Man, did I ever stink! However, my skinny chap had gotten it even worse. He had gotten a rather large dose of the spray into his eyes, which temporarily blinded him. He had also gotten about a gallon of the spray directly into his open mouth and was gagging like a person who had fallen into the open belly of a dead horse that had lain out in the hot July sun for at least a week. Talk about dry heaving, he reminded me of me when I was seasick while out on a marine patrol. But my lad did me even one better when it came to my seasick puking escapades. He was puking so hard over that mouthful of skunk stink, that he figuratively even upchucked his hip boots. Well at least that settled one thing for me. I didn't have to worry about him running on me again in his present condition...

Seeing my runner was incapacitated, I promptly backed off, took off my uniform shirt before its essence had penetrated the cloth and slopped onto my t-shirt and skin. As I did, I could see many torn places in my shirt where I had run through the grabbing limbs and brush in the earlier chase. Realizing the shirt was now an unusable mess, I removed my badge, tore off my fish and game arm patches, then pitched the shirt into an opening of an old sawed off redwood stump and left it there to stink up the rest of the forest. With voice commands, I got my still gagging chap to his feet, turned him around and the two of us left our little forested glen and its surprise ending smelling worse that when we had entered. Brother, did old Mother Nature sure create a stink... But it was a good stink because, like the R.C.M.P., I had once again caught my man. Course, I had some help from my striped companion, Mother Nature and her little surprise action cloud in the Redwood forest.

Walking back with my now much subdued chap, I had to grin. I didn't smell too badly and had only lost my shirt in the process. But it wouldn't be the only shirt I would lose before this little adventure was over... By now, my gagging chap had somewhat recovered and now he only needed a haircut, a few good meals and a long time in a bath tub with a goodly dose of old fashioned lye soap to clean off what ailed him. Walking back to where he had left his fish along the river, I discovered the large king salmon was now long gone! Someone seeing me chasing after my salmon snagging chap had slipped in behind me, stolen my evidence fish and split the scene. Nothing like honor among thieves on a salmon fishing river... In fact, most of my fishermen had left the river fishing scene as well. It was pretty obvious that they didn't want any of what had just happened to the skinny guy, stink and all, happening to them.

Undeterred, I guided my chap back to his vehicle only to discover that the three salmon he had caught and stashed earlier in his vehicle had also disappeared! He had placed them out of sight on the front floor boards of his old pickup. Those salmon in turn were discovered by another hastily leaving outlaw fisherman. That person had somehow observed my over limit chap previously lugging up his salmon to his truck. He had also seen the salmon subsequently left unguarded and decided to help himself. Once on the distant parking site and unobserved, my salmon crook broke out my skinny culprit's side window, unlocked the door and took what he wanted. As I said earlier, there wasn't much honor among thieves on the Eel River that fine day so long ago.

Somewhat dismayed over my evidence loss, I still cited my runner, the one and only who had obviously pissed off and then had been pissed on by an irate Mother Nature. He received a citation for taking an over limit of salmon and snagging. My evidence was obviously now long gone but I still had my testimony and that, because of a thing called 'Judicial Notice', where the court weighed more heavily the officer's testimony, was in good stead in any court of the land. Since all surprise had now been lost on the river with my appearance, I exited the area for home, a shower and a new uniform shirt. My skinny culprit had once again gone into his gagging and puking regimen and that was how I left him. But if one looked closely into the nearby tree line, you could see a wisp of a lady standing there who was a dead ringer for Mother Nature with a grin on her face...

Well two weeks later during a court trial, I discovered why the Statue of Justice wears a blindfold. My chap was found not guilty by the judge because I had no physical evidence! My testimony be damned, without the fish, the old judge found my outlaw innocent of the charges and had dismissed outright my testimony. Brother, that sure browned me off! That was the only time in my 32-year career that ever happened. I just had an old cantankerous Justice of the Peace Judge that day in court and he took out his wrath on the State of California and yours truly. Took out his wrath procedurally I might add, since any officer's testimony is at least as good as was any defendants. As I said earlier, losing my shirt in the chase wasn't the only 'shirt' that I lost in that adventure...

You know, Folks, one should never throw down the glove of challenge in front of a good game warden. Two weeks later while working undercover in Warden Hank Marak's Willow Creek district, guess who chanced upon my skinny chap with an illegally snagged salmon at Burnt Ranch Falls? Yep. You got that right. That time 'Skinny' did not escape because the female Willow Creek judge was a gunner and saw to it that my chap was fined $500.00 and received three days in jail for his little 'Boo-Boo'. The three days in jail part somehow came after I had made sure the judge was aware of my past snagging travails with my skinny violator and the lousy Justice of the Peace sentence on the first snagging and salmon over limit go-around. Gee, I wonder how that snagging and over limit information got out into the open court in Willow Creek? Well, since the Statue of Justice is wearing a blind fold, I guess she didn't see that one coming, did she?

As for the first Justice of the Peace where I had taken my skinny lad back in Fortuna with the salmon over limit and snagging case, I caught that same judge later that fall during the brant hunting season on South Humboldt Bay. It seemed that the old judge liked eating black brant and somehow had taken two brant over the limit in front of yours truly! Because he was the local judge who would have overseen the disposition of that current brant over limit case and was now a defendant in his own courtroom, I saw to it in that particular instance that the brant over limit case went to the Federal Judge in Sacramento to have this matter adjudicated.

There I filed the brant over limit matter under federal law. Under federal law taking an over limit of black brant, a migratory game bird, could also be a legal matter processed either state or federally under the Migratory Bird Treaty Act. Being a credentialed deputy U.S. Game Management Agent, I could legally file the above case in federal court and did. In short, since my local judge who presided over state court issues in that jurisdiction where the brant over limit case had been made and my lousy Justice of the Peace was now my defendant in that matter, that case went to federal court in Sacramento for obvious reasons. There my local judge did not skate from my black brant over limit charge and was fined $450.00 in federal court. After that, I just made sure I did not work in that county judge's jurisdiction because I figured he would not be very happy with me or treat any of my other cases fairly. Oh by the way, that Justice of the Peace lost his next election. I didn't realize that the hand of Mother Nature clearly extended into the murky depths of legal politics as well but that sure as hell tickled me to no end.

In the end, I guess one could say that Mother Nature had her say with a well-placed striped skunk, a persistent young game warden, a good Willow Creek Judge, the Federal Court system in Sacramento, and the ultimate dumping of a crooked Justice of the Peace from the bench. You know, Folks, it just doesn't pay to piss off Mother Nature or any of her minions. Be you a skinny runner or not. I guess one could say that is why the long arm of the law and that of Mother Nature is so long...

All you readers out there can surely smell the Flowers that sprouted up during this adventure. My skinny outlaw lost the side window in his truck, his three previously caught salmon were swiped by one of his kind and he had to pay an attorney big bucks to get off in his first case with yours truly involving his snagged salmon and over limit situation. There was a field of Flowers when I caught Skinny at Burnt Ranch Falls snagging salmon somewhat later. There were more Flowers when he had to come up with $500 big ones, plus take three days from off from his work while in jail to think about the error of his outlaw ways.

Additionally, there were the Flowers and their 'great fragrance' when I caught the judge with an over limit of brant in South Humboldt Bay that fall. You know, the one who had dismissed the first trial of Skinny over the issue of a snagged salmon and the over limit of salmon. I sure as hell got to smell the Flowers when that local judge ran afoul of Chief Federal Judge McBride in Sacramento over his little black brant over limit escapade to the tune of a $450.00 fine.

However, there were several Tombstones in this adventure as well. The Eel River wild salmon stocks have since been severely depleted as have that river's historic green and white sturgeon populations because of over fishing, snagging and environmental changes. That Tombstone more than likely represents something in the world of wildlife's long past adventures and probably never again to be experienced or enjoyed by those yet to come in the Eel River's population numbers and species diversity.

As a federal officer, I later worked with Judge McBride on a number of cases. As such, I found him to be one of the finest judges, state or federally, that I ever worked with! The man was brilliant, absolutely fearless in the face of political pressure, had the world of wildlife always in his heart, was firm but fair, and feared by those walking on the dark side of Mother Nature and the laws of mankind when such individuals' cases entered his jurisdiction. The great and friendly-to-the-environment Chief Federal Judge McBride for Northern California has since passed and is now under a Tombstone.

With him went all his years of great legal works and decisions! May the good Lord take a liking to the good judge and let him rest in eternal peace for the good work he did in and for, the world of wildlife.

No matter how one looks at it, there are always sunrises and sunsets in this world of ours. So it is also with Flowers and Tombstones in the struggling world of wildlife...

A GILL NET RUNNER'S SURPRISE

Returning to my hidden patrol vehicle after checking salmon fishermen while on foot along the Mad River, I went 10-8" or back in service on my fish and game radio. When I did, my radio quickly crackled to life once my signing back on duty transmission had ended.

"154-Eureka," came a return transmission to me as the voice of our radio operator back at our main fish and game office filled the airwaves.

"This is 154. Go ahead, Eureka," I replied.

"154, 156 has badly sprained his ankle and requests that you cover for him for a few days on the Eel River." (156 was Warden Herb Christie, the Fortuna fish and game warden.)

"Eureka, this is 154. Please let 156 know that I will be available to do so. Please also let him know I will land line him this evening for any patrol particulars he wishes to share. 154 out."

With that, I hung up the radio mike and proceeded on my way to check another part of the Mad River where I knew it would be heavily fished for the currently migrating salmon swarming upstream to spawn. Later that evening after I had finished my fieldwork, I contacted Herb via telephone to see how he was doing and glean any advice he might have on what in particular he wanted me to do or be mindful of when working in his district. As it turned out, Herb's salmon were presently running heavily in the Eel River and he wanted me to spend some time doing foot patrols on two sections of the lower part of the river that he felt needed more enforcement attention. After a few more suggestions on what he hoped I might accomplish and laying out the particulars of the geography on that part of the river he wanted heavily patrolled, I teased him for being so clumsy and turning an ankle like an old woman. Herb in turn told me that the next time we worked together and since I had such a smart mouth, I could pick up the lunch tab. He went on to say that when that event occurred, he would not eat for a week in order to stick me with a bill that was higher than a cat's back in a dog fight. We both laughed easily over the verbal antics of two close friends and then went our separate ways. Herb off and on his way to heal up and me making preparations for the next upcoming detail in another officer's patrol district.

Early the following morning, I passed through the town of Fortuna and headed south on State Highway 211 towards the small farming community of Ferndale. Crossing over the Eel River Bridge, I turned off highway 211 and began patrolling westerly on several smaller dirt feeder roads paralleling the Eel River as I headed for that portion of the river leading to its mouth on the Pacific Ocean.

I figured that those salmon migrating from the nearby ocean waters into the lower reaches of the Eel would be of the freshest quality and the most highly sought after as an eating fish by the locals. Those fish would be just in the early changes of physiologically converting over from their lives living in salt water into that of a freshwater critter. They would still be carrying their sea lice and that would be a good indicator of the fish being in their best physical condition for eating. Plus, those freshly arriving salmon into the river's habitat would still harbor a somewhat stronger desire to feed making them an easier fish to catch. With their bodies beginning to physically breakdown since all food consumption had stopped once they were in fresh water, salmon that had been in the river for a longer time would not be biting as much at a fisherman's bait and therefore harder to catch. I knew that many died in the wool salmon fishermen and those sometime wildlife outlaw dairy farmers in the area owning land along that portion of the lower river, would be aware of that bodily change over fact and the changed salmon feeding behavior. It was with those thoughts in mind that I decided where my patrol activities would be focused for the duration of my most recent assignment, which was also in accordance with Herb's wishes. Little did I realize that I was soon in for a unique and totally unexpected law enforcement surprise and learning experience.

Parking my marked patrol car in a grove of river-distant willows and throwing a camouflage parachute over it for good measure, I made ready for my patrol. Since I had planned a rather unique and extensive foot patrol for the day, I was dressed from head to toe in camouflage clothing in preparation for my salmon fishermen surveillance activities. My plan was to sneak along the Eel River from salmon hole to salmon hole and quietly observe the actions of any fishermen observed. If any chaps under observation broke the fish and game regulations, I would swoop down, collar their miserable carcasses and hang some paper on them for the error of their ways. If they didn't break the law, I would move on to my next fisherman without any person being the wiser as to my nearness.

Now all you readers out there, just you stop it! Yes, a chap my size could 'swoop' with the best of them! Just because I weighed in at a dainty 320 pounds, that didn't mean I couldn't do the quick step or a pirouette while in my combat mode. Shame on all you readers out there who doubted that the 'big one' (that would be me) couldn't do the 'river dance' and never be seen in the process by the outlaws.

For the rest of that morning, I quietly moved several miles up and down the Eel on foot glassing all the fishing waters and fishermen with my binoculars. I ran across about 20 or so fishermen and nary a one was breaking the law. That did my heart good to see such heavy use along a salmon stream and yet not discover anyone violating the law. After running out those portions of the Eel that held the best fishing waters, I reversed course and sneaked back upstream towards my patrol car. As I did, I continued quietly observing my salmon fishermen as they did their best to capture their elusive and soon to be great eating quarry, namely the king and silver salmon currently running in the Eel.

Stopping along a particularly dense stand of willows within a copse of Douglas fir trees, I paused to take care of a call of nature. By then the sun had burned off the north coast fog and steam could now be observed rising off the typical temperate Redwood's rain forest's perennially wet vegetation. It was then that Mother Nature went to work making sure I was earning my keep.

Finishing my call of nature, I started moving upstream. It was then that the sun warmed, heavy sickly sweet smell of rotting salmon graced my nose. *What the hell?* I thought. There were no spawning beds in that immediate area so I shouldn't be smelling rotting salmon like one would along a stretch of spawning gravel where numerous spawning fish would have died after laying their eggs. Stopping and dragging in several deeper breaths through my wonderfully shaped and sized Roman nose, I was again rewarded with the heavy sweet smell of death, namely that of rotting salmon. It was a unique smell that I had come to recognize after working one summer in Alaska conducting research work for the Bureau of Commercial Fisheries along many of Alaska's Bristol Bay's salmon spawning streams.

Following my nose, I soon discovered a pile of salmon guts in a dense stand of willows not 35 yards from the river! And

173

when I say a pile, I mean exactly that! Poking around in my unusual discovery, I counted a number of individual sets of innards and heads from silver and king salmon. No two ways about it, someone was harvesting more salmon than could have legally been taken by a sport fisherman over the short salmon season to date. In fact, the 51 sets of salmon insides and heads I had discovered, appeared to be just the minimum number that had been deposited in the brush patch. I could also see where numerous other sets of insides and heads scattered about, had been dragged off into the brush by numerous quadruped critters and scavenged. That second discovery of scattered salmon parts led me to believe that way more than just the 51 salmon parts discovered earlier had been harvested on the river near this spot by someone. Bottom line of reality, way more evidence of salmon piled about than could have been caught by a legal sport fisherman!

Looking around, I could see a well-travelled muddy farm road near the spot where all the salmon insides had been dumped to obviously lighten a load of fish someone had to move somewhere. Other than that, there were no other obvious clues that met the eye. As is typical for the temperate rain forest, a geographic area that gets 120-160 inches of rainfall a year, there was little left in the way of fresh footprints in or around the salmon parts dumpsite. Then my instincts and my two guardian angels quietly prodded me towards the river itself as if therein laid a clue to the extreme salmon harvesting that had previously occurred in the immediate area. I did so because based on the various decomposition rates observed of the remains, this salmon taking had been going on for some time and their numbers were way more in excess than one chap could reasonably do with just a rod and reel...

After looking all around to make sure there were no fishermen nearby to discovery me snooping, I walked out from my cover to begin looking for clues along the river. For the longest time I found nothing. Sure, I could see a few old footprints alongside the elongated pool in the river, a place where many salmon would normally pause during their upstream migrations to rest and rebuild their strength for more swimming upstream against the river's strong current. However, nothing more suspicious relative the perceived problem met my examining eyes at first glance. Taking more time and looking even closer, I could see that the long and deep pool was headed and tailed by extensive sets of long, fast flowing riffles. However, nothing else greeted my searching eyes in the way of any clues as to the extreme harvesting of salmon that had apparently previously occurred in the immediate area.

Damn it, I thought, *there just has to be some clues as to how so many fish were taken from this area and cleaned nearby*. But by damn, I did not see anything that rang my bell. Then, the sun finally shone on the manure pile behind the barn as I stood there by the river's edge looking for clues. Standing there on the sandbar edging the large pool of quiet water on the river, I discovered my first clue! Well actually to be fair to all you readers out there so you don't think that I am a whiz kid, I was standing in it! Scattered all over the sandbar on which I stood, was a mess of small twigs and a ton of red alder leaves scattered about.

Then it struck me! "Terry," I said out loud to myself, "remember what you learned while up on the Klamath River with Herb working the Yurok Indians and their illegal gill nets? One of the clues that Herb had told me to be on the lookout for was a mess of river borne debris that had been cleaned out of a finely meshed gill net and deposited along a clean sandbar where the net could be safely stretched out, examined and cleaned." *Hot dog,* I thought, as I finally looked down at my feet where I was standing on the sandbar next to the large eddy. With closer examination of the fine-grained sand at my feet, I could just make out numerous, barely visible, float and lead line impressions in the sand and some very faint footprint indentations. The lines in the sand indicated where the net had been laid as it was being cleaned of its debris after having been removed from the river after use. *Damn! Some puke is running an illegal gill net on this part of the Eel and, if all the piles of salmon guts and heads up on the riverbank in that stand of willows are any indicator of success, they have been knocking the hell out of the migrating fish!* I grimly thought.

It was at that moment of discovery that another issue hit me like a ton of bricks. I was standing out in the open in my illegal gill net use suspect area like a big bird. Out in the open, where if someone was watching their fishing hole to ascertain if anyone had discovered their dirty little gill net secret, the cat would be out of the bag. Taking one more quick look to make doubly sure I had seen faint net line marks in the sand along with all the debris cleaned from a suspect gill net, I vanished into the cover along the river like a puff of black powder smoke would make from a once fired musket in a forested glen during a slight breeze...

Turning around from my new place of hiding in the river's brush line, I glassed the entire area with my binoculars. The only living thing I observed was a large herd of brown Swiss milk cows peacefully grazing behind a barbed wire fence that paralleled the muddy road running high up on the bank alongside the Eel River. Other than that, there didn't appear to be another heart beat in the area other than the usual aerial critters found along such a densely wooded waterway and the cows in the pasture.

Good, I thought, *with a little luck, maybe I wasn't seen.* I then realized that for a gill net to be the most successful, it had to be run at night when the migrating salmon could not see the net's mesh lines. That being the case, my culprit running the gill net illegally more than likely would not be out and about until sometime after dark. More importantly, by running the gill net at night, every day fisherman passing by would not see the net floats, put two and two together and call in the law. Making one more quick check of the area from my location in the dense stand of brush, I fled the scene and headed back for my marked patrol vehicle. Shortly thereafter, I left the area with hope in my heart and nary a scent of trail left as to my earlier presence to betray the nearness of the long arm of the law.

That evening after dark, I parked my personal Jeep pickup in my usual hiding spot and quietly walked the half mile to my suspect gill net site. Since I considered running an illegal gill net a major case, I had used my own vehicle instead of an obvious fish and game patrol vehicle. That way I hoped if the gill net operator somehow ran across my vehicle, he would not be as suspicious as he would have been upon discovering a fish and game patrol vehicle. In case my culprit had a dog with him who could wind or hear me coming and give me away, I made sure I was moving along as quietly as a mouse does when pissin' on a ball of cotton. Finally arriving at my suspect illegal gill net site, I glassed the river eddy looking for the telltale sign of net floats. Damn, was I ever disappointed in what I did not see! Nary a net float did I see anywhere in my close at hand and suspect eddy. Thinking maybe my lad or lads running the gill net had yet to arrive, I settled in for a long wait because anyone running an illegal gill net along the Eel, a serious wildlife crime, would be as careful as a cat in a house full of mean assed pit bulls. An individual running such a net had to realize that getting caught would mean one hell of a fine and the possibility of a stint in jail. Running such an efficient killing device like a gill net would also be doing a heap of damage to that natural resource and my gill-netter had to know that in the shadows of his heart. No two ways about it, my gillnet operator would be extra careful in all of his illegal endeavors, even if he only had half a brain, because of the severity of the violation. However, I figured I was just the SOB to put a stop to such illegal and gross salmon killing behavior if given just half a chance and now, I would be there for the duration no matter how long it took.

Daylight the next morning found me heading for home with no outlaw gill netter in tow. No one had shown up the previous evening but that was all right with me. That meant a mess of salmon had successfully traversed that part of the river and that was a good show for Mother Nature and any future salmon runs. The next evening I quietly and patiently repeated my river watching actions. No cigar that evening either regarding my suspected illegal gill netter. The same stakeout procedure along the Eel River was provided by yours truly over the rest of that week. Again, no cigar for my persistence for that entire week was to be my reward for a stakeout well done.

In the meantime, I filled Herb in on what I had discovered but, because of his badly sprained ankle garnered during a foot chase with an illegal deer shooter, he was too crippled up to help so I was still on my own. Being that the salmon season was in full swing along the entire north coast set of river systems, there was no other help available from the rest of the limited numbers of my squad's crew mates either. Every officer in my patrol squad was up to his neck in salmon related problems and as a result, none could be spared to give this rookie a hand. Welcome to the wonderful world of conservation law enforcement, Folks, and why so many times the officers wearing the 'game warden greens' feel like Custer.

(If one is in the know, it is easy to see why help was not immediately forthcoming. For my readers' edification, there are only about 10,000 wildlife officers in ALL of North America! That means just 10,000 county, state, federal, Tribal, Territorial, Provincial and R.C.M.P. officers to keep about 350,000,000 million people in North America corralled within the world of wildlife in 2015 as these words are written! Hell, as I have said so many times earlier in my writings, Custer had better odds than that and look what happened to him...)

For nine days after I had initially discovered the illegal trappings of someone running a gill net on the Eel River, not a single black-hearted soul showed up at my suspect spot. I began to wonder maybe my gillnetting outlaw had somehow spotted me initially and had fled the scene for better shores. However, on the evening of day number ten of my stakeout, I struck gold! In fact, I struck more than that...

Slinking into my suspect area on the evening of the tenth day after my initial discovery of the evidence of a gill net being run on the Eel, my persistence paid off. Moving quietly in the brush along the river in the darkness to my chosen observation spot, I sat down, put a wad of chewing tobacco between my teeth and gums and made ready for another long and lonely, mosquito filled evening. As I sat down, numerous white-footed wood rats made many rustling noises close around me and I could hear the calls of a startled killdeer spooked off a marshy area near the Eel. But other than that, it was as quiet as a graveyard in the dead of winter in rural North Dakota.

Raising my binoculars to scan the suspect eddy where any gill net set would more than likely be located, I got surprised. THERE IT WAS! Sure as God made live crickets good trout fishing bait, there quietly laid a string of white net floats running about 30 yards out into the center of the eddy! An eddy in which the exhausted migrating salmon would more than likely pull off into to rest and gather up their strength for more swimming upstream against the current that was to follow. Several of the sections of the float line were violently moving up and down which signified a salmon or two were gasping their last as they hung there with the net's mesh firmly wrapped around their gill plates causing those critters so trapped to slowly suffocate to death!

Glassing the riverbank next to the float line, I could not see any movement indicating the presence of another human being who would more than likely be the net tender. I than began quietly moving up towards the head of the sandbar near the float line of the net so I could be closer to anyone subsequently discovered running the illegal net. As I did, I began stalking towards that area as my dad, Otis Barnes, had taught me. (In his youth, Otis, had been raised with a number of Maidu Indians in Plumas County in northeastern California, who had taught him their tracking techniques.) Walking as silently as any Indian stalking a deer, I slowly inched towards where I figured any illegal net runner would be seated and hidden watching his net's action.

After twenty minutes of quietly stalking a spot I had fixed in my mind as to where my culprit ought to be quietly sitting hidden from view, I found nothing! There wasn't another heart beat in the area except mine and the several dying salmon hanging in the gill net out in the river's eddy! *Damn,* I thought. *I was just sure there would be someone sitting there tending that gill net.* But once again, I was sadly mistaken and drew a blank for all my sneaking around efforts.

Then I put Plan B into action. I realized my net tender, if not on site, would have to come back sometime in the dark to tend his net before any legal salmon fishermen the next day stumbled upon his illegal activity come daylight. With those thoughts in the back of my mind, I took up a spot near the rotting gut pile of salmon taken earlier by my net-runner and dug in. If my net running chap was a creature of habit, he would return to his usual spot to clean out the fish. If he did, I surmised I would be so close to my culprit that I could nail his black-hearted hide to the wall in a heartbeat!

(To all my readers out there, there is nothing quite so patient as a good game warden on the hunt or the deadly South American bushmaster snake lying alongside a well-used game trail. You readers will have to read up on the life history of that snake to understand my comparisons. Word of the day, don't go to South America and try sneaking along any game trail unless the good Lord is your co-pilot.)

Around three in the morning as I dozed in my place of hiding with the nearby stink of rotting fish parts heavily perfuming the air, I suddenly snapped back to the real world with a start! I could hear the quiet engine noise of a nearby vehicle up on the farm road just barely idling along. Moments later along the muddy farm road up on the riverbank paralleling the river, I observed the darkened shape of a slowly and quietly moving pickup. I was so close that I could even hear my driver applying the emergency brake of the truck to stop, so he wouldn't have to use his foot brakes that would light up the area with his tail lights if he stopped normally. And in so using his brake's foot pedal, that would give away his presence to anyone who happened to be watching. *This chap is a real outlaw the way he is behaving,* I thought with a Cheshire cat smile of anticipation. (Don't forget that South American bushmaster lying alongside the game trail analogy, all my patient readers.)

Now stopped, my mystery chap just sat there in the truck for a long moment as if making sure no one was onto his little game. If they were, all he had to do was put his truck into gear and sprint off down the muddy farm road and into the nothingness of darkness. My suspect was pretty cautious and 'woods-wise', but so was the bushmaster lying in wait along the game trail wearing game warden greens and a big anticipatory smile over what was soon to occur.

Then the door to the truck quietly opened. I was close enough to see that my suspect had cleverly placed some tape over his dome light so it would not give away the driver when he opened up his door in the darkness. However, his taping job was second rate and a sliver of light still escaped from the dome light. As the man began exiting the vehicle, what a physical monster he turned out to be! The lad appeared to be at least a good 6-foot 4-inches tall and about the size of a well-built stone out house. *Pretty damn smart but not smart enough in the dome light taping department*, I thought as I now mulled over the man's size in my mind, figuring he would be a handful if he ever got riled. Especially when I dropped the hammer on his miserable carcass for his part in running the illegal gill net and placed him under arrest.

Stepping out from the truck and quietly pushing the door shut so he wouldn't make any excess noise by slamming it, my huge darkened shape of a man walked around the front of his vehicle and down to the sandbar. There I could see my monster of a man pulling in his gill net through my 7X50 Navy, high light gathering binoculars. I was a big man myself but the darkened shape bending over at the sandbar pulling in his net almost made two of me! Then my fascination with what was going on and what he was doing set in, so I watched.

My net-puller would drag in his net until he came to a dead or dying fish and then he would quietly untangle the fish. That salmon was laid on the grass next to the sandbar and the next fish would be dragged ashore and treated in the same manner. In the instance where he brought in several still live, very active salmon, I could see the glint of his knife in the light of the half-moon as he stabbed each fish in the head instantly killing it. That precluded a lot of flopping around on the riverbank and creating excess noises. He continued the fish removal process until he had pulled in and removed 22 salmon from the deadly gill net!

Following the fish removal process, my chap began shaking his net in sections as he removed many of the leaves and twigs that had floated down the Eel and snagged into the meshes of his net. When he had finished the cleaning process, he rolled up his net, struggling with its loose bulk as he staggered up the bank and quietly placed it into the back of his pickup. Back to the sandbar went my netter, whereupon he picked up two large salmon and began walking almost directly at me. Not moving or hardly even daring to breathe, I let my chap walk over to his fish gutting area holding all the rotting salmon innards and began gutting out his two salmon. Me? I was still trying to come up with a Plan A or a Plan B that would not get me killed in the process of trying to physically control my monster sized man when I made my presence known and placed him under arrest for the gill net violation. Moments later, he walked over to his truck carrying the cleaned fish and quietly laid them into its bed. This process was repeated ten more times until he had nearly gutted out all his illegally netted fish.

It was then that I sprang MY proverbial net. Quietly standing to let the blood return to my cramped legs, I waited until he had just finished gutting his 22nd fish. Stepping out from my place of hiding, I had the damn luck of those never-having-won-a-war Germans to nearly step on a big boar raccoon who was quietly moving up to the salmon gut pile for an early breakfast. When I made my move, so did the frightened raccoon and when he did, he alerted my monster sized chap. In an instant, my chap dropped his fish and tore off running for his pickup! However, guess who had luckily hidden in such a position that I was now in full motion on a classic intercept course of action? On went my Ray-O-Vac, five cell flashlight (we didn't have the good stout aluminum ones in those days like they do today) and the race was on!

Seeing that he could not make his pickup in time to escape because there was a rather large chap cutting him off at the pass all the while yelling, "State Fish and Game Warden. Hold it right there!" my chap turned away from running towards his truck. As he did, it seemed my bellowed out words only lent wings to his feet increasing his speed of flight.

It was then that the crap REALLY hit the fan! My damn piece of junk flashlight went out just as I hit my stride and had to be going at least 100 miles per hour! In front of me just out of arm's reach ran my huge man who surprisingly could run like the wind. But the SOB directly behind him had just lit up his after burners and I was moving like an F-15 fighter jet as the two of us thundered out across the muddy road and towards the huge open cow pasture to our front.

SCREEEEECH, went the unseen and forgotten in the darkness because of the emotion of the moment, four strand barbed wire fence as my monster runner got a painful surprise when he hit that immoveable obstacle running full tilt! OOOOFFF, went my lad as his mass painfully collided with an E-flat-tightly-stung-piano-wire, barbed wire fence! Fence screeching sounds filled the air as my moveable man hit an immovable fence, then came hurtling back towards me on his rebound. THUUUMMP, was the next sound filling the quiet morning air as my mass going 100 miles an hour inadvertently collided with my surprised runner's mass as he came rebounded back in my direction after initially hitting the fence. Man let me tell you, all we needed was some Uranium U-235 as an igniter and we would have created a mighty big bang upon the impact of two major sized men in that following collision.

I hit my man so hard that he was again propelled forward back into the fence and yours truly, now only going eighty miles per hour at that juncture, was flipped head over heels over the top of my runner, the barbed wire fence and into the cow pasture beyond! When I flipped over my outlaw and landed into the cow pasture, I landed flat on my back and had the wind knocked out of me for a brief moment. Realizing in the back of my mind I still had a monster sized outlaw on the loose and now on the truck's side of the fence, I choked down some air, scrambled to my feet and stormed back to the unyielding fence to make sure my chap did not escape. I knew if he ever did get behind the wheel of his truck and escaped, I would never see him again. However, there was no need for my haste. My huge outlaw was hanging on the barbed wire fence like a dead coyote or wolf hung on a fence out in western Wyoming in cattle and sheep country.

Since the darkened shape of my outlaw didn't appear to be doing anything but barely wiggling, I took my time crawling over the fence and letting my carcass get its wind back. Walking over to my now falling off the fence and starting to stagger around gill netter, I again announced who I was and slipped my set of Smith and Wesson handcuffs quickly over his wrists before he could say, "Howdy". When I did, I quickly realized my handcuffs just barely went around the man's huge wrists! When I closed them shut, I had to take a small portion of his skin along with it just to get the handcuffs to latch shut! Man, I wasn't any slouch for size but the lad I now had in tow was a bruiser. Truth be known, he was as big as one of those brown Swiss cows I had seen earlier in the day feeding in the pasture.

However my guy was whipped. He was hurting from the collision with the tightly strung fence and from the further surprise impact when my 320 beautiful pounds had slammed into his backside as he rebounded from the collision with the unseen and forgotten-it-was-there fence. Heck, he was a 'pussy cat' at that point. To be quite frank, my right shoulder hurt like hell as well from its impact slamming into the mass of my giant of a man. My chap was not only huge but he was as solid as a Durham bull. But like the R.C.M.P., I had my man! That was at least for now unless my monster decided to break my handcuffs and my head all in the same motion.

Walking my man in the dark back to where I had hidden my pickup so I could retrieve my extra flashlight, we had a chance to get acquainted. His name was Robert Glover and he was a dairy farmer who owned the land next to his gill net fishing hole. He had gotten the gill net from his brother-in-law, a Hoopa Indian, who had married his sister. After previously watching his brother-in-law successfully run a gill net on the Hoopa Indian Reservation, Robert felt he ought to give such a fishing device a whirl in his own back yard on the salmon infested Eel River. Since the river butted up next to his land, he figured he would be safe in illegally running such an efficient killer of fish. On the walk back to my truck, I discovered the reason he had not fished for so long a period when I had initially staked out the net. It was because he and his wife had been on a vacation and his hired hand was running the dairy in his absence but not his gill net. As for the fish, he had been running those he had caught back to his brother-in-law who had been selling them on the reservation and splitting the proceeds with my monster sized dairyman.

Back at my truck, Robert was snugly, and I do mean snugly, seated in the front seat and I drove back to the scene of the crime. There I loaded the fish and his gill net into the back of my Jeep and off we went to the sheriff's office lockup back in Eureka. On the way to Eureka, Robert asked if I was going to tell Herb he had been caught running an illegal gill net. I advised that since it was Herb's district, he would be notified of the circumstances of the arrest. With that, Robert just hung his head and swore quietly under his breath. I later discovered out why Robert was so concerned over letting Herb know he had been apprehended running an illegal gill net. Robert was a close friend of Herb's and was his number one hunter safety instructor in Herb's law enforcement district.

When I later informed Herb of my catch, he just roared aloud with laughter, cast or no cast on his damaged ankle. As it turned out, Herb's wife and Robert's were the best of friends and old high school pals. Herb, being the good human being he was, just continued his warm family's relationship with the dairy farmer and his wife because Robert dutifully paid his fine several weeks later. To Herb's way of thinking, Robert had settled up with the State of California for his misdeeds so everything was now a 'wash.' Other than sharing the information about Robert's brother-in-law illegally selling salmon on the Hoopa Indian Reservation with local warden Hank Marak who patrolled that area, my work was done on that Eel River detail.

(In writing this story, I just have to smile. I only knowingly caught two bona fide dairy farmers in my 32-year state and federal wildlife law enforcement career. In both cases, two high speed foot chases later, both had come to grief with a slow moving, tightly strung barbed wire fence. One was in Humboldt County gill netting salmon on the Eel River and the other in Glenn County in the northern Sacramento Valley night shooting snow geese under a full moon as they flew off the Sacramento National Wildlife Refuge to their nightly feeding grounds.

In the second instance, that farmer had a boatload of dead snow geese down in his cow pasture. In both cases, those issues turned into foot races in which I had inadvertently run the men full bore into unseen barbed wire fences. The only difference was that the Glenn County dairy farmer was injured when he had hit the tightly strung, external boundary barbed wire fence belonging to the adjacent national wildlife refuge. As in the current gill net runner's case, I had slammed into the back of my rebounding snow goose late shooting dairy farmer during that subsequent foot chase. But not until he too had slammed into a barbed wire fence and was violently recoiling when I collided with him running full bore and only feet behind him just as I was reaching for his shoulder. In that instance, my late goose-shooting runner had taken the top of a "T" post directly under his chin and ended up a bloody mess! I had to take him to the hospital in Willows to get him stitched up. They were both great cases in which the resource was being heavily impacted and the illegal activities had to be stopped. And subsequently in both instances, both violators were stopped dead in their tracks and in fine style I might add...)

If one looked closely enough, he would find the Flowers in this story. The first set of Flowers found in this story came from my Klamath River adventures when working gill netting Yurok Indians with Warden Herb Chrisrtie. There he had taught me many tricks of the trade employed by Indian gill netters and I had learned from those teachings. Months later, I had been able to apply some of Herb's teachings to my own successful gill netting case on the Eel River in Herb's own law enforcement district. Nothing like returning a favor of the same 'flavor' to my way of thinking...

Again as always in such adventures, the Tombstones reared up their marbled heads as well. Of the 22 salmon gillnetted that night and into the morning hours by Robert, 14 were big king salmon females in the 35-40 pound class! Multiply fourteen by approximately the 3,000 eggs each female would have laid had they made it to their spawning grounds of genesis and you can quickly see what a loss the wild Eel River salmon resource suffered. SADLY, THOSE EGG LOSSES COUNTED WERE JUST IN THAT ONE INSTANCE! Imagine the numbers of salmon eggs Robert destroyed before I discovered his dirty little secret and managed to put a stop to it…

But there were surprisingly other Flowers to this story as well. Herb and Robert remained the best of friends as long as they both lived. To Herb's way of thinking, Robert had learned his lesson very well relative to remaining within the fish and game laws of the land and the consequences if one did not.

And, there were additional Flowers in this story that soon followed. Those Flowers Robert incorporated into his following hunter safety instruction courses stressing the importance of protecting the natural resources of Humboldt County, especially the salmon. He used his sad story to show the farm kids the damage he had done to the salmon resource and what had happened to him after his apprehension. He even illustrated that point by explaining to the kids from his farming community just how many gallons of milk he had to sell in order to settle-up with the court for the evil of his ways. All those farm kids could clearly relate to Robert's illustration when it came to doing a wrong in the world of wildlife and his having to sell a lot of milk in order to pay the fine.

There was another set of Tombstones that pushed their marbled heads above the soil of the land several years later after this adventure had occurred. Both Herb and Robert have since passed, both men being lost to the ravages of cancer when they were in their prime.

Other Tombstones that have pushed their marbled heads above the 'topsoil of life' relates to the oft spoken theme I have mentioned many times in my other stories. The Pacific species of salmon are in trouble as these words were written in 2015. Their wild populations have plummeted and as a result, the salmon sport and commercial fishery have almost gone into the tank because of the low population numbers of wild salmon. This is an all too common sad Tombstone relating to man's inhumanity to man when it comes to the ravages taking place in the world of wildlife.

Ah, Man. What wonderful things he has historically brought to the natural resource treasure table and the storied world of wildlife for those folks yet to come to enjoy...or not...

Chapter Four: The Outlaw Bounty of California's Temperate Rain Forest

SNOW CAMP, "BRUSH OKIES" AND FOUR DEAD DEER

BOOM, BOOM,—BOOM! Shadow, my Labrador retriever who moments earlier had been sound asleep and loudly snoring in the backseat of my patrol car, jumped up and was now wide awake. She had been a constant patrol companion ever since my wife, Donna, had given her to me as a partner. Shadow had been on numerous law enforcement patrols ever since and the sounds of shooting or any unusual movement on my part, quickly galvanized her into her characteristic high alert mode. Now that I think back on it as I write these words many years later, it seems a law enforcement officer only gets one GREAT dog in his life. Boy, Howdy, Shadow was a good one! I am reminded in my computer room writing these lines about just how much I miss that dog. It has been almost 40 years since we shared a sandwich and like most good game wardens having great dogs, I still miss her dearly. I have never owned another dog after I lost her out of respect for the relationship the two of us experienced over those ten years we shared together hunting the lawless in the world of wildlife. Oh well, thinking about Shadow and the loss of my field partner only hurts, so, back to the story at hand.

As for me, I had been about half asleep myself when that shooting occurred. Suffice to say, I was now awake as was my ever-faithful dog. Glancing down at the luminous dial on my watch, I saw that it was two-thirty in the morning. Since there were no big game hunting seasons open at that time of the morning and the sounds of shooting came from two heavy rifles, I figured it was time to get off my dead hind end and go to work doing what the good people of the State of California paid me to do.

Fully awake, I quietly sat in my patrol car listening for any further clues as to who was doing what to whom. If there was any further shooting, I figured I would be able to echolocate on my shooters pretty darn quickly and more accurately since I now had all my windows rolled down and facilities in place. I had learned early on that patience was an absolute virtue if one was ever going to make a decent game warden. But by damn, it was also hard not to hustle right out and grab my night-shooting outlaws by their last parts over the fence and shake them with a vengeance before they did any more damage to the resident critter populations. However, that was not how it was done, so, I held my water and waited for any clues to come which would decide my next move.

As I sat there waiting for more clues, I ran the general set of known surrounding parameters through my mind's eye. I was in the Snow Camp area above the small logging and lumbering settlement of Blue Lake in Humboldt County, California. The general area in which I was sitting was in the heart of northern California's temperate rain forest of redwoods, Douglas fir, white fir and grand fir. That specific area was also rich in wildlife like Columbian black-tailed deer, Roosevelt elk, black bear, mountain quail, band-tailed pigeons, mountain lions, and every other type of creepy-crawler known to call home to such a wet coniferous forest environment. The distant town of Blue Lake held more than their fair share of ridge-runners, deer-shiners, late shooters, closed season shooters, and all other types of wildlife outlaws between 'A and Z' known to us officers of the thin green.

Throw into that illustrious mix the Friday night wild fist swinging loggers, out of work, tough as horseshoe nails lumbermen, several nearby tribes of wild as a March hare Native Americans and a nearby natural resources college with every type of young 'want-to-be' outlaw known to humankind and one could see that I potentially had a hat full of hornets when it came to wildlife protection. In short, I found myself within a sulfurous mix of humanity from the pot smokers of the 1960's to the potential run-of-the-mill trouble making wildlife outlaws known to frequent Humboldt County.

As for my current situation, from the pattern and sequencing of shooting I heard, I knew that there were two shooters. Weapons familiarity told me from the sounds of the rifles' fire that they were heavy hunting types of rifles. The shooting had come from the vast area to my west, which meant that my shooters were on a long, one-way backcountry road leading to a dead end mass of abandoned logging spurs. That also meant my mystery shooters would eventually have to come back through me on the same road on which I was now sitting in hiding if they wanted to get back to the Blue Lake area and home. The general area from which the shooting had occurred was a forested re-growth area, home to numerous Columbian black-tailed deer and Roosevelt elk. Historically, that area was a favorite haunt of many local wildlife outlaws because of its remoteness and high numbers of shoot-able wildlife critters. There had been three spaced shots fired from those two rifles. That either meant my shooters were of piss-poor quality when it came to their marksmanship or the outlaws had gotten into a number of deer and/or elk and had shot at more than one critter. Either way, the number of shots fired indicated to my way of thinking that I had a mess of poachers out of place in my neighborhood.

Most experienced night shooters characteristically restricted their number of shots fired while poaching the 'king's game' to avoid unwanted attention especially if there was the possibility of a game warden lurking in the area. With a little luck and a successful apprehension on my part, this little outing would ultimately come down to 'Lions One, Christians Nothing', figuratively speaking of course.

BOOM, went the sound of another heavy rifle being shot, presumably by poachers. With that shot, I was able to more accurately echolocate the area in which my shooters were illegally messin' around on the mountain with the 'King's Game'. That was all I needed, so, off Dog and I went. Leaving my hiding place, I kept my Mercury Comet patrol car in low gear so I could quietly sneak into the shooting area of my interest. Driving without using any lights and with my full set of cut-off switches thrown so lights of any kind would not show inside or out on my vehicle, Dog and I headed up the back country dirt road towards the sound of my shooters' last shot.

I marveled at just how quietly the engine ran in my patrol vehicle once I got up om my road of interest. On many previous night patrols, I had been able to run right up onto wildlife or violators before they even knew I was there. It was always nice, figuratively speaking, to have the sun at your back when working back country wildlife violators. 'Sun at your back', because back country wildlife violators were more often than not in the wrong, mostly armed, sometimes possessing dangerous attitudes, often times had been drinking, many times in possession of illegal game and almost every time outnumbered the arresting officer.

(Just for my readers' information, according to the most recent FBI statistics, wildlife officers have a mortality rate that is nine times higher than any other kind of law enforcement in America. Hence, the very real need to have the sun at your back at all times, if you get the gist of what I am saying...)

Five minutes later, I turned onto the one-way road that ran the full length of the mountain ridges skirting the Snow Camp area. Now that I was on the main road and the only escape for any outlaws to my front was through me, I relaxed a bit. I figured my shooters were about one mile away so I just took my time as I moved slowly along under the light of a partial moon.

My first contact of any kind came a few minutes later. Sneaking quietly along, I drove right up onto a huge porcupine rambling down the middle of the road. His darkened shape and familiar rolling gait gave away the presence and identity of that animal. Slowing to avoid injuring the critter, it finally ambled safely off the road. Then, with a smile on my face over that neat outdoor experience with one of Mother Nature's rather unique critters, I moved on down the dirt road towards my mystery shooters.

WHUMP! Damned if a surprised deer feeding along the roadside had not heard my vehicle approaching until the last moment. When that doe realized there was a huge object quietly idling down the road next to where she had been quietly feeding, she panicked and ran right into the side of my vehicle! That surprised the hell out of her and scared the dickens out of me! As for Dog whose head was hanging out the back window, I heard her teeth clack as she snapped at the nearby doe when it ran into her side of the car. That incident took a few minutes for Dog and yours truly to calm down after being blindsided by a critter I was trying to protect. Nothing like having Mother

Nature take us on for size and play a trick on one of her minions just for the hell of it to see if he was 'wide awake and bushy tailed'...

With that surprise out of the way, it was time to get down to the morning's business dealing with my wildlife outlaws at hand. BOOM! Through the open windows of my patrol car, I plainly heard a heavy rifle being discharged somewhere now close ahead of my position. Instantly stopping, I cut off my engine and just sat there listening. For about ten minutes, I heard nothing more from my mystery shooters. Then I quietly started up my patrol car and continued on making only a little tire noise on the roadway's graveled surface as I trickled along in destiny's direction.

Traversing about another eighth of a mile and slowly rounding a turn in the road, I became aware of a darkened vehicle like shape sitting dead center in the roadway about 35 yards distant! I immediately turned my vehicle sideways in the narrow road to block the roadway and any means of escape by my suspect vehicle, if that kind of action was to occur. Then I quietly shut off my vehicle's engine so my mystery shooters would not become aware of my nearby presence. Grabbing my binoculars from the seat, I scanned the older four-door sedan blocking the road ahead of where I now sat. Three of the vehicle's doors were flung wide open as if the sedan's occupants had left hurriedly. No one was in sight but sure as crickets made good trout bait, this had to be my mystery shooters' vehicle! To my game warden's budding senses, these chaps were serious outlaws. Even with three of their doors flung wide open, no dome light showed inside their vehicle. It was obvious these chaps had removed or taped over their dome light to remain unseen when they were illegally 'out and about' and needed to exit their vehicle in a stealthy manner. *Pretty damn clever,* I thought, *but not clever enough.* Then my survival senses kicked in over what I was seeing. There were three open doors on the vehicle sitting in the middle of the road, which told me I probably would shortly be facing three armed adversaries doing to Mother Nature what they shouldn't be doing.

Whispering to Shadow to remain in the backseat, I removed and pocketed my car's keys, quietly exited my vehicle, silently shoved my door shut and started slowly walking towards my suspect vehicle. Since my vehicle's windows were rolled down, I knew if I needed any backup that Shadow was only a quiet whistle or verbal command away. If called, in an instant she would be out the window and on her way to join in on any kind of unfolding fracas. Moments of quietly walking later, I could hear several hushed voices about 30 yards away at the edge of a meadow. Numerous times I swore I could hear several men talking and it sounded like a number of their words were coming from out of a whiskey bottle.

Great, I thought. *This is all I need to be faced with. Several obvious deer shiners armed and loaded to the gills with John Barleycorn.* (Many times when a law officer runs across a situation like this one portended to be, dangerous things can and do sometimes happen.) Sneaking up to my suspects' vehicle and making sure no one was coming out from the shooting area to catch me in the act, I took a quick look inside. That look was facilitated with a small amount of light from my flashlight filtered through my partially spread fingers. *Hot damn,* I thought. *Can you believe it? There, in front of God and everybody, laid a rifle on the front seat of the old sedan and another rifle was laying across the backseat with its stock sticking out of the open door of the vehicle!*

Well my mother, God rest her soul, didn't raise me as a ding bat! Reaching in, I removed both rifles and quietly headed back to my patrol vehicle to check the weapons for loaded cartridges in their chambers. Sure as all get out, both rifles had a loaded round in their chambers. *That is O.K. with me,* I thought. That just meant my shooters would also be looking at loaded gun charges once all the smoke had cleared away and the apprehensions made. After unloading both rifles, they were placed into the trunk of my patrol car for safekeeping and locked up so my poachers could not regain control of them and do something stupid.

Finished with that chore, I trotted back down the road towards my suspects' vehicle near where the voices were emanating from out in the brush at the edge of the meadow. Standing by my suspects' vehicle, on an oft chance, I looked at the steering column of my outlaws' sedan with my flashlight's light filtered through my fingers. And what do you think I discovered? There was a set of car keys in the ignition sitting there just as pretty as you please! Those I quickly removed and placed into my pants' pocket for safe keeping. Now if my suspects overcame me and tried to drive away, they would have one hell of a time doing it unless they hot-wired the car. Turning, I listened to get a better idea as to where my shooters were exactly located. With a quiet snap of my fingers to get my dog's attention, I heard toenails clicking as Shadow quickly exited my patrol car through an open back window. Moments later, she sat at my side as she had been trained. Let me tell you, my darling wife sure as hell knew what she was doing when she got me that big ole black as night dog as my law enforcement field partner!

With that, Dog and I began quietly stalking our ways through the dense brush towards the voices of what I figured were my mystery shooters. That stalking took about five long minutes as I cautiously inched my way sneaking silently towards the sounds of several voices. Moments later, I observed two men in the act of dressing out a deer in the feeble light from the partial moon above and from a three-cell flashlight held by another man who also was cradling a rifle in the crook of his arm. Realizing I now had an armed assailant to my front, I adjusted my stalk so it would place me next to

197

and behind him so I could immediately disarm him the moment my presence became known to all concerned.

As I moved in closer to the armed man from behind his blind side, Shadow just as quietly moved with me tightly positioned alongside my right leg as she had been taught. As I did, my chap with the rifle was in the process of verbally providing gutting instructions to the two men who were cleaning out an illegal doe deer. That armed chap never knew I was within a country mile until I reached out, quickly removed his loosely cradled rifle from behind and bellowed out all at the same time, "STATE FISH AND GAME WARDEN! HOLD IT RIGHT THERE!" I then quickly tossed his rifle off to one side out of the way and turned on my five-cell flashlight to illuminate the scene. Talk about taking a surprise dump in my outlaws' little deer killing punch bowl! I think it was safe to say that I had just ruined their little closed season deer shoot.

Surprised over me being so close, the fellow I had quickly disarmed exploded into a forward jump onto the top of his two deer-gutting cohorts that would have made a kangaroo proud. He landed squarely on top of his two just as surprised companions who were bent over gutting out their deer. That kangaroo move piled all the men onto the ground in one squirming heap. Talk about the crap hitting the fan, it blew everywhere! One man who had been previously gutting out the deer was the first to untangle himself from their frog pile. He jumped up and, in a panic without thinking about anything but flight, ran right down my flashlight's beam and straight into me!

At the second of that impact, the man realized that I was the one ruining their little deer-poaching outing. Purely out of defensive instinct, which I was sure had been fortified by many previous nips from a whiskey bottle, he took a clumsy swing at me. His swing missed and mine didn't. Swinging the butt end of my heavy five-celled flashlight, which I now held in my left hand, I cold cocked him! The other two lads had just scrambled back to their feet and were still in the moment of total shock. Then they saw their cohort in crime come flying back at them from the impact of my flashlight strike and collapsing in a heap at their feet. With that, the man who had been previously holding the rifle now wet himself as the front of his pants betrayed his reflex actions! Yeah, I would say I had ruined a perfectly good deer spotlighting outing, not to mention, was responsible for having a chap spotting' the front of a perfectly good pair of jeans.

Then the heavily bearded burley one, the man who had been initially holding the rifle before being disarmed, finally got his mental senses together and drew a long bladed knife from his belt sheath. He then menacingly took a step forward towards me muttering something I could not understand. Realizing his offensive move was more than likely brought on by his natural 'flight or fight' response, and fortified with a number of previous drinks of firewater, I made my move. 'Clearing leather' with my .44 magnum handgun, I leveled it accordingly at his center of mass! Plain and simple, when I drew my handgun, the man with the knife made an easy moving target illuminated by the light from my flashlight if I needed to pull the trigger!

That move was followed with a rather loudly bellowed command to drop his knife or die where he now stood! Once again I bellowed out, "STATE FISH AND GAME WARDEN! ALL OF YOU ARE UNDER ARREST FOR BEING IN POSSESSION OF AN ILLEGALLY TAKEN DEER!"

That second commands and the seriousness of the sight of a leveled handgun in the light of my flashlight shining on the man's chest finally sunk into the brain of the knife wielding man. He immediately tossed his weapon aside like the handle was red hot! I am sure looking down the rather large bore of a .44 magnum's barrel, which at that range was like looking directly into the opening of a garbage can, finally got his attention! Bearing that in mind, I think that 'gun barrel look' had more than something to do with his and his partner's immediate attention to my latest bellowed command.

"You two lads sit down and don't move or say a thing," I then commanded. Both men immediately dropped their hind ends onto the earth and sat there still as death in shock over what was now happening to them.

About then, the man I had clipped with my five-cell flashlight began moaning and coming out of his dreamland. Once he became somewhat more lucid, he was ordered to roll over and sit alongside his two companions in crime. It was then that I noticed another doe deer that had been previously killed and gutted lying off to one side of the men! I realized that was probably why I had initially heard three quick shots from two different rifles. My guess was the men had spotlighted several deer in a bunch and two of the men had fired simultaneously, possibly from their vehicle, killing the two doe deer.

"Gentlemen, so we don't have any further misunderstandings even though I am in full uniform, my name is Terry Grosz and I am a state fish and game warden. Since night shooting of deer is against the law and you three are in possession of two closed season dead doe deer in the dark of the night, I would say all of you have a legal problem. All three of you are under arrest and if any of you care to try and escape, I will sic my dog on you and that will be a most painful learning experience." It was about then that the three men noticed my dog still quietly sitting alongside my right leg. A dog who was intently looking at the three men, was as black as midnight and sitting by my side as still as death. Their collective sets of eyes said it all once they took a good look at a 100 pound Labrador quietly looking at them as intently as they were looking at her.

"Alright, Gentlemen." Pointing, I said, "You two lads grab those deer and haul them out to the road. Once there, you will be advised of your rights and then all of us are taking a ride to the Eureka Sheriff's Office where you will be booked for being in possession of closed season big game animals." Those words were followed by a good deal of grumbling about having to haul the evidence against them out to the road but that little chore was finally accomplished. On the way out, I holstered my handgun and picked up the third man's rifle that I had tossed off to one side when I had initially made my entrance into their little poaching party. Once back at their vehicle, I searched it for any other weapons, searched all the men, advised them of their rights and procured all their driver's licenses.

About then I got another surprise. Initially when I had walked by their darkened vehicle the first time, I noticed the trunk on their old sedan was open. Upon our return with the two deer and my three chaps, I took my flashlight and casually looked into the cavernous old sedan's trunk. There laid two additional, freshly killed doe deer! I could hardly believe my eyes! I now had three lads under arrest with four illegal deer! With a shake of my head, I had my three lads accompany me back to my patrol car. Loading Shadow onto the hood of the patrol car so she could keep an eye on my lads, they were walked and I slowly drove back to their vehicle. Once there, I had the men load the four deer into the trunk of my vehicle along with their remaining empty rifle. Suffice to say, my patrol car's trunk was more than a little full and the lid had to be tied down with a piece of rope to keep it from flying open.

I then individually searched the men one more time and then handcuffed them behind their backs. It was then that I paused and dug out the men's driver's licenses from my shirt pocket where I had placed them for safekeeping. Then I got another surprise for my already productive evening. The names of my outlaws were Gabriel Thompson, Joshua Thompson and David Thompson. All three brothers, possessing biblical first names but they sure as hell weren't biblical in deed by a long shot in what they had done that morning to Mother Nature. As I later discovered, they were from a rather large, religious family living in the logging town of Blue Lake and the entire clan had reputations as serious wildlife outlaws. Warden John Finnigan, the fish and game officer from the nearby town of Arcata, had over the years caught everyone in that wild and wooly clan and a number of them twice, as I later discovered.

Then came the fun. The men were squeezed into the rear seat of my diminutive patrol car. I had Shadow sit in the front passenger seat so she could watch my lads as we headed off to the jail. It is not smart transporting prisoners who are seated behind you if you are the lone arresting officer and driver all at the same time. But I didn't have any fish and game backup and was unable to raise any close at hand deputy sheriff as a transport officer, so, I did what I had to do. Before we left, I moved their vehicle off to one side of the road so other folks traveling in the area could get by, locked it up and left it waiting for another family member to retrieve at a later time. Following that, I called the sheriff's office dispatch on my fish and game radio and advised I was bringing in my three prisoners by name. I did so in case something happened and the sheriff's office needed a starting point to investigate what had happened to me in the event my prisoners made good their escapes and did something stupid to their arresting officer.

Two of the men were booked for possessing loaded rifles in a motor vehicle on a way open to the public and all three for being in closed season possession of a big game animal, To Wit: four female deer. Following the bookings, I went home to get some sleep because I had marine duty the following afternoon on our patrol boat.

The following morning of their arraignment, my three chaps pled guilty, were found guilty, fined $500.00 dollars each and had forfeited all three of their rifles to the State of California. Because of the high fines and the men being out of work, the judge allowed them to pay off their fines in installments. The four evidence deer were distributed to several needy families in Eureka and Blue Lake and to a couple of near starving college kids I knew living in Arcata.

Two weeks later, Shadow and yours truly were sitting in my patrol car in my same favorite Snow Camp area hiding spot near an old abandoned ranch house and apple orchard. I had been there since eight in the evening and was just now starting to relax as my world had begun to slow around me. It had been a long day and Dog and I were finding it hard to stay awake. It was a mild evening and I was truly enjoying myself within the surrounding, almost silent cloak of darkness.

About then, a spotted skunk ambled by my car around nine o'clock. The little critter stopped and investigated some sort of smell connected with my left front tire. Satisfied, my little spotted skunk walked about 40 feet out into the old moonlit apple orchard looking for something to eat when all of a sudden, there was a flurry of silent wings and my little spotted skunk was no more! Grabbing my binoculars from my front seat and taking a closer look, I could see a great horned owl sitting on top of his newly killed skunk dinner, waiting for it to die. The owl must have clobbered that little skunk in the back of its head so hard, that it didn't even get a chance to spray Mother Nature's style of perfume in self-defense.

Losing all interest in sleeping, I was now riveted on Mother Nature up so close and personal like doing what she did best. I had no more than settled in watching with my binoculars the deadly but natural event being carried out in the apple orchard, when all of a sudden from the dirt road below my hidden location, I heard a vehicle's engine laboring as it climbed the long hill heading in my direction. Soon a set of headlights swept into view as a vehicle continued laboring uphill on the road alongside my old apple orchard. Once it got alongside where my owl was obviously feasting in the moonlight on the spotted skunk just a few yards from the old adjacent farm road, it abruptly stopped.

Out from the rear passenger's side of the car came a pencil thin bright spotlight fully illuminating that feeding owl! With the bright flash of light, the owl, one of the fiercest aerial predators going, just ducked down and mantled over the dead skunk with its out stretched wings in order to protect its meal. Immediately from the front passenger side of the old sedan, came a bright orange ball of fire followed instantly by a loud BOOM! In that same instant, I saw my recently feeding owl exploding into a cloud of feathers telling me that skunk was the owl's last supper!

Shocked at what had just happened in front of God, Mother Nature and one very large and now pissed off game warden, my world came alive! Dropping my binoculars back onto my front seat, I started up my patrol car and burst out from my hiding place with my headlights on high beam, siren howling and red light glowing like a fiend. Everything happened so fast, that I was on my owl shooters before they could only pass as much gas as a constipated pigmy shrew.

Pulling up behind my surprised illegal owl shooters and bailing out with flashlight in hand, I ran up to the open driver's side window, opened his door and identified myself all in one fluid motion. Then I politely escorted his miserable carcass out from the vehicle and onto the ground as I informed him he was now under arrest. Quickly stepping over my prone driver before he could even wiggle and reaching for the back door of the sedan, I escorted the back seat passenger out the door and placed him somewhat roughly on the ground alongside the vehicle's driver. In the meantime, the passenger in the front seat who was my shooter, aware he was in deep do-do with the arrival of the law, was FRANTICALLY jacking shells out from the magazine of a Winchester model 94 lever action rifle. SUDDENLY THERE WAS A LOUD 'BOOM' IN THE

FRONT SEAT OF THE CAR AND A BLINDING WHITE FLASH, FOLLOWED BY A CONCUSSIVE SHOCK WAVE OF AIR, HEAT AND FLYING PARTICLES FROM THE INSIDE ROOF'S LINER!

During that microsecond of the rifle's blast, all I saw was a bright blue-white flash of light, heard a tremendous thunderclap, felt a blast of hot gasses, and became aware of cloth pieces of the car's roof lining peppering my face and body! Then I heard the most ungodly and inhuman howling and screaming coming from that passenger! Upon seeing the law's arrival, he had tried to unload his rifle before the game warden found it loaded in a motor vehicle on a way open to the public, a violation of the fish and game regulations. In his panic trying to unload the rifle, he somehow had pulled the trigger and the weapon had gone off inside the close confines of the vehicle! When it did, it was like being inside of a closed metal box, blast concussion, burned powder and all! When that happened, it did wondrous things for my shooter's eyes, eardrums, the roof of the vehicle and his underpants. Getting my shooter under control was a piece of cake after that once I had cleaned the parts of head liner off my face, shirt front, and cleaned out my shorts as well...

Removing the rifle from David Thompson's hands as he continued prancing about as if that would help still the loud ringing in his ears, I gently directed his dancing being over to where his two brothers, Gabriel and Joshua were standing. Yep, you Folks have that right. The same David Thompson and his two brothers I caught several weeks earlier with four illegal deer! Now I had all three again for additional wildlife violations. As things finally settled down and as a matter of procedure, I informed the three brothers as to my identity as a game warden. That was as if that was needed since they knew me from being previously booked for their several weeks' earlier closed season deer violations. After their driver's licenses had been procured, I retrieved my cite book from my patrol car and began writing my three familiar Blue Lake lads citations for possession of loaded firearms in a motor vehicle on a way open to the public, shooting from a public roadway, and taking a protected migratory non-game bird contrary to state and federal laws. They were not cited for a spotlighting offense because they had not used an artificial light to take a game animal (an owl was not considered a game animal under the fish and game regulations).

I then seized two still loaded and one recently fired rifle from my three lads. Those firearms were brand new because the lads had recently purchased them after they had lost their previous firearms which had been confiscated and forfeited by the court for their several weeks' earlier doe deer killing escapade. Their spotlight was also seized and the dead owl was retrieved to be used as evidence against my three still learning the hard way, Blue Lake "Brush Okies."

Three hardheaded Brush Okies went home later that night sadder, without their brand new firearms, wiser, and missing sizeable pieces from their last parts over the fence for night shooting a protected migratory non-game bird! In my book, such a Brush Okie moniker was attached if I caught the same wildlife outlaws doing stupid things and prosecuted such chaps at least twice for fish and game violations. Sadly to say, those three lads fit my 'moniker' billing perfectly.

About two weeks later, those three went before the same judge they had stood before for the previous illegal deer killing expedition up at Snow Camp. They did not fare as well before His Honor that fine day. Five hundred dollar fines were the word of the day for that little illegal night time outing and once again the State of California became the proud possessor of three brand new firearms. Two of the rifles had never been fired but were found loaded in their motor vehicle on a way open to the public at the time my three lads were apprehended, so, off they went. Oh by the way, the three brothers were also sentenced to thirty days in jail to think over the error of their ways.

By now, many of you readers can figure out where the Tombstones were planted' in this garden of sad adventures. Four Columbian black-tailed deer and one hungry great horned owl fell to the final rollcall of the Tombstones.

As for the Flowers in this adventure, the State of California became enriched with not only money taken from three dyed-in-the-wool wildlife outlaws twice, but added to the fish and game department's arsenal of confiscated weapons in Sacramento, times two! That arsenal was later auctioned off and the proceeds utilized within the State's National Rifle Association's initiated hunter safety training programs that helped teach youngsters proper gun safety and sporting ethics. Over the years, those programs have tremendously reduced accidental firearms related deaths. I guess one could say saving the Flowers of one's generations to come, namely our children, is a very special Flower and one in which to be thankfully proud!

The last Flower of this adventure was the fact that I had apprehended three wildlife outlaws who really needed catching. I had caught them by being in the right place at the right time and no one was injured in the process. After that, the local warden, one John Finnigan and yours truly, never again caught those three brothers in the backcountry doing things to Mother Nature that they shouldn't have been doing. If they had learned their lessons of not doing unto Mother Nature what they shouldn't be doing, maybe one could consider that a Flower of sorts. However, I have a feeling those three Brush Okies just went elsewhere to do their illegal killing and in so doing, left a trail of Tombstones throughout where ever they trod.

BLACK BEARS, POACHERS AND A SLOW MOVING REDWOOD

Clearing citations from my cite book one morning in the Eureka fish and game office, I heard Captain Gray tell our secretary to send me into his office when I was finished. Ten minutes later found me standing at attention in front of my captain waiting for whatever he had to say.

"I need you to go up to Klamath once again and give Warden Bill Williams a hand. He has been under the weather lately and could use some help corralling some of his illegal deer and elk poachers. Plan on spending a few days up there until Bill can get up on his feet and back into the saddle," ordered Captain Gray. With that, out from his office I went before the good captain who was already smelling strongly of cheap gin and slurring his words had anything else bad or good to say to me.

Bill Williams was the Klamath Warden whom I introduced to you readers in a previous story. He was an older man and for some time had been feeling under the weather, and for whatever reason, just couldn't seem to shake what ailed him. I had worked with Bill on a number of cases including one which required me to unlimber my .44 magnum for the first time in my earlier short fish and game career in order to punch holes into an oncoming speeding car load of suspected Hoopa Indians illegally running gill netted salmon off their reservation and into Eureka for sale.

The Indians tried to escape one of Bill's impromptu roadblocks at night in the backcountry and, in the process, had brush blocked his legs knocking him head over heels onto the roadside. With a man hanging out the passenger side window aiming a lever action rifle at me and a voice coming from within the vehicle screaming, "Kill him! Kill him!" the oncoming car then sped directly at me standing a few yards down the road with my hand upraised for them to stop. Even to my then rookie self, it was obvious the driver was trying to run over my miserable carcass as I stood there in the roadway with my upraised arm signaling Stop! A lot of good that did standing there like a dummy as the racing vehicle continued to 'bore sight' in on me! After the next six explosive 'reactions' from yours truly, the speeding car ran off the mountain road and was wrecked when it slammed into a Douglas fir tree. In the glare of my flashlight, the stunned carload of Indians fled down the mountainside on foot into the darkness and disappeared. With a gimped-up Bill Williams providing top cover from the roadway above, I went down the mountainside to the crashed car with its still steaming radiator, all the while reloading my .44 magnum handgun. Once there, I discovered that speeding car had eaten all six of my .44 magnum 255 grain bullets, in a process which had also blown out a portion of the driver's side windshield and holed the radiator. A perfectly good paint job along the rest of the side of that vehicle was ruined when I pumped the remaining four bullets into its side as it sped by me before going over the edge of the road and into a tree. Further examination of the crashed vehicle revealed that the trunk was loaded with a mess of iced down, gill netted king salmon (as evidenced by the net marks alongside their bodies), which were obviously being taken to an illegal market somewhere in the city of Eureka.

(In 1978 that totally unmarked, specially designed salmon running vehicle still sat on the mountainside where it had smashed nose first into that Douglas fir tree. There it sat quietly rusting away as a memento of a nighttime illegal salmon run gone really bad by a number of suspected Hoopa Indians and a pair of goofy damn game wardens. If you folks care to read the rest of that story, you will find it in my National Outdoor Book Award winning electronic book titled, *Wildlife Wars*, chapter two, A Carload of Indians and a Trunk Load of Fish.)

The morning after speaking with Captain Gray, I was heading north on State Highway 101 to the small north coast town of Klamath. There I met with Warden Bill Williams and he briefed me on where he wanted me to concentrate my work efforts and what he hoped I could accomplish. As we ate lunch, I found myself carefully studying my fellow warden and friend. He looked like death warmed over! It was pretty obvious that Bill was very sick but, like a lot of men of his ilk, chose to ignore his mortality and continue on like there was no tomorrow. To his way of thinking, he had a lot of wildlife law enforcement work to finish in his district and he wasn't going to let some damn sickness slow him down any more than it already had. The other thing that was driving Bill was his clientele. A number of wildlife outlaws lived in his remote district and took advantage of that remoteness and those critter related resources every opportunity they could. I could tell that being unable to hold the line against those poachers really bothered Bill as it would any good wildlife officer. I decided right then and there that a 110% effort on my part might just fit the bill and give my friend a little breathing space.

Working off a hand drawn map of the area that Bill supplied, he briefed me as to where a number of elk and deer had recently been poached. He figured they were somehow being marketed illegally based on the word from some of his informants and the numbers of gut piles being reported or discovered. It was into those general areas that Bill directed me to patrol heavily. He also gave me the names of some of his most dangerous hard cases and cautioned me to be careful if I was ever around any of that class of individuals. We discussed his local court times in case I ran across any of his outlaws and chose to cite those wildlife violators into his court. I was also given the address of his local lockup in case I decided to book any of his outlaws apprehended breaking the fish and game regulations. Lastly, he told me where to bring any seized wildlife for safe storage until any trials were completed. Parting ways somewhat later, I wished him well and began my next set of adventures in another officer's unfamiliar law enforcement district. Little did I realize at the time of those adventures, I would soon come to experience the ultimate sadness...

Leaving Bill, I rented a motel room in a typical rundown establishment smelling heavily of mildew and reeking of second hand stale cigarette smoke. When I first walked into my stuffy dump of a room I thought, *Welcome to the temperate rain forest where 100-140 inches of rain falls annually. No wonder the giant redwoods love it so much.* After unloading my gear in the room, I headed out into the area Bill had requested I keep a powerful sharp eye out for the welfare of his critters and the one frequented by his wildlife outlaws. In preparation, I took a book of citations along and an extra set of handcuffs for those who harbored illegal and deadly thoughts, along with Bill's kind words. Kind words for my safety because I had no backup, would be working in an area with little or no radio effectiveness and operating with limited wildlife law enforcement experience as a still learning the ropes rookie.

Later that first afternoon found me slowly patrolling the temperate rain forest's backcountry on its numerous muddy logging roads and abandoned logging spurs looking for Bill's illegal elk and deer poachers. The weather was typically foggy and drizzly with rain but I loved that kind of weather because it made all the critters move around a lot. And when they did, I got to see a lot of wildlife as did the local outlaws. With those factors rearing their heads, one can figure out what was coming next in the wildlife law enforcement arena.

The area patrolled that day was remote, cool, wet and held a deep forest quiet that was soothing to my soul. I loved that kind of solitude in a logged over second growth wildness left over from the late 1800's, where every turn in the lightly utilized back country provided a visual adventure of some sort. Be it the adventurous movement of the dainty Columbian black-tailed deer quietly slipping in and among the sword ferns, bald eagles flitting through the forest canopy or fishing along the almost deserted streams and rivers, the tan color quickly disappearing through the majestic redwoods of a large bodied Roosevelt elk, the ambling walk along the road of a surprised raccoon looking for his next meal or the rare glimpse of a river otter magically slipping under a creek's cold waters looking for a trout dinner without hardly leaving a ripple, I got to experience it all. It was great to be alive and surrounded by Mother Nature's bounty and majesty created by The Old Boy Upstairs!

Long about four in the afternoon on that first day, I was a good ten miles deep into the silent outback rainforest of Bill's district. I had observed little in the way of humankind showing any interest in violating the fish and game laws of the land and was now truly enjoying the solitude and wildness that came with such natural beauty and isolation. I could see why Bill was so worried over his elk and deer being poached in such a wilderness area. To put it mildly, I so far back in the bush that the chickens out there had square faces and human heartbeats were as scarce as frog's hair. That remoteness of the area and the richness of its wildlife perfectly fitted the kind of landscape frequented by dedicated and experienced poachers to my way of thinking. As I wandered and dreamed myself along in the outback that fine day, learned wildlife law enforcement information kept flooding through my active mind:

Rule # 1, as a poacher, stalk your quarry in an area not frequented by any other heartbeats other than yours and your target of choice. That keeps the possibility of discovery and apprehensions to a minimum.

Rule # 2, once your quarry is sighted, keep your shots fired to a minimum. Get into the area, get your deed done and get the hell out! By so doing, a patrolling game warden would more than likely not be able to echolocate in on you quickly enough to curtail your illegal activity.

Rule #3, load up your game and leave as quietly as a mouse pissin' on a ball of cotton.

Rule #4, once out and about after a successful illegal kill, keep your mouth shut!

About then in my travels, I chanced upon fresh muddy vehicle tracks leading to a green Ford 3/4 ton pickup parked barely visible along a brushed over and long ago abandoned railroad logging spur. Not seeing anyone near the rig after I had stopped for a closer look, I took a quick look with my binoculars from the main roadway. Observing nothing out of the ordinary and seeing a nearby stack of freshly cut redwood, I figured it was someone gathering winter firewood. That was typical behavior in that part of the country during that time of the year and with that, I moved on down the main muddy logging road. As I did, I sensed internally that my guardian angels were beginning to flit around as they would usually do when I had overlooked something of special interest or that which was illegal.

(Now to all you readers out there who may have read any of my previous works or other stories in this creation, you should be familiar with my guardian angels. However to my still doubting readers, I have always had two guardian angels in my life. Two because I am a plus sized fellow with an inclination towards always finding trouble with a capital "T". Secondly, two angels because I am blessed... I learned early on that when those angels begin fluttering around inside me, something evil or dangerous was in the wind and for me to get my tail end into a high alert mode. As a result of that early warning sense from within, I have survived many potentially life threatening situations and have only been shot once in the line of duty. And if any of you readers out there care to read that story, you can find it in my National Outdoor Book Award winning e-book titled, *Wildlife Wars*, chapter 12, Taking A Load Of 4's.)

Finding another heavily overgrown unused railroad logging spur nearby, I slid and slipped my patrol car down the barely visible two-track railroad bed and hid my vehicle out of sight from any prying eyes that might have been traversing along on the main road. Finding an old landing at the end of the road where the railroad cars had been loaded with redwood logs, I turned around, parked, rolled down all my windows and let Dog out so she could take care of business and explore a little. My angels began preening their feathers with that act and that usually meant I was making a mistake in not heeding their earlier call when I passed the previously observed green pickup.

In an attempt to placate my feathered friends and show them that they were wrong, I sat there figuring I would soon hear a chain saw cutting wood near the green Ford vehicle parked back down the road. When that occurred, the green pickup mystery would be solved and I could proceed with my afternoon patrol without any interference from my feathered friends. For the next ten minutes, I heard nothing except raindrops dripping off the nearby grove of red alders under which I was now parked. However, that did not stop my angels from trying to fly around inside me. As I have written oftentimes in my previous works, when they were that active something unusual and many times illegal was in the wind. Finally yielding to their now frantic call to arms, I slipped on my rain parka, left Dog in the patrol car with a window rolled down so she could come if I called, and walked back the short distance to the green pickup parked just off the main logging road.

Arriving at the logging spur's entrance leading to the pickup, I paused. Glassing the area for the longest time, I saw nothing nor did I hear anything out of the ordinary. Slowly proceeding down the logging spur to the partially hidden pickup, I stopped and put my hand over the front of its grill.

Engine warmth was still being emitted from the front of the grill, telling me the vehicle had been recently driven. Quietly standing there in the now lightly falling rain, I thought I could hear hushed human voices up in the brush a short distance away from the pickup. As I walked around the cab of the pickup, I did what all good game wardens do and looked inside. Boy, did I ever get a nice surprise.

There were three bolt-action rifles laid across the floorboards between the seat and floor mounted gearshift so as not to draw any attention by someone casually walking by or looking in. Quickly glancing all around looking for the rifles' owners and not seeing any other heartbeats, I tried the door handle and found it unlocked. Looking one more time to see if I had been observed poking around the now suspect vehicle, I quietly opened up the driver's side door, reached in and began checking the rifles. Every one of them was loaded with a live round of ammunition in their chambers! Realizing the possible illegal big game killing significance of those three hunting rifles and the possibility of their owners being up to no good since there were no open hunting seasons, I removed the cartridges and bolts from each rifle rendering them inert. Those bolts and cartridges were then placed into my coat pocket for safekeeping and as evidence of a fish and game violation. That way, if my three lads wanted to get deadly serious upon discovering there was another heartbeat in the area, they would be hard pressed to do that with those rifles since I carried their pertinent parts. I now had my rifle owners for the illegal possession of loaded rifles in a motor vehicle on a way open to the public, a violation of Section 2006 of California's Fish and Game Code. The 'dance in the forest' in deadly earnest had now begun and I apparently had 'three dance partners'. Those factors in mind, it appeared I was now more than likely 'hunting the lawless'.

Sliding the right side of my raincoat behind my holstered pistol in case I had need for a fast draw, I began slowly sneaking toward the distant muffled voices in the dense vegetation and timber down the logging spur a short distance away. Then it hit me! I could smell elk. To all my non-big game hunters out there reading these lines, yes, elk do emit a rather pungent and unique 'elky' odor when it moves around in its environment. To an experienced elk hunter, that unique odor should give him pause because that smell means elk are close by. I was getting an even stronger elk smell since it was now being pungently carried in the humid temperate rain forest air.

Remembering the three rifles back at the truck, I figured I had at least three suspect owners nearby. I further validated those thoughts when I shortly thereafter discovered three sets of fresh footprints on the muddy road leading away from their pickup. Coming to a large mud puddle that ran clear across the road, I further confirmed my suspicions. The water in the mud puddle water was not clear but cloudy which told me that somebody had just recently walked through and had stirred up the water.

Then my mind got to racing. I had not heard any chain saw running nor did I hear anyone splitting rounds of cut firewood with a mall the whole time I was in country. There had been three loaded rifles back in the pickup and this was late spring. There were no hunting seasons open that time of the year but, they could have been target practicing and, if so why the three loaded firearms still in the cab of the pickup? More importantly, my guardian angels were now having a fit. With those factors in mind, I sensed possible fish and game law enforcement trouble was in the wind. Trouble in the wind for an elk, trouble for me, trouble for my three chaps or trouble for the whole damned bunch of us...

Using every bit of vegetative cover that was available to me and I needed a lot to provide cover for my beautifully plus sized body, I continued stalking towards the distant voices that were now getting louder by the moment. As I continued stalking those voice sounds, I strained my eyes for any discernable movement in the forested area where the voices were located. Glancing around a large Douglas fir tree, I could finally see movement in the deep temperate rain forest brush from whence the mystery voices were emanating. I took three more cautious steps in the damp understory and then there were my talkers just barely visible in a large blue blossom thicket. What I saw going on in that thicket tickled the cockles of my heart...

There were three men deep into gutting out a huge cow elk and they had their hands full to say the least! Two of the men were holding the back legs apart and the third man was using a hatchet to split open the bony chest cavity of the animal. When he had finished splitting open the chest cavity, he took his hunting knife and began removing the elk's intestines starting from the throat and windpipe area and working his way down deep into the body cavity. One of the men whose back was to me told the one gutting out the elk to be sure and save the heart and liver and to be careful when he got near the pelvis area so as not to puncture the bladder and spray urine all over the best meaty parts of the animal. (To my non-hunters out there, the hams on the hind legs are the best parts for steaks and roasts on a big game animal.)

Figuring I had seen enough to make an easy case on my three chaps for the illegal possession of a closed season elk, I started to make my approach. Then I changed my mind, decided to stand my ground and continue watching the three men and their cleaning actions. That way I let my three outlaws do all the work, thereby keeping my hands free and clean for the surprise enforcement action that was soon to follow. Then if I had need for the eventual use of a handgun, it would not be healthy trying to rapidly grip and use a firearm if my hands were covered with slippery elk fat and bodily fluids acquired if I had been the one gutting out the animal.

It was at that very moment as I stood looking on at the elk gutting events going on around me, that I got Mother Nature's surprise of the day. I saw movement a short distance away coming through the dense brush toward my chaps who were still deeply engrossed in quickly gutting out their illegal elk. *Damn,* I thought. *I hope to hell there aren't more of these elk killing chaps associated with this first group of men coming this way!* It was already three to one and I had no backup. Additionally, one of my three elk killing chaps looked so damned stout that he could have eaten hay and pulled a fully loaded beer wagon down the cobbled streets of Philadelphia all by himself during the 1700's, if you readers get my gist. He was a Man Mountain Dean if I ever saw one. Comparing him physically to me and my beautiful 320 pounds, I was a wimp!

The man doing all the cutting and gutting on the elk finally finished his task. Then he cut off the animal's head and with difficulty, lobbed it behind him into the brush in the direction of and oblivious to the brush-busting arriving newcomers. That was when all hell broke loose! The mystery movement I had seen in the brush coming slowly towards my elk killers just seconds earlier let out a loud WOOOFFF! The tossed elk head had landed right next to the arriving company, which just so happened to be one hell of a large sow black bear! In short, guess who was coming to dinner? You got that right! Additionally, that damned black bear had company! As it turned out, the black bear was a giant female and with her were three previous years' cubs that weighed over 150 pounds each! Next thing I knew, the four black bears simultaneously stood up in the dense brush some six to seven feet away from my elk killers to get a better look at the humans and that good smelling dinner-for-the-bears to be. That was the last calm moment before the coming storm!

Instantly I had an explosion of three elk killers running for their lives right at me just as the female bear aggressively dropped to the ground from her standing position and charged the elk, its gut pile and the man previously doing all the cutting and gutting. That was extremely unusual behavior for black bears, which are usually quite timid, especially around humankind. However, that was not the case when it came to that female and mother of three. She and her cubs had the bit in their teeth and they were flat out coming to dinner! It became obvious to me during that microsecond when the explosion of elk killers occurred, that the bears had heard the shooting, smelled the elk and had come to investigate. Because of their highly developed sense of smell, as they got closer, the sow recognized the smell of death. That smell was all they needed being perpetually hungry as most bears are and they came 'hot-footing' it in for dinner. From their bold actions, it was apparent that they were hungry and aggressive as all get out. To me standing off to one side and getting ready to run as well, it was apparent that Goldilocks and her three kin were not easily going to be detoured from that inviting dead elk and its gut pile until they were satiated.

Back at the ranch, I had three chaps fleeing for their lives as they stampeded in my direction where I was standing still partially hidden. Stepping out in front of my terrified runners from my hiding place behind a tree, I foolishly held up my hand and bellowed, "State fish and game warden. Hold it right there!" How was that for being such a a stupid rookie trick and being dumber than a box of river rocks in a dry creek bed?

I just as well should have peed into the wind and tried to keep my pant legs from getting wet for all the good that command did in trying to stop the stampeding terrified elk poachers coming my way. With terror in their eyes, all three men roared into my little world and, from their panicked looks, none of them had any intentions of stopping until they got into the next county! As they blew by me, I managed to grab the largest man mainly because he was the closest and usually big guys are the slowest. As circumstances dictated, I had grabbed the Man Mountain Dean of the group. You know, the one who was so damned big that he could eat hay and pull a loaded beer wagon all by himself. However, he had a full head of steam up and in the ensuing collision, we both rocketed off into the brush and onto the muddy ground in a squirming clump. As for my other two lads, they disappeared off into the temperate rain forest's dense vegetation like a wisp of black powder gun smoke after shooting at a deer in a howling windstorm...

However, for the moment, I still had my man. In fact, he was funny. He was lying on the ground underneath me and still trying to run in his deep fright over being charged by the huge sow black bear and her three oversized cubs. I finally got him calmed down and with a quick look back at the four busily arguing black bears over who was going to eat what part of the elk carcass, we two began slinking off backwards making sure we weren't being followed and on the bear's menu as well. But not to worry. That tan colored dead cow elk had turned completely black buried under those four hungry bears, so we made good our escape.

Then my other two elk killers rose to the forefront of my concerns. Letting my man know he was under arrest for being in possession of an illegal elk, I hustled him back to his group's pickup. As expected, no one else was standing around their means of vehicular escape for me to soothe their savaged feelings. My two runners were still running or hiding now that they knew of my official presence, especially in the light of being caught red-handed with an illegal elk. So, I kissed the apprehension of those two chaps off for the moment.

As luck would have it, I discovered that I had captured the owner of the pickup. That meant the other two runners were now out of luck when it came to making good their escape. Especially since they were at least ten miles away from the nearest other human heartbeat in the outback with an oncoming rainstorm looming just over the tree tops. It appeared that the elk God had smiled upon me. I had one wildlife outlaw in the bag and two others with nowhere to go except eventually down.

Handcuffing my captured lad for the elk possession violation, I gathered up the three rifles from the floorboard area of his vehicle and locked up his pickup. Then we walked back to my hidden patrol car and he was seated inside with Dog as his partner in the backseat. Their three rifles were placed into the trunk of my patrol car for safekeeping as were their previously removed bolts and then I drove back to my Man Mountain Dean's vehicle.

There I searched his cab more thoroughly, all the while keeping a wary eye on the nearby, still madly feeding black bears and lo and behold, did I ever get a nice surprise. To all my budding game warden readers out there, guess whose two wallets were found inside the glove box? Yep, you folks got that right. Maybe you readers will make good game wardens yet. Apparently, my two runners had placed their wallets into the glove box after the elk had been killed so they would not lose them during their labors to gut, hurriedly drag out and load their illegal elk into the back of the pickup. As I later discovered, the small pile of redwood was then to be placed over the elk's carcass in the back of the truck in order to make the whole mess look like a load of freshly cut firewood. Pretty clever, but their loss was now my gain. Well, I can't quite say that without including my four dinner guests…

With that lucky find in hand, I now turned to the problem with my evidence quickly being demolished by my four hungry bruins. Leaving my chap in the care of Dog, I carefully walked back close to the original elk kill site. Sure as God made grasshoppers good German brown trout bait, my four bears showed no inclination to leave their newly found meat market. Removing my .44 magnum from its holster and standing on the logging spur in plain view, I yelled in the hope they would leave the kill site. Instantly my four bears were standing up on their hind legs looking my way like they were saying, "Just who the hell do you think you are?"

I thought of firing one shot into the air in an attempt to run them off so I could preserve what was left of my evidence. Then it dawned on me that I had a six shot revolver in my hand. Shooting one shot into the air would leave five remaining cartridges. That left four very aggressive and determined bears at the dinner table. If I shot and the bears decided to charge simultaneously, that would mean I had better be a damn good shooter since that only left me five bullets for four bears in the defense of my beautiful carcass. That just did not leave me much of a margin for safety if this issue devolved into a shootout. Come to think of it, black bears eat humans, don't they? Well, my mother didn't raise a turnip. Besides, I was not in the mood to kill four perfectly healthy bears who were doing nothing more than trying to stay alive and enjoy their hard fought for dinner. I decided that for the moment, the bears could 'guard' my evidence elk and I would try to intercede again later after they had finished with their meal.

Returning to my patrol car and lone prisoner, my thoughts now ran to my two runners. A good game warden does not like to lose any of his catch of the day when it comes to bad guys. And I might not have been much of a game warden in those days but I sure as hell did not want to lose any of my elk killing miscreants either. I was sure my two lads were watching me from a safe place of concealment but I could not see them so we were at a draw. Plus, I damn sure could not leave my prisoner all alone and go looking for them either. Stymied for the moment, I opened up the two wallets I had discovered in my prisoner's pickup and removed their driver's licenses. The wallets belonged to one Dale Adler and Darrel Jenkins. Both men according to their driver's licenses resided in the small town of Requa. As it turned out, Requa was near the small town of Klamath where Bill currently resided so I figured he more than likely knew the two subjects.

Standing by my patrol car, I shouted out the names of the two men, letting them know I had their wallets and that I expected them to surrender. I received no response to my shout out. Shouting several more times and urging the men to surrender, I let the lads know it was no use in trying to run and hide from me. Quietly waiting, I received no response. Walking back to my patrol vehicle, I got my prisoner to yell out the rear window to his fellow elk killers to surrender. He let his partners' in crime know that I had them cold for the illegal elk killing and now had their wallets in my possession. Again, there was no response. Sensing my lads were going to tough it out, I acquiesced after I bellowed out for their knowledge and information that the dark of night and the now intensifying rains were on their way. I further advised that I would be waiting for them at the end of the road when they tried walking out or if they hitched a ride out with someone, I would be checking every vehicle that would be exiting on the main road looking for them as well. Seeing that my lads were still going to tough it out, I quit yelling. The rains now came down with a soaking vengeance as if the storm clouds had been listening to my prediction of their coming. It was now only a matter of time before I would catch my two remaining at large elk killers, unless they wished to drown in the coming downpour.

Not having any luck in capturing my two remaining outlaws and with a Plan B swirling around in my head, down the road Dog, my Man Mountain Dean prisoner and yours truly went. Once in my vehicle out from the drenching rains and out a ways from the radio-dampening effect of the nearby mountains, I got on my fish and game radio. Soon I was in contact with the sheriff's office and they rolled a deputy my way in order to transport my prisoner to the lockup. Coming to an all-important set of cross roads that would give my remaining outlaws several ways to go to evade the man in game warden greens, I stopped. As far as I was concerned, I still had my two outlaws trapped. They would have to come through me if they wanted to get out of the rain, off the now rain slathered mountain, and eventually home. Settling in, there I quietly sat watching my back trail and listening to the drumming rain on my roof top until sometime later when my requested sheriff's deputy rolled up.

After introducing myself and transferring my prisoner into the sheriff's unit, the deputy and I walked off a ways out of earshot of the prisoner and discussed the situation. Taking out the two wallets removed earlier from the pickup, I handed them to the deputy. He looked at the names of the men and then looked back at me with the strangest look on his face. In fact, he had the same look I would imagine would be on someone's face when in a crowded room full of people, had accidently messed his britches with last night's greasy rich dinner.

Then slowly my deputy said, "Darrel Jenkins is my brother-in-law! That damned fool! I always knew he had a little outlaw blood in his veins but my sister married him just the same against all the family's wishes. Now, I have to hunt that puke down. You can bet your bottom dollar that if I am the one to collar him, he is going to get the royal treatment from his brother-in-law. Then my mom and dad will blister his ass for indirectly involving my sister and their three little kids in something as stupid as killing an elk during the closed season."

Me, I just stood there in surprise over this new turn of events! No way did I ever expect such a happening. However, with that happy turn of events, I could not have been more pleased. Turning to my deputy, I said, "I have an idea. What do you say if the two of us drove back to the area where they killed the elk? There you can use your patrol car's outside loudspeaker and call for my two outlaws to surrender. Especially since one of them knows you and you are now aware of what he has done this day contrary to the fish and game regulations. Additionally, that outside loudspeaker may just scare those bears off what is left of my evidence elk so I can retrieve it for courtroom use if necessary."

With an affirmative nod of his head, the two of us boarded our vehicles and headed back to the kill site. Once there, the deputy tried using his loudspeaker several times to coax my two outlaws out from hiding in the brush. He had no luck, even when he announced that he knew who they were and if Darrel knew what was good for him, he had better damn well quickly surrender. We later had as much luck scaring off my hungry bears with the loudspeaker as we did in forcing my two outlaw elk killers to surrender.

Having no luck, the deputy headed down the mountain with his prisoner and yours truly left the area as well. However, my leaving was only a ruse. Driving further down the mountain, I found another old abandoned logging spur and backed my patrol car into it and out of sight to the casual eye of anyone driving down the logging road. I figured I would sit there until my two lads who had left their raincoats back in the now locked pickup 'drenched out' and, deciding they had enough of standing around in the down pour, tried walking out. When they did, guess who would come crawling out from his hiding place on the logging spur and put the grab on the two of them quicker than can a German brown trout put the catch on a grasshopper floundering in the water nearby?

By ten o'clock that night, it was so damn dark out in those mountains that I could hardly see my hand held in front of my face! But, there Dog and I patiently sat like two spiders at the edge of a web. I had no more than put another hunk of chewing tobacco into my mouth to help keep me awake, when I heard a slow moving vehicle quietly coming down the logging road to my front. Quickly grabbing my binoculars and looking road ward, I could just barely make out the darkened shape of a pickup slowly coming down the graveled road. That vehicle was running without using any headlights and I could hear it was running on compression on the steep down hills so brakes would not have to be used, whose taillights would quickly give away the vehicle's location.

Reaching over and flipping my cut-off switches to the 'on position' so no lights would show on my patrol car when I used my brakes, I started up my engine. Giving what I figured had to be my elk poachers in a now hot-wired truck a little lead as they headed down the road, I quietly slipped in behind my suspect outlaws running without lights of any kind. I now realized that my two elk killing lads apparently had broken into their friend's pickup, hot-wired it and were trying to sneak off the mountain and make a run for home. Why else would an individual be driving on a dangerously narrow mountain road in the dark of the night running without using any lights? I then had to grin over my last thoughts. One guess as to who was wearing the game warden greens and doing the same damn silly and dangerous thing on a narrow logging road in the dark of the night dogging a couple of closed season elk killers?

However, there was now a rather large fly in the ointment. And that fly was packing a badge and a gun along with two more pairs of handcuffs for my elk killing outlaws' unfettered wrists. Carefully trying to keep my patrol car on the darkened, muddy roadway and not running over the edge, I just crept along a short distance behind my suspected elk killers as they drove slowly off the mountain. I could just picture my two elk killing lads nervously trying to keep their pickup from running into the ditch or over the side of the road and into the canyons below. Especially since they were not using any lights and the rain clouds covered up any help coming from the moon.

Keying my radio's mike, I called the sheriff's office and asked for an intercept vehicle at the road's end where it met the main highway. I figured my chaps would run once I was discovered following them or made myself known, so having a little help at the end of the road would be nice. Then lo and behold, guess who was still on duty? Yep, you readers got that right. The brother-in-law with the family bit in his teeth wearing the deputy sheriff's badge. Soon the deputy had the outlet road blocked and our trap was set. Down the narrow logging road the two of us slowly came as I kept the sheriff's office informed about the changes in my general location via my fish and game radio. Then the sheriff's office would pass my information onto the deputy in the field since my fish and game radio did not have direct contact with their field unit.

Then the crap hit the fan! As we passed a lit up farm house adjacent to our road, my two elk killing outlaws spotted my darkened patrol car following a short distance behind them. All of a sudden on came their headlights and the race down the mountain was on! On went my red light and siren and the two vehicles slipped and slid down the muddy logging road like one lizard chasing another across a sandy beach.

I then called the sheriff's office and let them know the chase was on and to alert their deputy waiting below at our road's outlet. The sheriff's office responded that the deputy had just driven his patrol car across the logging road effectively blocking it and was now standing off to one side with a loaded 12 gage shotgun in case he needed to shoot out the fleeing vehicle's tires!

With that bit of information, I backed off from my pursuit of the green pickup but only just a tad. However, my two culprits didn't back off one bit but kept the pedal to the metal. Down the muddy logging road the two of our vehicles plunged like two crazy bull elk in heat after a cow in estrus. As the green pickup slid the last turn before reaching the distant highway, its driver all of a sudden realized a white sheriff's office patrol car was completely blocking the road ahead! On went the pickup's taillights and then it began 'fish-tailing' on the road's muddy surface, since he was travelling to fast under a full head of steam. In short, too much speed and driving a

227

pickup with a light in the ass rear end was just too much for good traction and my outlaw driver lost control of his vehicle. Overcompensating from his initial slide, the driver of the green pickup now found himself dangerously out of control and hurtling off the steep road and into a thick grove of redwood trees below!

Even as I brought my sliding vehicle under control realizing the chase was over, I heard the green pickup hurtling off the roadway, crashing down the road bank and smashing hard into a second growth redwood tree with a loud WHOOMP! Moments later, the deputy and I arrived at the place where our fleeing elk killers had exited the roadway, crunched their way down the road bank through the brush, and had smashed nose-first into a large redwood tree at their final landing point! Both the deputy and I scrambled down the muddy embankment to the smashed beyond all recognition pickup below. Both of its doors had been blasted wide open upon impact and THERE WAS A PARTIALLY EATEN ELK LAYING FLAT OUT ON THE PICKUP CAB'S ROOFTOP!

What the hell? Those two damn knot heads must have gone back for the elk remains after the bears had eaten their fill and retrieved what was left for themselves to eat. Well, that just makes my evidence gathering all the easier, I thought with a grin, as I hustled up to the cab to see if everyone was still alive and kicking. Brother, what a mess of broken steel and outlaw carcasses greeted my eyes! Darrel Jenkins, the driver, was tossed upon impact through the front windshield and was a bloody mess as he sat on the ground in front of the crashed truck holding his bloody hands to his bleeding head! Dale Adler was little better off. He had smashed his face into the dash upon impact, leaving one hell of a dent in the metal (that was before seatbelts in those days). Upon closer examination under my flashlight's glare, I could see that Dale's face had one hell of a dent in it as well and he was incoherent! Both men were alive but in one hell of a mess. With that, the deputy scrambled back up the road bank and called for an ambulance.

Thirty-five minutes later our cut all to hell and busted up elk killers were on their way to Crescent City and the hospital. Once our two chaps were hauled off, the deputy and I dragged the half of a mostly eaten evidence elk up to the logging road, quartered its remains and placed it into the trunk of my patrol car. Well to be truthful, the damn thing still hung out both sides of the trunk even after my four bears had eaten more than half of the animal. Finally around four in the morning, I hung and seizure tagged what was left of the elk in Bill's evidence shed. The next morning, I reported to Bill on my capture of the three elk killers. He was tickled-pink to say the least. It seemed that he had been after Dale Adler for his reported wildlife thievery ever since he had moved to Klamath as its resident warden. With that capture, Bill now felt vindicated for all the hours he had selflessly worked in trying to catch Adler in the act of killing off a number of his big game critters.

Later that day, I went to the hospital and issued citations to the two men who had run from me and had met a slow moving redwood tree at a high rate of speed. Then it was off to the county jail to take care of the administrative business involved in the booking of Carl Bartlett or the one known to me as Man Mountain Dean.

For the rest of that week, Dog and I patrolled Bill's backcountry on the hunt for Bill's elk poachers. None did we find but Dog and I did manage to scratch three other outlaws with two illegal deer and put the snatch onto one lone lad shooting blue grouse off the logging road from the open window of his pickup during the closed season. As a result of those adventures, I managed 'to pay for the gas and oil' used in those patrol endeavors to coin an old game warden adage relative to one's successful work efforts while on a patrol...

Three weeks later, my three elk killing lads were found guilty in a court of law and each were fined $350.00 dollars for their parts in the possession of the illegal elk and an additional $50.00 dollars for having loaded rifles on a way open to the public in a motor vehicle. All three firearms were ordered confiscated by the court and the State of California later sold them at auction. The proceeds from the sale went into California's National Rifle Association's initiated hunter safety training programs.

As for my illegal deer killers, two pled guilty and were fined $250.00 dollars each and suffered the loss of their rifles as well. Since neither of my deer-killing culprits were employed, both of those men served out their time in jail. The third man of that party of deer killers skipped town and a warrant was issued for his arrest. When I left the fish and game department four years later in 1970 for a position as a U.S. Game Management Agent with the U.S. Fish and Wildlife Service, my remaining deer killing chap had yet to be arrested and to my knowledge, remained on the run.

My blue grouse killer was fined $200.00 dollars and lost his .22 caliber bolt action single shot Winchester rifle to the State of California. The grouse, deer and elk remains went to several needy families living in the town of Klamath as per Bill's instructions.

There weren't many Flowers in and for the world of wildlife in this adventure. I had managed to snag seven wildlife outlaws doing what they did best, namely stealing wildlife from the American people. Wildlife outlaws who needed catching and thankfully were. Monies accrued from the sale of the violators' weapons went into the fish and game accounts to be used in the hunter safety training programs and the evidence critters went into the cooking pots of several needy families residing in the area. Four black bears had a delightful elk dinner handed to them on a silver platter and they made the most of it. I think that could be called a Flower even in the bear world. The last Flower in this great little adventure was yours truly. I was now well on my way to becoming a better hunter of wildlife outlaws and there would be many more good days, like experiences and adventures yet to come before I limped out the door in retirement in 1998 on two destroyed knees and a bad back from the rigors of my self-ascribed vision quest in and for the world of wildlife. But you know something, Folks, knowing what I now do, I would do it all over again in a heartbeat if the Good Lord and Mother Nature would give me just half a chance and the healed up body required for the work at hand in hunting the lawless…

As for the Tombstones in this story, the two deer killed by the three outlaws were pregnant and that meant instead of only killing two deer, the outlaws managed to scratch four from the herd if one counted the unborn. My grouse shooter also did well in the Tombstone department. Three of the five blue grouse he killed were females. Two were active egg layers and the third already had a clutch somewhere as evidenced by her brood patch. That meant the loss of all those eggs and potential young, about 20 plus, from the future blue grouse population. The cow elk taken was also pregnant at the time and that meant not only the loss of the adult but the young one she was carrying from the overall population. Not a lot in the wildlife-loss department in numbers but a loss just the same when one takes everything else into consideration.

The last Tombstone really hurt. Warden Bill Williams, the one I had been with in my very first shoot out with a carload of Indians and a trunk load of fish, was sicker than he let on. He died shortly thereafter this adventure occurred from cancer of the pericardial sac which is a vital organ that surrounds the heart and one without which man cannot live. There was no treatment at that time for such a malady and I am not so sure one exists today as well. May God rest his soul and THANK YOU, Bill, for teaching me some valuable tips of the trade on some of our earlier shared wildlife law enforcement adventures in the wilds of Humboldt and Trinity Counties.

AN OLD FASHIONED PIGEON SHOOT

Leaving my home in Eureka one fine late spring morning, I headed north driving alongside Humboldt Bay. Warden Warren Duke, a college classmate majoring in fisheries and a rookie hire same as me, was taking a short four-day vacation with his family. Duke was the backcountry warden in the mountainous Pacific Coast Range and cattle ranching Kneeland area located to the east of Eureka. Since my duties required I backup absent resident officers, into his area I was now driving. Turning eastward from the shores of Humboldt Bay, I headed through the small north coast town of Freshwater towards the mountainous Kneeland area.

Somewhat later, I slid to a stop in the driveway of my friend, Deputy Sheriff Glenn Ragon's home on my way into the backcountry. Glenn was the local deputy sheriff in that part of the country and knew not only the area like the back of his hand but everything that went on within that remote part of Humboldt County as well. Glenn was an ex-UDT man during his stint in the Navy during the Second World War, had the build of a cast iron fire plug and was as horseshoe nail tough as they came. My main reason in stopping for a chat was for some backcountry intelligence gathering before I started my fish and game patrol into the Kneeland area, which was also his sheriff's patrol district.

Glenn's law enforcement area of responsibility was a mixture of large cattle ranches, isolated farms, redwood forests, logged off forests, and a remote stretch of the Mad River that was home to seasonally migrating salmon and steelhead trout. Resource wise, his patrol area was rich in mountain quail, Columbian black-tailed deer by the hundreds, salmon in the Mad on a seasonal basis, the majestic Roosevelt elk, feral hogs by the score, black bear at most every turn in the forested road, seasonally migrating band-tailed pigeons and about every other kind of creepy crawler in between. In short, his was a remote area rich in wildlife that also attracted some of the areas' most daring strain of cattle rustlers, 'druggies' and wildlife outlaws known to modern day man.

An hour later after leaving Glenn's home, Dog and yours truly were deep into our patrol. I drove through broken stretches of old redwood and Douglas fir forests initially and then into the rolling Pacific Coast Range grasslands of the Kneeland hilly back country. There stretching before me were the large old established cattle ranches from the earlier part of the century. Like most 'cattle people', folks living and operating those individual ranches were a hardy lot. They represented fine old pioneering stock, were for the most part straight as an arrow and did not tolerate much in the way of trespassing wildlife outlaws or the frequent cattle rustlers on their ranches. Bottom line in most cases, if the ranching community heard about a strange shooting incident, they saddled up and rode out to investigate. I say that in most cases because there were a few of those hardy folks who were not above killing a deer or two outside of the law themselves. They just figured that since they were feeding the deer on their home ranches year around, they were entitled to take an occasional deer every now and then as payment for the cattle feed those critters had consumed on the ranges of their ranches. That and the fact that fired deer steak, fried potatoes, buttermilk biscuits, eggs, hot coffee and a hunk of homemade apple pie, can sit a cow 'punchin''cowboy all day in the center of his saddle on his favorite saddle bronc.

As I drove along, I let my eyes drink in the day and its happenings going on around me like a kid does when he is in a candy store. The first thing I noticed as I moved deeper into the forested areas, was covey after covey of mountain quail crossing the road in their hurry to get somewhere. With feathered topknots held high and blurred legs speeding underneath their beer keg shaped little bodies, the mountain quail were on full display for a much appreciative visiting game warden. The air that morning was clean and fresh, unlike the perennial fog off the coast in the city in which I lived, seasoned with the constant smell of the fumes from the nearby north spit pulp mill. The sky was clear of any clouds, as blue as was the color in my wife's beautiful eyes and the warmth of the sun allowed me to joyfully drive with all my windows down. That 'windows down' thing also pleased Dog riding in the backseat of the patrol car to no end. She was standing up in the backseat with her head hanging outside the window and her tail was in a happy constant wag mode as she sampled the many different smells in the air.

Throughout those hilly rangelands, I could see numerous quietly feeding deer scattered about and heard the frequent melodious calls of the western meadow larks flooding through my open windows as I slowly ambled down the road. However, you can bet your bottom dollar that I was quietly alert as a shrew and as quick to react as a long-tailed weasel chasing a field mouse if someone pulled a trigger when they shouldn't have been so doing.

Turning off onto another road, I travelled down through the Kneeland grasslands towards the Mad River flowing in the canyon below. Running along the bottom of the range of hilly grasslands, I paralleled the Mad River looking for any sign of early season salmon or steelhead fishermen or anything else out of place. Finding that area along the river quiet as a tomb, I continued until I hooked up with the back road leading up into the Snow Camp region because that area was usually frequented with local, mostly out of work lumbermen and the run-of-the-mill Blue Lake wildlife outlaws. As I continued climbing upward out of the Mad River canyon and back into the second-growth coniferous forest, I noticed numerous flocks of band-tailed pigeons nervously flitting from tree to tree as they observed my close at hand moving presence below. *Typical band-tails,* I thought. Every time I saw them, they always appeared to be as nervous as a cat on a hot tin roof. However, that was a behavioral trait common to the species. They were always very alert and ready to leave the country at the first sign of danger. *Too bad the now extinct passenger pigeon hadn't been as cautious as my current day band-tails during the last century in America,* I sadly thought.

Finding some high ground with a commanding view of the area, I did what many good game wardens would do. I stopped, sat, looked, and listened for anything out of the ordinary or out of tune in my world of wildlife. As I did, I let Dog out so she could take care of business and then investigate all the unfamiliar smells that abounded around the patrol car. Since the area appeared to be quiet as an Egyptian tomb, I placed a chew of Levi Garrett chewing tobacco between my teeth and gums and then lit up one of my mean-assed little Italian cigars that many of the nearby Pacific Coast's Italian commercial fishermen smoked. Man, to my way of thinking, I was all set. I held the high ground, Dog was out and about enjoying life, the air was clean and faintly smelling of the oil aerosols being emitted from the nearby conifers, pigeons were noisily flitting from tree to tree in my immediate neighborhood and not a suspicious sound of illegality was forthcoming. Brother, it felt good to be alive and doing what I dearly loved, namely being out in the quiet of the wilderness, hunting my fellow man doing what they should not be doing to Mother Nature.

For the next half an hour, nothing out of the ordinary rocked my little world. Shadow had since climbed back into the back seat of my patrol car and was now snoring loudly. *Typical lab,* I thought with a grin. Then I had two doe deer daintily step out from some blue blossom bushes just a few yards away and quietly lie down in the rays of the sun in front of my patrol car. When they did, I just had to smile. That was the safest place in their little world for them to lie down and sleep. That is, right next to the world's largest and most beautiful game warden who was now on the hunt, hunting the lawless.

Stretching out as best as my 6-foot 4-inch frame would allow me to do in the front seat of my 1964 Mercury Comet patrol car, I drew deeply on my cigar and let the smoke curl slowly out through my nose. *Life can't get much better than this,* I thought with a big ole grin. BOOM! BOOM!—BOOM! The sounds of faraway shooting sure took a dump in my heretofore quiet wilderness mess kit as I shot upward in the seat of my patrol car. Especially since there were no hunting seasons open at that time of the year! Listening like a red fox would do to a mystery rustling in the tall grass at its feet, I hardly even dared to breathe for fear of messing up my now more than peaked senses.

Nothing of interest greeted my ears for the longest time after that initial barrage of shooting. Then there it was once again! BOOM! BOOM!—BOOM! BOOM! BOOM! As Shadow stirred in the backseat over her now heard suspicious far away sounds, I honed in on the shootings' location with the built in mental directional compass sported by most good conservation officers. I noticed that my two nearby resting doe deer had since risen and nervously disappeared back into the nearest dense brush patch for the cover and protection it offered.

Sure as hell, that last series of shots came from two different guns! I thought. That shooting came from across the Mad River and, as near as I could figure, was located on one of the distant cattle ranches in the Kneeland area. Trying to remain as quiet as I could, I sat there in the front seat of my patrol car and continued listening. Nothing further greeted the airways or my ears, NOTHING! It was as quiet as a mouse pissin' on a ball of cotton once again. Then I got to thinking that maybe it was a rancher shooting a coyote or maybe at a feral hog. BOOM! BOOM!—BOOM! went three more quick shots. With that latest string of shooting, I finally had it figured out. The deep booming sounds from that series of shooting had to be coming from a shotgun. With that last series of shots, I found myself surrounded high in the air by numerous flocks of nervous band-tailed pigeons. They obviously were alarmed by the far distant shooting and were taking to wing from in and around the forested area where I was now quietly sitting.

I had heard all I needed to hear as I got out of my car, walked to the back and shut the rear door that I had left open so Shadow could exit and enter at will. The only road leading to my suspect shooting area was back the way I had come. With my patrol car engine springing to life, I turned around and headed back down the road. Down the mountain, across the Mad River and back up into the Kneeland grasslands I once again sped.

Whomever those folks were firing those last heard sequenced shots, had to be doing more than just target shooting. I had hunted enough in my lifetime to recognize the last heard spaced shooting as that coming from a hunting situation. To my way of thinking, whoever was doing that shooting was either shooting mountain quail or band-tailed pigeons. They were the two most abundant and commonly found species in the area normally taken with a shotgun. Being that it was late spring, there were no open hunting seasons for those species of game birds in California. That meant that the hunt for my fellow man was now on!

Finally arriving as near as I could tell to the approximate location of the mystery shooting, I parked the car, got out, looked, and quietly listened. For the longest time, I saw nothing out of the ordinary through my searching binoculars other than numerous flocks of band-tail pigeons flying about the distant timberline. No matter how quietly I listened, I heard nothing further in the way of any kind of my earlier mystery shooting. My long moments of silence stretched into even longer periods of hearing only bird songs and the quiet sounds of the winds moving across Kneeland's prairie-like mountain grasslands.

BOOM! BOOM!—BOOM! There they were again! Three more quick shots from two separate shooters and whoever they were, I now knew they were absolutely using shotguns. It was then that I noticed large numbers of individual flocks of band-tailed pigeons getting the hell out of Dodge from across the way near a distant line of timber. Glassing the area hard with my 7X50 binoculars, I could see nothing in the way of an off road vehicle in the area from whence the shooting had occurred. Bottom line, there were no roads in that part of the ranch's grasslands leading up into that ridge of timber that skirted the open range.

For me that meant only one thing. It would be up to me and 'Shank's mare', to get off my dead hind end, head across the rangelands on foot into that ridge of timber and investigate. As near as I could tell, I was looking at a good mile walk just to get into the general area of my mystery shooters. But, that is why the good Lord gave me two strong legs and what the people of the State of California expected and were paying me to do. So, getting it into gear, I got up and went.

Hopping a barbed wire fence as Dog crawled underneath the bottom strand, we began our mile-long hike across the rangelands bordered to the northeast by heavy stands of conifers. Realizing I was pretty much out in the open, I tried staying down in the gullies and grassland draws as much as we could as Dog and I hoofed it across the open rangelands at a right sprightly pace.

Twenty-five minutes later, Dog and I were at the edge of the timberline walking cautiously towards the area where I had finally located in on my mystery shooters. Continuing to walk cautiously and glassing every few yards as I went, I saw nothing other than band-tailed pigeons radically flying into or away from my suspect timbered area. But, I damn sure could hear the heavy shooting action close at hand and that spurred me on. In the process of sneaking towards my gunners, I counted nineteen more shots that were fired by my two distant shooters as I continued moving towards their exact locations!

When I had moved into the area earlier, I had discovered nothing of consequence while I was looking for any kind of vehicle which would have brought my shooters into this remote area. Either my shooters had walked all this way from the nearest ranch house or they had 'flown'. But no form of land transport did I see, nor did I observe any fresh vehicle tracks coming across the open range country. *Boy, this sure is an odd one,* I thought as I creeped along. After looking around, I knew there were no roads in which for my shooters to drive within miles of the backside of the ridge of timber from whence they were having such a field day obviously shooting pigeons. But sure as God made green apples, my shooters were now in my neck of the woods and having a 'shooting' field day. Every time they shot, the dense tree line of timber just exploded scared all to hell, previously nesting band-tailed pigeons scooting out in every direction of the compass! *Well, that closed season pigeon shooting is soon going to come to a BIG DAMN screeching halt or I am not the largest and most beautiful game warden in the world,* I thought with a grimace as I continued sneaking along.

Then located off to one side of my direction of travel was the answer to my question regarding the mode of travel into the shooting area by my shooters. Standing calmly off in the distance in a stand of timber and brush stood two horses tied to several low-hanging tree limbs! *Well, I will be damned! Those chaps have ridden horses high up into the backcountry, apparently from a nearby cattle ranch, and are now closed season shooting what I know are nesting band-tailed pigeons!*

With that 'horse moment' fixed in my mind and being on foot, I quickly realized I had some unfinished business with my

239

horses.... A few minutes later, I had unsaddled both horses and hidden their saddles behind a distant tree just in case my shooters got wind of me and fled to their horses before I could stop them from escaping the long arm of the law. If they did get to their horses before I could put the grab on them, I couldn't just shoot them off their horses as the law did in the cowboy movie days of old, now could I? But, do any of you readers out there know of any REAL COWBOYS who will leave without his much beloved saddle behind? NOT ON YOUR LIFE WILL SUCH A HAPPENING OCCUR! With that thought in mind, hence my removal of said items and the hiding of the same.

With that horse discovery under my belt and the hiding of their saddles completed, Dog and I continued into the area at the head of the timber above where the horses were tied off. In so doing, I made sure the horses, my outlaws' main means of escape, were between me and my closed season pigeon shooting son-of-a-guns, precluding their easy escape. That way if I was discovered and my shooters made a run for their horses, they would have to come through me as they tried to flee. As I continued moving upward into the line of timber, I came across numerous splashes of feathers on the forest floor where a pigeon had met its demise. Then my wildlife outlaw 'treasure hunt' got even more profitable. I began following a trail of recently fired, bright red paper Winchester shotgun shells lying on the ground. (To all you budding game warden types out there, those shell casings, as expected had been recently fired. That was determined by smelling the empties.)

About then I hit a bonanza! Lying underneath a large easily recognized Douglas fir tree because of its towering size in a forest of trees upon returning after the pigeon shoot, was a pile of freshly killed band-tailed pigeons! Sneaking over to the pile of pigeons and keeping an eye peeled so I wouldn't be discovered prematurely by my shooters, I moved to the downside of the tree for cover. Checking one more time for my shooters and still hearing them off at a safe, out of sight distance banging away, I crawled around the tree to the recently discovered pigeon pile. There I quickly counted 23 freshly killed band-tailed pigeons and my damn knot head shooters were still blazing away!

That really browned me off. The pigeons were nesting and raising their young during that time of the year. That meant my shooters were killing mated pairs. That also meant if the shooters were deadly at what they were doing and from all appearances they were, they could be killing both parents! If that was the case, that meant the eggs or young of the year back at the nest would die a slow death. A happy camper I did not make over that wasteful thought!

Looking back at Dog in order to tell her to heel so she would be close in case of any apprehension action, I got surprised. There, Dog patiently sat waiting for me to give her instructions, as she held a dead, freshly killed pigeon in her mouth. Just being a typical Labrador, on the way up to my location, she had discovered a dead pigeon that had been overlooked by our shooters and retrieved the same. Well, that was O.K. with me. I just added that bird to the pile of 23 already discovered pigeons for the later come to Jesus meeting between yours truly and those closed season shooting boneheads pulling the triggers on their shotguns.

Locating my two shooters again, Dog and I began our final stalk. About fifteen minutes later of carefully stalking my shooters, all the while trying to keep trees between us, I finally spied my first lad. He was so busy looking skyward for pigeons to shoot that he never even knew I was in country. That was until I sneaked up to him from behind, reached out and tapped him on his shoulder. He let out a scream like a terribly frightened woman and then jumped at least ten feet. In his moment of terror after being surprised from behind, he fired his shotgun into the air when he landed. I figured from the magnitude of that leap of surprise when I tapped him on his shoulder, my poor cowboy shooter had come as close as one could to messin' his britches...

Quickly disarming my chap before he could gather his wits about him, I identified myself even though I was in uniform. Without further ado because I still had another pigeon-killing son-of-a-gun on the loose, I requested my shooter's driver's license. It took a few more moments for my unsettled lad to get over his 'scared' and then he complied. In the meantime, his partner in crime kept on blazing away at any pigeons that overflew his immediate area and were within shotgun range.

Ten minutes later as the two of us walked towards where the last shooter was still eagerly looking for more pigeons, the crap hit the fan. That shooter just happened to turn and see the two of us slowly approaching through the trees. I could see him taking a second look at me and then realizing who the hell I was and what I represented. Without a second look, off he went like a shot down the hill and through the timber in the direction of his horse!

Down through the timber Dog and the two of us now raced as well! He had about 40 yards head start on me but I could run in those days like the wind. OK you disbelieving readers out there. Even at 320 beautiful pounds, I could run. When playing college football, I could run like the wind. Alright, alright, maybe like a BIG wind... But my speeding cowboy wasn't any slouch either. He made it to his horse before I did and with a giant leap, he was on his critter and reaching over its neck to untie the animal from its tree branch. About then I burst out from the timber and bellowed, "Hold it right there! State fish and game warden and you are under arrest for killing pigeons during the closed season. If you try to run, I will see to it that your saddle is forfeited to the State of California!" I said what I said in that moment of time because I did not know who my mystery shooter was. That being said, I figured if he escaped,

I would sure as hell seize his hidden saddle and try and have it forfeited to the State of California in his absence. As I did all that bellowing, I continued quickly narrowing the distance between the two of us.

About then, my lad came to the realization that he was bareback. If any of you readers out there know anything about REAL cowboys, remember this. Cowboys will give up their wife, first born, even if a son, or favorite Winchester rifle before they will let anyone take their horse or saddle! That in mind and to be quite frank, the saddle I had earlier removed from that cowboy's horse was one hell of a nice looking and high quality silver inlaid saddle. Instantly his hands shot up into the air and when he 'reached for the sky', he dropped his shotgun to the ground.

When he did, the damned thing went off when it hit the ground and the load of shot plowed up the ground under his nearby partner's horse's belly, throwing dirt and sticks all over that horse's underbelly! Well, that did it! The other horse was already made nervous by two men running in his direction and now with the shotgun blast tearing up the turf under his belly, that sealed the 'composure' deal! Back that horse reared breaking the tree limb to which it had been tied and down it raced off the side hill like a mountain lion was hot on its trail. (As I later discovered, that horse ran clear back to the home ranch before it was stopped near its familiar corrals by another ranch hand.)

Getting my lad under control, the two of us and Dog then walked back to where I had left my other pigeon killing lad. With the men's driver's licenses now in my shirt pocket and their shotguns in tow, we walked back to the pile of dead pigeons Shadow and I had discovered earlier under the Douglas fir tree. THEY WERE GONE! In the moments it had taken me to corral my running cowboy, the other lad had run to the pigeon pile and had hidden what he had considered was the evidence against them so I couldn't find them. When questioned about the absent pile of pigeons, he of course knew nothing! Well, not to worry, Folks. Three minutes later Shadow had discovered the pile of freshly buried pigeons and we were back in the game. When Shadow started returning with the dead pigeons, spitting feathers every which way but loose as she came, my cowboy who had hidden them looked about as badly as did the dead pigeons.

After gutting all the pigeons, the one cowboy retrieved his still tied up horse and then the three of us walked over to where I had hidden their saddles. The one cowboy saddled his horse and the horseless one had to carry his saddle as we began our long walk back to my patrol car. After getting over the fright of being caught in the act for the illegal pigeon shoot, my two cowboys finally relaxed a bit and then began laughing at the mess they had created for themselves. It was then that their story came to light. Seems they were riding the range checking all the cows that were calving at that time of the year and had run across the huge numbers of nesting band-tailed pigeons high up in the timber at the edge of their ranch's property. Since neither had ever shot or eaten any pigeons, at the end of that first day's ride back at the bunkhouse, they had unlimbered their shotguns and placed them in their rifle scabbards for the next day's cow-calf checking detail. Subsequently, they had their shoot, the pigeons paid the price, and the game warden had his closed season pigeon shooters. Seems the reason for the old fashioned pigeon shoot was to have a big pigeon BBQ with the rest of the folks back at the ranch along with a few beers at the end of the day. In the end, they both were to 'eat' citations for taking migratory game birds during the closed season with unplugged shotguns instead of eating band-tailed pigeon BBQ out on the range.

When we finally arrived back at my parked vehicle, citations were issued accordingly and then one Randy Dutchen rode his horse back to his home ranch, sadder but wiser. As for

Steven Addisen, the horseless one, he rode back to his home ranch in my mechanical horse along with his saddle, seized dead pigeons and confiscated shotguns. A month later when their citations had cleared the court, each man had paid $450.00 for their little afternoon illegal pigeon shoot and their unplugged shotguns were duly forfeited to the State of California.

As for the Flowers in this story, even though it was springtime, there were few in evidence. I had managed to snag off a couple of closed season pigeon killers that were as dedicated to the killing as was I to their apprehension. The word soon got out in and around the ranches in the Kneeland area that the hills were crawling with game wardens on foot. Because of that word racing around on the rancher's 'jungle telegraph', I heard from Glenn that the occasional early season shooting of pigeons in his outback ranches had quickly withered on the vine. I guess one could call that a Flower.

Oh by the way, that was the only wildlife case I made in my 32 year state and federal law enforcement career in which I apprehended two clever cowboys a-horse way back in the bush closed season shooting wild band-tailed pigeons. Perhaps there is a Flower in that rather unique, once in a lifetime adventure and apprehension as well, eh?

As for the Tombstones, they were there as usual. My two pigeon-shooting cowboys only made $200.00 per month plus board and found. Looking at a $450.00 dollar fine meant that for the next two plus months, my pigeon-shooting cowboys worked for nothing. As for my band-tailed pigeons, 44 of them paid the ultimate price. That number included the other twenty my second cowboy had killed that Shadow and I later collected after the fact. Statistically, half would have been females and the other half would have been males. Had they lived, the females would have produced only one egg per female. That meant the approximate loss of 22 young of the year had all of them survived. Today the band-tailed pigeon population, because of habitat destruction and over shooting, has dwindled dangerously so that bag limits in many states in which that species of bird lives, have been restricted to only one bird per day! Today's populations of band-tailed pigeons do not show any signs of recovering back to their old population numbers like I can remember in my days as a young man from the 1950s.

I can remember back as a boy during those years the many band-tailed pigeon shoots I had in the oaken forests of Plumas County in northeastern California. Many times, many times, I can remember flocks of 5,000 or more birds passing directly overhead during pigeon season! As a 12-year-old boy who would shoot at anything, I would just stand there in awe listening to the whistling wings overhead and never fire a shot! Today in that same area when I return home for visits, I see no band-tailed pigeons anywhere. Today they are mostly gone from those halcyon days and old oaken forest haunts of yore! Talk about a real living Tombstone in an old man's sad memory...

As I walk in those old oaken forest found in the land of the fabled California gold rush days of '49,' where I walked as a young man, I still see the real life fire brick black ink-lettered Tombstones of the Chinese gold miners who scratched the earth for pay and were buried where they fell. I can also visualize the many smaller Tombstones in each of the oak forests representing that rich natural feathered band-tailed heritage that once flourished high up in their tops by the thousands and now are no more...

Speaking of Tombstones, have any of my readers ever even seen a stuffed passenger pigeon from that extinct uniquely American species? They used to number in the billions when America was young and were at one time the largest flock of birds in the world! The last one, named Martha, died in 1917 in the Cincinnati Zoological Gardens. An estimated four to six billion birds were gone in a few short years when our country was young, the shooters possessed only black powder guns and conservation laws pertaining to that species were non-existent. That species of bird was shot year around by the millions, even during the nesting season and right off their nests. Many times hundreds of thousands of the young birds called squabs were scooped right off their nests, killed, salted down and shipped by the barrels full to major city centers like that of New York for food. So many living birds were destroyed that tons of those critters were shot and even fed to the farmers' hogs... I often thought as a young boy in northern California when those huge flocks of band-tailed pigeons flew overhead, did the sounds their few thousands of wings made resembled anything like those during the day of the now extinct passenger pigeon? Ah, man's inhumanity to man and the natural beauty and heritage that surrounds us all...

A HELPING HAND FOR MOTHER NATURE'S LITTLE ONES

I managed to make it up one more time to help Bill, the Klamath warden, before he died of cancer when he was just in his mid '40's. During that latest detail, I found myself roaming many of Bill's backcountry roads within the Pacific Coast range in my patrol car to show the flag in his absence while he was resting at home ill. During those patrol adventures, a number of out of work loggers, lumbermen and run of the mill wildlife outlaws failed to take heed of that flag passing by on parade and paid the price for being slow of step.

Arriving mid-morning on that first day of my latest Klamath patrol assignment, I checked into a motel and then 'hit the bricks.' Being there was a multitude of backcountry logging roads throughout Bill's Klamath patrol district, I just fueled up my patrol car and headed out at random. When confronted later with a patchwork quilt of roads and logged off areas, I just let my curiosity and interest in what that' neck-of-the-woods' had to offer in the way of law enforcement adventures lead the way. Up into the Pacific Coast Mountain Range I climbed, enjoying the early morning air and the lack of fog. It was beautiful out! The air was clean, the sun's rays were filtering through the massive redwoods and dense stands of Douglas fir, raindrops glistened off the leaves of the brush from recent rains, and the musty smell of the forest's decaying vegetation scented the warming air.

Then, there was Mother Nature's bonus laid out for the whole world to see. It was one of those unique days in the world of wildlife in which mountain quail seemed to be everywhere moving 'to and fro'. Legions of their little coveys sprinted across the muddy logging roads on which I patrolled that sunny day. My guess was that the rain-soaked little birds were happy as clams at high tide to be out in the sunlight and having a chance to dry out their feathers from a spat of the temperate rain forest's 100+ inches of annual rainfall. Four or five times that morning as I climbed ever upward into the dense forests of the coast range, I had to abruptly stop and let my mountain quail or the "Little Ones" as I called them, skitter across the road in front of my patrol car. As they did, it never failed to bring a smile to my face seeing those strings of wildlife on parade. Those little guys would sprint across in front of my vehicle with their top knots held high and their little legs just a-blur underneath their typically beer keg shaped bodies. A riot of life from Mother Nature in one of her finest hours seemed to greet my eyes at about every turn in the road that morning...

(Being a wildlife biologist by academic training with B.S. and M.S. degrees in Wildlife Management from Humboldt State College (renamed Humboldt State University today), I had more than just a passing interest in what I was enjoying during Mother Nature's moments in time. Early on in my life as a one-parent kid because of a divorce, I often found myself wandering alone and enjoying myself in the outback. In so doing, I discovered I found joy and solace immersed in a passel of natural wonders in the world of wildlife on every occasion. So much so, that it wasn't long before I knew where almost every trout lurked in the nearby streams, where every covey of mountain quail called home and could even mimic the little bird's plaintive calls and in so doing, have them come a-running in short order.

Conversely, I grew up as a sportsman and could mimic those mountain quails' calls so well that many times I could call them to my gun during the hunting season. I also knew where the elusive California mule deer would more than likely be lurking and was deadly in shooting the quick as a moving bullet mourning dove and band-tailed pigeons in my backcountry Plumas County haunts as well. Unbeknownst to me at the time, the good Lord was branding into my soul what was to come in the future when it came to me and the lifelong love and protection of those in the world of wildlife who had little or no voice. Somehow, I think the Chief Game Warden in the Sky had preordained the placement of those feelings for all things natural for something He had in mind for me in my later years as a state and federal wildlife officer.

As an example of that preordination, when faced with a four-year college choice after completing my first two years of junior college, my guardian angels saw to it that style of life decision had been previously made for me. Walking into my junior college's library one afternoon, I was confronted with a long table deeply loosely stacked with hundreds of various college booklets advertising the wonders of going to their particular college. The booklets had been arranged for us graduating sophomores to thumb through and select the next college of our choice in order to complete our four year degrees. Reaching out and grabbing the first college booklet off the top of that huge pile at random, I opened it up somewhere into its middle pages. There before my eyes was one program of study at Humboldt State College titled, *Wildlife Management*. "There it is!" I said. "That is what I want to do." Not many people can do that, namely decide on a dime your life's profession and know that was the correct selection. As I said earlier, I think I had a little help from that Chief Game Warden in the Sky.

I had no idea what that field of study meant, what kind of career field opportunities it offered, the difficulty of study or anything else. I just knew, with a little help from my guardian angels, that I had made the correct choice for a college and had chosen the right field of study. The following semester I transferred to Humboldt State sight unseen and subject matter or career opportunities unknown. After 32 successful and fruitful years later in a wildlife management/conservation officer career field, both nationally and internationally, the rest is history. I guess one could say, I had more than just a passing interest in the world of wildlife. Once I was involved in that wildlife management career field, it became a matter of dedicating my life and soul to those in the world of wildlife who had little or no voice as a law enforcement officer. And in so doing, I took it personally when anyone did unto Mother Nature other than what they should have been doing. I think in the days of old, the American Indians called that a 'vision quest'. Hence my extreme joy that fine day in Bill's district watching the world of the Little Ones unfolding all around me in its purest of forms. (As an aside, in 2008, the Humboldt State University Alumni Association presented me with its "Distinguished Alumni Award"!)

BOOM! BOOM!—BOOM! BOOM! *What the hell!* I thought, as I snapped back from my dawdling and daydreaming as I drove along another muddy road. Those shooting sounds bursting through the open windows of my vehicle seemed to be coming from two shotguns. And the sounds of that shooting were coming from above me further up on the mountainside. Looking upward through the front windshield of my patrol car, I spied an old red pickup sitting in the middle of the switch-backed logging road about 100 yards away. Both of its doors were wide open as if the occupants had disembarked quite suddenly. Grabbing my binoculars from the front seat, hurriedly stopping and exiting my patrol car, I looked upward once again. Not a thing greeted my eyes except the majesty of the old-growth forest around and beyond my suspect vehicle.

BOOM! BOOM! *Damn it!* I thought. There aren't any hunting seasons open this time of the year! Jumping back into my vehicle, I slipped it into low gear and began quietly stalking up to the area of the suspect red parked pickup. Climbing ever upward on the muddy logging road, I was one switch back below the pickup when I saw a loaded logging truck coming down the road from above. About the time I rounded the last turn in the road, the logging truck was fast approaching the suspect pickup still sitting out in the middle of the road with both doors flung wide open and blocking the road!

Seeing the pickup blocking the road, the logging truck driver coming downhill with a load of logs laid on his air horns! Noticing how narrow the haul road was, I pulled over and partially up onto the road bank in order to let the loaded logging truck pass when it eventually arrived at my location. I put my rig into 'park' and jumped out with my binoculars just in time to see one heavily bearded and skinny-as-a-rail lad emerge from the roadside brush at a dead run. In one hand appeared to be a Winchester Model 12 pump action shotgun and firmly clutched in his other hand was a bunch of dead, wildly flopping, dead mountain quail! Running to the driver's side of the pickup, my lad dove into the front seat and quickly moved his pickup off the road so the heavily loaded logging truck could pass. As the logging truck came my way, Mother Nature interceded. The logging truck now blocked my marked patrol car from being viewed by anyone in the location of the red pickup, as it continued thundering downhill travelling to a far off mill. The positioning of the logging truck on the roadway was perfect. My quail shooter could not see my nearby parked patrol vehicle and did not realize the long arm of the law was close and about to render the shooter some much needed personal attention because quail season was closed.

When the logging truck passed me standing alongside my vehicle with my binoculars in hand the driver decided to put the screws to me. Upon recognition of who I was and what I was about to do, he laid on his air horns again as if to warn the chap on the road above with the illegal quail that the law was close at hand. "Too late," I said to myself as I gave a friendly gesture (no, not that one) to my truck driver trying to be helpful to the outlaw holding the illegal quail. As the logging truck noisily rumbled out of sight running under full compression and liberally using his Jake's brake, I had my binoculars up and on my man of interest once again. My lad was bent over in the front seat area as if he was doing something below the dash or around the floorboards in his vehicle. When he looked up again, he saw what had to be his worst nightmare considering the circumstances! Trotting towards him was a man dressed in game warden greens wearing a silver star on his left chest. I was sure that I was not what my closed season quail shooting chap wanted to see even on his worst day.

Upon seeing me approaching, my chap quickly ducked back down again inside the cab of his truck and with that, I picked up my pace. Short moments later, I was upon my still bent-over man watching him trying to madly stuff a mess of dead quail up under the springs of his seat. "Morning, how is the illegal quail hunting going?" I asked with a grin in the tone and tenor of my voice.

Rising up from his quail hiding activity, all my now captured chap could do was just look back at me in shock with a baleful looking set of eyes. Then instantly gaining his composure, he regrouped with an original wildlife outlaw response. 'What quail?'

"Well, you can start with that one quail next to you with his foot sticking out from under the front seat of your pickup," I responded with my most original Walt Disney Cheshire cat smile and, of course, a wonderfully endearing voice. With that, my lad just dropped his head on the side of his steering wheel in total resignation. He did so because he had just been caught with his hands in Mother Nature's cookie jar by the largest and most beautiful game warden in the world of course.

"Hand me your shotgun and make sure it is stock first," I ordered.

When my now captured chap handed me his shotgun from the front seat, he had doom and gloom splashed clear across his face. Jacking open the chamber, I not surprisingly discovered a live shot shell in its chamber! *Well, well,* I thought. *Nothing like having a loaded shotgun in a motor vehicle on a way open to the public.* And of course, that being another violation of the fish and game regulations.

"You're not going to give me a ticket are you? I was just trying to get something so I could feed my family," he continued with a voice that reeked of hoping the game warden was a charitable soul and just this one time would look the other way when it came to all the dead closed season quail hidden under his truck's seat.

To me, I had labeled that story 'Number Four B.' I had heard that story so many times already in my short career that I now gave such stories a number. "Well, it is either citations for taking and possessing quail during the closed season and possessing a loaded gun in a motor vehicle or, I can place you under arrest and take you forthwith to the county jail," I responded.

"No, no, no," he blurted out! "I am already on probation for knocking my old lady around so I can't be booked again. If you do, I will be in violation of the terms of my probation and be ordered back to the county jail to serve a six months' sentence," he exclaimed with real concern rising up in his voice.

BOOM! BOOM! BOOM! went three more quickly fired shots by what I now assumed was his partner in crime up in the brush some thirty yards distant. WHIRRRR came the sound of a set of fast flying quail wings as the little bird sped by overhead escaping from the dangers behind him. And in so doing, almost as if pointing out the direction I needed to go in order to save some of his brethren from a further killing fate.

"Hand me your driver's license and pickup keys," I quickly commanded.

Man, you never saw someone get out his wallet and hand me the requested identification item and his pickup keys so fast. It was obvious the driver didn't want to piss me off and have me haul his miserable carcass off to the slammer, forcing him to end up in serving out an earlier sentence for beating his wife.

Grabbing his driver's license, truck keys, and taking his shotgun along with me for my own safety, I trotted up into the brushy hillside after my second shooter before he shot to hell all my Little Ones. About then, my remaining lad shot one more time at a rising quail and, in so doing, provided to me his exact location. Two minutes later, like the R.C.M.P., I had my man. My second shooter was an older man, badly in need of a bath and several good meals, if you get my gist. I identified myself and commanded him to drop his shotgun. One look at me and what I represented and like a shot, that old bugger took off running downhill like he had been shot out of a Civil War cannon.

Surprised over his 'flight' response to my verbal command, I hesitated. Then realizing the race was now on, I finally got my beautiful 'tail-end' into gear. Moments later, since I was now running downhill, it didn't take me long to get up on step. Down the two of us stormed off that brush-covered hillside like a couple of maddened Durham bulls.

"Roger, Roger, let's get going! Game warden, game warden!" that old bugger yelled just like the devil was hot on his trail. Well, one couldn't really say it was the devil. I was a lot prettier than that damn old horned devil but I did have evil intentions in mind once I caught my quail-shooting runner doing everything he could do in order to escape.

At that moment, Mother Nature intervened on behalf of the Little Ones and yours truly. My fleeing chap, now just a few scant yards in front of me, stormed up over the road's berm next to the pickup, caught his foot on a root and speared himself straight into the side of the parked pickup going full bore! WHOOOMP! went my old lad, making a solid metal-hammering sound as he knifed himself directly head first into the side of the pickup's door! Suffice to say, all the 'run' was out of my second quail shooter upon his high-speed contact with their truck. But the funnies didn't end there. When my "Javelin Man" struck the side of the pickup, his still loaded shotgun discharged and it blew a hole into the front end of the bed of the truck!

Me? I got a face full of flying paint chips because I was so close to reaching out and grabbing my runner. Roger, the other closed season quail shooter still sitting in the front seat of the pickup, bailed out from the cab as quickly as a rattlesnake can strike upon hearing the shot and feeling the concussion. After the other quail shooter had quit running down the road in fright, he realized he had some work to do when it came to cleaning out his shorts. As for me, I wasn't so far behind him in the shorts cleaning-out department either after the shotgun had gone off in my such close pursuit proximity to my runner!

Checking over my now inert runner, I could see that he would have a nasty facial bruise and cut on the top of his head from spearing the truck but other than that, he appeared to be alright. So with all that in mind, I commenced with the official business at hand. Digging out my book of citations from my coat pocket, I ticketed one Roger Gilpin citations for possession of closed season quail and for possession of a loaded shotgun in a motor vehicle on a way open to the public. During that flurry of activity, I put Roger's shotgun into the trunk of my now just recently moved up to the scene patrol car for safer keeping.

About then I could hear my Javelin Man starting to come around. Walking around to my lad still lying in the mud alongside the pickup, I identified myself and could see that he now realized his hind end was clearly hanging out over his little closed season quail shoot. I requested his driver's license and as he was digging around for his wallet, I let him know I had already seized and had his shotgun in custody. Still a bit groggy from the 'header' he had taken into the side of the pickup, the man eventually dug out his driver's license and handed it up to me. Looking down at the man sitting on the ground alongside the truck with a groggy look still in his eyes and a stream of blood trickling down the side of his head, I advised him to continue sitting on the ground until he felt better. Then I began writing Darrell Jenson citations for taking and possessing quail during the closed season and using an unplugged shotgun.

In searching Roger's pickup after all the smoke of the moment had cleared away, I discovered 39 quail hidden under and behind the seat of his vehicle! Damn, my Little Ones sure paid the price that day before I could physically intervene on their behalf. But my lads' problems didn't end there. I had Dog bail out from the open window of my patrol car and told her, "Get the duck". (That was her standard command to find any game close at hand.) Twenty minutes later, Shadow had retrieved six additional dead quail and one cripple from the hillside which I dispatched. All of those quail were also added to my culprits' total kill for the day.

When all was said and done, you could bet your bottom dollar that both men were going to pay a pretty penny for their little illegal quail-shooting escapade. In fact, Bill, the local warden, later told me that each both man were fined $450.00 dollars for his offenses and, since they could not pay, were jailed. There, both men had to work off their fines at $10.00 per day of incarceration. Additionally, Roger served an extra six months in jail in order to satisfy the requirements of his earlier sentence for being convicted of domestic abuse. Well, at least the skinny one in bad need of a shower and a few meals, Darrell Jenson, got his wish when it came to a shower and three squares a day…

After my cited chaps had left the area in their pickup, I gutted my 46 evidence quail and iced them down in my ice chest. Washing my hands from the melted ice drain water in the ice chest, I took out a cold Coke Cola and just stood there quietly with my dog in the solitude of the moment. As I did, I drank in all the beauty and quiet of the temperate rain forest surrounding me that I could. There was no fog and the sun was beating down on the dampened soils causing streaming mists of vapor to rise into the air in exotic plumes. Gosh, except for all my Little Ones getting killed earlier, it was a beautiful day to this rookie game warden's way of thinking. Finishing my Coke, I let Dog back into the patrol car, shoved a wad of sweet tasting Levi Garrett chewing tobacco between my teeth and gums, and set out to see what other devilment I could get into. Well, that next wildlife law enforcement adventure was just a short and totally unexpected ways down the road.

I drove out the logging road until I came to a logging show in full swing. There, I pulled off the road at the edge of the landing and watched the "high-lead" operation in fascination.

(I had lied about my age when I was just sixteen in Plumas County so I could earn enough money to go to college and in so doing, got a job as a logger during my summer months with Meadow Valley Lumber Company. It was a job I truly enjoyed, especially being out in the bush day in and out. I earned a whole $2.02 ½ per hour and that was good money for a kid my age in those days. As long as I could do a man's work, I received a man's pay. The work was hard and dangerous but it later helped pay for almost six years of my college for which I was most thankful.)

Watching this new type of high-lead logging whose basic operations I was unfamiliar with, I sat there fascinated. Huge redwood, Douglas fir and grand fir logs were just a-flying down to the landing on the high-lead, overhead cable outfit and the landing was a whirl of activity. Then the crap hit the fan! Walking onto the landing came a choker setter who was happily holding aloft and showing all around what appeared from a distance to be a dead blue grouse! Grabbing my binoculars from the front seat, I took a gander at the man carrying the mystery bird. As I looked, I could see that the man carrying the dead grouse had no idea I was even in country and even worse, watching him!. *What the hell!* I thought. *Blue grouse season is not open and what the dickens is that logger doing with what appears to be a freshly killed bird?* It didn't take long for one 'Great Grotz', that's me, "To hit the deck a-runnin' and spin the guns around", to quote the words from an old Marty Robbins' song on sinking the German battleship, "The Bismarck", by the British Navy during the early part of the Second World War.

Thirty minutes later, I had just finished gutting one seized blue grouse and putting it into my ice chest so it would not spoil. Back on the landing was one unhappy logger now holding a citation in his hand for the illegal possession of a closed season blue grouse instead of the dead bird which was to be his supper later in the evening. Like I have often said regarding life's circumstances, 'Sometimes you eat the bear and sometimes he eats you.'

As the story went, my logger, Cole Jefferson, had seen the blue grouse with a mess of chicks up where he was setting chokers. (That means he was putting chokers or wire cable nooses around the sections of downed and sectioned logs so they could be lifted up off the ground with the high-lead cables and lofted to the landing below to be loaded onto the waiting logging trucks.) Jefferson had gathered up a mess of rocks and walked up to the gentle blue grouse, also named the Fool Hen because of their gentle nature around man, and stoned it to death! Then Jefferson, feeling guilty, shooed the chicks off into the brush to die without their mother around to show them the way. Well, in the wonder of her wisdom, good old Mother Nature found a way to have me sitting and watching the logging show at just the right time. Who says the blue grouse don't have a god of some sort watching over them? (As an aside, over the 32 years of my career as a conservation officer, I made at least a dozen such cases. Cases involving individuals seeing and killing blue grouse with a handful of rocks as their weapon and not having any idea I was in country and watching them performing their illegal deed. In each of those cases, I was able to avenge the poor little blue grouse with a rather fine-hefty citation before all was said and done.)

Realizing I was no longer wanted around the logging show by the company of loggers after catching one of their own in a fish and game violation and ticketing the man, I took off. When I came to another fork in the road, I took it and headed into another unfamiliar part of the Klamath Warden's District. Feeling proud over all the good game warden work I was doing, I was drifting along like a downy duck feather in a slight breeze as my head expanded at least two hat sizes larger because on my day's law enforcement successes. As was many times typical in the world of wildlife law enforcement, the rest of my day did not produce any miscreants skating across the line of legality.

Come nightfall, I closed up shop and headed back to Klamath. There I conferred with Bill over the day's events, stashed my seized evidence in his fish and game freezer and headed for my mildew smelling motel room for a night's rest on a bed that was far too short for my 6- foot 4- inch frame.

As for the Flowers in this story, they were there. The first Flower was for my friend, Bill. As sick as he was, I was sure I had brought some relief to his tortured soul knowing there was some law west of the Pecos roaming out and about in his district. And the Outlaw Flowers I brought back in the evening certainly lit up his day, deep chest pain or not.

The other Flowers that come to mind were those of humankind plucked from the wilds and cited for killing my little mountain quail and the blue grouse during the closed season. Those Flowers needed plucking and deserved all of the legal consequences that followed. Plainly and simply, they were wildlife killers and they were struck down by the sword of Mother Nature at an opportune moment in time. At least that one fellow's wife wasn't getting knocked around during those additional six months her husband was in jail serving out his sentence for violating the terms of his probation.

As for the Tombstones, they were there as well. In my first instance with the 46 mountain quail illegally killed, remember the male to female ratios. Half and half and that meant 23 of the 46 quail statistically were females that had illegally been killed. And that being the case, with those birds laying from 5-15 eggs per clutch, you folks can do the math on the birds potentially lost during that breeding season. Additionally, that was their nesting season. Any eggs previously laid and any chicks, not having a mom to care for them and show them the way, either died of exposure or starved to death. It is amazing what one thoughtless act by man can so quickly lead to so many other deadly moments.

As for the Tombstones in the blue grouse situation with the logger, its life situation runs the same. That female blue grouse would have laid from 5-10 eggs and would have had the same number of chicks. In that case, it was late in the season and my money would have been on the grouse already having a large brood of youngsters. With the logger removing that adult female, that left the chicks defenseless without a mom to show them the way and suggested that they were soon to perish. All of this because one logger having such stupid thoughts of removing a female blue grouse from the wild during breeding season for a damn evening meal. Go buy a hamburger! They only cost twenty-five cents in those days which was a hell of a lot cheaper than receiving a citation for killing a game bird during the closed season.

THE PIGEON KILLER WAS A "SPIDER"

The following morning on the second day of my Klamath detail, I arose to hear heavy rains hammering on my motel's rooftop. As it turned out, heavy rains and winds were my constant companions for the next two days. In short, those weather events pretty much foiled any meaningful daytime anti-poaching patrols in the backcountry. As for any nighttime patrols, they were out as well. With such heavy rains, use of a spotlight to take deer or elk was useless because the light from a spotlight was diffused by the 'curtain' of raindrops and its rays bounced back to the sender. However, I did use my time to get even better acquainted with other parts of Bill's district so when the heavy rains stopped, I would be out the gate with the bit in my teeth in fine style ready for another meaningful wildlife law enforcement patrol.

Thursday finally dawned brightly with a slight breeze coming in off the ocean. Finishing a lumber jack's breakfast of fried spuds, four sunny side up eggs and' half a hog' of bacon at the nearest small north coast eatery, found Dog and yours truly more than ready to 'hit the bricks'. Once again, into the forested backcountry with all its muddy logging roads Dog and I went. Soon it was warm enough to roll down all my patrol car's windows and Dog and I were almost set. Stopping at a narrow pull-off, I let Dog out to take care of her 'daily dozen' and then do some smelling around. As for me during that interlude, into my mouth went a large chew of Levi Garrett chewing tobacco and to my way of thinking, Dog and yours truly were set for our next set of adventures. The hunt was on again and deeper into the wet and steaming temperate rain forest of the Pacific Coast Range we ventured.

Gosh, it was great to be alive that fine day so long ago. There were birds everywhere flitting about in the over and under stories, several Columbian black-tailed deer were out in the sun drying off and feeding and the quail were once again almost under-foot and wheel as I slowly drove along keeping out a sharp eye and a tuned ear. Proceeding inland after crossing over one ridge of mountains, Dog and I dropped into a small, almost hidden valley. At the front end of the valley was an old ranch house that had seen better days and, in the adjacent several pastures, ran a mixture of horses and a few head of Angus beef cattle. *A beautifully tranquil scene,* I thought, as Dog and I quietly passed by the ranch house toward the far end of the valley and whatever adventure awaited us lurking in the wings.

Stopping at the far end of the small valley in its quiet isolation, I attended to a call of nature. Finished, I figured it was time for one of my wicked little Italian twisted, 'dog's droppings look-alike' cigars. Out from the box one came and after wetting it with the juices from my mouth, I lit it up. Drawing in the acrid smoke from my first puff and letting it pour out through my nostrils, I grinned. A nosy mosquito just happened by honing in on the CO2 being emitted from my body and flew into that cloud of cigar smoke by mistake as she looked for the CO2 emitter. That was all it took. My winged visitor dropped like a 'car hit chicken' when she entered the acrid cloud of cigar smoke and landed dead in the grass at my feet. *Serves her right,* I thought with a grin. Then the thought crossed my mind as to what that smoke and its associated nicotine was doing to me... In fact, even Dog stayed away from me when I smoked those wicked little twisted Italian cigars but by damn they sure were good.

"POW," came the sound of a shot from a light caliber firearm clear back in the area of the ranch house just passed! Spinning around as Shadow shoved her head out the rear open window to hear better too, I quickly 'eye-balled' the area from which I had just heard that single shot. I saw nothing but a few band-tailed pigeons speeding away from the ranch house area like their tails where on fire. *What the hell?* I thought as I stood there in silence waiting to see if I was going to hear another shot. Nothing but silence followed the sound of that first shot! For the next twenty minutes or so, Dog and I stood at the far end of the valley on the deserted road and just listened. Finally figuring the rancher had probably shot at a crow or maybe some other pest, Dog and I prepared to leave. Then a flicker of movement caught my eyes. Back at the isolated ranch house, I saw a pair of band-tailed pigeons dropping into the rear area of the ranch house like a pair of feathered rockets. Pausing because my guardian angels were now fluttering around inside me, I just quietly, stood, looked and listened.

"POW," went one more shot from a light firearm and that time, I only observed one pigeon hurtling skyward and disappearing over the canopy of trees by the old ranch house instead of the two I had originally observed dropping into the area! *Well, I'll be damned. I wonder if that rancher living out here in the middle of nowhere in almost total isolation is shooting pigeons during the closed hunting season? Because if*

263

he is and I am able to catch him, he is going to tumble just like those two pigeons did moments earlier when they dropped into his back yard, I thought.

Driving down the road a piece towards an old hay barn that had seen better days, I carefully pulled in behind it so I would not be observed by anyone casually driving down the road. In short, I didn't want anybody driving down the road, seeing my marked patrol car sitting there, then stopping and warning the rancher at the suspect ranch house that the fish and game warden was in country. Locking the car, Dog and I headed towards the isolated ranch house at the far end of the valley on 'Shank's mare'. Dropping down into a creek bottom and using a line of trees for cover, Dog and I began our long walk to the suspect area of our mystery shooting. That turned out to be an arduous walk because everywhere I looked or walked were numerous patches of poison oak. A plant because of its poisonous oils, that did not like me nor did I like it. Thirty minutes later Dog and I were about 100 yards from the backside of the old ranch house. We couldn't get much closer because the rancher had a couple of dogs running around in the backyard. So with that ranch dog 'early warning system' in effect, I just settled in with my binoculars in hand with my back resting against an old fern and moss encrusted redwood stump from which Dog and I could watch, learn and listen hidden from sight.

Then I got a visual break. I noticed at one end of the rancher's backyard was a tall stand-alone post. Sitting on top of that post was a flat piece of plywood about four feet in length. Closely watching that area with my binoculars, I observed a Steller's jay landing on that piece of plywood atop the vertical post and begin feeding. *That piece of plywood is being used as a bird feeder. That would account for those two pigeons diving into that backyard as if it was old home week for the seeds scattered atop that feeder,* I thought. Soon other birds like starlings and black birds had descended onto the bird feeder and were eating away like it was their last supper. Moments later, five band-tailed pigeons dropped from the sky onto the piece of plywood like they had been there before and began eating with all the other birds atop the makeshift feeder.

"POW," came the sound of a single shot as the birds atop the feeder scattered like someone had just dropped a bomb into their seed bucket! That was except for the two pigeons blown off the feeder like they had been shot from out of a cannon in a flurry of feathers. In a millisecond, those two pigeons dropped lifeless to the ground in a puff of feathers instead of getting the hell out of Dodge as that species was want to do in the face of danger.

Pushing away from my redwood stump and telling Shadow to heel, off I began sneaking towards the ranch house to put the snatch on my mystery closed season pigeon shooter, loose dogs running around or not. After I heard that last shot and observed the two pigeons falling, I never did see my shooter. It became apparent to me that my secretive shooter was shooting at the birds from out of an open window or a back door just cracked slightly so the barrel of the firearm in a non-alarming fashion could be secretly extended for shooting. That way, the normally careful and observant pigeons would be none the wiser and would make easy targets. Quietly moving to within fifty yards of the house, I took up a position behind an old Ford tractor and began doing what I did best. I was now quietly waiting like a South American bushmaster lying along a game trail waiting in ambush for my quarry...

I didn't have long to wait. Out the back door came a middle- aged woman wearing a red apron. She strode over to the bird feeder, picked up four dead pigeons from the ground (two from apparently earlier shootings), turned and walked back to her house as if it was an everyday event hardly worth mentioning. She was so bold about it that it just seemed like breaking the fish and game regulations was nothing more than old hat.

Well, I knew just the medicine to use for what ailed her miserable law- breaking carcass. With that little performance firmly fixed in my mind, I instructed Dog to sit. Then off I went to confront the mistress and apprehend the same in her lair. Getting closer to the ranch house but still in cover and using my binoculars, I looked through her kitchen window as the lady with the red apron began plucking her illegally killed pigeons. However, her two dogs running lose on her property winded me and bayed out a racket that would have woken up the dead in the nearest cemetery. Figuring the 'jig was up', I walked up to the back door and knocked like any gentleman would. Soon I could hear someone coming to the back door and lo and behold, it was my pigeon-plucking 'lady of the house'.

Opening the back door, she said very sweetly, "Good morning, Officer. Is there something I can do for you?"

"Yes Ma'am," I said. "My name is Terry Grosz and, as you can see, I am a game warden. I was passing by and heard shooting coming from the house earlier. Curious about what someone in this house might be shooting at, I stopped and listened. I heard someone shooting several times from this ranch house killing a number of band-tailed pigeons in the process. Since pigeon season is closed, I came over to investigate. When I did, I observed you from a distance retrieving several pigeons from below your bird feeder and taking them into this house. Then later I observed you through your kitchen window with my binoculars picking those closed season pigeons."

"No, I don't think so. I really don't know what you are talking about. I haven't shot or picked up any pigeons," she very sweetly advised. But when she mouthed those words, I could see worry moving fleetingly across her face and hear the same concerns in the tone and tenor of her voice. About then, looking over my diminutive shooter, I observed a .410 shotgun standing in the entryway behind her back door. *That has to account for the light report I heard several times earlier when it came to shots being fired,* I thought. Ignoring her earlier denial, I pointed to the shotgun standing along the wall behind her asking, "Is that the gun you used to shoot the pigeons?"

Without thinking about her response, she said, "Yes, it is. Oh, darn it, I didn't mean to say that! Well, you got me."

"May I see the man of the house," I asked.

"Only if you have x-ray eyes, Officer. He has been dead several years now and I live here alone," she quietly replied. "My husband had been loading our cattle for the market in one of our big trucks when a steer charged back out from being loaded. When the animal did, he smashed my husband against the sidewall of the cattle truck rupturing his spleen. He died before he could be operated on," she sadly and quietly offered.

Man, those words sure took the wind out from my toughest game warden in the world sails... Changing the tone and temper of my voice after I had offered my condolences, I said, "Ma'am, may I see the birds you were cleaning in the kitchen sink area of the house?"

"Yes, you may, Officer." With that, she turned and led me into her kitchen. On the top of her stove, she had a huge pressure cooker canning away. On the counter next to her sink were eight cooling quart jars full of previously canned pigeon breasts! In a pan in the sink lay six more pigeons in various stages of being prepared and on the other side of the counter were six more open jars of just pigeon breasts ready to be brined and later placed in the pressure cooker to kill any and all botulism spores contained in the canning jars! *Damn, this lady is not only a killing machine but a canning one as well,* flooded through my amazed mind at the cutting and gutting operation I was now witnessing.

Almost at a loss for words, I said, "Ma'am, you can't do this." Talk about being a rookie. How was that for a dumb statement? Hell, she already had and if I hadn't intervened, she would have been up to her elbows in even more dead pigeons!

"Well, I have to eat too," she stoutly maintained. "Ever since my husband died, I have been trying to hang onto this ranch and it has been hard. And when I saw those band-tailed pigeons coming to my bird feeder to eat the sunflower seed I had put out for the other birds, I got the idea of shooting them for food. They came so fast and frequently, that I decided I would do like my folks did back on the farm in North Dakota with their young chickens. I just would shoot those pigeons and then can them. Then I would have meat enough to last me all winter and I wouldn't have to butcher my precious beef cattle for personal consumption but could keep them for the market."

Brother, was I ever in a pickle. Here she was all alone and there I stood. All of 6-foot 4-inches tall and weighing in at what one of her steers probably weighed, just a-glowering at her over her attempts to make ends meet and save a little on her food bill. Boy, I felt just like a heel. But, I had a job to do and commenced. "Ma'am, I am going to have to issue you a citation for taking and possessing band-tailed pigeons during the closed season. I will also have to confiscate all your jars of pigeon breasts that you have canned or are in the process of canning. I have to do so because any game animal illegally taken cannot be possessed under state law. As for any canned pigeons you might have stored away, I will leave those because they are not in plain view and in order for me to legally go after the other out of sight jars, I would need a warrant, which I do not have." That decision I made because she had been so sweet up to that moment and seemed to be appreciative for anything that I could do for her in which to aid her in her survival.

"Thank you, Officer. That is so sweet of you to leave me with the food I have already canned," she cooed with a smile that would have wilted any other heart not as black as mine.

"In the meantime, I need to get a count on the evidence birds in your kitchen that are to be seized. When I am finished with that, I will walk back to my patrol car and return shortly. Then I will load up the items to be seized and issue you a citation for the violations you committed as we discussed earlier," I said.

"O.K., Officer," she said very sweetly as if trying not to piss me off for what she had been doing contrary to the law.

Standing there in her kitchen, I got a count on the jars and numbers of pigeons contained therein and of those in the sink being prepared for canning. It was a good thing I had stumbled onto this situation when I did. My charming Lady had 20 quarts of pigeons in total holding 86 pigeon breasts sitting in her kitchen! Turned out, my little gal was some sort of a pigeon killer...

Once finished with the evidence count, I excused myself, walked out to the road and headed for my hidden patrol car. As I passed the Ford tractor where Dog was still sitting as she had been instructed, I whistled. Boy, here she came at a dead run. I guess that old crap of being left behind while her master got to do all the neat things wasn't her cup of tea. Retrieving my patrol car, I drove it back to the ranch house and then backed it into the rancher Lady's driveway for easy loading. After opening up the trunk, I entered the ranch house and began bringing out the jars of previously canned and ready to be canned pigeon breasts.

Once all the canned pigeon breasts had been loaded, I sat down with Mrs. McMaster, my nice little pigeon shooter and issued her just one citation for the illegal possession of closed season band-tailed pigeons, To Wit: 86 pigeons! I let her skate on the taking charge because as she had said, she was struggling and I could see no use in rubbing her nose in another potential charge of closed season taking. Especially since I hadn't seen her personally kill or take any pigeons.

I know, I know! To all my budding game warden readers out there reading these lines, she was the only person in the house so who else would have killed all those pigeons? Right? Well, I was always a stickler for enforcing the letter of the law and since I had never witnessed her actually taking any pigeons, she was not cited for such an offense. That was my legal option to do and I did so. Plus, she had been really nice so why trample a down and out person any further? So there, 'how do you like them apples'!

After explaining the citation to Mrs. McMaster, I also handed her a seizure document attesting to what property of hers I had seized as evidence. With that, she just sadly shook her head and quietly asked to be excused as if she was going off to be alone and cry. She had been so nice the whole time, I did not fear that she was going to get a gun and cause me any further problems, so, I headed for the kitchen as she headed elsewhere into the back rooms of her house. Once in the kitchen, I put the remaining feathers, insides, body parts and whole bodies from the pigeons lying in the sink in a plastic garbage bag. Washing my hands, I gathered up my last sack of evidence and headed for the front door of the ranch house.

Approaching the front door, I heard Mrs. McMaster's soft voice hailing me from her hallway. Turning around, I was confronted by Mrs. McMaster who had since changed her clothing from jeans and a sweatshirt into a long blue house robe... Her hair had been let down from her earlier ponytail and it was now all brushed out. She now had on bright lipstick and its color framed a very 'special' kind of smile...

"Officer Grosz, can we settle this matter in another and more friendly way other than an expensive citation? One in which I won't have to drive all that way into town, go to court and yet can have all my canned pigeons back?" With those purring sounding words, she loosened the belt around her robe and let it fall to her sides revealing a long and slender leg when the robe partially opened after the belt had been untied and the flap pulled slightly back!

Realizing I was in a very touchy situation, I blurted out like a 13-year-old on his first 'sash-shay," "No, Ma'am, I have got to go," and whirled and stumbled my way out her front door and into my patrol car in what had to be a microsecond! Fumbling for my keys, it was all I could do in getting the engine started and getting the hell off her property and back onto the county road. Looking back in my rear view mirror as I pulled away, I could see Mrs. McMaster standing there demurely on her front porch with her robe flung wide open for the whole world to see the beauty she was... Almost as if that last piece of bait would drag me back into her lair and exchange a citation for, well you know... And let me tell all you readers out there, she looked a damn site better standing there demurely on her front porch than any of those plucked and canned seized pigeons that I had in the trunk of my patrol car!

Although needing some extra patrol help, Bill's district could go to 'hell in a hand basket' in that area of his district holding that pigeon shooter as far as I was concerned. That was the last time I took that road driving into that little almost hidden valley! If there were any bad guys **or gals** out that way, they could kill anything that suited their little hearts- desire as far as I was concerned...!

Bill later told me that Mrs. McMaster appeared in court and explained to the judge her living situation. The Justice Court Judge surprisingly lowered her fine from a previous $500.00 because of the severity of the violation to a mere $25.00! Then according to Bill, His Honor admonished her in open court for killing the state's scarce band-tailed pigeons during the closed season and later, because the judge had also known her husband, took the Lady out to lunch. Bill further advised that all the canned pigeons I had seized, were returned to Mrs. Mc Master after she and the judge had 'lunch' later that afternoon...

As for me, as this adventure is being put into words in 2015, I have been happily married for 52 years and counting to the same gal! Donna, my wife, is the love of my life and the light in my world. I will love her forever and a day. And, no amount of killing band-tailed pigeons during the closed season is ever going to get me to change that mind set...

As for the rest of the Flowers in this story, I kept mine...

As for the Tombstones in this adventure, there were plenty. As I explained the natural ramifications in earlier stories when wildlife is destroyed, statistically half of the 86 band-tailed pigeons Mrs. McMaster's had killed were females and the other half males. Those females, had they lived, would have produced 43 young of the year. That doesn't sound like much but to a species that only lays one egg per year and is already in trouble population and habitat wise, that loss is problematic. As is usually the case, there is more in that numerical loss than meets the casual eye. Especially when one factors in the overall loss of that species genetics, national, and natural heritage. Remember, folks, the eventual extinction of the fabled passenger pigeon, a flock of birds that went from billions in number to zero in a few short years, started initially with just a few pigeons being killed for food a long time ago by a hungry settler. As history has shown many times over, the road to extinction starts with just the first death of a species...

THE COAST GUARD SHOULD HAVE STAYED AT SEA

Towards the end of my most recent Klamath assignment, found Dog and me quietly sitting out of sight at the edge of an old logged off brushy clearing that was full of feeding deer. We had arrived long before daylight in an area in which I had scouted out the day before that was full of many good eating critters of interest. Sitting there hidden at the edge of that logged off area full of inviting rolling fat Columbian black-tailed deer and coveys of mountain quail (or Little Ones as I called them) waiting for any low-life poacher who just happened to wander by with an itching trigger finger, Dog and I quietly waited. My sitting there that morning in hiding brought to mind the comparison of a 'spider and his web' comparison. Across the canyon from where I lurked was another logged- off and cut over area that was also loaded with a ton of deer, blue grouse and several coveys of my much loved mountain quail. No matter how one looked at it, my temporary home was a perfect set-up for a game warden who was hunting the lawless. And believe you me, Humboldt and Del Norte Counties had more than their fair share of rank and file wildlife outlaws of the worst degree.

The day before while roaming or free-lancing the area looking for any folks doing to Mother Nature what they shouldn't be doing, I had observed a fair amount of suspicious looking activity in the geography I was currently sitting in. None of that human traffic previously observed in the area the day before appeared to be logging related. They just seemed to be the kind of those folks who were just suspiciously looking around, hence my patrolling effort that fair day so long ago in such a wildlife target rich environment.

For an hour, not another human heartbeat moved within my stake out area. Wearying of the lack of activity and bored over hearing no sounds other than my dog snoring loudly in the backseat of my patrol car, I headed out. Moving away from my initial stakeout area, I meandered into a complex series of old logging roads and abandoned railroad spurs used at one time to spirit out the heavy redwood logs to the nearby mills by narrow gage steam locomotives during the late 1800's.

I had not been moving through my new patrol area very long when I came upon an old, early fifties model Dodge four-door sedan. As I approached, I could make out a blue print over a white sticker proudly proclaiming "U.S. Coast Guard" plastered across its rear bumper. About then, that vehicle's passengers crawled up to the roadway from trout fishing in the canyon's stream located far below. As they walked to the rear of their vehicle, they appeared to be very interested in a recently spooked covey of quail landing all around them on the road. I made it a point to just slowly pass by, wave and kept on going. I did so because my sixth sense did not seem to be too interested in my three fishermen at that time, so I did not stop and do a fishing license check. Watching the men in my rear view mirror as I passed, I could see them ignoring my marked patrol car and just innocently preparing to leave.

Continuing to work the rather large area and seeing a lot of wildlife in those locations after the recent rainstorms, I decided that I would work the rest of that day on site and then return the next. Since the following day would be a Saturday, to a game warden's thought processes, that meant more people than usual would be out and about recreating or gathering up free firewood. When they were 'out and about' on a weekend, the better possibility existed that a goodly number would be up to no good. Especially in the remote outback I now occupied which was more than cloaked with wildlife and the other necessaries appreciated by any violator, namely isolation and remoteness from any other watching sets of eyes.

Come the following Saturday in the same area, other than observing two fishermen working the trout stream in the canyon below, most everything else was pretty quiet on my morning's patrol. That was except for the numerous coveys of mountain quail I had observed on the muddy roadways throughout the morning. The rains the day before had been pretty drenching. Even a day later, all the vegetation was still dripping like that from a nose with a bad cold. All the critters with feathers seemed to be moving out from under such wetting vegetation and into the open sunny areas to try to dry off. Anytime such wildlife is out in the open like they were that morning, they are potential targets for those who walk on the dark side in the world of wildlife.

That went double for the little quail because of their excellent eating qualities and their propensity to run down the road in plain view of an oncoming vehicle in closely grouped coveys. This the quail did because their feathers were so wet from recent rains, it was easier to run instead of trying to fly when spooked. To any run-of-the-mill outlaw, it is very hard to resist shooting into a mess of closely bunched, running-out-in-the-open-birds which, when ground-sluiced', provided an excellent opportunity for more than one kill per shot.

Around nine that the morning, I saw that same Dodge vehicle I had seen the day before with the Coast Guard sticker on its back bumper, pulling into the parking pull-off alongside the road it had occupied the day before. Three men exited the vehicle and walked back to the trunk of their car. Opening up the trunk, the men started getting out their fishing gear when one of the men noticed the two fishermen I had observed earlier fishing in the creek below. With that revelation, the men hesitated in getting out their fishing gear as they were in obvious discussion over the fact that the other two fishermen were already in their hoped-for fishing spot.

Then the crap hit the fan! A large covey of quail flew off the side hill above my three chaps and landed onto the road about ten yards in front of their car. What followed next caught me completely off guard. My three chaps crowded around the trunk of their car and the next thing I knew, they were all armed with shotguns and blasting away at my still bunched up little covey of quail in the middle of the road! Quail hunting season was closed and I happened to really love my Little Ones, the mountain quail! With that barrage of shooting, I could hear my dog stirring in the back seat of my patrol car as I focused in on my three shooters from a distance away with my spotting scope. Moments later, I could see all three men hurriedly picking up 18 quail they had just shot out of that large covey that had originally numbered about 30 birds!

Those damn knot-heads! I thought. *They just shot the heart out of that large covey and, being that it is spring, many of those birds those dopes just killed have to be breeders or already are nesting birds!*

Getting out my U.S. Forest Service map, I quickly laid it on the hood of my out of sight patrol car and located the road onto which sat my three illegal closed season quail shooters across the canyon from me. *Damn it,* I thought, *in order for me to catch those lads, I am going to have to backtrack about five miles to get back onto that road!* Where I now sat looking across the deep canyon separating my position and the road across the way was only about 800 yards. But to get over there would require me to backtrack several miles and then head down their particular road before I could put the snatch on my closed season quail shooters.

Swearing under my breath, I realized I also faced another hurdle. If I left my place of hiding now in front of God and everybody and headed down the road so I could collar my lads, I would be out in the open with an obviously marked game warden green patrol car. If they saw that, my lads could quickly disappear into the maze of logging roads webbed throughout that area they occupied before I could even get close to them. That would make any apprehensions regarding their closed season quail shoot problematic.

With that 'in plain view' circumstance in mind, there I sat like a big assed bullfrog on a lily pad with a large and hungry northern pike slowly circling the area. I then discovered that all was not lost with me not being able to burst from my place of hiding and pursuing my quail shooting culprits. Watching from my place of cover with the spotting scope, I saw my lads remove the rear seat from the back of their old Dodge sedan and appeared to place all their illegal quail under that seat. Then the rear seat with all the illegal quail was replaced as if nothing out of the ordinary had just happened. Following that, my lads piled into their sedan carrying their shotguns and headed out down their road at a slow rate of speed like they were looking for more exposed quail. No two ways about it, it now appeared they had forgotten all about going fishing and were on the hunt for any other closed season quail foolish enough to cross their paths. When I saw that, the hunt was now on in both of our worlds...

Once my quail-killing lads had driven out of my sight, yours truly hit the road like a whirl wind and down the road I went speeding along like the Roadrunner of TV cartoon series fame. Well, a rather large and most beautiful Roadrunner as most of my older and familiar readers out there have come to know me. Soon I was at the first set of cross roads. From there, I turned and headed back in the direction towards where I had last seen my illegal quail-shooting lads. Arriving somewhat later, I stopped at the site where my lads had shot into that first covey of grouped quail in the roadway and picked up their nine empty shot shells laying scattered about. Those went into the glove box of my car as future evidence and then I remounted my trusty 'metal stead'.

That turned out to be my last contact of any kind with my three quail shooters for hours. That was because my shooters had faded into an area that was a maze of forest service and private logging roads with their associated logging spurs like I had never seen before. I knew what I was looking for so the elimination process began of running out every road that I possibly could looking for my shooters. Brother, talk about muddy roads! How I wished for a four- wheel drive vehicle that day as I spun my way up one muddy logging road and down another. Frustrated over not finding my illegal quail shooters, I finally took to the time worn game warden trick of stopping and listening for the sounds of shooting. No such luck in that law enforcement 'tricks of the trade' maneuver either because of the vast mountainous sound-deadening environment I found myself in. Then it was back to thundering down every logging road I had not earlier traveled looking for my quail shooting chaps and getting more and more frustrated by the moment as I drew a big goose egg for my efforts.

A little after noontime, I was zipping along one forest service road that was so far back in the bush that all the chickens located in that area had square faces. It was then that I finally struck game warden 'gold' when it came to the success of my hunt. Barreling around a muddy turn, I saw a pair of fresh automobile tracks leading off the main road and onto an old, heavily overgrown logging spur. As I did, I just got a glimpse of what I thought was a silver 'flash' from a chrome bumper partially hidden in the dense temperate rainforest vegetation! Locking up the binders, I skidded to a stop that was so abrupt that it sailed Dog out from her spot of standing up in the back seat of the patrol car into the front seat! Snapping my patrol car around, I headed back until I was about 30 yards from the entrance to the suspect logging spur. Stopping, I got out, quietly shoved my door shut (an old game warden trick to avoid making any loud and unnatural sounding noises) and began walking back towards the logging spur's entrance and the mystery vehicle partially hidden therein.

Just as I got to the spur's entrance, I heard a vehicle's engine start up and, as I entered the densely wooded logging spur, I found myself confronted by an old Dodge sedan slowly exiting from its previous location. Stepping in front of the old Dodge, my eyes went to its bumper. There was a U.S. Coast Guard sticker on the front bumper that I had also seen the day before. Standing in the middle of that logging spur, I raised up my hand for the driver of that vehicle to stop. He did so and what a surprise registered all across not only his face but on the faces of his two passengers as well.

Once the driver had stopped, I walked over to his now open driver's side window and introduced myself even though I was in official uniform. That way, there would be no mistaking my identity and the purpose for making such an unorthodox stop out in the boondocks. During my greeting and salutation, my eyes quickly scanned the interior of their vehicle. There were two shotguns propped up in the front seat between the vehicle's two occupants and one propped up alongside the passenger occupying the rear seat. All three men appeared to be in their early to middle twenties and every one of them had a 'cat with a canary in his mouth' look smeared all across their faces.

"Gentlemen, starting with the driver, I would like you to hand me your individual shotguns, stock first, out the nearest window. Make damn sure when you do that the barrel is not pointing at you or your friend and you are keeping your fingers away from the triggers. Alright, Driver, hand me your shotgun first please." As he did, I watched my other two passengers for any furtive movements like they were trying to quietly remove a live round from the chambers of their shotguns. I also closely watched which way the barrel was pointing on any shotgun passed my way. I had been in situations before when the requested weapons had discharged inside the vehicle while going through such inspection drills. Let me tell you, that later requires a shorts cleaning out action when one of those smooth bore cannons goes off in such close confines as in a car and one is not expecting it.

Receiving and checking that first shotgun handed out to me, I found it to be loaded with a live round in the chamber! That gun was then laid with an open action upon the hood of the Dodge and then that checking action was repeated for each of the other passengers. In their two remaining cases, their shotguns were loaded with a live round in their chambers as well!

Now that I had control of the shotguns, I began my questioning. "Why the need for the loaded shotguns in a motor vehicle on a way open to the public in violation of the fish and game regulations?" I asked. They all fumbled around for answers and none came up with a plausible explanation. Now the looks on each man's face registered that they all had just developed a BAD case of the BIG EYE over the unfolding fish and game violation events at hand.

"You boys been hunting?" I asked. Denials were instant and in a flurry. You know, it is amazing the 'tells' one gives off when a violator's hind end is hanging out. "You boys sure you haven't been hunting?" I asked with my Walt Disney Cheshire cat all-knowing smile running from ear to ear.

"No, Sir," came a number of repeated responses. Well, to be truthful, they weren't really hunting. The word 'hunting' connotes fair chase and killing a species during the open season and it is certainly not fair chase when a protected critter is taken during the closed season.

Then the driver spoke up saying, "Sir, we all are with the U.S. Coast Guard. They don't allow us to break any kind of laws. If we do and our commanding officer finds out, we will be cleaning toilets on board our ship for the next month. They really want all of us to realize the Coast Guard stands for community service and that includes not breaking any laws." With those words, I noticed that the driver was now beginning to sweat like the proverbial southern Baptist preacher at election time.

Then I switched horses mid-stream and went to one of my sure-fire, old faithful tricks of the trade taught to me by my friend and long- time Arcata warden, John Finnigan. A trick of the trade that when properly applied, always brought forth the 'violator's' gold. Especially since I had observed my wildlife outlaws hiding their illegal mountain quail earlier in the morning under their vehicle's back seat. "Say, Boys, I swear I can smell the bodies of dead quail. Can't you guys smell what I am smelling?" I asked all innocent like. I had used that 'I can smell dead game' trick a number of times during my short career and it was amazing what results it could engender from guilty culprits. That 'trick' when used also provided a good learning lesson to 'outlaws in training' when it came to understanding just how good a game warden's nose really is when around dead, illegally taken critters.

Immediately a flurry of denials of 'utter seriousness' regarding the smell of dead quail fluttered through the air like leaves in the autumn from an aspen thicket during a strong breeze. I just had to grin inside knowing what was coming next in this outlaw roundup. I knew I had my quail-shooting chaps and was now just going to make them sweat and remember this moment for the rest of their evil lives. If they were going to shoot my Little Ones, then they were going to have to pay the piper. And, that 'piper' was soon coming in the strangest of configurations.

"Are you guys sure you haven't killed anything illegally today," I stridently asked in an offhanded and semi-accusatory tone. All I received was a chorus of weak-kneed verbal denials. You know, my readers, people are truly amazing sometimes. They think we game warden types are stupid when in reality, good game wardens do this kind of thing every day, all of their lives. In just about every case, we know when you are 'telegraphing' and we generally can figure out where you are hiding the evidence of your guilt. That is because we have been through this drill a million times before.

As an aside, it always used to tickle me upon discovering the over limits of fish or ducks in a toilet bowl in an RV during a roadblock and the looks of surprise on the suspects' faces once that fact was seeing the light of day. They would be so amazed over how we discovered the over limits in the toilet bowl thinking we would never look in such a smelly damn place. Or, when it came to finding the extra deer in the shower of the RV or in a sleeping bag on a bed in the RV's bedroom. Well, it is because we have found such items a million times there before stashed in such wonderful places on the likes of campers and other types of recreational vehicles.

"Well, I will tell you what, Boys. If you have any illegal game in this vehicle, you had best give it up. If I find any, your commanding officer will be the first to hear about it," I said in my most terrifying sounding voice. Now remember, my readers, I had observed my lads earlier illegally killing and then stashing a mess of mountain quail up under their back seat on the old model car that they were now occupying. The seat had since been replaced and no one was any the wiser except God, the One who had created all the critters and the game warden who had been given the job by God to protect those Little Ones without a voice.

"Honest, Mister. We just came out to target practice and find a good place to go fishing," continued the driver. He was the man whom I now took for the leader of this Coast Guard assembly and was named John Gibbons as I was soon to discover.

"Are all of you sure?" I asked, "because the smell of dead quail is really strong in your car." I continued that line of questioning trying hard not to laugh over the funny I was now playing on my three trigger-happy, outlaw, closed season quail shooters, but it took all I had to keep a straight face in so doing.

"No, Sir. Maybe that is the smell of my aftershave," hopefully retorted Gibbons. You know, folks, John Gibbons was sounding just like I would expect to hear coming from an outlaw under like circumstances. He was displaying the time worn fact that even a drowning man will grab for a sharpened spear when it is thrown directly at him under like circumstances.

"All right you guys. Everyone out so I can search for any quail in the car. I know my nose does not lie so I need to search your car anyway," I responded now thoroughly enjoying my little, nose like a bloodhound charade.

My lads all happily bailed out from their car, confident in their knowledge that they had hidden the dead quail taken earlier up under the springs in their back seat of their car. They just knew that the quail would never be found out or discovered by anyone once hidden in such a fashion. And sure as hell upon inspection and for another 'learning reason,' I didn't find any quail. For reasons known only to me, I purposely didn't look under the back seat of their vehicle during my first inspection.

"Well, Guys, I guess you were right. But just to make sure, are all of you positive there are no quail in your car? Because sure as hell is a hot place in which to linger, I can smell dead quail," I advised rather forcefully. Their negative assurances to my question flowed like water in a fast flowing brook after they thought I had struck out in my search. "Well, may I have a look in your trunk?" I asked, full- well knowing no quail would be there either and did so just to drag out the suspense. In short, I was just continuing to put constant pressure on my three quail shooters for the learning lesson that was yet to follow.

"Absolutely, Officer," said the driver as he fumbled for his car keys and then dropped them into the mud in his hurry just to show me I was wrong. Opening the trunk as I already knew, there were no quail there. Just a mess of hip boots, fishing poles and other related fishing gear laid all jumbled up in the trunk of their car.

"See, Officer, we were just looking for a good place to fish and a place to target practice. Nothing more, nothing less," said the driver and suspected ringleader, now starting to get a bit of the smart mouth and the 'I told you so' type of smirking attitude.

"O.K., guys. You have one last chance to come clean. I still can smell the dead quail. This is your last chance to drag them out or else," I said with my now most serious sounding voice. Damn, I was sure enjoying this moment knowing what was coming next. (All you readers out there, remember my earlier warning about paying the piper? Well, some pipers have four legs and a long tail don't they?)

"Officer, I don't mean to be a hard ass but why are you harassing us. We told you we don't have any illegal game in the car. You yourself have looked all over in our vehicle and have found nothing but a suspected dead bird smell. And personally, I think you need to check your 'smeller' at the door next time you search a vehicle. I think I would like your badge number and the name of your supervisor so we can call him and complain about what is happening here," said my now getting really mouthy ringleader and driver, one John Gibbons. In the meantime, his other two friends in crime said nothing. They just kept their mouths shut hoping I would go away. Was that another 'tell' , my loyal readers or, was this just the start of the much needed learning lesson sinking in?

"Well, you know my name and my badge number is here on my badge fastened to my shirt. You can take the badge number from it if you like and call my captain. But before you do, you have one more time to come clean regarding those illegal quail I keep smelling. Are you interested in doing the right thing and digging them out for me?" I asked.

"Nope! Just like I said, we are clean. Now let me have that badge number so I can call your captain and let him know just how unprofessional you have been. Sure, we had loaded guns. But, that doesn't give you the right to badger us over a mess of non-existent quail you claim we have in our car," sharply advised the driver while his two cohorts remained as silent as a field mouse in a tomb.

"O.K.," I said. "Now we shall see." With that, I gave a low whistle and could faintly hear toenails clicking on the sides of my patrol car parked out of sight as Dog bailed out the open back-passenger door window and came a-barreling my way. When Dog turned the corner on that logging spur, you should have seen the faces of my outlaws. It looked like a shark had just bitten off some very special private parts from each of the killers of my Little Ones.

Shadow ran to my right side and, as trained, immediately sat down. "Find the duck," I said which was her normal command for finding any game and off she went. Running through the open back doors of the old Dodge, she took a couple of sniffs and then immediately stopped. With that and another quick smell, she looked back at me as her tail wagged like crazy!

"Well, Boys, Dog tells me the quail I have been smelling are under the rear seat. Do you want to get them out for me or do I have to call a wrecker and have your car towed all the way back to Crescent City and then have them tear out the seat after I get a warrant (which I didn't need)"? I casually asked, knowing all I had to do was lift up the seat to get at the quail. But the threat of a potentially expensive towing job dropped on a few 'poor as church mice' Coast Guard Seamen who made very little money, had the desired humbling effect I was looking for. Plus in the process, I would be able to drive home a damn good lesson when it came to not being truthful to an officer of the law.

As expected, all I saw were all eyeballs and hind ends flying towards the backseat of the old car as Shadow exited and soon I had 33 freshly killed quail laid at my feet. Not only did I have their original kill numbers but it seemed others they had killed along the way after they had left the first kill site earlier in the morning.

An hour later after issuing citations to each man for possessing a loaded shotgun in a motor vehicle on a way open to the public, for taking a protected game bird, To Wit: quail during the closed season and for jointly possessing 33 quail during the closed season, the citation paperwork was finished. Then each man was presented with a seizure tag for the quail and each man's shotgun was seized. Talk about long, hang-dog' faces present on each man's face! John Gibbons, David

Olmstead and Darrell Whitaker, U.S. Coast Guard Seamen stationed at the U.S. Coast Guard facility at Requa, California, all had the look of seasick lads riding on a destroyer in a Type 8 Typhoon in the South Pacific.

Finished with my lads and they having no questions other than would their commanding officer discover they had been apprehended and cited into court for closed season fish and game violations, I let the lads hurry on their way. But as I was soon to discover, my day with one of the quail-killing lads was not yet over. Not by a long shot, no pun intended...

About three in the afternoon, the sheriff's office in Klamath called me on the fish and game frequency. They requested that I call Warden Williams by landline as soon as possible. Being still back in the bush on patrol and before we all carried a pocketful of cellular phones, I hustled off the mountain and back to the nearest form of civilization. Stopping off at the first gas station I ran across, I called Bill on the telephone. When I did, I got a pleasant surprise. It seems Bill had received recent information of a fish and game violation from a neighbor who lived across the street from John Gibbons. You know, my Coast Guard quail killing Seaman, who lived in the small northwest town of Requa.

Apparently, when John had gotten off the mountain after having been ticketed by me for the illegal take and possession of closed season quail, had shot two quail in his front yard in front of his neighbor. John picked up the birds just closed season shot and as he was walking back to his house with the two quail, upon seeing his neighbor intently looking askance at him, John had told him, "Mind your own business!"

Whereupon, Gibbon's neighbor had called his local game warden, namely Bill Williams with that information. Bill, still too sick to work, in turn had called the sheriff's office and asked them to raise me on the fish and game radio. And in so doing, ask me to land line the Klamath warden. In that subsequent conversation, Bill briefed me regarding what his informant had told him about John Gibbons killing the quail in front of the informant during the closed season. I could not believe what I was hearing! Here just hours earlier, I had written that same chap for doing the same thing, namely taking quail during the closed season. Now my sea going lad was at it again!

Hustling into town and meeting the neighbor at a gas station away from the house of the shooter, I listened to his story and had him write down what he had seen in my notebook. Then I beat a hasty retreat over to the county attorney and filled out an affidavit for a search warrant on the John Gibbons' residence. The county attorney reviewed my affidavit, signed off on it, and off I went to the nearest local judge. There the judge examined my affidavit, asked me a few questions regarding the address of the residence to be searched in the warrant and then signed off on my warrant. With that, off I went to see John Gibbons before something happened to my two evidence quail.

Arriving at John's Klamath River riverside rental with a search warrant to search his home, I knocked on the door of my earlier Dodge car driver, the one's vehicle that had held the 33 illegal quail hidden underneath the back seat. Now I was looking for the two quail the neighbor had observed John killing in his front yard earlier in the afternoon. When John opened the door, I gave him the surprise of his young life when I served him with the search warrant enabling me to look for the two quail. Suffice to say, John had a fit! After he got over 'pissing down his leg,' or so I thought, I was admitted to his home and the search began since John had once again denied any wrongdoing.

For the next two hours, I tore his house completely apart looking for those two evidence quail. No quail could I locate no matter how hard I looked! No guts, feathers or carcasses anywhere to be seized, was my reward for all my search efforts. I was dumbfounded to say the least over my lack of success in my search! I had searched all his garbage cans, his kitchen, garage, his car parked in the garage, brought Shadow into his home to search for the illegal quail, all with no success.

Finally coming back to John's kitchen, there he sat. Knowing I had found nothing that I was looking for under the authorization of the warrant, he sat there at his kitchen table and just smirked.

"Well, Asshole. How about leaving so I can shower, eat my dinner and get on with my shift at the Coast Guard station?" said John with an obvious smirk in the tone and tenor of his voice.

Damn it, I thought. I had searched everywhere! I had even checked out John's dinner cooking away on the stove. On that stove he had a pan of freshly baked cornbread he had just removed from his oven, immediately after I had walked into his kitchen and served the warrant. He had a cooking pot full of ham and beans simmering away on the stovetop as well. However, I found no quail anywhere. I knew if he had killed a pair of quail in his yard, he more than likely had not tossed them away. But by damn, I had looked everywhere even under his bead, in the shower, under his sinks, in his washer and dryer, refrigerator, in the toilet, in all the kitchen drawers, throughout his car and garage again, under his couch and the like. No luck on my part did I have in finding the damning evidence. Evidence of the two dead quail that I needed in order to file additional charges against John without having to bring the informant in to testify against John as to what he had observed. (Keep in mind my readers, it is never a good practice to involve your informants unless you absolutely have to. Keep exposing your informants unnecessarily to testifying in a court of law and soon you will discover that you have no more informants stepping forward to give you a helping hand in catching outlaws.)

Foiled, I stopped in his kitchen only to face an overly smirking John with a few more biting comments. "Well, Asshole. Since you can't find anything, you can get the hell out of my house and if you ever come back, you and the governor of this state will hear about it!"

Pissed off by an obvious hind end, mad at myself over not discovering any evidence of the crime and because my guardian angels were still fluttering around inside me telling me I was 'hot on the trail', I was now being forced to leave. My Teutonic magnificence had met its match and I had been foiled in my endeavor even with a warrant in hand. DAMN! Starting to exit John's kitchen just as he filled his soup bowl with a big scoop of beans and ham, I stopped dead in my tracks. Taking another moment, I ran the entire search scenario through my memory banks looking for any over looked clues. As I did, John sat his bowl down on the kitchen table and went over to cut out a piece of cornbread from the baking pan sitting cooling on the stovetop. That piece of cornbread he took over to the kitchen table and his bowl of beans and they stood looking at me.

"Well, what are you waiting for? I have no plans on inviting you to dinner. Get your ass out of my house and don't ever come back," he snarled just like any outlaw hind end would do when he felt he had the upper hand in a bad situation that he had created.

Then a smile of memory-realization slowly crossed over my face. Approaching John's front door earlier in the afternoon with the warrant, I had to walk up a long walkway to get there. Just for an instant, I thought I had seen a flash of John's face watching me approaching his home through his front door's window curtain. Seconds later, his face disappeared as fast as it had appeared. Getting to the front door, I had observed John through the window pulling out and checking a pan of cornbread from his oven. Then after John answered my knock at the door, I again identified myself and served the warrant. When I had initially walked in after announcing I had a warrant to serve and began doing so, John, after glancing at his copy of the warrant, laid it down on his kitchen table then casually walked back to his stove. There he took out the hot pan of cornbread he was checking when I had knocked on his door and placed it onto the stovetop to cool. With that, he turned off his oven. Then he walked back to his kitchen table and just sat down in apparent resignation over the legal actions taking place. From there while I searched everywhere, he had not moved. Now my guardian angels were really flitting around inside me as my memory revisited the scene sifting for any detail I had inadvertently over looked.

Without a word, since my warrant and the authority to search was still valid and my recall memory was working overtime, I walked across the kitchen to the stove/oven complex. As I did, I noticed that John's eyes never left me or the direction in which I was moving for a single moment. John watched me like a red-tailed hawk would do a prairie dog about dinnertime. Stooping over, I opened the oven door. There sitting in a pan of water sat two completely cleaned quail with all their feathers and guts lying off to one side in the pan! Turning, I just looked at John. Have any of you ever seen what a deer mouse looks like when it is being confronted by a long tailed weasel from just two feet away? That had to be the look on John's face the very instant of my quail-in-the-oven discovery.

Apparently, John had identified me coming up his long walkway and, suspecting my mission, had grabbed the pan of cleaned quail, feathers and entrails out from the sink and shoved it into the hot oven still cooking the pan of cornbread. Then he answered the door as I came knocking. When I had walked in, John, after reading the scope of the warrant, excused himself, calmly walked over to the oven and, standing in front of the now open door shielding it with his body, had removed his freshly baked pan of cornbread and sat it on top of the stove to cool. Then he shut the oven door and turned off the oven. That was why I had never looked in the oven. Why should I? He had just removed a pan of freshly baked goods from it and casually walked away after placing the baked item on the stovetop to cool. Since I couldn't see into the oven because his body had blocked my view and it had a solid front door (no window), I found no reason to look into a hot and just vacated oven for any freshly killed quail since it obviously in the instant case, had been baking a pan of cornbread.

Boy, did I ever learn a lesson there. So did John. I later booked him since he had not learned a damn thing about killing quail during the closed season. I guess one could say, I also booked him because he had taught me a damn good lesson about thinking outside the box.

My two quail killers, Darrell Whitaker and David Olmstead, each paid $400.00 for their closed quail season hunt and for possessing loaded shotguns in a motor vehicle on a way open to the public violations. John Gibbons also paid $400.00 for the first set of citations I had issued him and an additional $500.00 for the second two quail he had taken in front of his neighbor. His neighbor was a man who also liked the Little Ones, especially the two John had shot. As it turned out, that same pair of quail who had been peacefully nesting in the neighbor's yard and had been much loved by the man. And when John intentionally killed those quail in front of the man during the closed season, he 'saw red'! As it turned out, the same two quail I had discovered hidden in a pan in the still cooling oven.

A subsequent trip to John's commanding officer introduced to him what kind of a chap John's character represented in my eyes over the day's series of criminal events. Somehow, I forgot to mention to the commanding officer David's and Darrell's involvement in the illegal quail shoot since I figured they had learned a good enough lesson from their experience and needed no more punishment. Besides, cleaning the toilets on board a 110-foot Coast Guard Cutter, only required the labors of one man and I had just the man the Coast Guard needed for such important duties…

After that lesson, I figured my three closed season quail shooters of U.S. Coast Guard flavor and fame, probably should have stuck to riding the waves instead of tangling horns with a game warden land lubber who had a penchant for seasickness. But to put the whole episode into U.S. Coast Guard perspective, shoot my Little Ones and you are in for a Type 8 Typhoon if I am close at hand, have my druthers, AND CONDUCT A DAMN GOOD AND THOROUGH SEARCH IN THE PROCESS…

For the Flowers in this story, there are a few. Hopefully, my three closed season quail killers learned a damn good lesson. I was pretty sure John had when it was all said and done. Especially when it came to his overall fine of $900.00 dollars which would take a few months to pay off on a Seaman's lowly salary in those days. That plus the '10,000' toilets he had to clean during those two months of 'swabby' duty on board his coast guard rescue/patrol vessel, surely added to that lesson learned… As for me, I had learned a hard lesson that went on to serve me well over the next thirty years of state and federal wildlife law enforcement service. Never quit on any kind of a law enforcement detail and always think outside of the box were my lessons for the day. I learned and I carried that Flower throughout the rest of my career. Suffice to say, I learned it well and a number of outlaws paid the price thanks to a lesson learned from one quail-killing son-of-a-gun named John Gibbons early on in my career…

The last Flower in the bunch went to the kids of California. Since I had seized my quail shooters' shotguns, they were ordered forfeited by the court and ultimately went into the National Rifle Association's initiated hunter safety training programs for the aspiring hunters of tomorrow. A hunter safety training program that teaches sportsmanship, firearms safety and sports afield ethics. Not a bad return, I must say, for an original bad act on the part of my quail shooters.

As for the Tombstones in this adventure, they were there as well. Statistically, 16 of the 33 dead quail seized were females. Had they lived, each of those 16 females would have produced anywhere from 5-15 eggs and young. Multiply those numbers by the number of birds killed and you get the idea of the real loss that occurred. Taking it one step further, multiply the probable 150 young quail produced in that first nesting season by the following years' nesting success numbers and one can see just how fast an animal population can recover or... decline. A little loss here and there is all it takes sometimes in the world of wildlife for **extinction** to rear its ugly head.

I know I have mentioned this before but, the last Tombstone in this story was my friend, Bill. He never recovered from his cancer. I lost a good friend and the world of wildlife lost a hard working officer who was always there for the critters, all of the time. That was evidenced by his working for those 'voiceless ones' right up to the last few days just before the Grim Reaper stepped in and did what he does best... Rest in peace, my friend, for many of your teachings were carried forth by me over the next three decades in the fight for those without a voice. I only hope I did you proud.

I continue to mention the loss of good wildlife officers related to these stories because I want all my readers out there to realize the value of those lost ones and what they were fighting for against such overwhelming odds that the Creator threw our way on a daily basis. Sometimes those odds do not just relate to the critters in the world of wildlife but to those defenders of the voiceless ones as well. Remember folks, **extinction** cuts both ways. It just depends upon the sharpness and the placement of the 'blade of life'...

Hence the many times I remind my readers in these adventure stories of the 'badge carrying' loss of humanity who served you folks and yours so ably and well. Look at any wildlife officer who has made it to his or her retirement and now you no longer have to ask yourselves why that officer walks with a limp or with bent and stooped shoulders shoulders. It is because while many of you were sleeping, he or she was not...

When you sing your song of death, sing it as if you are coming home...

Chapter Five: The Sacramento Valley's Outlaws' Horn of Plenty

THE COLSA DISTRICT, MEMORIES AND MILESTONES

In the early summer of 1967, I transferred from the Region I North Coast fish and game squad under Captain Walter L. Gray into the Region II Sacramento Valley squad under Captain James Leamon. In short, I transferred sight unseen into a new district in order to be out from under my drunken and alcoholic fish and game captain in Eureka. My new duty station was located in the northern Sacramento Valley town of Colusa, California. Not knowing the particulars of the town and surrounding area, I soon came to understand that my new duty station was located in the heart of the northern Sacramento Valley's agricultural country. Driving through some of its rich rice country travelling to my new duty station, my law enforcement and wildlife management mind began to wander and race before I even got my feet on the ground.

Being an academically trained wildlife biologist with my major interest of study on waterfowl management, I could see problem war clouds forming on my new law enforcement horizon as I drove through acres and acres of beautiful rice country in route my new duty station. It was simple math when it came to knowing what would be some of the first wildlife management issues I was soon to encounter. Ducks and geese historically wintered in the Sacramento Valley by the millions in those days and they loved to eat rice. Even as I drove into my new district, I began reviewing my memory banks to ascertain what agency management measures needed to be instituted to alleviate what portended to be a massive waterfowl rice depredation and public relations problem between 'farmer and fowl'.

In those days, a farmer needed a federal migratory bird depredation permit in order to begin herding depredating waterfowl off his crops. That required a state game warden to visit every complaining rice farmer, examine his crop damage and then issue the federal permit so he could legally chase the offending feeding waterfowl off his croplands. Being that game wardens were routinely extremely busy with just their criminal enforcement responsibilities and terribly limited on the ground numbers, I could see that I would soon be so busy in my new district that I wouldn't be sure 'if I had found a rope or had lost my horse'....

I recalled that the U.S. Government early on had established four national wildlife refuges running strategically down through the center of the northern Sacramento Valley. This they had done to lure the millions of historically wintering hungry waterfowl onto those refuge lands instead of having them sallying forth into the adjacent rice fields and eating those farmers out of house and home. That noble effort of refuge placement may have just had the opposite effect to my budding initial way of thinking as I continued through thousands of acres of brilliant green colored rice country. The placement of those refuges gave millions of migrating waterfowl a safe place to gather and rest in the heart of the rice country! As those ducks and geese ate out the refuges and as newly arriving, hungry winter migrants continued adding into the Valley's already tremendous waterfowl numbers, into the adjacent unharvested rice fields to feed during daylight and darkness the winged critters could choose to descend. As I was soon to discover, wintering waterfowl would begin arriving in August into the Sacramento Valley, weeks before the rice had been harvested.

For the rice farmers, it was a race against time to get their crops harvested before the hungry masses of waterfowl ate out their refuges and then streamed off from those sanctuaries into the adjacent croplands to feed. Man, before I even physically got to my new duty station, my hair was almost standing straight up over the anticipated waterfowl versus dirt farmer encounters I would soon be facing. There goes that 'rope and horse thing' again that I mentioned earlier when it came to being so busy one did not know if he was afoot or on horseback.

Putting those potentially time consuming depredation issues aside for the moment, I discovered that Colusa County is approximately 1,200 square miles in size. My newly assigned fish and game patrol district encompassed the northern half of that county and was approximately 600 square miles in size. My district was not very large size wise in comparison to some others in the state but was extremely resource rich and because of those resources, would be terribly wildlife-protection busy in both scope and degree. Geographically speaking, my new district ran from the mountainous region in the western portion of the county to the vast and rich Sacramento Valley farmlands and orchards in the eastern half. In short, there was enough potential wildlife law enforcement opportunity for even the most energetic game warden to enjoy.

The mountainous region of my district as I was soon to discover, was dry, hot and timbered with conifers in the higher elevations. Understanding my ecosystem layouts and their general wildlife species' distribution patterns, the mountainous portion of my new district would be home to the tule elk (the smallest of North America's three elk species), California mule deer, black bear, mountain lions, mourning dove, a few band-tailed pigeons, increasing populations of feral hogs, some rainbow trout in the high country and a few recently introduced wild turkeys. I would soon come to learn, that there was plenty enough wildlife to keep even the laziest game warden hopping when it came to wildlife law enforcement.

The Sacramento Valley portion of my new district, according to my college studies and other information I had previously gleaned, was simply a "Horn of Plenty". That was especially so when it came to the world of wildlife and the sporting and recreational opportunities the area offered for sportsmen and women of all shapes, sizes and flavors. As I was soon to discover and much to my surprise, that eastern area of my law enforcement district sported monster sized California mule deer because of all the available great eats and favorable habitat. However, monster mule deer and their related illegal gunning issues aside, I would soon to be confronted with the specter of historically wintering flocks of ducks, geese and swans by the millions and a plethora of gunners to match! When it came to enforcement problems, sliding into second place behind my waterfowl issues were the many thousands of Chinese ring-necked pheasants calling the Sacramento Valley home. If all of the above mentioned wildlife and enforcement issues were not enough headache generators, I also had California valley quail by the many secretive coveys underfoot, the graceful little mourning dove throughout the district, wintering sandhill cranes by the thousands, bull frogs by the gunny sacks full, scads of warm water game fish in every drop of water scattered throughout, a river full of striped bass, white and green sturgeon, salmon and every other kind of creepy crawler and finny critter in between! As I described earlier, the Sacramento Valley was a Horn of Plenty, that many times had the potential to be interlaced with a Bed of Thorns when it came to related wildlife law enforcement issues.

Little did I realize at my first blush, that associated with all those natural resources was a world of dedicated, born and breed in the valley, wildlife outlaws that would put all of those in that historical category of 'Bad Men of the Old West' to shame! Oh, I had heard the whispers from many of my counterparts about the lawlessness that historically abounded in the Sacramento Valley in the fall and winter months with the waterfowl and pheasant populations. However, they were just whispers and I was young and innocent when it came to the actual reality of the Valley's lawless history. And in those whispers, no one said anything about all those enforcement problems associated with the warm water game fishery, the mobs associated with pheasant season, the problems associated with all the fishermen on the Sacramento River, the over limit problems associated with the local bull frog populations and on it went... However, my education as to all of those potential wildlife related law enforcement issues would soon be heading my way.

Since the days of California's occupation by the Native Americans, Mexicans, Spanish, Mountain Men, European pioneers, and the gold rush crowd of '49', the Sacramento Valley's resources were the 'go to' place for subsistence. As California's populations explosively spread into every nook and cranny, so did their demands, both legally and illegally, for the many and varied resources found in that Horn of Plenty. Historically, as the protein starved peoples' appetites from the rapidly developing cities and state dictated, the stain of commercial market hunting reared its ugly head. All manners of fish, millions of ducks and geese, deer by the gross, and bales of hides from endemic furbearers soon flooded into and graced the big cities' market places. That predilection to supply the demanding food- hungry markets and the monetary gain it supplied, persisted from the 1700's until the late 1960's in its many evil forms. Into that caldron of historic folkways, mores and mind-sets, stumbled one still learning, green as a gourd, game warden with all his warts, hopes, dreams and desires. Poor old Mother Nature, if she had only realized the kind of chap she had been saddled with as her new Sacramento Valley 'Sword for Mother Nature'.

Finally arriving in Colusa, I found the usual problems associated with a duty station change when moving into a small community. The town of Colusa was small and the availability of housing was an issue right off the bat. In short, there weren't any reasonable housing accommodations available. Well, I can't really say that. There was ONE house available for rent for my family and its last occupants appeared to be a flock of Rhode Island Red chickens! That place was so bad, that it even had living plants growing through the walls into the living quarters! But it was a roof over our heads and my great little wife put on her best face and made the most of it as she always did.

(That is one of the wonderful things in life. If one marries well, he or she can weather most any of the storms that roll across one's threshold. And in the case of my marriage, hell, with the great little wife I had, I could have weathered a Type 8 Typhoon. In fact, just weeks later my wife had landed a teaching job as an elementary school teacher in the small town of Williams located ten miles west of our 'chicken hutch' home in Colusa. How was that for working through the crazy life as a game warden's wife in a small town and landing on her feet in fine style?)

Then it was off to inventory the fish and game equipment left to me by my predecessor. The game warden who had preceded me in my part of the county's fish and game law enforcement district was a chap named C. J. Winn. As I quickly discovered, he was a legend before his time and, what a legend he was. Many of the people in the county I later came into contact with, had laughingly nick named him "Feather Foot" for his lack of adroitness 'afoot or on horseback'! From what I could tell from all the derisive stories about him, Winn had a predilection for not only being a noisy, loud, bumbler but not necessarily very light of foot and somewhat clumsy. But what the hell did I know? After all, folks were entitled to their opinions. Well, I was soon to find out my new neighbors were pretty damn astute when it came to judging human nature, especially those wearing 'the game warden greens'.

Driving down to the local sheriff's office to retrieve my assigned patrol vehicle where Winn had left it stored when he had moved on to another duty station, I was amazed at what I saw. Sitting forlornly in the parking lot sat an old Dodge two-wheel drive pickup. One that had surely seen better days. Its right front fender had a large dent in it advertising that it had met something tougher than it was. The vehicle was filthy both inside and out and further checking revealed that the oil had not been changed in the last 12,000 miles! That was in the day when one religiously changed the oil in their vehicles every 3,000 miles. All four tires were well worn, semi-flat and needed replacing, including the two with bulges in their sidewalls. The rear bumper was wired up on one side so it would not drag in the dirt and poorly done at that. Starting up my new patrol truck, I discovered it ran as quietly as an old fashioned thrashing machine in the grain fields of North Dakota.

Realizing that vehicle would be my home on wheels and lifeline until it was replaced sometime in the future, down to Joe Willow's Garage I went for a health care checkup on my new patrol truck. In so doing, I discovered the truck needed an engine tune up, oil change, radiator flush, lube, fluid changes in the transmission and rear end, and a new set of tires along with a front end alignment. Inspecting the undercarriage while the truck was up on the grease rack, I discovered additional signs of gross neglect and misuse. A number of the welds in the frame were busted loose signifying that the truck had been abused numerous times when it came to running over immovable objects like large rocks. Imagine that, busted welds on the frame and a number of them at that! As for my truck's muffler, it was wired to the frame and had long ago burned itself out. Now I was beginning to understand why the folks I had met so far were rolling their eyes when I was introduced as the new game warden replacing C. J. Winn. I could just imagine what many of the good people of Colusa County I had just met were thinking of me. My thoughts ran to: *Oh, no. Here is another one of those fish and game jerks, only this one is big enough to eat hay and pull a wagon.*

But that wasn't the worst part when it came to the equipment department. I was also aware that I had a patrol boat that was to be shared with the county's other newly assigned game warden who was to patrol the southern half of the county. Between the two of us, we had the mighty Sacramento River running through part of our districts to patrol and check numerous stripped bass, salmon and sturgeon fishermen when those species of fish were migrating in the river.

So, down to the local marina I went to inspect my Sacramento River patrol boat. Brother, what a surprise I got upon my arrival. There moored to the marina docks was a tired and dirty looking boat. It was a Chrysler 18-foot inboard/outboard with an 8-foot beam and it was about half-sunken alongside the marina dock! Stepping aboard into about eight inches of standing putrid algae-green looking water, I tried to see if I could pump the bilges on the half-sunken, rainwater- filled boat. However, the battery was as dead as a river rock. With a new battery borrowed from Don, the marina owner, who by that time was clucking his tongue over the state's mistreatment of a perfectly good boat, I managed to pump the bilges dry. Starting the engine, I discovered the plugs were badly fouled and needed changing. By the time I had purchased new marine spark plugs and changed out the old ones, it was almost dusk. But, I now had the vessel up and running as it now continued charging up its own battery. Other than that and it being dirty as all get out, the State of California finally had a naval presence once again on the Sacramento River. That was, once I had replaced the old, badly damaged propeller with a new stainless steel one.

With those small details taken care of, off I went to meet the local law enforcement community. Starting with the sheriff's office, I introduced myself and quickly discovered I had an outstanding group of officers to work with. From the old sheriff, Alva Leverett, on down, I had a bunch of topnotch professionals with which to work and depend upon. That initial assessment of the officers was validated later with sterling back-up performances by such deputies as Fred Pilgrim, Delbert Garrison, Peter Grieve, Ray Murillo, Carter Bowman, and Del Nannen among others.

Then it was off to meet those officers in Colusa's small police department. Once again, I was not disappointed. Chief Oliver was a down to earth sort of chap and I liked him right off the bat. He advised that I had a tough job as a game warden ahead of me because of the county's ugly past history involving commercial market hunting and duck dragging (illegal duck shooting at night into the feeding masses of ducks on the harvested rice fields). A number of its hard case outlaws, according to Bill, had previously been apprehended and had even been sentenced to federal prison for their waterfowl related violations. A number of which were doing 'hard time' for felony sale of migratory game birds, which had left bad tastes in some of the convicted outlaws' mouths and a continuing meanness of mindset and spirit when it came to interactions with the wildlife law enforcement officers. Chief Oliver made it very clear that if I ever needed a backup no matter where I was in the county, his officers would stand ready to leave the town's city limits and roll to my aid. Some of the best of those officers who came to my aid several times were Officers Eloy Zaragoza and Ken Kagehiro. A man can't beat that kind of assistance when one realizes wildlife officers have a mortality rate that is nine times higher than the next class of law enforcement officers in the United States! And those statistics are not mine but from the files of the Federal Bureau of Investigation!

The next day it was off to meet the other part of my new legal community. Meeting with the county's district attorney left me not impressed. The Colusa County attorney, to my way of thinking, was a standing invertebrate. I did not get a good feeling about that man's 'amount of sand' if and when it came to a tough legal fight with some of the county's most politically influential people or notorious wildlife outlaws. That became even more apparent if and when that county attorney had to deal with one 'crackerjack' defense attorney in the county with an aggressive and winning reputation. As for his assistants, most looked like they had yet to shave. And as for the young assistants' practiced experience levels in the courtroom's legal traces, well, that too left something to be desired...

Then it was off to meet with the judge located in the town of Colusa. Judge Weyand was a kindly old gentleman whose office was staffed with two outstanding cracker-jack court clerks. One of those clerk's I liked right off the bat. Court Clerk Bonnie Grussenmeyer was open and welcoming with a genuine smile to match. With a wink and a nod, she told me to always come to her if I needed any advice on how to work with the sometimes cantankerous old judge on any legal issues. From my time in the county from 1967 until I went to work with for U.S. Fish and Wildlife Service in the spring of 1970 and began using the Federal Court systems, I found Bonnie to be not only an excellent court clerk but a great friend. We are still great friends as of 2015 when these words were written. My meeting with the judge went as was expected. Judge Weyand was quiet and respectful during that meeting and gave me some advice on what he expected of his officers. Then we both split for previously planned meetings

Next, I went to meet my other judge in the small town of Williams on the western side of my patrol district. I first met the court clerk, a young lady nicknamed 'Tinker'. What a great little gal she was. Always helpful to me and one who could read the judge and pass on to me any court related issues that I needed to be made aware of. She was a real jewel when it came to being such an outstanding court clerk. As for her boss, Judge Gibson, what a winner! Before it was all said and done over my 32-year career in law enforcement, Judge Gibson turned out to be one of the finest judges I ever worked with in either the state or federal court systems. He was brilliant, quick as a cat when it came to getting down to the bottom on any legal matters, and as forward thinking as any judge I ever worked with. He was a hell of a good man, a great friend and an outstanding judge. All officers in the field of law enforcement hope for a firm but fair judge being present in their professional lives. I was legally, professionally, and personally blessed to have that man on my legal side in a county that had more than their fair share of wildlife outlaws. Without a good judge and the people on the side of their local law enforcement, the officer will not have a successful enforcement program in his jurisdictional arena no matter how hard he or she tries. I still relish those bygone days when I brought the good judge a ringer of a stem-winder damn good case and detected a small smile of approval on Judge Gibson's face upon hearing the particulars. Those were what I came to call my 'two-fisted' and 'runnin' and gunnin' days' and what great times they were, knowing I had Judge Gibson 'flying top cover' for me…

Next, I took a look at my bail schedule which is the level of fines associated with any of the fish and game violations. It was from the fourteenth century when it came to having any kind of lasting 'don't do it again' effect on any outlaws brought before the mast because the penalties were so low. It seemed a $25.00 fine was a big one and it went downhill from there! Working with the county attorney and my two judges, I finally got the fines raised for fish and game violations that represented what one could expect to find in the twentieth century when compared to the other fish and game legal jurisdictions around the state.

As I was working through some of my administrative problems and getting used to the county's system of doing business, I began noticing a general standoffish attitude with a large number of its people when it came to doing business with their local Colusa Game Warden. It soon became apparent that a number of the folks of the county did not like game wardens, what they did for a living or what they officially represented. Additionally, a number of them seemed to have a more than general disregard for the fish and game laws of the land. Part of that disregard for the fish and game laws of the land stemmed from Colusa Counties historical past associated with market hunting and duck-dragging. Once ingrained, the blood sport of market hunting and the killing of hundreds of thousands of God's creatures, primarily waterfowl, just became so ingrained, that it became part of the general fabric of life in the Valley… It was also obvious that my fish and game predecessors, other than old time Colusa Game Warden Taylor London, had not been very highly respected for their efforts nor for the wildlife laws they enforced. That was pretty concerning to me! If the law of the land does not have the strong backing, support, and belief of the people, you won't have any kind of a successful resource protection program. As a result, there will be no law west of the Pecos. With those dark histories in mind, I just figured my family life would have to be 'second fiddle' and protection of the critters would have to be 'first chair' in the 'music of life' in the Sacramento Valley. Thus became the real start of my lifelong world of wildlife's law enforcement vision quest. A quest that was to last for the next 30 years of my life as a state and federal conservation officer, both nationally and internationally.

As for my new Sacramento Valley fish and game squad mates, it was as to be expected. Namely a duke's mixture of the poorly led, young, old, worn out and, in one case, a physically broken down alcoholic. At first glance, there were a few fireballs like Warden Bob Hawks and Wally Callan with the rest running the gamut of excellent to worthless as teats on a side of bacon. Gosh, it is nice to be 'sooooo' perfect that one can make all those kinds of value judgements about your fellow wildlife officers. But I had earlier learned that wildlife dies without making a sound. That the only voice it has is yours! And unless an officer is squalling like a smashed cat, then he or she is part of the problem! With that problem in the world of wildlife law enforcement being destruction or extinction of a species if protection is lacking, there in my mind was no place for 'also-rans' or second place! However, 'all in all', my fish and game squad mates were O.K. guys and we got along just fine. We all had plenty to do being that we worked in the famous resource rich Sacramento Valley (except for two officers assigned to mountain districts) but we generally still had time to assist each other when needed or requested.

When it came to assessment time for my new captain, it soon became apparent that I had drawn another lemon. Captain Leamon was highly political, drifted with the political winds of change like a downy duck feather in a gentle breeze, played favorites, and loved to hunt pheasants and fish all on the state's dime. Those last two categories caused a lot of friction between the two of us because I stood for enforcing the law of the land no matter who got in the way. I did not make a real effort to take him hunting and fishing on private lands like he would have liked in my assigned district because I considered that unprofessional. I knew that I could pinch a landowner for a fish and game violation one day and in the next be put in the unenviable position of requesting from that person the right to hunt and fish on his land so my captain could have a good time. No, I don't think so! I just felt that was a little too much and just stayed away from such activities as much as possible.

Don't get me wrong. I liked to hunt and fish as much as the next sportsman. But not when I had work to do and not unless when I got invited to recreate on someone's private property, it was with the understanding that if I caught that landowner or his friends violating the fish and game laws, he or they would be treated accordingly. Besides, there was so much work to do in the county, one could work day and night and that I did many times and never did get all the work done. Hence, hunting was many times not an option when there was so much work that needed doing.

However, where ever he is, I would like to thank Warren Davison for letting me hunt on his east side duck club on the off shoot days. Warren was one of the most honest and genuine men I ever met in my life. Honest as the day was long, considerate and as good a man who ever crapped between a set of boots, that was Warren! I had helped him through a difficult situation, even loaned him one of my handguns for protection and shortly thereafter we became the best of friends. Warren seeing me dragging my behind from so many long hours worked, one day offered to let me hunt on his private duck club on the off shoot days and what a gift of life that turned out to be. Many a day did I sit in one of his duck blinds when there was no duck hunting on the commercial duck clubs and just watched Mother Nature do her thing up close and personal like without any other human interference flooding into my life. Those short interludes of total quiet never failed to allow me to 'charge up my batteries' and then I was good for another 20-hour day or night in the rice fields of Colusa County chasing the numerous outlaws always found swarming around the ducks. Where ever you are, Warren, may God take a liking to you for your act of kindness. It allowed me to work a hell of a lot harden when it came to protecting those voiceless ones in the world of wildlife...

A great number of farmers and ranchers that I ran across early on in my district were obviously not too impressed with game wardens in general and me in particular. But, there were also many farmers and ranchers that were key to my law enforcement programs in the Valley as well. Those folks turned out to be the salt of the land and damned good friends once we got to know each other.

I remember the first time I ran across rice farmer, Leonard Beauchamp. He boiled out from his pickup and began yelling at me even before his feet touched the ground. The depredating ducks had been into one of his growing rice fields and had raised hell with it. I finally got him calmed down, introduced myself to him, and saw to it that he was issued a federal migratory bird depredation permit, as was required in those days, to herd the ducks off his rice. He was also issued several boxes of herding rockets with which to scare off the ducks feeding out in the middle of his larger rice fields. He was finally somewhat calmed down when he drove off but I got the feeling that I was still considered as a 'class of game warden person' lower than whale poop in the Marianas Trench!

Somewhat later, I met Leonard's wife, Millie. She was a great gal with always a calming voice when Leonard was in one of his yelling moods or rants at me for what 'my' ducks were doing to his rice. Being a government parasite in Leonard's eyes, I always rated a damn good sand papering from him for even the smallest of reasons like driving in on one of his muddy farm roads. But, I did respect him. He was hard working, stood his ground, was a solid part of Americana and I suspected, part of the Sacramento Valley duck dragging sub-culture in his younger days as well. I wish we now had more of his kind and mettle in 2015 in America as I am writing these words in the next to the last year of the gutless and divisive Obama Administration…

Another farmer of note on the east side of my district was Terrell Sartain. He was also a farmer who had a 'firecracker' fuse. I soon experienced his temper when I arrested one of his farm hands for killing ducks during the closed season. Instead of herding the ducks off Terrill's rice fields, his farm hand was killing and eating them. When that 'duck-killing' farmhand saw me coming for him late one evening in the darkness, my illegal shooter bolted. Well, a foot race did not suit my duck-killing lad as he was full force tackled moments later just prior to being marched off to the jail for closed season killing of ducks. When that happened, the ducks stormed back onto Terrill's rice fields since there was no one there to keep them at bay and they made a mess of one of his 40-acre rice fields. That was when Terrill let the local game warden, namely me, clearly know that I was lower than whale poop in the Marianas Trench. Before it was all over, we became good friends and he started backing and supporting what I was trying to accomplish in the Sacramento Valley in the way of my wildlife law enforcement programs. And that was going some because Terrill, according to his own words, had shot and sold ducks illegally in order to pay to keep his farm afloat during the hard times when he was just getting started. By the end of my stay in Colusa, if I ever needed any help, Terrill would roll out his considerable resources in order to give me a hand. We didn't always agree or see eye to eye but we worked together where it counted because I wanted to keep what we had in the way of resources and he wanted to keep more of what was left compared to what he had experienced in the good old days of his youth.

Another set of farmers I ran across were the Dennis brothers. Charlie and Linc Dennis lived in the small town of Maxwell on the western side of my district. They were the first two rice farmers I met that seemed to be respectful of not only me but my fish and game law enforcement work in general that I was attempting to accomplish. Neither brother seemed to have any agenda other than being good farmers and solid citizens in and for their community. Both were always very helpful and I came to quickly like and respect the two men for whom they were and what they stood for. Years into our relationships, I became fast friends with Charlie Dennis's son, Tim. Tim and I went on to become fast friends and I was responsible for getting Tim credentialed as a Deputy U.S. Game Management Agent. When that happened, the two of us chased the hell out of a number of the locals, causing a number of them to hang up their shotguns or give up their illegal shooting styles.

As for Linc Dennis, I saw to it that he eventually partnered-up with the U.S. Fish and Wildlife Service and farmed a portion of the Delevan National Wildlife Refuge so the ducks would have more to eat on the refuge and leave the adjacent farmers' rice crops alone. And it was always nice to visit with Linc's brother, Charlie, and listen to his tales of the old days when as a younger man, he shot hell out of the ducks and then ran from the long arm of the law to avoid the embarrassment of being apprehended. For to the locals' way of thinking, it did not bode well for one to get apprehended by the local game wardens or 'Tule Creepers' as we were called in those days. I guess one could say it left an unenviable and embarrassing stain on one's kilts if caught by one of us Tule Creepers.

Over my Sacramento Valley career, I met a number of farmers and orchard men in my stint in Colusa County as a game warden. Once they got past the game warden thing, most were pretty damn good people. Even those who were somewhat inclined to do a lot of harm to or night shooting of my waterfowl, they were all right as human beings as well. Especially during the daylight hours when I wasn't chasing them around the rice fields at night. Right, Gene, Gordon, Tony, Del, Peter, Harry, David...?

All of my rice farmers had difficulty with the ducks eating their rice crops and we worked together to stem the hungry tide of feathered ones out looking for a free meal. In the end, although many of the locals held to their old beliefs and shared little history of their killing ways during the days of old with me, like two Durham bulls in the same pasture, we managed to get along.

Then there were the 'million and a half' duck clubs I had in my district, or at least it seemed like that number on any given shoot day or during windy, foggy, and rainy weather events. In fact, during the waterfowl season on a shoot day, which was every Wednesday, Saturday, Sunday and holiday, I would have at least 10,000 sportsmen in my half of the county pursuing the elusive duck, goose or wily pheasant. Trying to keep a handle on such a mess of humanity was like pissing in the wind and trying to keep it off your pant legs. Hell, Custer had better odds! I had deep-water duck clubs, shallow-water duck clubs and numerous rice farms that allowed waterfowl hunting on their flooded harvested properties during those shoot days. As I said earlier, trying to hold the legal and common sense line of defense with so many sports afield was more than a chore that necessitated me often times working seven days a week and putting in many 16-18 hour days for weeks on end during the 107 day long waterfowl hunting seasons that existed during the 1960s and middle 1970s.

If the above activities were not enough to keep me active, I had what I called the 'creepers'. There were still a few of the old time commercial market hunters left in the Sacramento Valley when I arrived in 1967. In addition to those insidious duck-killing chaps, I also had numerous, what were termed 'duck draggers'. In both instances, those groups of folks would venture forth once the cloak of darkness had descended over the land and began creeping about looking for masses of nighttime feeding waterfowl. They did so because the hundreds of thousands of birds wintering in the Sacramento Valley, especially ducks in those days, would stream off the refuges in long strings and descend into the harvested rice fields at night to feed. It was common to have many thousands of ducks feeding so closely packed together that they looked like a living carpet as they moved across the fields gleaning every grain of rice spilled by the harvesters. Being in such close physical proximity to each other, they became inviting targets for outlaw gunners to sneak up on and ground sluice as they fed. As told to me by numerous old timers from the 'Valley,' groups of experienced outlaw gunners could end up killing anywhere from 300-800 ducks in such a successful night shoot!

When shot by commercial market hunters, the birds would then be gathered up and hustled off to a middle man buyer or transported to the San Francisco Bay Area by the shooters themselves for resale into the illicit restaurant trade for $2.50 to $5.00 per duck depending on the species moving in trade and whether or not picked or cleaned prior to sale. In short, the larger ducks like mallards, canvasbacks and northern pintail brought more money than did the smaller ones like the widgeon and teal species.

It the shooters were the common garden variety of duck dragger, the sneaking upon and shooting into method of killing would be the same but generally those birds would be for one's freezer or for the freezers of their friends or other family members. Either way, during those halcyon years of the commercial market hunter and duck draggers in the Northern Sacramento Valley, millions of ducks fell to the lethal streams of lead shot in order to grace one's table, be it in a restaurant or at home, with an excellent eating rice fed duck for dinner.

I had one outlaw gunner from the small Sacramento Valley town of Gridley tell me on his better days with a 'Long Tom,' (a modified model 11 Remington semi-automatic shotgun capable of shooting from 11-15 shells with the use and aid of an extended magazine), routinely killed 1,000 ducks per shoot! Those ducks were then bagged up in gunny sacks and shipped by train to the Bay Area of California for sale into the food trade. (To see what an old time Long Tom looks like, check out my e-book *Slaughter in the Sacramento Valley*.)

I won't bother to name some of the better duck draggers I missed from the towns of Maxwell, Delevan, Williams, Willows, and Princeton but, if any of you are still alive and reading these lines, please try hard to stifle any grins you might have. Maybe I didn't catch all of you but just remember that when you night-shooting chaps die, you have to stand before the Creator who graced the earth with such fine feathered critters. When that happens, He just may give me another go at you high up in the clouds and hopefully I will be fleeter afoot than I was here on earth. You shooters may also discover yourselves in that ethereal go-around being caught and then sent back to earth as a duck feeding in a rice field somewhere in the dark of the night in Colusa County. That being your punishment for being a little quick on the trigger in your previous life in the cold and damp rice fields of the Sacramento Valley.

As for the violations I came to grips with in the waterfowl arena, they ran the gamut of the stupid, bad and just plain damn ugly. I don't remember how many hundreds of citations or bookings I initiated working my waterfowl sports and outlaws but they were considerable. I experienced extreme cases of early and late shooting, numerous monster over limits of ducks and geese, unplugged shotguns by the ream, no hunting licenses by the bushel basket, shooting over baited areas by the score, no federal duck stamps by the fistful, shameful wanton waste, illegal untagged birds in temporary storage or in transport, sale of waterfowl, closed season taking and the illegal list of events experienced in the Sacramento Valley are legend!. Before my stint was over in Colusa County, my largest duck over limit case was 158 over made in the Butte Sink on a wealthy duck club committed by just two shooters! My largest goose over limit which took place on Sartain's Ranch was 198 snow geese over the limit by four shooters! My best Long Tom seizure case was one that held 15 shells taken from one of my dear friends who was a 76-year-old market gunner on the Newhall Farms property at the time. My earliest early shooting case was one where the gunner shot six hours early. The case of my worst late shooter was for shooting six hours late. In my eight years in the Valley as a state and federal officer, I always ANNUALLY exceeded citation issuance for 1,000 collective minutes in the early shooting department and in excess of 5,000 minutes for late shooting! As I mentioned earlier, Colusa County was a resource rich area and almost every year when I was a either a state or federal officer working in that area, my fine totals exceeded $60,000 per year JUST for violations committed in the waterfowl arena!

Then there were the pheasant hunters. Ah, the pheasant hunters and poachers of Colusa County, they were legend in and of themselves... When I arrived in the Sacramento Valley in 1967, the farming methods were such that there were thousands of acres of weedy upland game bird habitat scattered about on most farms. That included fencerows, weedy corners in fields, grass covered rice checks, wooded lots, fallow lands and every other kind of waste cover land in between. Into that prime habitat moved what is considered the number two upland game bird of America (the mourning dove being the number one game bird), namely the ring-necked pheasant. The pheasant had been transplanted from such areas like Pakistan, China and India into the United States in and around 1872 into Washington State. Finding a wonderful home in all the above types of habitat, those few initially transplanted birds quickly spread into every type of favorable environment until they became a wonder bird for the upland game bird sportsmen. Literally hundreds of thousands of that great eating little game bird fell to the sportsmen's gun over the years in the Sacramento Valley. Additionally and sadly, other untold thousands fell to the outlaws guns, nets, .22 rifles, and illegal live traps.

Once the young birds of the year reached eating age, they began falling to the outlaws and the illegal taking went right on into and through the legal hunting season. When it became seasonally legal to hunt pheasants, my law enforcement district would look like we were in China population wise because there would be so many pheasant hunters 'out and about'. On the opening day of the hunting season once the shooting started, it would sound like the battle at Gettysburg in 1863 there would be so much shooting in the area. In fact, I remember my first pheasant season as the Colusa game warden when I wrote so many tickets for violations of the law, that I seized 167 illegal birds that very first day of the hunting season! Every pheasant season I worked in the valley as a badge carrier, I issued over 150 pheasant related citations per year! Pheasant oddball cases ran the gamut from use of live traps, catching pheasants on baited fishing hooks and lines, to shooting pheasants over a heavily baited area. And of course, there were over limits of pheasants taken by the score by those who had flunked Mrs. Wilson's third grade math class.

But times have changed. I am now told by such folks as Wayne Oliver, So Han Sonny Park, Fred Pilgrim and others during my book signing in Colusa in 2015, that farming methods in the Sacramento Valley have drastically changed from the earlier days. When I was there in the 1960's and early 70's, there were lots of wasted corners and weedy ditches and therein resided the wily ring-neck pheasant. The birds had the habitat type they preferred, a place to forage for seeds and insects and a quiet place to lay their eggs and safely raise their broods. Many weedy places favored by the ring-neck are now gone with the new and improved methods of farming, which leaves little in the way of waste habitat for those in the world of wildlife in which to call home. The dozens of rooster calls in the spring of the year when a loud noise was heard are now almost stilled. The numerous bunches of roosters observed openly vying for a nearby female are also almost non-existent. Numerous young of the year pheasants running down the farm roads and trails in front of trailing farm equipment are experiences appreciated less and less because the runners are basically no more in observable numbers.

Come the summer months in Colusa County, the work of a game warden was never finished as one might think. I had two major areas requiring just about every minute of my time come the summer months. In late summer, I had an early deer season ongoing in the far western part of my district and salmon, striped bass and sturgeon fishing seasons ongoing in the eastern part of my district on the mighty Sacramento River. Both of those geographic areas were many miles apart. Now I was a rather large fellow but, even at my weight, such divergent seasons and geographic areas of sporting endeavor spread my miserable carcass rather thinly.

Arriving in the early summer in the Sacramento Valley of 1967, I quickly discovered that I would soon have an early deer season ongoing in the western portion of my district. That sure didn't give me much time to learn my district, so I completed my duties in the house moving department and then headed for the hills to get better acquainted with my deer hunting public, local area ranchers and the geography in general. Talk about a handful of learning. Initially, I had to learn all the back roads in those areas in which my deer hunters trod. Then came the more complex part of my learning curve being that of understanding the life history habits of my local deer population and where to be when they needed me the most.

I had transferred from a temperate rain forest where the deer behavior was far different from those critters living in the hot and dusty California foothills. I did a lot of scrambling quickly learning about the day and night activities of the deer populations as well as those of my night-active humans. In order to be effective in wildlife protection, the officer has to get in between man and his prey. I couldn't do that without learning about the hunting methods utilized in such a hot and dry environment and the movements and habits of my targeted species of animals.

I soon discovered that I had two different types of human predators when it came to adding venison to one's menu. I had at least a jillion city slickers for the most part pursuing the wily deer during the hot summer days, especially on the weekends. Anything went with that class of sports. The most common faults were trespassing, killing the wrong sex of animal, not tagging the animal in accordance with the fish and game regulations, shooting up the road signs, loaded rifles in a motor vehicle, firearms accidents, shooting from a public highway, investigating hunter safety accidents and settling numerous fistfights over who had killed the deer. Into that squirming mess of humanity, I found myself rapidly thrust just a few short weeks after my arrival as the new Colusa game warden.

Then I had the night shooting crowd. Note that I didn't call them hunters because of the illegality and the lack of fair chase. Again I had those trespassing, shooting from a public highway, spot lighting deer with the use of artificial lights, loaded guns in a motor vehicle, shooting from a motor vehicle, over limits, cattle rustling, taking closed season species like doe deer and destruction of private property such as fences and gates. I had a hatful of night shooting outlaws like nobody's business. Just to give you an indication of the illegal night shooting business in my district, the average for ALL of California's game wardens in those days for apprehending night shooters of big game animals was around six cases per officer per year. I averaged 48 in my lowest year of apprehensions and 54 in my busiest year when it came to apprehending deer spotlighters in Colusa county and sometimes in Glenn County! That not only made me happy but the resident Stonyford deputy sheriff as well when it came to stacking up and transporting the bad-guys to Colusa and inti the lockup....

Now there was a REAL man! Deputy Sheriff Carter Bowman was always there for me when I needed assistance or a deputy as a prisoner transport officer. And let me tell you, that was one man who took no guff or lip from anyone! We made a good pair, just like 'Lenny and Squiggy' when it came to catching deer poaching outlaws.

So when it came to resource rich Colusa County, the local numbers and temperament of the county's home grown outlaws, the numbers of visiting big game hunters for the early deer season and the perennial night shooters, one could see that any game warden worth his salt had little moss growing under his feet. And I can remember many 23 hour days because the smell of gun powder, both legally and illegally, was hardly ever stilled in the hot and dry foothills climate when the mule deer season was open and the big bucks were on the move.

And for you water warriors, don't forget I had a portion of the Sacramento River running through the eastern side of my district. Come the summer months, as if I didn't already have my hands full of gun smoke and wildlife outlaws on the run during my ongoing early deer season, I had my river crowd of happy fishermen having a go at it, both legally and illegally. In fact, I many times would catch a person violating the big game

319

regulations in the western portion of my district and later that night or in the early morning hours, catch that same person violating the fishing regulations on the Sacramento River! Boy, did that ever surprise those folks who had violated the law on one side of my district and then did the same on another side of the county in a different environment, only to see my happy arriving face. Then to be captured by the same officer for breaking the fish and game regulations twice in one day! My river crowd was drawn to the Sacramento River by the hordes of salmon, striped bass, white and green sturgeon all running the waterways. And let me tell all you good folks out there, when the fish were running, I had a boat load (no pun intended) of fishermen on the river of every cut of the legal and illegal cloth. Many of those folks apprehended illegally fishing, had a bad case of the 'uglies,' not only in their violations but many times their temperament as well. Those cases of the 'uglies' ran the gamut from no fishing licenses, short striped bass (had to be a minimum of 15 inches in length), short sturgeon (sturgeon had to be at least 48 inches in length in those days), using more than one pole, illegal terminal gear, snagging, over limits, bringing fish ashore where size or length could not be determined, chumming with live or dead bait, failure to show their terminal gear upon demand, and littering. Suffice it to say, a long day on the river was as long as it took to get the job done. Then remember, I still had to drive clear across Colusa County to my foothills and work my illegal deer spotlighters throughout many nights and into the early morning hours as well.

Or, I could work my warm water game fish, fishermen along the many hundreds of miles of canals, streams, ponds, duck clubs, marsh edges, creeks and the Sacramento River within my district, *when I didn't have anything else to do!* And in those days, I had many died in the wool warm water fishermen pursuing the several species of catfish, bluegill, largemouth bass, crappie and monster bull frogs. It would not be unusual on the weekends for me to check a hundred fishermen and/or froggers in a night!

Then throw into that mix what I considered the insidious commercial froggers. In the case of those lads, finding them with five to seven gunnysacks full of live bullfrogs was not only common but disgraceful! Why the hell the State of California allowed commercial frogging was beyond me. The most money for such species was in the illegal restaurant trade and not for sale in the biological supply houses as originally planned and with that, the race was on. The race being yours truly catching every one of those black-hearted commercial froggers breaking the law that I could. Of the original 26 commercial froggers that were originally licensed in California, I caught 24 of them! Too bad I didn't make a clean sweep of those rascals... Those I caught lost their commercial fishing licenses. But as I have been told over the years since my leaving Colusa County, the bullfrogs are no longer there in such numbers as in the days of old. Just another valuable resource lost to the ages due to the deleterious effects of humankind and a short thinking game and fish department...

My warm water fishermen were like every other group of sporting humanity that I worked. I had my good, bad and the ugly type chaps when it came to crossing over the line of legality. Gill netters, set-lines, over limits, sale of game fish, illegal terminal gear, snagging, live traps, fishing with more than one pole, no fishing licenses, trespassing, taking ducks during the closed season while fishing, deer poaching (yes, while they were fishing), use of drop-lines, assault and battery, prostitution (yes, by pimps pushing their women into the arms of the visiting fishermen), and littering led the pack of violations of my warm water game fish fishing crowd. And, it was always exciting working by myself at night and coming upon 20 or so fishermen from the inner cities of Oakland and San Francisco. Especially those folks who thought that they had been hustled and harassed by the local police in their home cities and were now being hassled by a lowly game warden in the darkened hinterlands. In the 1960's, there was a lot of unrest among the Bay Area folks. When those folks came into the hinterlands, they did so in order to be left alone and just fish, drink and have a good time. The last thing they wanted to see was another damn badge carrier. When things got a wee bit touchy as I went along checking my city fishermen, which commonly happened, I was glad I was carrying a .44 magnum handgun on my hip and had my 100 pound Labrador dog along for company. Only had to draw my gun in deadly seriousness a number of instances but most of those stories are for another time...

So as far as Memories and Milestones go when it came to being a rookie game warden dumped into another whole new world in Colusa County, you can see why I had eyes as big as dinner plates and needed roller skates on my feet to keep up with my crowd of chaps mucking around in the world of wildlife. But I was young in those days, had the world's best supportive wife (still do), was in pretty damn good shape where walking up to five miles per day was nothing, could get by on four hours or less sleep at night, was well trained, loved hunting my fellow man, and was at home with the odds, challenges and dangers of my chosen profession. Plus I still had my two guardian angels protecting me and carrying me through many of my actions, so I thought, *bring it on!*

As for the Flowers in the above memories, they are many and sometimes subtle. My time in Colusa County was a crucible for me. There were so many resources and wildlife outlaws of every kind that such interactions between the two, meant being almost overwhelmed on a daily basis. My many thousands of hours spent in the saddle leavened me into the person and the professional that I became. That leavening certainly can be counted as a Flower for all seasons. I was blessed with untold numbers and species of magnificent resources in the world of wildlife on a daily basis. Those Fields of Flowers are treasures that many from this day and age will never see but are memories that I will carry to my grave of what Fields of Flowers used to look like.

Those Fields of Flowers were also the many sunrises and sunsets filled with the aerial wonders from the world of waterfowl that still grace my memories today. I met and worked with many of the local populace finding them to be the salt of the earth Flowers and the type of human beings that I would have wanted my children modeled after. Many of my Colusa County folks I found to be hardworking and honest folk of the land and proud of it. I also personally met and came to call my friend many of those from times past. Commercial market hunters, duck-draggers and those who lived off the land and the rest of the world could go to hell if they didn't like it. Although I did not support their philosophies of what was right and wrong in their world of wildlife and their killing bent, I still found many of them a part of Americana to be cherished for their sub-cultural history they left behind. And like many other of my experiences, those are just some of the Flowers I will carry to my grave.

The Flowers I came to know and love as a fellow law enforcement officer were my counterparts in the legal world. My sheriff's officers and local police department folks were some of the finest I ever worked with over my 32-year state and federal wildlife law enforcement career. They were just solid, common thinking, down to earth people who were always there for me no matter the odds. The inner feelings of closeness that all of us shared were genuine and always service oriented when it came to doing for the American people.

As for the Flowers discovered in the legal jurisdictions, they for the most part, were exceptional. Be it court clerk to judge, all provided me with a wisdom and humanity that I carried both nationally and internationally for the next 28 years throughout my federal law enforcement career. Those things learned and practiced in Colusa County, kept me alive and successful as a professional law enforcement officer.

Because of my work successes in the Sacramento Valley, I was subsequently selected to be one out of a total of only 178 federal wildlife officers of their kind to serve this great nation of ours in 1970! A Flower of greatest importance because it ultimately led into what I considered an outstanding career. (Subsequently my older son, Richard, has successfully followed the federal call into the world of wildlife law enforcement and is now serving the American People, as did his father as a Resident Agent in Charge in the States of North and South Dakota as these words were written in 2015. That is what I would call a Field of Flowers.)

As for the Tombstones in this story, there are many. Many of the critters I saw and lived with in the world of wildlife are now reduced in numbers for a multitude of reasons. Loss of habitat, over gunning pressures, drought on the nesting grounds, reduced stream and river flows, and changes in agriculture practices have pushed many wildlife species downward in numbers and variety. Clouds of many hundreds of thousands of ducks in the Sacramento Valley are no more! Drastic changes in the farming practices that have reduced the weedy areas have severely reduced the numbers of pheasants at every turn in the trail. Bullfrogs, an invader species from east of the Mississippi but one that was much loved by many folks of the night, have also been severely reduced in the Sacramento Valley. Those patterns of species and numbers reductions are not just symptomatic to the Sacramento Valley but many times a symptom of the times across the United States.

Another Tombstone I deeply feel are the numerous losses of folks I came to respect and love as I labored on in the Sacramento Valley as a game warden and special agent. Folks such as, judges, law enforcement officers, farmers, orchard men, business men, hunter safety instructors like my old friend, Angelo, mechanics, market hunters, duck draggers, deer poachers, informants, Mexican farm hands and many others that I have sorrowfully forgotten. All part of the fabric of this great nation of ours, whose 'camp fires' have now gone out. I guess the bottom line is, never ask for an easy life, just the strength to get through the one you are given. Then when it is 'said and done', bow your head and thank the good Lord for all the sunrises and sunsets you were privileged to have experienced. Then 'hang onto the willows" and make sure you are 'sitting center' on your horse…

THE GAME WARDEN 'HOPS TO' FOR THE FROGS

One hot Colusa County summer afternoon I was driving down the farm road paralleling the 2047 Canal not far from the backside of the Gunner's Field properties. As I did, I kept noticing the upper torsos of bloated bullfrog bodies either floating in the canal or lodged in the vegetative growth along the water's edge!

What the hell? I thought, as I slowed to a stop and then got out from my patrol truck for a closer look. Walking over the edge of the canal bank, I quietly looked at nine bloated bullfrog torsos quietly bobbing in the water along the shoreline. I also noticed that gathered around the floating frog carcasses were a handful of crawdads helping themselves to a free meal. However, what I saw next shocked, saddened and sickened me all in the same rush of emotions. Lying in the water at the canal bank's edge was a live bullfrog. It was nose in to the dirt bank and hanging on to some grass with its front feet because IT HAD NO REAR LEGS! Looking closer and trying not to alarm the already deep in misery poor damn critter, I could see where its back legs had once been joined to the rest of its body. From what I could tell, someone had cleanly chopped off the animal's hind legs and then tossed the unfortunate, still living critter back into the water to fend for itself. With that look, my temper flashed hot even in the valley's already intense summer heat. Whoever had done such a thing to that bullfrog was the lowest form of slime I could imagine. If one wanted a bullfrog's legs to eat, the humane thing to do would have been to knock it in its head killing it outright first before cutting off a living animal's hind legs!

What my already disbelieving eyes saw next really sickened me. Considering my profession and the things I had seen as a result of my activities, that was pretty hard to do since I had already seen more damn human caused wreckage in the world of wildlife during my short career than I really needed to see. There laying in a pile on the bank a few further yards away were marks in the mud where a boat had pulled up onto the shoreline and there laid an even larger pile of legless bullfrog torsos! As if that wasn't enough misery, in that pile of dead frogs were three more that were living without their hind limbs as well! Taking a stick, I dispatched the four recently discovered live bullfrogs in what had to be their utter agony as they waited away their lives after being live-chopped in two by a human savage.

With my stick, I began separating out the bodies from the huge pile of dead frogs in order to get an accurate count. After my count had ended at 97 frogs, I just shook my head! The sport limit of frogs was 25 per person per day. Whoever was responsible for that pile of frogs on the bank was more than likely grossly over the limit. Most of the frogs' bodies looked like they had been dead at least a day or two except for the four live ones I had just dispatched. Figuring backwards, I deduced whoever had done this had more than likely had frogged along the 2047 Canal during the previous weekend.

Now I had a number of folks in the valley who really enjoyed frogging for the delicacy such a sport ultimately offered. The frog leg dinners that would have emanated from such a successful frog hunting expedition as I was now witnessing, would have made many a tasty repast for those kinds of discriminating pallets whoever they were. But therein laid a slight problem. My two guardian angels who had been sleeping in the heat of the afternoon were now stirring. When they chose to arouse themselves, that usually meant there was trouble brewing in camp.

Seeing there was nothing more I could do about my pile of legless frogs, I hopped (no pun intended) back into the truck and left the bodies for the numerous local quadrupeds, like the hungry skunks and raccoons, to find and feast away. However when I left, I mentally was still intensely cognizant of that grisly scene. Now more alert in the summer heat than earlier, I slowly drove down the east side of the 2047 Canal looking for anything else in the world of wildlife that was out of place. Well as usual, my now aroused guardian angels were spot on. A half mile down the canal, I chanced upon another smaller dump of legless bullfrogs! Those bodies were in more advanced stages of decomposition and it was obvious that many had already been feasted upon by various land and aerial predators. That aside, I managed to count 54 legless bodies or what was left of them! Imagine just how many more had been there before a number of the bodies had been eaten, were carted off by scavengers or had floated away down the canal…

Later that evening around the supper table with my wife, Donna, and two sons, I just picked at my food as my mind searched for clues or a law enforcement answer to the legless frog issue.

"What is bothering you, Honey? Did you miss a clue or lose a case this afternoon?" my great little wife, Donna, quietly asked.

"Yeah. I think I have someone taking huge over limits of bullfrogs and then cutting off their legs either for their freezers or re-sale somewhere," I said as I continued toying with my

327

food. "Do you have any leads?" Donna continued, knowing me as she did that my mind had to be racing over the issue at hand for some kind of solution to the problem.

"I have very few leads. It looks like the chaps taking such big numbers of frogs are coming into the area on the weekends, which makes sense. Especially if the person or persons are fully employed and that is the only time they can be out most of the night frogging. There were boat pullouts and piles of animal parts at both of the sites I discovered. So, I am hoping they come back this weekend because I will be working that side of the valley and that will enable me to check the canal off and on as the night wears on. Besides, the bullfrogs are thick as thieves in most everybody's adjacent rice fields right now, so those frogs will be migrating back and forth and the canal will be constantly restocked with more of them no matter how many are taken. Plus, Delevan National Wildlife Refuge is just next door to the canal and it is loaded with a million frogs as well. Either way, there will be lots of frog feeder resources reloading the canal with fresh targets and that will make another trip for my outlaws a paying proposition and will pay them big dividends," I said.

For the next few nights I worked a number of warm water game fish fishermen in my district and managed to quietly skirt the 2047 Canal on several occasions looking for any fishermen frogging. As I did, I could see numerous bullfrogs resting and feeding along the canal banks on both sides. That was good, because if my suspect lads came back, they would have a lot more bounty to take a whack at on both sides of the canal. And if they did, those mysterious bullfrog leg-chopping chaps would get a chance to meet me up close and personal like.

The following Friday night yours truly was working the Lambertville area in northern Colusa County and points east. Several times that evening I made it over to the 2047 Canal but had no luck locating my suspect chaps taking such large numbers of frogs. All I discovered were a few catfish fishermen working the area of the dam adjacent the Delevan Refuge. Around three in the morning, I shelved my patrol efforts and went home to get some sleep knowing Saturday would be another day and another battle.

Saturday produced a negative capture performance on my part when it came to my frog hunters, as I initially worked my illegal night hog hunters south of Highway 20 on the Colusa National Wildlife Refuge. Tiring of that detail, I broke off my stakeout of the refuge area and slipped up along the 2047 Canal running along the many adjacent farm roads and dikes without using any lights. Nothing got my attention other than a pair of lads hand-frogging along the canal and they quit without either of them catching limits of frogs. Sunday was more of the same nothingness when it came to capturing my suspect 'frog-chopping' outlaws.

The following weekend I made sure I kept a close eye on the canal. My guardian angels were 'all-a-flitter' the whole time and I felt my frog hunters would show for sure. Friday night along my many waterways was a bust and I broke off my patrol efforts around four in the morning. In so doing, I got home just in time to shower and fix breakfast for my bride. Then out Dog and I went into my western foothills to work my early deer season sportsmen. Sleep would have been nice but at that time of the year, 'hell was a-popping', the critters were a-dying and I simply needed to be 'out and about' since I was the only fish and game law in my heavily utilized 600 square mile patrol area.

When things quieted down around noon in my backcountry working hunters because of the heat and the deer had quit moving, I hid my patrol truck out of the way on a back road and slept alongside it on the ground with the rattlesnakes for about two hours. Following that, back into the saddle I went and continued checking my deer hunters until dusk. With the arrival of darkness, I slid into a favorite alfalfa field that was heavily used by feeding deer and spotlighters, then staked out the area until around eleven. Because of the evening's heat which had to be still above 90 degrees and lack of sleep, my old bottom needed a roller skate attached to it to keep from dragging on the ground and wearing out the hind end of my britches. But bottom dragging was not to be. Popping another hefty chew of Levi Garrett chewing tobacco into my mouth to help keep me awake, off I headed for the Sacramento Valley and the still worrisome 2047 Canal and its suspect froggers.

Without using any lights, around twelve-thirty I quietly slid into a location across from the backside of Delevan National Wildlife Refuge where I could watch the canal frogging area both north and south. Exiting my truck, I stretched my tired frame and let Dog out so she could attend to business. Making sure there were no froggers in the immediate area, I lit up one of my Italian cigars to help keep the hordes of mosquitoes at bay and use its nicotine to help keep me awake and on my toes for whatever the good Lord was to throw my way.

Approximately one-thirty in the morning over the sounds of a million mosquitoes buzzing in and out of my open-windowed patrol truck where I was sitting, I heard the quiet purring sounds of a small outboard motor. As near as I could tell, it was far off and south of my position on the canal. Around two forty-five, I finally saw a flashing light from a small boat slowly moving upstream. Putting my binoculars to work, I could see two individuals in the oncoming boat. One chap was running the small outboard and the other was lying in the bow of the boat with a high- powered head lamp shining and catching bullfrogs sitting along the canal bank with his hands, which was a common practice.

Then abruptly after catching and bagging up another bullfrog, I could hear the men talking and it sounded like their lingo was in Chinese. It was then that their little boat pulled over to the refuge side of the canal and anchored. Since I was on the opposite side of the canal, all I could do was sit, watch with my binoculars and wait for my lads to come over to my side of the canal or try and intercept them at some choke point further down along the waterway. Either way, they had me over a barrel if they became aware of my presence and decided to motor off. Since they had a boat and I would of had to move around and across numerous farm roads to eventually get to them, my best strategy was to remain hidden and hope to ambush my froggers at some later time.

My plan was to surprise and ambush my chaps so they would not have the chance to dump any illegal frogs they might have in their possession. That strategy was made all the more important because now my guardian angels were really letting me know a special moment was close at hand and needed my attention. And to be quite frank, I figured these lads may very well be the ones who had cut the legs off the bullfrog bodies dumped into the canal that I had observed days earlier.

About then, the man in the bow of the boat with his back to me made a quick move and then I heard a muffled WHUMP! Using my binoculars, I could see my person of interest chopping the legs off live bullfrogs on a board laid across the gunnels of their boat. Aided by his headlamp's illumination, I could see my chap laying the bullfrogs taken from a nearby gunny sack on a small piece of plywood and, using a hand ax, chopping off their legs! The legless frog torsos were then tossed overboard into the canal and the legs went into an ice chest that was sitting open in the bottom-center of their boat between the two men.

With the headlamp-assist from my chopper, I managed to count 61 frogs chopped off at their torsos and their bodies thrown overboard. Since the limit was only 25 per person, these chaps were way over their legal sport limit! Now I found myself trying to figure out how I was going to successfully head these guys off at the pass in such a way that they would not see me coming and be able to preclude them from dumping overboard all my evidence. Realizing they had motored up from the south on the 2047 Canal, I got an idea. Since I was still far enough away from my lads busily chopping off frog legs, I started up my patrol truck, backed away from the canal levee and then quietly fled south on a maze of farm roads as I headed for the Highway 20 bridge which intersected the 2047 Canal. There I figured is where my two froggers had launched their boat earlier and, if so, once I got there, I would have them trapped upon their return.

Twenty minutes later, I was at a pull off spot that widened into a mess of willows just south of Highway 20. Pulling back into the depths of the wide out, I discovered a blue Ford pickup parked even further back into the darkness of the bushes! Figuring that truck belonged to my two froggers still upstream on the canal since they had hidden it so well, I just 'grinned my spider to the fly' grin. Parking my patrol truck directly in front of and blocking the Ford so it could not leave without driving over the top of my vehicle, I left Dog in the bed of my truck and took off heading north on the eastside dike of the 2047 Canal on foot.

It would be daylight soon and I figured I would just out wait my lads and eventually set up an ambush near their vehicle. In the meantime, I hotfooted it north on the canal until I could see my chaps from afar slowly coming downstream. Watching them with my binoculars, I could see that they were frogging all the way down the canal as they came my way. Just before they got to my hidden position, they once again stopped and chopped off the legs from another mess of just freshly caught frogs. Once finished, they shoved off and here they came down the canal heading for their pull out spot. Out of sight, I quietly followed them back down the canal on foot. Since I knew they had an over limit of frogs, I just figured my surprise and speed would rule the day when it came to capturing them with the goods. Well, that and I had pulled a wire from the coil on their Ford pickup. Even if they did discover me and tried getting away in their boat, they sure as hell weren't going anywhere in their truck without a coil wire. And as for trying to escape me in a boat, well, they after all were in a two-way canal... Plus, I had written down their license plate number and figured I was ready as all get out to close the gate on my two illegally frogging Celestial Sons of Heaven. So now the trap was set and all I had to do was intercept my chaps as they motored down the canal towards their pickup and wait until they had disembarked. Then I would close the ring on their miserable carcasses and, figuratively speaking, my bullfrogs would have their moment of justice for the cruelty they had endured. With that capture plan set in motion, I trotted back down out of sight to their vehicle parked along Highway 20.

About thirty minutes later, I could hear the soft purring sounds of a small outboard motor coming my way. The sound was coming from upstream as I quietly waited with a big Walt Disney Cheshire cat grin. Man, did I ever get a surprise just moments later! All of a sudden, the noise from the outboard motor stopped and there was nothing but abject blackness down in the depths of the canal channel and no further directional noise for me to hone in on or any sign of a light from my froggers to follow. Even my binoculars were of no further use to me at that moment in locating my two frogging suspects.

But I damned sure wasn't going to lose my suspect froggers over a little darkness, so, I fell back to the side of their parked vehicle and then lurked in the bushes. A few minutes later, I could just make out the forms of two chaps coming my way and from the sounds of it, they were lugging something heavy. I let them cross the highway and head for their vehicle as I simultaneously slipped around the rear of their truck and waited. As I did, my two lads slipped into the deeper darkness of the pull out in the trees and then I heard them stop and once again, it got as still as death. I figured they had spotted the darkened shape of my patrol truck and had heard Dog stirring around in the back of my vehicle when she discovered people were coming her way.

It was at that point I figured it was time for the party to begin and I lit my two nearby chaps up with the light from my 5-cell flashlight. Man, you talk about a blow up when that light illuminated my two froggers, they jumped like a bug on a hot rock! My two chaps had heard my dog stirring in the back of the patrol truck and all their heightened senses had to be focused on that foreign suspicious sound along with the discovery of the darkened shape of another vehicle parked next to their Ford. Then came the surprise of the 'light of day' via the light from my flashlight. "HEY-HEY-HEY!" one of them yelled and, between the two of them, they flung the heavily laden ice chest they had been carrying to the ground. One man sprinted for their Ford and the other for some damn reason ran directly right at me and my flashlight in terror. Course that was a short run because I was now only six feet or so away when I had turned on my flashlight and illuminated my two frogging chaps!

My runner was a short stump of a man and as he ran by me, I neck-tied him with my left arm as I got the words out, "Game Warden!" My chap was running so fast that he hit my rather sizeable arm and flew up and over the arm and landed flat on his back with a soft THUMP, followed by a loud OOOPHFF!

Suffice it to say, my lad who had tried to run through my arm found himself immediately physically controlled by a man who was three times his size. That being the case, he went nowhere except where I wanted him to go. And sure as my wife makes the best pies in the world, my captured lad was a diminutive chap of Asian descent. As for the other runner, once he discovered that his Ford was blocked by my patrol car and there was a HUGE dog sitting in the back of that truck closely watching him, he came stumbling back to me in the light of my flashlight.

After identifying myself again and asking them for their driver's licenses, I discovered I had David Chow and Raymond Chin, both from the nearby city of Marysville. We three then walked back to the spilled open ice chest. Therein and splashed across the ground were a mess of frog legs and I do mean a mess! Reloading the spilled legs back into the ice chest, I carried it with an effort back to the bed of my truck and began counting. Not a word was said by either of my two captured Chinese culprits as I counted out my now evidence frog legs. When the count was finished, I had leg parts of 99 bullfrogs! Since the limit was only 25 each per frogger per day, my two lads were in legal hot water to say the least.

In short, my two chaps of Asian descent were facing a major legal problem with the potential of a rather large fine at the other end of their little illegal frog-killing escapade. That problem was that the 2047 Canal was the most eastern legal boundary for the Williams Justice Court administered by Judge Gibson, who was a no nonsense judge somewhat like Judge Roy Bean of historical Texas fame. That was especially so when it came to prosecuting the fish and game laws of the land to their fullest extent of what the law allowed. Gee, from my experiences in taking cases to Judge Gibson concerning gross over limits of frogs, the sentencing results had to be right up there along with cattle rustling...

My two Chinese lads were ultimately cited for jointly possessing 49 frogs over the limit that morning since they could legally take only a total of 50 between the two of them. Following that bit of administrative action, all the frogs were seized and my two chaps were provided with seizure papers regarding the frog legs removed from their possession. A week later, Chin and Chow forfeited $500.00 each for jointly possessing a gross over limit of 49 frogs. They also forfeited their frog catching apparatus, their boat and their 9 ½ horsepower Evinrude outboard motor! All of which was later auctioned off by the state during one of their auctions of seized and court forfeited property.

Since both men listed their occupations as cooks and worked in a Chinese restaurant in Marysville, it didn't take much of a brain to figure out where their frog legs were going. After citing my two chaps, seizing all the frogs, their boat and outboard motor, I released my two somewhat contrite outlaws. Once they had replaced their coil wire, it didn't take any time for them to disappear into the dawns early light as they headed for home. Watching their tail lights disappearing off into the pre-dawn darkness, I got into my truck, pulled up onto the highway and headed for my evidence facility in which to store the frog legs, boat and motor.

My wife was up early that morning and had made a nice breakfast for me after the sheriff's office had called her earlier and advised that I was finally on my way home. That breakfast included a rather large slice of her wonderful homemade pie. Since I was a little shy in the sleep department over the last few days, after finishing breakfast yours truly crashed. But I did so knowing that fantastic slice of pie eaten earlier was now where no one else could have at it and, there was more of the same in the refrigerator.

Never again did I run across those two Chinese lads frogging in Colusa County. Additionally, never again did I run across a mess of legless frogs discarded along the bank of the 2047 Canal either. Gee, you think maybe the word got out in the nearby Chinese community to get their frog legs in someone else's law enforcement district other than mine?

I guess one could say that I quickly 'hopped' to the legless frog problem at hand and solved the mystery. Then if nothing else, made sure my other amphibians were able to hop around and enjoy life in the rice fields and canals of Colusa County. Especially so, after I had taken a nick out of the hides of my two Celestial Sons and the word had gotten out in the rest of the Asian restaurant community in the nearby towns of Marysville and Yuba City to forego Colusa County frog legs on their dinner menus....

As for the Flowers in this story, they are obvious. I had managed to remove from the world of wildlife two very serious illegal froggers who were more than likely commercializing in the sale of frog legs. That made life a little easier in the amphibian world along the heavily utilized 2047 canal for those remaining web-footed chaps still swimming around.

As for the Tombstones in this story, they are obvious too. Do any of readers out there have any inkling on how many eggs a frog will lay if given a chance? Me neither. But the number of eggs laid by a mess of frogs has to be a bundle! And just imagine how many future frogs were lost by the destruction my two Chinese lads caused during their gross illegal killing sprees in Colusa County. Even more importantly, imagine how many frogs they illegally took before I finally got my hands on those two killers! Then take that frog-killing issue one- step further. Imagine how many frogs they took in a lifetime of illegality in other areas of the Sacramento Valley when they frogged elsewhere for the restaurant trade... As told to me by some of my friends back in Colusa County during a recent book signing, one now has to listen hard to hear the familiar 'JUGGA-RUM' in any of the valley's waterways now in 2015. To many amphibians, their saving grace in the form of a rather large game warden hunting the lawless had come too late...

EIGHT LIVES LEFT, NOT NINE!

One summer evening I pulled off onto Art Andreotti's Ranch located just south of the Cook's Spring Road turn off. Moving past his darkened old home ranch, I turned and drove through an open gate just off the Ladoga-Leesville Road. Running with lights, I hustled my patrol truck around the north side of an old, past its prime alfalfa field and over a slight bank near the edge of a small creek. Quickly turning my patrol truck around, I parked it out of sight from any potential searching 'eye' of an illegal spotlight but yet where I could still see the entire alfalfa field usually full of night time feeding deer. As I did, the turning sweep of my headlights illuminated about 20 quietly feeding California mule deer. In that quick look, I observed two very large buck deer and several smaller antlered males as well. *Big bucks are always big draws for any poacher who just happens to wander along with a killing heart and an itching trigger finger*, I thought as I quickly dumped my lights and shut my truck's engine down. In so doing, I found myself immediately enveloped in the soft blackness of a near moonless night. *The best kind of dark,* I thought with a grin. As black as it was out, any deer spotlighted will stand longer when blinded by the beam of a powerful spotlight making any kind of a kill much easier for the shooter.

For about twenty minutes, I quietly sat in my patrol truck to see if anyone had observed me entering the ranch's alfalfa field as I let my eyes begin adjusting into their night vision mode. That particular alfalfa field was fast becoming one of my favorite spots to set up on a stakeout in the hopes of corralling anyone foolish enough to spotlight my field of deer located on the western side of my patrol district. I had come to realize that many a city slicker who had yet to fill their deer tags, often took a chance in spotlighting my past its prime alfalfa field for the numerous feeding deer it historically held. I had discovered the area quite by accident and the business of putting those in the 'spotlighting' business of extinction out of business through apprehensions had been good when it came to my now favorite alfalfa field. As it turned out, my old alfalfa field, even though past its prime, still held enough succulent green feed to attract just about every deer within calling distance. That greenery with its attraction for every neighborhood mule deer, also seemed to lure every itchy trigger fingered lad who had yet to fill out their deer tags. With that California mule deer lure and attraction, came the local game warden and then the circle of life in the often times lawless backcountry was complete. Those last thoughts followed many others, as my mind quickly ran through several recent earlier captures of night shooting outlaws that had taken place in this same field. Those illegal night shooters had run the gamut of the good, the bad and the ugly, running from priests to big city policemen but they all were booked the same once the dust had settled, if you readers out there get my gist. However, all you budding game warden readers out there need to look behind the above described scenes. Working deer spotlighters at night mostly by one's self because of less than adequate numbers of supporting game wardens can be risky and many times dangerous. That becomes even more so when one realizes most deer poachers do not work alone. Under those circumstances, 'death can ride a dark horse' and in the covering darkness, will often not be seen coming one's way. Keep those dangerous thoughts just mentioned in mind as you continue reading the rest of the lines in this story…

Satisfied that I was not observed, I exited my blacked out truck, then let Dog out so she could stretch her legs and take care of business. In order to safeguard her from the popcorn dry terrain's ever present plethora of rattlesnakes, when she had finished I had her jump back into the safety of the bed of my patrol truck. That way, if I had to leave in a hurry in order to chase down an outlaw, she wouldn't be left behind in a field of deadly rattlesnakes.

(As an aside, Shadow had been a gift from my wife early on in my career so I would always have a partner in any adventure undertaken. As it turned out, what a wonderful partner Shadow turned into being and would continue to be throughout the rest of her life as the two of us tromped through our adventures in the world of wildlife. Especially so when she had saved my life after I made an ill-advised, head-on car stop on a carload of drunken Indians in the backcountry of Trinity County early on in my career. That event occurred early one morning when I was by myself and out of radio contact. As it soon turned out, I found myself out- numbered by six deer killing Indians just off the Hoopa Indian Reservation. They were spotlighting deer late at night and caught me in a position of having to make a dangerous head on car stop. Before that adventure had run its course, I had five healthy Indian prisoners, six illegal dead deer and a sixth fellow from their party who had tried to knife me from behind. In so doing, that Indian chap ended up chewed all to hell by my eight month old female Labrador dog, who had exited my patrol car uninvited and joined the fight. But if you readers are interested in the rest of the story, you will have to read about that adventure in my EBOOK, *The Thin Green Line*, chapter eight titled, "Dogs.")

Hours earlier before ending up at Andreotti's ranch, I had been working in the eastern agricultural portion of my district checking numerous warm water game fish fishermen and folks frogging. Tiring of the heat, humidity and hordes of mosquitoes found within the Sacramento Valley's agricultural areas, I opted for dark of the night big game duty in the bone-dry, mountainous western portion of my patrol district. However, evading the county's intense summer heat was a horse of another color. It was still summer-hot in that part of western Colusa County, maybe in the middle 90's, as I sat there sweating in the cab of my patrol truck late at night.

However, I had early on learned a trick of the trade when working at night in the western portion of my patrol district during the hot and dry summer months. Tiring from the stifling in-cab heat, out from the back of my truck came a lawn chair, which was then positioned twenty yards in front of my hidden truck. Sitting in that type of chair away from the truck, I would be as cool as I could be and not hear all the clunking and clanking of my vehicle as its engine cooled down. That way, I could remain as cool as possible and would not mistake a cooling down sound coming from my truck engine for a faraway distant rifle shot.

Soon I could hear my bored dog snoring in the back of the truck as I quietly sat there in my lawn chair safely out of sight from the view of any deer spotlighter or his searching spotlight. As I typically did when sitting in such a position, I was listening quietly to the sounds of night going on around me. Soon I could hear some sort of critter messing around in the nearby creek bottom like that from a raccoon. That was soon followed by the far away familiar three-note hooting of a great horned owl, the bark from a nearby fox scenting my quiet presence and the snorting of occasionally disturbed feeding deer in the darkened alfalfa field to my front. God, it was great being surrounded by those in the world of wildlife. At that moment in time, I realized I was part of the natural world and now benefitting from its bounty…

I liked the night. As any law enforcement officer knows, the onset of the night brings out a different class of people and problems. The law enforcement officer must adapt his style, manner and alertness to a much different level if he wishes to be able to retire from the job uninjured or suffer death before his time when working at night. The quiet of the night also brought out every kind of creepy crawler known to man. Collaterally with the advent of the creepy crawlers, a good game warden's hearing reaches deeper into his soul and soon he can hear many things that an ordinary everyday person will never hear. It was into that world of silence with all of its related 'sounds' that I found myself magically drifting.

For the longest time, I only observed the occasional vehicle traveling to or from on the Leesville-Ladoga Road that bordered my staked out alfalfa field. Being that it was so quiet and my hearing had sharpened so tremendously, I could hear vehicles coming from a long ways off. As was typical on most stakeouts, as folks drove by, none were aware they had been watched by Mother Nature's silent sentinel. Soon the quiet of the night, oppressive heat and the many long hours previously spent on patrols in the valley, began smoothing out my wrinkles into a quiet relaxed calm. As such, I found it difficult to stay awake. That is when the Levi Garrett chewing tobacco came out, a wad went between my cheek and gum, and shortly thereafter, the nicotine rush brought me back into my world of the living, alertness and soon to be possible adventures.

Around one o'clock in the morning, the road's traffic picked up as the local bars began closing and clearing out. For about thirty minutes, I had a few vehicles pass my backcountry alfalfa field and then quiet reined again. For the longest time, nothing stirred in my world of darkness except for a great horned owl who had now chosen to set up shop in one of the tall oak trees behind me along the barely flowing creek. His rhythmic hooting filled the air and my thoughts quietly turned to my academic training received as a college wildlife management student in an ornithology class. Drifting through my mind like wisps of fog, came taxonomic data, physical characteristics of the species, food habits, life history information and predation behavior of my nearby serenading aerial killer. One that was uniquely qualified for a life as a small to medium sized animal predator.

What the hell? I thought, as I instantly rejoined the real world! I swore I could hear the faint distant strains of Herb Alpert's Tijuana Brass lilting through my world of night and darkness. Minutes later, a four door Buick sedan drove south down the Leesville-Ladoga Road, which paralleled the entire length of the deer-filled alfalfa field I had now staked out. As the vehicle drove slowly by, I could hear Herb Alpert's catchy strains of music flooding out that vehicle's open windows and into the dark of the hot summer night. Looking through my binoculars at the passing vehicle, I could make out a passenger and driver in the front seat and what appeared to be a single passenger in the back seat. But other than that, nothing out of the ordinary occurred! They never slowed down from their normal speed and didn't even seem to be interested in the alfalfa field full of feeding deer just illuminated by their vehicle's headlights as they passed by.

I thought their behavior was a little strange because almost everyone liked to stop and look at buck deer illuminated by their vehicle's headlights. Especially now since that alfalfa field held two large and heavily antlered bucks easily observed as they fed not far from the barbed wire fence surrounding the alfalfa field at the edge of the road. My Mexican music lovers just toddled on down the road without a backward glance. *Damn*, I thought. *I sure thought for a moment I just might have a taker on at least one of those big bucks feeding in the field. Or at least a looker.* To be frank, I was a little disappointed that my Mexican music lovers didn't fancy busting a cap and giving me some excitement in which to drown out my 'tired' and boredom, as I quietly sat there in my lawn chair.

Long about two in the morning, I heard a single shot way far away somewhere in the distant Bear Valley to the south. No other shots followed that one and I just figured some traveler passing down one of the graveled backcountry roads in the area had run across a rattlesnake crossing the road, stopped, gotten out and had shot it. With nothing more to go on, I sat back in my lawn chair, loaded up a fresh chew of tobacco into my mouth and hoped Deputy Sheriff Del Garrison on his nightly routine patrols back in the Valley was swinging by my home in Colusa occasionally to make sure my family was safe and sound.

Then my mind ran to my dear friend, Deputy Sheriff Del Garrison. He was a big old dude and just a gentle old bear of a man. I had liked him from the onset and we had become great friends over my short time living in the Sacramento Valley. When I needed a sheriff's office prisoner transport, it always seemed to be Del showing up to haul my miscreants off to the slammer. When he did show up in response to my call for transport assistance, it was always led with the words as he unfolded his huge frame from behind the steering wheel of his patrol car, "Well, well, well. What do you have for me tonight, Little Buddy?" Whenever he was on patrol he always swung by my house to check up on Donna and our two boys (that was before Donna and I had adopted our Vietnamese daughter) because a game warden was not the most loved type of law enforcement officer in the Sacramento Valley. Especially since a substantial number of the locals who had grown up with the stain of commercial market hunting or dragging ducks in their souls, had come to legal grief with some of my predecessor fish and game badge carriers.

As a result of those encounters, a number of the Valley's wildlife outlaws had been convicted for their crimes and sent off to federal prison. Can any of you readers out there imagine that? Being sent off to the 'Big House' for selling sport shot waterfowl. Even worse, when a convicted murderer in that joint asked you what you were in for and you had to tell that killer of humans that it was for selling a measly bunch of ducks. Can any of you out there reading these lines imagine what that killer of humans had to be thinking when you told him you were there for killing and selling ducks? Since many of those convicted lads found that their resultant bad feelings died hard when it came to game wardens, Del always took it upon himself to keep an eye on my little family during my many absences. Even better, the local hard-case outlaws knew that the sheriff's deputies religiously checked my home for any problems. So if any of those previously convicted Valley outlaws harbored any bad thoughts relative to the welfare of my family, they had to check it at the door…

In fact, on one of his late at night house checks, Del had stopped by and had tried all the doors to make sure they were locked. When he did, my wife, Donna, heard the doors rattling. Not knowing I had asked the sheriff's Office to check my place, the sounds of someone trying the doors scared the hell out of her! Doing as I had taught her, Donna retreated to our bedroom fearing the worst and retrieved my Colt model 1911, .45 A.C.P. Then back to the end of our long hallway she went where she was between the one rattling the doors and my two young sons. There she set up shop' with the .45 in hand waiting for the one rattling the doors to break in and come her way. But in so doing, she discovered that she could not pull back the hammer on the single action .45 (she had such small, delicate hands that she had a strength issue)! Man, being unable to do that scared the hell out of her. Finding everything OK, Del left and Donna settled down. But, I sure caught hell when I got home over a gun left for her to defend herself that she could not get the hammer back so she could shoot. In the future, I left her a double action revolver for her use because it took less strength to index and fire...

There it was again, suddenly snapped through my mind! I heard Herb Alpert's familiar strains of catchy music wafting through the air. It was amazing just how quickly the adrenalin surged through my body along with the strains of that music. When it did, I noticed that my guardian angels began fluttering around inside me and even Dog quit snoring and quickly stood up in the back of the truck so she could see and hear better.

Moments later the Buick I had observed earlier surged around the southern corner of my alfalfa field and passed on by heading north. Ten minutes later, it came back heading south! Now to set the 'stage', remember folks, it is past two in the morning and we are out in the bush! Only that time, the Buick glided up to the center of the alfalfa field and then quietly drifted to a stop. BING! Out from the backseat of the Buick, came a pencil thin white stream of light, which quickly swept the field and passed over a large, feeding buck deer. Then as if almost realizing what it had just illuminated, the light quickly came back to the big buck and anchored its beam on the animal's head! The blinded buck dropped its head down as if to escape the uncomfortable blinding light and began walking away. BOOM, went the report of a heavy rifle fired out from the driver's side window, as a large orange fireball instantly followed the sharp report! Down went the big buck kicking in the dry dirt as it became evident that my shooter had scored a direct killing hit on the unsuspecting large animal!

Then the dome light of the Buick went on and I saw the backseat passenger vault out the door, run to and athletically vault cleanly over the four-foot high barbed wire fence. All of that man's actions were caught with the use and aid of my trusty binoculars as I watched in fascination at the unfolding events taking place on the south end of the field. With my back seat passenger's exit, the Buick took off like a striped assed ape and the forward rapid lurch of the car slammed shut the open back passenger door. Down the Leesville-Ladoga county road flew my Mexican music playing car as it careened out of sight and sound to the south. In the meantime, I continued glassing my chap out in the field. All I could make out were faint movements of a darkened shape but it appeared my lad was in the process of gutting out his deer in the light of a small pen light held in his mouth.

Having seen and heard enough, I quietly rose and laid my lawn chair off to one side so I wouldn't run over it upon leaving. I had been to this rodeo many times previously and knew what was coming next so I did not hurry in any of my actions. Getting back into my patrol truck, I quietly keyed my radio mike's transmission button. With my radio transmission receipt volume turned to low, I called the Colusa County Sheriff's Office and requested that they contact the nearby Stonyford deputy, one Carter Bowman, and alert him that I would need a prisoner transport vehicle for an illegal deer-killing incident near the old Andreotti Ranch headquarters. Moments later, the sheriff's office responded that Deputy Bowman was on his way and would hide in his usual place off the main road until I contacted him for immediate prisoner transport assistance or backup as needed.

With my Plan B in place, Dog and I patiently waited. Twenty minutes later, I could hear a vehicle coming my way on the Leesville-Ladoga county road. Soon I could see what I suspected was the darkened shape of the old Buick sedan slowly making its way back to Andreotti's alfalfa field and their partner who had jumped into the field to gut the downed critter. It was the old Buick alright but it surprised me and just continued north on the main road and shortly was out of sight and sound once again. Fifteen minutes later, the Buick ambled back into sight and sound, as it headed south on the main road like it was on a mission.

As the Buick slowly ambled down the road as if looking for their chap, I heard a yell coming from the field telling the car to stop. On came the tail lights and, using my binoculars, I observed a man jump out from the front driver's seat, run to the trunk of the car and snatch it quickly open. Then that man quickly jumped back into the driver's seat. However, when he had opened up the trunk of their vehicle, the trunk's light illuminated a rather large man struggling with the huge just killed deer as he tried to quickly heft it over the barbed wire fence. With a lot of struggling, grunting, swearing, and groaning noises, that man, with an assist from another man from the front passenger seat of the Buick, finally hefted the deer over the barbed wire fence. Then the man in the field adroitly hopped over the barbed wire fence as if it wasn't even there. From there, the deer was lifted up and flopped into the spacious trunk of the sedan by the two men and the lid shut. Then both men ran around the car with one getting into the front passenger seat and the other into the back seat. With the slamming of their doors, the headlights went on and I could hear the Buick's big engine roar to life as it began motoring down the Leesville-Ladoga county road towards Bear Valley to the south.

That was when I keyed the mike and asked the Colusa County Sheriff's Office to send Deputy Bowman the direction in which the Buick had fled and to let him know I was in front of his position and in a quiet and unlighted pursuit. Dog and I headed out the gate and down the county road after the Buick without using any lights. I hoped to be able to get right up onto my quarry before lighting them up with my headlights, red light and siren. That way my underpowered two-wheel drive pickup would not be out run by the Buick with its bigger and more powerful engine.

For the next mile or so, I sped down the road using only my night vision adjusted eyes to steer me clear of any obstacles in or alongside the roadway. Soon I could see my Buick scooting down the roadway ahead of me. Closing, I waited until I had them on a narrow portion of the county road where side road escape would not be an option and then lit them up. Talk about human movement in the light of my headlights in their car! It looked like a three ring circus in the car in front of me with the movement of three surprised bodies moving wildly all around like they had just overturned a nest of hornets inside their vehicle and were now all trying to escape.

Finally the Buick slowed and then stopped in the middle of the county road. Stopping a short distance behind them and using my open door as a shield, I yelled at the driver that I was a state fish and game warden and that he was to throw his car keys out his open window and onto the pavement. You talk about obeying. Those keys were airborne in an instant and I suspected I had a mess of not only totally surprised chaps but scared all to hell rookie poachers as well.

Then I could hear the unmistakable sounds of a lever action rifle being rapidly jacked open and shut repeatedly! Realizing someone in the car was jacking out live rounds from his rifle and not wanting to lose a loaded gun charge against those chaps, I started walking quickly towards the back of the Buick. I figured if I could catch the chap jacking out live rounds before he had emptied all the rounds from his magazine, I would have him with a loaded gun charge as well. With those thoughts, I quickened my step so I could witness my chap unloading his rifle.

BOOM! In an instant, I had my face and hair filled with flying glass chips as the back window in the Buick exploded outwardly into a million sparkles of 'diamonds' in the light of my flashlight and headlights of my patrol truck! Unfortunately, that sparkle-load of diamonds blew across my body as I was hurrying forward towards the suspect's vehicle! Spitting out glass fragments and wiping them quickly off my face and away from my eyes, I realized just how lucky I had been. When I heard the report of that rifle going off in the backseat of the Buick, that sound was preceded by a 'ZIPPP-POP,' as the bullet that had shattered the Buick's back window, passed within inches of the right side of my head! In fact, that bullet was so close, that I felt a sucking of air from around the side of my head as it passed within inches of my right ear... Then a second realization hit me. I had fortunately been wearing my Bausch and Lomb shooter's glasses with yellow lenses because they helped me see more clearly in darkness and in any low light conditions. If I hadn't been wearing those glasses, my eyes would have likely been filled with sharp glass shards! I had glass fragments spread clear across my face, blown across the front of my shirt, in my ears and down the neck of my shirt but nothing in my eyes. In fact, the entire area around my eyes was clear of any glass shards but the glasses I had been wearing were now nowhere on my face! Apparently, the concussive force of the nearby rifle blast exploding out the back window of the Buick had blown my shooter's glasses clear off my face! Sure, my hair and front of my shirt glistened with glass chips and I was spitting out glass chips but my good parts were O.K.! Once again, thanks to my two guardian angels, I had slipped by the Grim Reaper and his 'rider on the dark horse' in fine style.

(As an aside, in 1978 as a Special Agent for the U.S. Fish and Wildlife Service on special assignment in South East Asia, my group of Thai wildlife officers and my Marine guard from the Embassy, were by sheer chance ambushed in our vehicles by marauding Burmese insurgents while traveling along a jungle trail near the town of Kwai, to check a crocodile farm. In that ensuing shoot-out, I again experienced the sounds of a too close for comfort bullet as it tore off my shirt collar! But if you folks wish to read about that wild adventure, you will have to read it in my EBOOK, *Defending Our Wildlife Heritage* in the chapter titled, "Asia, 1978". That is unless you can now find that out of print book listed for sale on Amazon.)

Realizing where one bullet had come from and not wanting to experience another, I quickly stepped up to the back of the car, ripped open the back door with my pistol in my right hand in case the shot fired had been intentional. At that point, I just wanted to get control of the situation before it got any further out of hand. There I discovered a Mexican fellow rolling around on the back seat as if he just had his head blown off. He was screaming and yelling in Spanish and squirming around like he had a live rattlesnake moving around in his pants near his family jewels. Then I saw why. He had a huge red and black powder burn alongside the left side of his neck and cheek! Laid on the seat was a Winchester model 94 lever action rifle. Grabbing it off the seat so my lad would have no more opportunity to use it, I holstered my handgun and jacked open the rifle's chamber. Out flipped a loaded cartridge, 32 Winchester Special in caliber.

Hearing the siren and seeing the red light illuminating the Buick's rear window, my chap in the back seat had tried to quickly unload his rifle. Instead of just flipping the lever open and leaving it in that configuration, he had nervously continued jacking out live shells from the rifle's tubular magazine. To facilitate such rapid, awkward action in the confines of the backseat, my lad had laid the rifle's barrel over his left shoulder, held it there with one hand and continued jacking out shells from the magazine with the other. He somehow had pulled the trigger in his excitement and the rifle had gone off. Since the end of the barrel had been laid on the man's left shoulder next to his head, he got a beautiful powder burn on the left side of his neck and cheek along with a loudly ringing left ear as a reminder of his stupidity to boot!

Seeing my lad in the back seat was a mess and now no further threat, I turned my attention to the driver who was still yelling, squirming around and holding his ears over the concussive effects from the rifle blast in the back seat. It was apparent that he too would not be able to pass much of a hearing test for the next few days because of his buddy setting off his rifle unexpectedly in the close confines of their vehicle.

Then it dawned on me. Where the dickens was my lad who had recently occupied the front passenger seat? The one and same man who had originally helped spirit the deer over the fence. HE WAS NOWHERE TO BE SEEN OR FOUND! Figuring the back seat rifle blast had spun him out from his front seat and onto the ground, I ran around the car looking for him. The car had been full of Mexicans. Yet, my front seated passenger was now nowhere to be seen. Looking all around the Buick with my flashlight and with the help from Carter who had just driven up, our third lad was still nowhere to be found. It became apparent to the two gringo law dogs that our other lad, who was more than likely an illegal alien, had fled off into the night to avoid capture and forcibly returned to Mexico. Twenty more minutes of looking produced nary a third lad.

Getting back to my remaining two captures and still trying to dust glass chips off my clothing, Carter and I searched our lads, handcuffed them after placing them under arrest for taking a deer illegally and put them into the backseat of his patrol car. Then I got an idea. I had the driver of the Buick call out in Spanish for the other long gone chap to surrender and come forward. Nary a chap produced himself for us to see and capture. For all intents and purposes, he was lost to the ages.

Opening up the Buick's trunk so I could retrieve the buck that had been killed in my presence, I discovered the fresh hindquarters (the meaty parts) from three other deer in the trunk of that car! Where those deer parts had come from the now tight- lipped Mexicans from the nearby town of Williams wouldn't say. So, I had Carter haul them off to jail in Colusa. I then called the sheriff's office and had them get Joe Willow out of bed and have him come with his wrecker to meet me in order for him to haul their Buick off to the sheriff's office impound lot in Colusa. That way, our suspected illegal Mexican was not going to be able to sneak back to the car after I had left the field of battle, hot wire it and flee the scene if I had anything to say about it.

When Joe finally arrived, it was already daylight. After I helped him hook up the Buick, I took off and ran all the roads in the general area looking for my third poaching son-of-a-gun Mexican deer killing chap. Nothing was ever found of my escapee.

Later during daylight hours, I tried to find my B&L shooters glasses with the yellow lenses. You know, the ones that had protected my eyes from the flying glass shards when the Buick's rear window had exploded into my face from just a few feet away with a million flying shards of glass. Like the third Mexican, they were nowhere to be found either.

Giving up my quest to find the third leg of my Mexican deer-killing trio, a thought suddenly hit me. When I had originally walked up to the rear of that Buick and the back window had exploded, I was directly in the line of fire. I could still feel that bullet's air-sucking sensation as it sped by my right ear and then experienced the following blast and explosion of glass fragments that followed. Yet, I was unhurt except for a few glass scratches on my face. Talk about the beauty of having two guardian angels watching over me. I guess one could say, like a cat and being a game warden performing a sometimes dangerous job, I had to have nine lives in order to survive the long haul. I figured I had just used up one of those nine lives when that bullet sped closely by the side of my head that morning and now I figured I was down to just eight....

A month later, my two forlorn looking Mexican chaps who were American citizens, trooped forward into the Williams Justice Court and laid their heads down on the chopping block. Judge Gibson found both men guilty of casting an artificial light upon a game animal and having a weapon capable of taking that game animal in their possession, taking a deer during the closed season and possession of a loaded rifle in a motor vehicle on a way open to the public. The two men were fined $750.00 each and the judge allowed the men, who were nearby well known farm hands, to pay off the fines in installments. Their spotlight and Winchester rifle were forfeited to the State of California where they were later sold at auction. Ironically, as for the deer and the hind quarters of the other deer discovered in the trunk of the Buick, I delivered them to several needy legal Mexican families with a hat full of kids on the east side of my patrol district.

I still think back with a smile over the looks of all those 13 Mexican children when they saw all that deer meat dropped off into the kitchen of their home. No more JUST beans and tortillas for a while had to be going through those kids minds. Looking over at the smiles on the parents' faces, I already knew what they were thinking...

Flowers and Tombstones

As was the case in all of my law enforcement adventures, there were always Flowers and Tombstones. As for the Flowers during this latest adventure, I was still maturing and learning just what it took to become a good wildlife officer. Additionally, I still had the world's best supportive wife who let me run in my world of a wildlife vision quest until my tongue dragged on the ground. I was also discovering that I was more than successful in putting a mess of those chaps in the business of extinction out of business when it came to night shooting deer. And, I know of 13 little Mexican kids who ate one hell of a lot better once several hundred pounds of good eating venison was dropped off on their doorsteps by the local game warden. Years later I found out that all of those 13 children had gone off to college and graduated because of their parents' dedication to them and their educations. That is what I would call 13 sterling American citizens living the American Dream in a field of Flowers!

As for the Tombstones in this story, the constant lawlessness against those in the world of wildlife generated by my locals and others of like ilk, continues to grind against the critters population numbers and their genetic qualities. As I was later to discover, the war against those walking on the dark side in the world of wildlife would ultimately not be winnable. The odds from the 'dark side' and the 'man on the black horse' were just too much for the law of the land to overcome and win the battle in the world of wildlife. But, that sure didn't stop me from trying, sacrificing my body, my family times, and giving my all every time I ventured forth. No matter how one looked at it, life is not measured in time. It is measured in what you do with the time you have been allotted. Before it was all said and done some 32 years later of state and federal wildlife law enforcement experiences, I would have to say like a smashed cat, I am now down to just one life left to live... The other eight out of my nine lives were expended in other like law enforcement adventures but what a great ride it has been!

The last Tombstone to be noted in this adventure was that of my dear friend, Deputy Sheriff Del Garrison. Years later he contracted a fast moving strain of diabetes, eventually lost most of his fingers, both legs and a lot of feeling in his body. He died shortly thereafter from complications of that disease. I lost a dear friend and buddy when he died. May the good Lord take a liking to Del for he was a good man and I miss him dearly to this very day. I still find it hard to see through misted eyes as these words are written about Del many years after his premature passing... Like Del, I am now also a diabetic. Hell, anymore it seems just about everybody has diabetes. That being the case, I wonder if that disease will use up my last life out of the nine I had been previously allotted and present me with my own Tombstone...? Wouldn't that be a hoot? Dumped by a useless, non-functioning pancreas instead of a flying bullet fired through the back window of a Buick or in the jungles of Thailand after being ambushed by Burmese insurgents and almost killed...

THIRTEEN SHOTS ARE THE DOWNFALL FOR THREE WILDLIFE OUTLAWS

Arriving at the Goat Mountain Road turnoff in western Colusa County, I turned and headed up into some of my mountainous backcountry in order to check my early deer season hunters. Rounding a turn near the Trough Spring Road somewhat later, I came upon a chap hurriedly dragging an untagged forked horn buck off the hillside above the road. Down that high bank he came at a trot dragging the small buck like the devil was on his tail. Losing his footing on the lose substrate, he plunged head over forked horn buck off the bank and onto the Goat Mountain Road in front of me in a cloud of dust, flying elbows and tumbling deer carcass! For a moment my chap lay there on the roadbed getting his wits about him and then seeing the nearness of my game warden green patrol truck slowly approaching, flew into action! With the realization that a game warden was close at hand and knowing that he had an illegal deer in his possession (untagged), he jumped up, reached for his rifle laying on the roadside and his wallet holding the needed deer tags all in the same panicked motion.

"You are a little late," I said, as I stepped out from my truck and began approaching my now in a panic lad. Not heeding my words, the man frantically tried removing a set of unused deer tags from his wallet so he could quickly punch them in accordance with the fish and game regulations and attach them to the deer's antlers. To you non-deer hunters out there, upon killing a deer in California in those days, one had to **immediately** fill out and punch the month and date of the kill on his deer tags and attach them to the animal **prior** to transport. Normally I wouldn't have been such a hard ass in the deer tag punching detail and given my chap some latitude. But in this particular case, my guardian angels were all a-twitter inside me letting me know all was not square with the deer hunting world. Walking forward, I now became keenly aware of my lad's vehicle sitting off to one side on the road's edge. And in the front seat of that vehicle sat a young woman who by her dress, was also a deer hunter. My being a hard ass over the untagged deer violation was later justified when I reached my slightly banged up sport who had just taken a tumble off the hillside. One who was now clutching a set of unused deer tags in his hands with a desperate look spreading across his face. Upon examination, the unused tags he was holding turned out to be his wife's unfilled deer tags! That situation was further exacerbated by the fact that my sport had already taken his deer and it currently was lying in the bed of his pickup all legally tagged!

Understanding what had just transpired, I asked for his driver's license. Once that was in hand, I walked over to the young lady sitting in the pickup with a set of eyes the size of dinner plates and a look of concern splashed all over her face as she firmly clutched her hunting rifle between her legs.

"Ma'am, did you shoot that deer laying over there in the roadbed?" I asked.

It took my young woman a moment to recover from what was happening and then she replied, "Yes I did, Officer." When she spoke those words, I noticed that the tone and tenor of her response left a lot to be desired in the truthfulness of her statement department and so did her lack of eye contact.

She was sitting on the passenger seat of the pickup with a bolt action Winchester held between her legs. Let me tell you, she was shaking like a dog passing peach pits over my unexpected presence and the questioning situation now at hand. Folks, when someone is that nervous in the presence of a peace officer, most of the time something is dead wrong (no pun intended) and needs further exploring.

"Ma'am, may I see your rifle so I can check to see if it is loaded?" I asked in such a manner in order to calm her down.

Without a word, she stuck the rifle barrel out the open window directly into my face! Quickly reacting and ducking below the end of the rifle barrel, I just shook my head in disbelief as I quickly reached up and controlled the direction in which the weapon was pointing. I am sure the young woman who had just unsafely handled her firearm saw the disgust of that careless moment splashed across my face. Lifting the bolt to check to see if the rifle was loaded, I discovered a live round in the chamber of the rifle with the rifle's safety on the off position!

It sure was nice having a loaded rifle dangerously poked into my face, I disgustedly thought. It was a good thing I had ducked when I did upon receiving her rifle because in her state of extreme nervousness anything could have happened. Chalk

357

that survival moment up to having two protective guardian angels at my side.

Putting the live round in my shirt pocket as evidence for a loaded gun citation to follow, I lifted up the rifle to my nose and smelled the chamber area. All I could detect was the faint smell of gun cleaning solution and no smell of a freshly fired shell. That told me she had not shot the rifle recently nor the deer now lying dead in the road. Removing the bolt, I reversed the rifle and looked down the barrel to see how clean it was. There was no powder residue in the barrel indicating that the rifle had been recently fired. With those facts in mind, that told me more than likely my pair had been 'road hunting' down Goat Mountain Road, observed a buck deer standing on the hillside and the male of the pair had shot the deer for his wife. Since California law required each person to take their own game, another more serious violation of the fish and game regulations was now in the mix in addition to the loaded gun violation.

Laying her rifle on the hood of their truck where I had earlier laid the man's rifle after making my initial contact, I checked her hunting license against the set of non-validated deer tags I had taken from the man. As suspected, the deer tags numbers matched those recorded on her hunting license. Since my fellow had a freshly killed buck deer in the back of their pickup and another one lying on the road, it was apparent to me what had just transpired. Bottom line, I now had a chap with one buck deer too many lying on the road since the limit was one buck per season in that district and his previously killed and tagged deer now laid in the bed of his truck.

Further discussion with my two deer hunters revealed that my assumption was correct. Both people admitted under questioning, that the man had legally killed and tagged the buck in the bed of their truck earlier in the morning. Later when driving down the road on the way home, he had spotted another buck on his side of the road, quietly gotten out from his truck in order not to spook the animal and had shot it from the roadway. He had done so because his wife still had an unfilled deer tag and he figured since another buck was so close at hand, that was better than 'one in the bush.'

Twenty minutes later after seizing both deer, I issued the man a citation for possession of an over limit of deer, To Wit: one over the limit. Following that, his wife received a citation for being in possession of a loaded rifle in a motor vehicle on a way open to the public. I didn't say anything to her about her careless handling of the rifle when I had asked to inspect it to see if it was loaded. I just figured I had survived another dangerous episode in my life and better to let sleeping dogs lie.

With that bit of administrative work out of the way and a seizure tag issued for the two deer and the man's rifle used in the killing of both deer, I sent my two contrite folks down the road 'kicking rocks'. Following that, I gutted the second deer alongside the road and tossed the innards over the bank for any hungry critters to enjoy. I then washed my hands off with some water drained from off my ice chest's melting ice. After putting seizure tags on the two deer now lying in the bed of my truck, I let Shadow out so she could take care of her business. Taking one of my ever-present ice chests from the now getting crowded bed of my truck, I let more melted ice water flow into a pan for Shadow and set it down for her to drink. As she drank, I took out a cold Coke for me to slack my thirst. (This was before the days of commonly bottled water.)

Standing there in the day's dry heat and quiet, I took a long pull on my Coke and refilled my dog's water pan so she could have another drink. It had to be hot riding in the back of my truck and I made sure every time we went by any clean standing water, she got to take a swim. However, when I stopped elsewhere where no swimming water was present, she got a drink. Shadow was a damned good dog and I treated accordingly. (Besides, if I had come home without her for any reason, my wife would have shot me and my two boys would have disowned their dear old dad...)

BOOM, BOOM, BOOM, BOOM, BOOM,.. went a series of thirteen quick shots from what sounded like they were being fired from three separate rifles. As it just so happened, I was looking right in the direction from where that explosion of shooting had come. From where I was standing on Goat Mountain Road looking over into the area where Trough Spring Road ended, that was where I had echo located onto that series of wildly fired shots. I knew damn well that intensity and sequencing of shooting was not target practice or any kind of random target shooting at tin cans and the like. The frequency, sequencing and number of guns shooting told me a group of shooters had gotten into a mess of deer and were making the critters pay.

Jumping back into my truck after reloading Dog, off we went in the direction of the shooting. Turning off Goat Mountain Road onto Trough Spring Road, I slowed and began looking for a point where I could stop, get out, listen and scope the suspect area with my binoculars. Finding a wide spot in the road with an adjacent high point, I bailed out grabbing my binoculars as I went and sprinted to the high ground. From there, I discovered I had a good view of the area I figured from whence had come all the earlier shooting.

For the longest time I saw nothing except two pickups parked a ways off down Trough Spring Road. Then I spotted a man without a rifle hurrying down through the wooded terrain, as he left the approximate area of the suspect shooting. Watching him closely, I could see that he was hastily moving towards the two parked vehicles with the 'bit in his teeth'. When the man arrived at the vehicles, he looked all around as if to see if anyone was observing his actions. Seeing no sign of outside recognition, he opened a door on a blue truck and extracted a large backpack. Turning, the man slipped one of his shoulders under a shoulder strap and then hurriedly reversed his course and went back up onto the ridge like a man on a mission. You good folks out there reading these lines know what happens when a prey species quickly moves away from a predator... You guessed right, with what I had just observed, the 'prey' species had just split the scene and the hunt was now on.

Still not seeing anyone else moving about in the suspect area from whence had come all the shooting, I figured I would just keep my eyes on the chap with the backpack to see if he would lead me to the scene of the shooting. That way, my suspect man with the backpack could lead my eyes to what I needed to see. For the next twenty minutes or so, my fellow with the backpack struggled uphill and then disappeared over a ridge that led into a small canyon. Taking that as my cue, Dog and I headed further uphill so I could occupy the higher ground and be better able to look back into that small canyon into which my chap lugging the backpack had just disappeared.

Soon I was sweating like a pig at a slaughter house and feeling the excess body weight I was packing as I hurriedly climbed higher and higher in the eighty degree heat and higher elevation. Stopping at a high point at the head of my suspect canyon, I slid in behind a large Douglas fir tree for the cover it offered, sat down and took a quick look into the small canyon below. There about 150 yards below me were four individuals in a group. Three of them appeared to be older men and one individual appeared to be maybe a boy of eleven or twelve years of age. All four individuals had gathered around a pile of dead deer and were beginning to process the same! From my location with the binoculars, I could not make out a single set of antlers on any of the critters lying on the ground, which made all of those deer illegal and my lads as well!

With the exception of the younger lad, the three older appearing men were skinning out the illegal deer. Once a deer was skinned out on one side, the men began boning out the critter and placing the piles of meat on a white cloth which had been extracted from the backpack of the man I had earlier watched returning to the scene. When finished with boning out one side of a deer, the animal was turned over and the meat boning-out process on the other side was repeated. With that maneuver, it became apparent my three men were boning out their illegal deer to make hiding and transport of their meat easier. As for the boy in the group, he was now holding open white cloth meat bags as the men filled them with chunks of doe meat. This illegal butchering activity went on for over an hour until the men had boned out a total of five doe deer and placed all the meat into white cloth meat bags for easier transport. That boning out process told me my chaps had intended all along to kill whatever they saw that day, legal or illegal, and then sneak out the meat. That preplanning and field butchering made it easier to carry the best venison eats off the mountain in amounts small enough to hide once they got back to their rigs. Pretty damn clever idea boning out the meat and all but my outlaws had just one major problem. There was a chap sitting off at a distance on the far hillside now fully aware of their little plan and, he didn't approve...

When finished with the butchering and the meat sacking, the men urinated on their hands apparently to wash off the telltale smears of deer blood. *Pretty damn clever,* I thought. *But, I would bet a plug nickel that they didn't take the time to clean out the tell-tale signs of blood from under their fingernails...* As an aside for all you budding game wardens out there, looking under a suspected wildlife outlaw's fingernails is always a good bet and a commonly used game warden trick of the trade. A good bet because without vigorously washing one's hands after a kill, there will always be blood remaining under one's fingernails.

Finished with the meat boning out process, everyone hefted a bag of meat and made ready to leave the scene of the crime. With 'Backpack Man' in the lead and the others following cleverly about 50 yards behind him in case the first man was intercepted by a game warden, out they headed. With a plan forming in my head as to how I would approach the situation, off the mountain Dog and I trotted. Once back at my truck, I reloaded Dog, got a quick drink of Coke and kept watch for the arrival of my four chaps back at their vehicles still parked off a distance away.

About 30 minutes later, I observed Backpack Man carefully approaching their two parked vehicles. Through my binoculars I could see the man looking all around to see if anyone was watching. Satisfied that he was alone, he ran the final few yards to the blue truck. He then unloaded the white sacks of boned out meat from within the backpack and hid all of them behind the seat of his pickup along with the telltale bloody backpack. Finished, he gave another look all around and then got out a drink from one of the ice chests in the back of his truck. He kept looking all around as if expecting the game warden to appear at any moment. Little did Backpack Man realize that little moment in time was later to come... Finishing his drink and satisfied he was alone, I saw him raise his arm and wave to someone in the forest's cover on the mountainside.

Out from their hiding places in the forest trotted the remaining three chaps carrying the white bags of boned out doe meat. Those chaps ran to the two vehicles and quickly hid all their ill- gotten gains behind both pickup's front seats. Soon, nary a sight of anything being illegal or out of place greeted any casual eyes that might come along. Taking another long look at my chaps, I observed that they had all gathered at the tailgate of the green pickup. Draining melted water from an ice chest, they again washed their hands clean of any evidence of wrong- doing. But once again, I didn't see anyone taking out a knife and cleaning underneath their fingernails.

Talk about outlaw smart, I thought, *my killers sure as hell know what to do in order to throw off any unsuspecting game warden making a routine check.* By washing off their hands in the manner in which they did, there would be no obvious bloody hands to give away their little secret. Well, my outlaws in their haste to appear all legal like and innocent as a new born lamb, had forgotten one thing. They had the timber's cover to hide their black deeds but they had forgotten to put a roof on their little forest fortress. That allowed unwanted eyes to have a clear view of what not to do when the game warden was in country and on to them...

By holding the high ground and being able to look down upon my wildlife outlaws without being seen in the process, I now had the goods on my lads. Then just at that moment, I got another one of my goofy damn ideas that would teach the young man in the bunch a unique lesson. I knew I couldn't teach the older dogs of their party any new tricks but I sure as hell could leave the youngster of the group with a damn good life's lesson in wildlife conservation and that crime does not pay. A lesson which I would hope teach him in the future to obey the laws and not follow in the footsteps of the outlaw bunch of adults he was currently running with.

It was then that I observed my outlaws getting out a lunch for the group and placing it out on a lowered tailgate. Satisfied with their day and the fruits of their labors, they began their little tailgate celebration over having pulled the wool over the Face of God and his 'Tule-Creeper' game warden minions. Finding that as good a time as any to rain on their little doe killing parade, I figured 'we' would make our grand appearance acting like nothing out of the ordinary had just occurred. As we did, my little Plan B on the trick I was about to pull on my deer killing outlaws whirled around in my head. It would soon be Plan B lesson time for my wildlife outlaws, especially for a still impressionable young man.

Driving slowly into view, I saw everyone's eyes fly to looking at my approaching marked patrol vehicle like that of a flock of Rhode Island Red roosters would be looking at something moving on the ground close to them like a succulent worm. Approaching slowly so I wouldn't spread road dust on their picnic lunch, I pulled in behind their pickups and stopped. Stepping out and acting like any other dumb as a rock game warden not knowing what was going on, I said, "Afternoon, Gents. Have any luck this fine morning while deer hunting?"

"Never saw a damn thing this morning, Officer. I guess it is just too hot and the deer are feeding at night and resting out of sight during the day," said a bearded one and, to my way of thinking, maybe the patriarch of the group from his taking the lead actions with an obvious foe.

"Dang, that is too bad. You guys should have been where I was this morning. I ran across a sport who had one too many. Now both of his deer are in the back of my truck," I said as I began leading into my lesson soon to be learned by the group.

"Really," said the bearded one.

"Let's take a look and see what a deer looks like," said a tall chap with a smirk splashed clear across his face like he knew something that I didn't. Then he said, "Come on, Son. Let's go and see what this game warden has in the back of his truck."

Just as I had suspected, I thought. *The younger lad is that outlaw's son and one who is soon going to get a message in just how sharp these game warden types can be*, I thought with a grin in my mischievous heart over what was coming. (I think some of my sharper readers out there can see what is coming, especially if their noses are working...)

With that, my outlaws went to the back of my truck and stood around admiring the two bucks that I had seized. Then it was back to their picnic with a lot of talk centering about where I had seen deer in my travels and was there any area in which I could recommend where they could go and try their luck on an afternoon hunt. As the five of us visited back and forth, I made the rounds checking their rifles to make sure they weren't loaded where they had been placed on the hoods of their vehicles. Following that, I made a perfunctory check of their hunting licenses and deer tags, just like a game warden with only an I.Q. of 4 would do. Every now and then I could see small smirks and sly smiles coming from the faces of my outlaws like they knew something that the dumb game warden didn't.

Having been there before, I let my chaps play their little game but I noticed the boy had little to say and just kept looking at the adults so he could follow their leads on what to do or say in the presence of a 'hated enemy'. Since my youngster seemed to be taking his cue from his outlaw companions, I figured it was time for the lesson formulated under my Plan B to make the scene in all its glory. So with that, I let her rip.

"Say, Guys, do any of you smell that?" I casually asked in a phony quizzical tone of voice.

"Smell what?" asked three of the men all at the same time with their mouths full of sandwiches. (By the way, I hadn't been asked to join the men in their repast. What does that tell you about their respect for the law or another possibly another hungry human being? What it told me was they wished I would get the hell out of their lives and the quicker the better.)

Looking all around like I had missed something obvious, I said, "I smell venison. Say, those aren't venison sandwiches are they?"

"No," said two of the men, "they are ham and cheese."

"Well, I sure can smell venison and to be frank, it smells like fresh venison now that I think about it," I continued. When I uttered those words, I made it a point to smell big snoot full of air in front of my lads like I was trying to concentrate and scent the 'air' that I was now smelling.

366

"Well the only thing fresh about venison in this camp is the deer poop I stepped in this morning," said the bearded one with a big know-it-all sly grin like I know something that you don't know smile slowly crossing his face.

But when he responded, just for a second, I could see a flash of surprise and then worry skip across his eyes over my unusual question and sense of smell. Boring in, I continued with my little lesson the boys could share back at work on Monday about the local game warden and his tremendous sense of smell...

"I need to step back so the smells of what you fellas are eating doesn't goof up my 'smeller'," I said, as I took several exaggerated steps away from the food spread out on the tail gate. Then for God and all the forest creatures to see, I made a big issue of me smelling deeply into the air up high and then down low, as if the smell might be on their boots or on the ground. When I did, it was like every one of my lad's heads moved up and down following my every smelling movement. It was a riot and I really had to stifle an urge to laugh loudly at the antics of my four chaps in response to my obviously goofy behavior. Hang on tight my patient readers, there is more to come in the offing besides just a 'smell' in the air...

"You sure you boys didn't kill any deer this morning? I ask because the sweet smell of fresh venison is sure heavy in the air around us." With those words, I let my eyes move from lad to lad as if looking into their inner beings for answers to my goofy damn questions. When I did, not a single man could look directly into my eyes. Talk about a guilty and nervous 'tell' now being exhibited by down cast eyes from everyone present, including the youngster. Plus at that stage in the conversation, I had my doubts about any of them being able to pass any gas at that moment in time because of my odd-ball behavior. Especially in light of what I was apparently smelling and what they were hiding...

Then there was the young lad and the looks he was carrying on his worried face. His eyes betrayed the fact that he looked like a trapped mouse looking at a close at hand, hungry long-tailed weasel. It was obvious that the young man had such a tight hind end over the events now unfolding and his knowledge of the illegal deer hidden in their pickups, that he couldn't have passed any gas even if he had eaten a dinner plate full of fat back and Navy beans.

By now, everyone had seemingly lost interest in their picnic as they waited for the goofy damn game warden in front of them to make his next move. And it wasn't long in coming... "Damn, Guys. That smell of freshly killed venison is hanging so heavy in this dry mountain air that I can't understand why you can't smell it," I continued as I now gave all of them a real searching look. When my eyes fastened onto those of my young lad, it was obvious he was ready to run for cover or cry.

It was then that the bearded one I considered the leader of the bunch, came up with a brilliant and surprising response that almost caught me napping. Almost... "Hell, Man. All you are smellin' are those two damn deer in the back of your truck you seized from that other deer hunter with the over limit earlier in the day."

With that seemingly brilliant observation and verbalization, you could just see the response relief flooding across the other doe killing lad's faces including that of the youngster.

But hang on my readers, your gorilla sized game warden was no slouch either when it came to being a 'trickster'. "Guys, I hate to tell you this but that smell isn't coming from those two bucks. Yes, they have their own venison smell but what I am smelling is coming from doe deer not males of the species!" I brilliantly countered. Just think, folks. Who the hell can tell the difference in smells between a male and a female deer? No one to my experienced way of thinking and extensive college book knowledge except that of a buck deer when the doe deer are in estrus during the rut that is.

At that moment, I could sense that each of my adult outlaws felt like a tiger shark had just clamped onto their family jewels! As for my youngster, he looked like a T-Rex was gumming him. And he was looking at his dad like he would lose him forever if their dirty little doe killing secret was ever discovered by this monster sized game warden confronting the four of them. You know, the warden who has a nose like a shark when there is blood in the water.

Then came the game warden's grand finale! Bending over like a damn fool and making very loud sniffing sounds like a bloodhound trying to sniff out his quarry, I moved around the men's two pickups. As I did, I continued taking in loud and deep snoots full of air like a marathon runner at the end of a long race. I stopped at the open doors of each truck and made sure they heard and saw me taking in an extra loud snoot full of air. I hoped my lesson of 'cold tracking' a venison smell was being taken in by the youngster for the lesson that was to come. If I could somehow convince him of a game warden's super sensory smelling powers and prowess, maybe he would go straight in the future. And if so, I would have won one for the Gipper in the world of wildlife law enforcement.

Walking back around to the front of the group, I casually said, "Gentlemen, that fresh venison smell of doe deer is coming from the insides of your pickups, as well as from your hands! Let me see all of your hands," I said abruptly. For the longest moment, each man withheld his hands out of fear they might lose them to the crazy game warden at hand. Finally their hands were proffered and I took great pains to smell each man's hands. "That is where some of the fresh venison smell is coming from!" I loudly blurted out. When I said what I said, each man jumped like I had just clipped off one of his fingers per hand. "It sure looks like fresh deer blood underneath each of your fingernails," I continued like it was a real revelation.

By now, my group of lads had grown as quiet as an Egyptian tomb and no one was paying one bit of attention to their ham and cheese sandwiches....

"For your information and I won't tell you how we game wardens do it, but we are taught back at the fish and game academy about various animal smells. With that scope and degree of training, we are able to use those senses routinely when working sportsmen, especially when it comes to search and seizure. Plus when I was sniffing around your vehicles, I noticed several drops of blood on the door sill of the brown truck. That blood is still sticky to the touch, which tells me there are fresh deer parts or meat behind the seats of your vehicles. I can also see several partially covered white meat bags that are bloody looking and stashed behind the seats. That tells me there is fresh meat of some kind inside and if I was a betting man, I would bet it is deer meat." Of course, I did not tell them what I had observed earlier on their doe butchering detail on the mountainside and how I had observed them subsequently depositing the meat behind the seats of their pickups. To do so would have spoiled my fun and ruined the lesson I was hoping to teach the youngster.

"Now we can do this one of two ways. If there are parts of deer behind your seats and you come clean, we can settle this up with just a citation. However, if you want to be difficult here is what I am proposing to do. I will arrest the lot of you for possession of illegal deer and I will seize your vehicles and have them towed back to Williams for impound. You will be handcuffed and taken to jail in Colusa and booked for possession of illegal deer. On top of that, the owners of these pickups will be liable for the rather expensive towing charges. What call do you guys want to make? The easy way or the hard way if confessions are not forthcoming?"

Brother, my tough guys weren't so tough. They all broke like an egg with their lame 'we needed the meat to feed our families' justifications and soon the back of my patrol truck was again graced with more illegal deer. Good to my word, all three adults were issued citations for taking and possessing illegal deer, To Wit: four doe deer. I also seized their rifles and issued seizure tags for the deer and their rifles. You talk about a contrite bunch. They all were as quiet as a bunch of mice pissin' on a ball of cotton when their little secret was out of the bag and the citations were issued.

As for my young man, he sure got an eye full! Since he was under the age of 16, he was not cited for his actions. However, my hope was he had learned a lesson regardless of what his father had done and that lesson would stick with him throughout the rest of his life. If the looks on that youngster's face said anything as to lessons learned, I had been a good teacher. My smelling abilities still had him stumped from the looks on his face and they were more than compounded when the citations were issued all around and the men's rifles and deer meat seized.

Over the next two weeks, my three lads individually trooped into the Williams Justice Court, left $500.00 each with the state's coffers, lost their hunting rifles and were surprised by Judge Gibson's ruling that the three men be barred from hunting deer in California for the following three years! Like I said earlier, Judge Gibson was a good man. I never ran across those three doe killing chaps in Colusa County again nor did I ever see that youngster afield. I sure hoped he had learned a damned good lesson on just how sensitive a game warden's sense of smell can really be...

As for the Flowers in this story, they are many. I was able to teach a husband that his wife needs to kill her own deer and the wife needed to remember the same. As for my three doe slayers, their crime, no matter how slickly thought through, did not pay. No matter just how devious you might think you are, there are badge carriers out there who are 'slicker than cow slobbers' when it comes to having a better sense of smell than the average Yogi Bear.

Additionally, another Flower was my ability to add to the mystic sensory powers of those of The Thin Green Line. In the years that followed in my law enforcement career, I have used that Flower of my mystic smelling ability on numerous cases with the same wonderful teaching results. And with a three-year moratorium on any deer hunting in California, I was sure that lesson of Flower power gave pause to my three doe killing outlaws come any future poaching ideas or outings they might have had in the back of their minds.

The Flowers continued when the State of California sold the confiscated rifles later at auction and the money secured from such sales was utilized within the statewide hunter safety training program. A program that my young accompanying lad with the doe slayers had to participate in if he wanted to be an ethical, legal and safe hunter.

As for the deer and their parts seized, Flowers were spread all around. I distributed those stores to four hard working Mexican farm families with children in Colusa County. Those meat stores I am sure were happily utilized and preferred over a steady diet of beans and rice.

California lost a total of six deer taken illegally that day but here is a case of a Tombstone being turned into Flowers. Hopefully in this illegal deer killing affair, a father learned never to take his child along and try to teaching him how to be a wildlife outlaw. I also hope my youngster learned in the above lesson that one's life is not measured by the time spent in the traces but what you do with that time.

A DAY WITH 'DOG,' OVER LIMITS AND OUTLAWS

Leaving my home in Colusa around two in the morning, Dog and I headed north on Highway 45 to the small

Sacramento Valley town of Princeton. Once there, I turned east on Norman Road and, before crossing over Willow Creek, turned off my lights on the county undercover truck so I would not be seen while sneaking around in the dark. At the intersection of Young Road, I turned south heading into many acres of recently harvested rice fields. The evening before, Dog and I had observed at least 50,000 mallards and northern pintail flooding into several adjacent harvested rice fields just west of Young Road. If I could see that many ducks flooding into the harvested rice paddies so could the local outlaws from the towns of Princeton and Delevan as well as all the other black-hearted duck killing souls driving the backroads at dusk looking for feeding hordes of waterfowl to illegally blow up later under the cover of darkness.

Driving out into a recently harvested rice field, I parked my truck in among several Hardy Harvesters and a bank out wagon like any dirt farmer would do. This I did so my truck was hidden in plain view from those illegal duck and goose killing souls that I figured I would soon be pursuing. Stepping out into the cool darkness of the morning's air, I could hear the flowing water sounds made by thousands of madly feeding ducks several hundred yards distant in an adjacent rice field. With the feathered ones located, Dog and I slowly and quietly headed out into the rice fields so as not to disturb the thousands of feeding ducks or anyone of my local night shooting, duck-dragging clientele stalking the birds as was I.

Sneaking about 300 yards away from where my truck was parked using numerous rice checks for cover, Dog and I moved to a hidden position near approximately 10,000 happily feeding ducks. There we dug into the water grasses and damp mud on the back side of a rice check for the cover and concealment such a water control structure and its accompanying vegetation offered. Then we laid in wait to see if anyone was putting a sneak on the nearby feeding birds with the idea of blowing them up as they fed in their traditional, snake-like moving, living carpet style across the harvested rice fields.

Within 30 minutes, Dog and I were totally surrounded and, in a sense of the word, buried in madly feeding ducks. And, when it came to huge numbers of feeding ducks, I do mean buried! As it turned out, the hiding place we had chosen inadvertently placed us directly in front of the living carpet of madly feeding ducks. Initially in the darkness when we arrived at our hiding spot, I could not see or tell by listening which way the ducks were moving as they fed. The air was full of whistling wings by the thousands, with many zipping by just head high, precluding me from standing up and exactly locating the path of my feeding birds. There were numerous adjacent bunches of feeding ducks on the ground all around us, and there were more birds constantly winging into the area. In short, it was an aerial madhouse and the ground was literally alive with the critters, and as we quickly discovered, soon to be moving our way! Let me tell all you good readers out there, the experience of being that close to so many living critters that did not know we were there, was a memory and adventure I will carry to my grave. It was soon to be a magnificent living moment in time in our memory banks!

Lying as still as death itself to avoid alarming the close at hand madly feeding ducks, Dog and I soon found ourselves literally buried with the arrival of tens of thousands of ducks feeding across the rice check where we laid hidden. When they arrived, they were physically bumper to bumper because they were feeding so closely together! Those birds were so hungry and greedy for any rice grains left on the ground by the harvesters that their bodies literally were touching one another! And in their feeding frenzy, here they came! That moving carpet of ducks, feeding into a soft southern wind, quickly fed up to the rice check we were lying behind. Then without hesitation, they flooded right over Dog and me lying motionless on the backside of the rice check like the living, breathing, feathered carpet that happy mess of ducks had become.

Dog was well trained as a retriever and lay still as a stone with my hand resting comfortably on her head as the horde of living critters mowed right over the top of us, our rice check and into the harvested rice field beyond. That being semi-squashed by thousands of happily feeding ducks lasted about 15-20 minutes before they thinned out and the carpet moved off to feed elsewhere. Not only did Dog and I have that experience to log into our memory banks but both of us were now covered with rice field mud from the ducks' feet, a blanket of loose feathers, and a ton of duck poop as mute testimony of that memorable event. What a glorious moment in time that was for us two crazies laying out in a muddy rice field!

(I had experienced that kind of duck feeding mass movement several times earlier in my career while lying out in rice fields full of feeding waterfowl in my meager attempts to apprehend duck-draggers or any surviving commercial market hunters afoot and afield. EVERY TIME when such an event occurred, it was a powerful memory making moment in my soul! Today as I am writing these words in 2015, I can still feel the ducks' bills poking me as they felt along in the darkness feeling for any rice grains as they swept over me in a huge living mass. Along with the sensation of being almost buried alive by living bodies, came the world of wet of duck poop being dropped on the surfaces of Shadow's and my body. Every one of those floods of ducks moving over the top of Dog and me memories, sure made the journey sweet and the getting there memorable!)

Dog and I lay there in the mud, poop, duck feathers, dead crawdads that had perished when the fields were drained prior to harvest, and dampness of the rice field mud until about five in the morning without human induced incident. About then I spotted just the parking lights of a vehicle slowly moving south on Young Road in our direction. Soon its parking lights were extinguished and then nothing. About ten minutes later, I saw the dome lights of that vehicle briefly go on as two subjects bolted from their pickup, quietly pushed the doors shut and then sprinted out into the same field into which Dog and I were hiding. That vehicle and its driver moments later exited the area using only his parking lights once again for illumination. To me, that was a sure sign that something dark in the world of waterfowl was soon to be in the wind...

All the above had been observed through my binoculars and I soon found myself shivering but not from lying in the cold and damp rice field mud for such a long period of time. I loved hunting my fellow man and the rush of excitement I felt over what was about to transpire was truly unique. With the arrival of those two shotgun-toting chaps long before legal shooting hours rushing into rice fields still holding thousands of feeding ducks, told me that the HUNT was now on for BOTH parties!

From that moment on until just before daylight, I saw or heard nothing more of my two shotgun-toting chaps. Those two lads had gone to ground and, in true Colusa County outlaw-style when moving in on the ducks in order to kill as many as they could, they became like a 'will-o-wisp'. If my chaps were there to blow up the ducks, not an evil heartbeat would be heard or 'hide nor hair' of such evil intentioned beings would be seen if they were true to the Valley's illegal gunner's travels and traditions! At least not until it became time to pick up all their ill-gotten gains after a shoot on the massed and feeding ducks had been accomplished.

Right at daylight in the area south of our position but closer to Willow Creek, the damp morning air exploded! When it did, it sounded like someone ripping a heavy sheet because the sounds of shooting came so fast. For the briefest of moments, the air blew up with the thundering sounds of ten shots fired so closely together that one could hardly separate the individual explosions. Then utter silence followed from the shooters. However, a micro-second later, the thunder clap of 20,000 madly beating wings exploding up off the rice ground into the air as their owners headed for the safety of nearby Sacramento National Wildlife Refuge. That moment in time and the spectacular crime of such a killing event, was almost lost to the world that morning, except for its greeting the ears and eyes of one particularly rather large nearby individual and his dog...

As part of the living aftermath of that shoot, the air was full of the sounds of whistling wings, soft croaks, quacks, whistles and peeps from all the different species of confused ducks fleeing the area for their lives and the safety of the nearby wildlife refuge. Me, I was shaking before from my long hours of exposure in the damp cold and now the excitement of the coming chase and its felt cold, totally manifested itself in my winter rice field mud numbed legs. Not having working legs because of the cold damp of lying too long in a winter rice field without movement, especially when it subsequently came to a foot chase, was problematic. I had early on discovered that lying on the cold and damp rice ground for hours on end really stiffened up my running muscles. Just the opposite was happening with my constantly moving outlaws who were keeping warm in the process. In their movement, they were keeping warm and able to move faster if surprised over the appearance of a wildlife officer. So if a chase was to occur, I had to carefully pick my targets of opportunity and moderate my pursuit due to my rice-field-cold running muscles. Dog was also shaking because from her many previous hours of 'practice', she knew what was coming next and couldn't wait to get it into 'gear'. No matter how one looked at it or felt, the hunt was now on, BIG TIME! Moving westward along the backside of my rice check in a crouch, Dog and I trotted right along as I warmed up my cold legs. I needed to get as close to the immediate area from where the explosion of shots had come and do so quickly, because the light of dawn was on its way and so soon would be my shooters. Remember, Folks, once it is light enough to see, one could also be seen. And if that person was my size, it was easy to be seen even when bent over and moving slowly. I could sneak with the best of them but it is damn hard to hide a 6-foot 4-inch framed person weighing as much as I did behind a blade of water grass...

I had now located the specific area of the early morning shooting and was now within chasing distance of anyone involved behind those shots fired 35 minutes before legal shooting hours. (Legal shooting hours for all migratory game birds is one-half hour before sunrise until sunset.) Then Dog and I dug in behind our closest rice check and quietly waited for the known action to come. However, during the whole time, I kept glassing the suspect area with my binoculars looking for any sign of my early shooters picking up the killed birds. In the meantime, hundreds of ducks continued flying over the area they had just vacated after being surprised by the string of early morning shooting but none landed. They just looked for more of their kind feeding below and finding none, along with now being gun shy, left the area for the safety of nearby Delevan and Sacramento National Wildlife Refuges.

Finally, I briefly saw a suspect-shooter peering my way through the water grass over the top of a nearby rice check. For a moment I thought, *'By Gum', I have you now,* because the face peering over the rice check appeared to be a local chap I knew. He looked like Dave Fonseca who was from an old Princeton family of renown from the days when the Sacramento Valley was full of ducks and those who commercially market-hunted them for a living. After looking around and making sure the coast was clear, my suspect stood up and I could see that it was not Dave at all. Dave was a slightly built lad, not one who was all of 6-foot 4-inches to 6-foot 5-inches tall as was the fellow I was now intently eyeballing through my binoculars. Not only that, the chap I was looking at outweighed me. Then another big fellow stood up from behind the same covering rice check. Both men looked all around for any signs of trouble in the form of someone like yours truly being close at hand.

Seeing no one of the local game warden flavor, my two lads dropped their shotguns on top of their rice check and began running around in the field picking up dead and wounded ducks as fast as they could. That was my cue to get my miserable carcass in gear and beginning the process of apprehension. Dog and I then began stalking our duck shooting chaps from behind our covering rice check like there was no tomorrow. We sneaked as close as we could get and then held our ground as our two shooters continued stacking their morning's kill behind the rice check they had previously occupied. Then my two shooters dropped down out of sight behind the rice check and I saw no more of them for the longest time. Fearing they might be crawling away behind their rice check, Dog and I rose and headed at a trot directly toward the last spot where I had seen my two chaps ducking down behind their rice check the last time.

Let me tell you folks out there reading these lines, I could move in those days on my size 14 EEEE hip boots. Hell, even in college weighing 265 and playing football, I could run an eleven-second flat 100-yard dash! Not like I am today, all busted up with two replaced knees and a back that isn't worth a tinker's damn. But in those bygone days, I could run like the wind and go the distance if necessary. Alright you disbelieving readers out there, maybe I ran like a big wind...

However, my earlier concerns about my two shooters' escaping were baseless. My two early shooting chaps had only laid down behind their rice check to get their wind after racing all over the muddy rice field picking up the ducks they had previously ground sluiced in the pre-dawn darkness of the morning. Over the top of their rice check I came like the

Charge of the Light Brigade. Only, unlike that infamous moment in history, I didn't charge into massed Turkish machine guns like an idiot but simply raced across a muddy rice field and stormed over a rice check like a German Panzer tank across the Steppes of Mother Russia. Talk about two surprised chaps! One lad, the huge tall one, damn near wetted himself because he was still in the process of putting his plug back into his shotgun when I busted over their rice check almost directly on top of him! Suffice to say, that silliness of re-plugging his shotgun stopped right then and there.

Before the smoke had cleared and all my suspects' feathers had settled to the ground, I had David Jenkins and Peter Townsend who were both from the nearby town of Willows. Seems they couldn't find enough ducks in their own back yard to kill up in Glenn County, so, they had to give my county a try. Sitting down on the side of the rice check so I could still keep my eyes peeled for their drop-off driver whose name my lads chose not to reveal, I began the paperwork. Both men received citations for early shooting, using unplugged shotguns to take migratory waterfowl and taking over limits of ducks, To Wit: 84 ducks or 68 ducks over the limit! (The daily bag limit was eight ducks per day per shooter when legally taken in those days.)

My two lads were cited accordingly into the Williams Justice Court located in the nearby town of Williams. Days later, Judge Gibson found both men guilty of the charges and levied individual fines of $95.00 for the early shooting violation, $50.00 for taking migratory waterfowl with an unplugged shotgun, and $500.00 for taking a gross over limit of ducks. (Just to give one an idea of how much those fines had to really hurt one's pocketbook, I made just $566/month in those days as a game warden. My two subjects on the citations had listed their occupations as 'farm hands'. Farm hands in those day in the Sacramento Valley made around $300 per month. As one can see, my two early shooting chaps worked a number of day as farm hands for nothing.) The judge allowed them to keep their shotguns because neither man had any fish and game priors. Suffice it to say, my little two o'clock venture that morning had paid off rather handsomely. I would ultimately secure a total of $1,290.00 in fines from those two miscreants and my single day afield with Dog was just beginning...

After I had finished the paperwork with my lads, the three of us packed out all the ducks back to my hidden vehicle. Because their pick-up driver had seen his boys captured by the law, he had chosen not to make his appearance. In so doing, that left David and Peter walking towards Princeton where they could get to a phone and call home for a ride. Me? I spent the next hour or so gutting all the ducks so they would not spoil and could be properly disposed of for the needy in the county to consume. As a reward for being a good dog when we were buried earlier with all those 'offending,' to Shadow's way of thinking, ducks walking all over us, Dog got to eat all the warm duck guts she could hold. Since Shadow weighed at least one-hundred pounds and was as firm as a rock, she could literally eat a barrel full of guts! Afterwards, it always amazed me just how much terrible smelling gas a one-hundred pound Labrador dog could generate within hours after eating a barrel full of warm duck grits!

However, cleaning all those ducks in the field that morning brought unexpected dividends. To the west of my duck cleaning location near the old Willow Creek Gun Club on the Colusa and Glenn County line, it sounded like one hell of a shoot was going on. Pheasant season was in full swing and from the sounds and frequency of shooting, there was a huge gang-shoot going on for such in season upland critters. Hurrying through my duck gutting duties, I washed my hands and hit the road because a good game warden always moves to the sounds of the guns. As I was later to discover, it was a damn good thing I headed to the sounds of all those guns shooting...

Heading west down Norman Road, I finally spotted a mess of vehicles parked in two large groups. One clump of vehicles was clearly parked in Glenn County to the north by a huge fallow field. The other vehicles were parked just north off the Norman Road in Colusa County. Between the clumps of parked vehicles was one monster sized fallow weed field. Through my binoculars, I could see about 30 sports surrounding that large field having what appeared to be one hell of a pheasant shoot. It was plain to me from the outward signs of camaraderie among the shooters, that the shoot had been well planned and thoroughly executed by a number of family members and close friends. The huge weed field was surrounded with active gunners and many of the shooters were working their dogs in concert with the shooters. Watching the whole spectacle in my binoculars as I sat alongside the Norman Road, I could see that the air over the weed field was clear full of pheasants trying to escape! As I said earlier, the sportsmen were organized and knew what they were doing when it came to bringing the wily pheasant to gun and their game bags.

Then I noticed several not so nice things outside of the law that were occurring. Several times, I saw totally protected migratory non-game birds like bitterns fall to a fusillade of shots fired by the now field-circling shooters. (Note that those chaps weren't called hunters not after what I had seen illegally occurring.) Then I noticed almost every time a pheasant went into the air, it exploded into a puff of feathers and dropped. It didn't take a dummy like me long to realize that I had a field of excellent marksmen. However, that wasn't the most egregious part of what I was seeing taking place once the birds were airborne. Every time when that group of shooters saw a bird take to the air, it was killed outright! Than meant the shooters were killing both male and illegal to take females every time they took to wing! Under state law, female pheasants could not be taken for any reason. Seeing enough of that kind of 'horsepucky', I got my miserable carcass into gear and began hunting the lawless once again.

Moments later, I had quietly slid into the parking lot holding the southernmost group of shooters and, letting Dog out from the truck, quickly headed into that gang of 15 or so field-surrounding chaps. The first surprised group of four sports I officially confronted, were totally in violation! Between the four of them, they had over limits of roosters and a sizeable number of illegal hens in their game bags! Gathering up their California driver's licenses and writing out their violations on its blank backside in ink, I told all of my sports to meet me back at the parking lot with their birds. In the notebook that I always carried, I also recorded what evidence birds each of my previous shooters were carrying when ordered back to their vehicles in the parking lot by species so I could compare numbers of critters killed when I arrived later with my cite book. With that, I headed for my next group of errant gunners spread out line abreast just to my north.

The second group of two shooters I contacted were illegal as all get out as well! Both men had over limits of ring necks and totally restricted hens in their possession! Additionally, they were using unplugged shotguns while taking upland game birds. Repeating what I did with my first group, I gathered up all their driver's licenses, recorded their violations on the backside, sent them packing to the parking lot, recorded the same in my note book and zeroed in on another bunch of four nearby shooters who were now starting to get "spooked" over my unusual, 'gathering up everybody in sight' presence.

By now, my huge group of remaining shooters to the north realized there was a turd in their 'pheasant shooting punch bowl'. Small groups of shooters on the north end of the large field began breaking off and making tracks for their vehicles as I approached the next group of nearby shooters in the southern half of the field. Every one of those in that next group contacted were in violation of the fish and game regulations as well! Unplugged shotguns, hen pheasants, untagged birds and over limits ruled the waves with that group. Grabbing up those chaps, taking their driver's licenses, recording their wrongs by name on the backs of their driver's licenses, noting in my notebook and sending them packing to the parking lot, I managed to keep moving through the now diminishing in size group of violators.

By now, EVERYONE on the north end of the huge weed field was moving like the wind towards their vehicles so they could escape the obvious presence of a game warden in their midst. Running after the next closest group of three shooters trying to flee and hailing them down, I was not surprised at what I found. Every man jack one of them were in violation of the hunting regulations. Just like the earlier shooters, they had killed everything they could hit. They too were sent packing for the lower parking lot after being processed, as I watched the last of the outlaw lot of shooters on the north end of the weed field get into their vehicles and hurriedly drive off into Glenn County never to be seen ever again! Looking at some of the local familiar names of the shooters already contacted on the seized driver's licenses, I realized that this organized family shoot had to be an annual thing and 'Katy bar the door' when it came to the legality of what those shooters were taking.

Back at the south parking lot, I confronted 13 mad as hell, 'flaming' hind ends. All of them had been previously drinking, were from a group of in-laws and outlaws from several nearby valley towns like Princeton, and every one of them were in serious violation of the fish and game hunting regulations!

Angry at losing so many outlaws from the north end of the shooting area because I was unable to raise the Willows game warden and have him come in from that side of the huge field to round them up, I was pissed to say the least! 'Right off the bat', I shut down all the lip from my 13 chaps now standing impatiently in the southernmost parking lot 'grousing' at me and what I represented. I think after that, they all deduced that I was an unhappy camper over their complete lack of sporting ethics. Secondly, I made sure that their grouchy attitudes and verbalizations would not fly with me because I had lost the greater number of outlaws at the north end of the field and that did not set well with me.

For the next two hours, I issued citations to the various shooters in the southern parking lot. Those citations by shooter ran from possessing untagged roosters (male pheasants in those days had to be tagged with a paper tag wrapped around the leg of the dead bird); over limits of roosters; taking and possessing protected hen pheasants; unplugged shotguns; no hunting licenses in one's immediate possession, and the taking of protected migratory non-game birds (like owls and bitterns)! Then to top off my being miffed, several of the lads did not show up with their evidence birds back at the parking lot after I had originally contacted them, recorded the same and then sent them packing. Dog saw to rectifying that little issue in short order and then those chaps were cited for wanton waste charges as well. Bottom line, it is not good to piss off Mother Nature... or any of her minions!

When that smoke had cleared several hours later, I had issued 13 citations to my group of shooters for possessing over limits of rooster pheasants; 12 citations for taking protected hen pheasants; two citations for not having a valid hunting license in one's immediate possession; two citations for wanton waste of a game bird; seven for possessing untagged roosters; three for taking a game bird with an unplugged shotgun, and two for taking protected migratory non-game birds. In the end, I seized 30 illegal rooster pheasants, 12 illegal hen pheasants, three unplugged shotguns and two totally protected bitterns... (To speed up on the writing process, I would double up on the citations and just fill in the specific violations since I already had all the identifying information written on the initial violation issued to each chap.)

That wasn't the bad part when it came to dealing with my set of outlaws. When I had finished with my lads and they had left the area, Dog and I walked the field my shooters had earlier shot over. In so doing, Dog picked up a dozen lost roosters, 14 dead hens and two more dead bittern! For the next hour or so, I gutted my evidence birds and then took all of my duck and pheasant seizures over to the Sacramento National Wildlife Refuge. The refuge manager, Ed Collins, let me use the federal agents' evidence freezers to store my birds so they wouldn't go to waste.

Man, was I pissed over such a stupid showing of lousy sporting ethics and waste of perfectly good game birds. I made sure that Judge Gibson became aware of what had happened that day and of what I found left in the field to rot. As it turned out, none of my cited chaps chose to contest any of the charges levied against them that 'fine sporting day'. Every one of those shooters chose to forfeit bail as opposed to telling their sordid stories to the judge. The result, $500 fines were levied across the board for each of the 13 chaps I had managed to apprehend before the rest of the rats abandoned ship and headed for the hills. In that fiasco, I had at least another 20 lads escape who needed my attention as well. However, I gladly settled for $6,500 in fines for that brief adventure into frustration over the sporting ethics of my fellow man. In that fiasco, I learned a lesson in how to prevent losing so many chaps in the future. That lesson learned was turned into a game warden's trick of the trade I am not prepared to share with you folks at this time because it is a good one. One trick of the trade I will not share because I am not sure who all is reading these lines…

(Oh, the hell with it! The worst of you wildlife outlaws reading these lines will finds out how I did it anyway, so, here goes. If any of my readers are interested in learning how I managed to trap 45 illegal shooters in one swoop in the Stockton, California area a couple of years later for shooting dove over a baited area, you will have to read that story in my e-book at Amazon titled, *For Love of Wildness*, chapter two, 'Forty-five Italian Shooters and Plan B'. It was a hoot and will leave the reader smiling from ear to ear on how just one officer of the law waylaid and rounded up 45 Italian shooters with a historic propensity to run once they knew the law was close at hand, all for shooting dove over a baited field.)

By now, my bottom was beginning to drag and even Dog looked a little whipped. Especially after her exhausting run through the dense weed field retrieving all those lost and illegal pheasants. In fact, she had run through so much vegetative roughage, her nose was no longer black but pink and she didn't have any eyebrows left! But we still had work to do and I could still hear the booming of numerous shotguns going off throughout my zone of hearing. So, loading back up into our trusty truck, off we went into our next set of adventures in the wildlife wars, all framed by the sounds of shooting.

Leaving the Sacramento National Wildlife Refuge after putting my evidence birds into the federal agents' freezers, Dog and I headed for Newhall Farms located almost due south of the refuge. Did so because the sounds of frequent gunning over the harvested rice fields told me I had more pheasant hunters afoot and obviously having one hell of a good shoot.

Finding a pull off along the Four-Mile Road paralleling Newhall Farms properties, Dog and I took a breather. During hunting seasons, any good game warden worth his salt is still aware of and moving towards the sounds of the guns. That morning was no different, because it found me standing alongside my truck glassing six pheasant hunters on the southern side of Newhall Farms, hunting just north of Linc Dennis' farm properties.

My shooters were line abreast afield and working three Brittany spaniels like there was no tomorrow. With six shooters working a good pheasant area with three dogs, that told me I had some serious hunting folks that needed watching. Watching the dogs work and the killing accuracy of my shooters every time a rooster went aloft, further validated my suspicion that my group of sports rated more than just a casual look-see. That look-see they were now getting, as I settled into my 60 power spotting scope so I could watch their shooting success actions even more closely.

In those days, the daily bag limit on pheasants was three per sport per day. When my six chaps had cleared the field they were currently hunting, each man had a least one pheasant that I had observed falling to that individual's gun. That was the least they had because remember, I had just arrived and chanced glassing them at that moment in time. The accuracy in which my suspect shooters shot, told me that they had to have way more pheasants than I had observed being taken in such a short period of time. Especially when one realized I had just arrived after hearing them shooting numerous times earlier that morning.

Making a drive on the next harvested rice field, my six chaps limited out over their hard working dogs and KEPT SHOOTING! Upon reaching the end of that second field, each of my six shooters had taken over limits of pheasants! Pausing back at their vehicles parked at the end of a long field, my lads broke out the beers from one of their ice chests and relaxed. Taking that as my cue, I took off for their 'out in the bush' location so I could inspect what they had taken. Trying to find the farm trail they had used to get out to where they were currently located took some time on my part. That gave my lads the opportunity to view my truck suspiciously moving closely about as I tried to find the exact farm road they had used so I could inspect their shotguns for plugs, check their bags and issue the appropriate citations for their over limits.

In trying to find the right road leading to my chaps, there were several times I was out of sight of their location and actions. Finally finding the right farm trail leading to where my suspects were parked, I zeroed in on my lads whom I had observed through my binoculars taking over limits of pheasants. Driving up to my lads and getting out like any fat, dumb and happy game warden, I walked up to them as I looked for any 'tells' on their faces regarding the over limits they had taken earlier. I was surprised. Not one of my lads showed any signs of nervousness over their previously taken over limits. Kind of like they had nothing to hide in the way of pheasants even if I was to check them out thoroughly. I found that a little strange but was accustomed to such looks of not guilty. That was especially when working real hard cases or genuine wildlife outlaws, so I kept on trucking.

"Good morning, Lads. How is the hunting?" I asked all fat, dumb and happy like.

One chap dressed to the nines in his expensive Eddy Bauer clothing responded with, "Who the hell wants to know?"

What the hell! There I stood dressed in the full field uniform of a real-life game warden and with the man's questioning words, realized I had stumbled upon some very rich chaps who cared little about being confronted by such a low-brow type like myself. Further discussion revealed I was in among a rather haughty and well off bunch of 'Patricians' who resented having a 'Plebeian' like me interfering in their little private pheasant hunt...

But you know, Folks, as I have told all of you before in some of my other stories, it is not nice to mess with Mother Nature or her minions. Especially if your hind ends are hanging out with over limits of pheasants and such! I had observed every man of that crowd of chaps I now confronted kill an over limit of pheasants. Regardless of their stations in life, they were going to pay the piper, come hell or high water! I ignored some thinly veiled comments they made about being bothered in the middle of their hunt, one that they had paid a fortune to enjoy and, being the good citizens that they were, resented my interference. I happily continued on ignoring their biting remarks, knowing what ultimately was coming down the pike for some rather haughty, pheasant over the limit killing chaps.

"Gentlemen, I would like to check your hunting licenses, pheasant tags, birds and your shotguns if I may", I advised in my most professional 'spider to the fly' tone. Damn, I sure loved my job as a game warden! Loved my job especially when someone was dead wrong and did not know that I knew just how far their butts were hanging out into the wind.

That request for compliance was met with more open grumbling about ruining their hunt as they deliberately took their sweet time in producing the said requested sporting items just to show their disdain for me and the moment at hand. Well, I had worked rich hard cases before and had a formula for such obnoxious behavior. I had the knowledge of their violations and they were clueless of that fact, so, armed with that information, guess who held all of the aces?

"Do you know who we are?" finally acidly asked one chap with a faked smile signifying there was a taipan snake in the grass behind that smile.

"No, Sir. Not until I have a chance to examine your hunting licenses. But it makes no difference because I treat everyone the same," I more than sweetly replied in kind.

About then, the man with a pot belly like mine who had remained quiet up until that moment rose up from his seat in his Remington folding chair and ordered me to get done with what I had to do and to brief about it! Be brief about it because I was interfering with their perfectly good pheasant hunt since my arrival and because of that, my presence had not been appreciated.

"Yes, Sir," I said as if his out-of-line order would make me hop to and follow his commands. By now, I had a gut full of their better than thou attitudes and found myself really having to rein in my feelings and bite my tongue. But, my mother, God rest her soul, didn't raise a turnip so I continued checking the licenses and such as my eyes swept the tailgate area of their vehicle. There were just twelve rooster pheasants all laid out for me to see and nothing more. Well, I had observed my six chaps killing 24 roosters earlier and I guess the tailgate display was just for the benefit of one like me. Especially since they had seen me a long time in coming and had plenty of time to hide the rest of their ill- gotten gains. Well, I always liked a good mystery as to where the extra birds were hidden and, as such, the 'game' of hunting the lawless was now on!

Having checked everything out in the open that needed checking, I thanked the men for their patience. With those thanks, I got more less than thinly veiled grumbles hurled my way once again. Then I made sure they quickly discovered that they now had a turd in their punch bowl.

"Gentlemen. I need the extra birds that you shot earlier this morning," I quietly said.

Talk about a joint explosion of denials and other derisive comments, I got an ear full in short order. The man with the potbelly and full of his self-importance, bellowed out, "I want your badge number and the name of your immediate supervisor and I want it now! This harassment crap has and is going to stop right now!"

"Yes, Sir," I replied. "My name is Terry Grosz. My badge number you can get off my badge that I am wearing. The name of my supervisor is Captain James Leamon and he lives in Yuba City. But before you blow your stack there is something all of you should know. I have been watching all of you shooting this morning with my binoculars and spotting scope. During that time, I watched the six of you kill 24 roosters when you were only lawfully allowed to take 18. That puts you folks six birds over the limit and those numbers only accounted for the short period of time I was actually watching you hunt. I have no idea on the total numbers of pheasants all of you took before I arrived on the scene and began watching you hunt but we will get to that in a moment."

Brother, there were more explosions of denial and even more strident language about my lineage and even one threat of placing me under arrest for trespassing on the land they had leased for hunting if I didn't leave and find someone else to harass. You know, folks, you don't ever threaten a bull-headed German. 'Me, myself and I' being of full-blooded German descent, well, how far do you think those threats got my six shooters?

"Gentlemen," I began once again. "I would like you to gather up those extra birds for me because, if you don't, I will have to find them for myself. If I have to do that, you will also be charged with an additional violation of 2012 of the Fish and Game Code for Failure to Show Upon Demand."

By now, the air around my six chaps was blue with every word used normally around a logging camp after one had smashed his thumb with a hammer, if you readers get my gist. Then I got an idea. Since I had not observed where they had hidden their extra birds when they saw me coming from a long ways off, I tried an old ruse. Ignoring all the bad language directed at me and their following threats, I walked back to my truck and extracted my Super-Eight movie camera with its telephoto lens and returned to all the bad language about me still being flung around and about.

"Gentlemen. Earlier today I filmed all of you killing the over limit of birds I spoke about earlier." I really hadn't done so but figured my bluff might just smoke out the extra birds and then after citation issuance, I could be done with my foul-mouthed chaps and be on my way. With that unexpected revelation, the really vile language somewhat abated as I could now see some small signs of concern clearly sneaking across several of the lads' faces. Then the pot-bellied one whom I figured was the leader of the bunch, boiled over and spouted off once again.

"There is no way this son-of-a-bitch saw anything. If he had, he would be writing all of us tickets as I speak. Go ahead, Mr. Game Warden, fire your best shot." With that, Pot-Belly sat back down in his Remington chair and ordered another of his friends to get him a beer, saying, "As I watch this piece of crap game warden make an ass of himself trying to find some extra birds that he says we killed and, then when he is done, we will have his ass." You know, folks, some people just needed to be grabbed by their necks and squeezed until their eyes popped out.

Well, I had fired a fake bluff across the men's bow and no one blinked. But that was O.K. with me because I still had my ace in the hole, namely the 'Shadow Factor'. Turning, I gave my dog a low whistle and out from the bed of my truck bolted Shadow. She ran to my side and in that split second of time, I saw six sets of eyes following her every inch of the way like all of them had just spied a grizzly bear in their midst! My six pheasant hunters trailing sets of eyes now began showing signs of worry around the edges and I swear, every one of them were now breathing more deeply over the dog's presence in 'the field of battle'.

"Last chance, Lads. Produce those extra pheasants or I put the dog on their trail and she will find them. When she does, there will be extra charges added and I will seize your shotguns as well," I advised. When those words left my mouth, I saw two of my six chaps quickly glancing worried looks towards Pot-Belly who was still sitting in his chair with nary a single look of worry on his face.

Well, that tells me they have hidden the extra birds in such a manner that he doesn't think the dog will find them, I thought. However, Shadow had a great nose and knew what to do, so, I turned her loose on the trail of the missing pheasants.

"Find the duck," was the standard command given by me and off she went at a dead run looking 'for the duck'. First, she sniffed all around the men's vehicles and found nothing of interest. Then, she expanded her search area along several adjacent weedy ditch banks and found nothing of interest hidden there as well. Following several of my hand signals, out along several nearby rice checks she sped and in that ensuing search found nothing either.

"Come on, Boys. This turd has nothing on us. Since he ruined our hunt, let's get the hell out of here and go elsewhere where we can be left to continue our hunt in peace. And just as soon as we can get to a phone, I will call my friend Ronnie, the Governor, and give him an ear full about what a lout this game warden was in ruining our day," said Pot-Belly. With those words and while Shadow was still searching, two of the men kenneled up their dogs as the rest of the men began bagging up their shotguns, closing up their ice chests and generally making ready to leave.

About then Shadow stopped poking around in the adjacent rice field and stood there looking back at me as if to say, "Where do you want me to look next, Boss." Damn, I was dumb founded! I **knew** these chaps had extra birds and yet my dog had found none of them. That was not like Shadow to return empty handed after making a search for illegal game. I gave her a 360-degree swing of my arm letting her know to keep searching, so she did as I instructed.

In the meantime, I brought everyone's leaving preparations to exit the field to a screeching halt. "Gentlemen. No use in getting in a big hurry to leave. Since I observed and recorded every one of you killing over limits of pheasants, you will be cited accordingly. Birds or no birds, all of you will be receiving a citation for the taking over limits and the birds you now have will be seized in order to show that over limits were taken."

At that moment, Pot-Belly blew his stack! "You son-of-a-bitch, my attorneys will see you in a court of law for harassment. You think you have had a bad day here today? Just you wait until they get through with you. They will see to it that you won't have an ounce of skin left on your ass, much less keep your job with the State of California!"

Ignoring his lip, I retrieved a cite book from my truck and began the process of collecting driver's licenses all around so I could at least issue an over limit taking citation to each man for what I had observed and recorded earlier in my note books. As I did, the men ignored my earlier commands and continued preparing to leave, loading up their vehicles with their goods and placing their shotguns in the back of an adjacent Suburban. In the meantime, here came Shadow with a genuine look of disappointment on her face. She had been sent out to 'get the duck' and had discovered nothing in the way of evidence birds. Knowing my dog the way I did, I could tell she was ashamed of herself for not minding her master.

Then my guardian angels began flipping around inside me with the approach of Shadow. With that warning, I began taking second looks all around as to where those extra birds might be stashed. It was then that I saw Shadow sitting quietly behind the one Suburban whose back door was open so the men could continue loading up their gear. *Why the hell is she just sitting there?* I wondered. I had earlier quick-checked the back of that vehicle and only saw the men's luggage stacked inside the rear compartment and a mound of clothing loosely tossed into the second seat. But, Shadow had 'that look' on her face as she quietly sat there looking back at me for my next command.

Setting down my cite book on the hood of one of the men's Suburban, I walked back to the rear of that vehicle for one more look. I saw nothing but some loose hunting gear, four suitcases and several cased shotguns. Looking down at my patiently sitting dog, I got a knowing nod that I was on the right trail from one of my angels (or sixth sense to you non-believers). A nod that told me I was on the right track, just slow on the uptake and approach on what needed doing...

"Find the duck," I ordered once again. With those words, Shadow barreled into the back of the suburban and stood there nosing one of the men's rather expensive alligator skin suitcases.

"Get that God-damned filthy dog out of my clean Suburban," shouted Pot-Belly as he blew up out from his chair and quickly trotted over to where I was standing. And when he did, I could see concern 'spelled out' clear across his face in CAPITAL LETTERS! Not to mention, he was really picking his feet up and laying them down in order to get to the back of his vehicle as if there was a bomb inside ready to go off!

Standing there, Shadow looked back at me like she always did when she had found 'her duck'. Reaching into the back of that Suburban, the one with all the various conservation organization decals plastered over the rear side windows showing what great sportsmen my 'Patrician' pheasant shooters were, I extracted the alligator hide suitcase Shadow was looking at. When I did, she barreled out from the Suburban and sat alongside the suitcase when I set it heavily down on the ground. When I hefted that suitcase from the back of the vehicle, I had noticed that it was more than heavy. Looking the suitcase over carefully, I noticed THERE WAS A SINGLE ROOSTER PHEASANT BODY FEATHER STUCK BETWEEN THE UPPER AND LOWER PORTIONS OF THE LIDS ON THE SUITCASE! It was then that I realized all six of my heretofore antagonists had grown as silent as a graveyard in the dead of winter. No longer were they bitching at me but every one of them had fastened their eyes onto the now suspect suitcase like it contained a bomb!

Then, the sun finally shone on the manure pile (that would be me) behind the barn! Piled up there in the third seat of the

Suburban laid a mess of loose clothing. Probably about a suitcase full to my way of reckoning! Since it had initially taken so long for me to get to my pheasant shooters' location, they had apparently suspected my intentions, quickly emptied out the suitcase, filled it with their over limits, and shoved it back into the vehicle when I was out of sight of the men. No wonder Dog couldn't find anything in the way of evidence birds hidden in the fields. Earlier, since the rear loading door on that Suburban had been closed and one of my chaps was standing nearby, Shadow had missed the suitcase inside with all the illegal pheasants. Well, I wasn't going to miss what came next. Opening up the suitcase after I had pocketed the tell-tale feather removed from the two portions of the lids, out dropped 27 additional freshly killed pheasants and not a tagged bird among the over limit!

With that revelation, you could have heard a shrew passing gas the next county over among my six violators. Especially when it came to any sounds emanating from my shooters when they observed me discovering and then unlocking the secret to their little stash of a major over limit of birds.

After making a count of the pheasants and telling Shadow to sit alongside the pile of illegal birds, I casually returned to my open and unfinished citation book like I had known what I was doing all along. To that and the following five citations, I added collective possession charges of 21 illegal pheasants over the limit! Twenty-one because each man was allowed three pheasants per day and they now had a total of 39 pheasants in possession. Since the group was 21 over the allotted daily bag limit of 18, they had a collective problem. They each were collectively assessed the joint overage because I did not know exactly who had shot what bird regarding that bunch of 21 illegal pheasants.

Talk about silence in the rice field except for other far away shooting and the sounds of the nearby songbirds once those extra birds came to light, it was deafening! Finally each

397

man trooped up and admitted getting carried away and shooting over limits as they signed on the 'Promise To Appear' line on the citation. None could remember just how many each man shot, hence the 21 collective birds in possession assessment on each of their citations. Their reasons for going hog wild and shooting so many pheasants over the limit was that they had a company party coming up and were going to serve their guests and fellow workers a pheasant dinner. That plus they had paid a lot of money for their pheasant, duck and goose lease and felt they had spent so much money that they needed to come away with a collateral amount of value in wild game! It was also plain from the men's top-of-the-line clothing and expensive equipment, that all of them were so well off that they could have purchased a mess of pen-reared pheasants for their dinner instead of illegally killing the same. It is always amazing to me just how much greed and ego influences the illegal taking of wildlife.

As my sad six but now silent shooters drove off, they left behind all of their pheasants and their beautiful and expensive Browning over and under 12 gage shotguns as evidence of their wrong doings. That and the silence that came from such mouthy rich chaps after an 'alligator' had figuratively clamped down hard onto their collective hind ends. That gator thing became more than true when two San Francisco attorneys showed up later to contest the charges in a court trial in front of Judge Gibson.

To make a long story short, my chaps were found guilty and the judge only fined each man $500 for their offenses. However, good ole Judge Gibson had all of their expensive Browning over and under shotguns forfeited to the State of California! And in those days, a Browning over and under shotgun cost about $800 each at Chick Montgomery's Sporting Goods in Colusa, or, about a month and a half's gross salary for me.

Following that adventure, Shadow got to eat all the pheasant guts she could hold for making our case when I cleaned the birds so they wouldn't spoil. Once again, I trooped back to the Sacramento National Wildlife Refuge and availed myself of the federal agents' evidence freezer in which to store my recently seized, second batch of pheasants.

By now, it had been a pretty long day. But, my work was not yet done. I had driven way south because I could hear a constant flurry of shooting just north of Tennessee Ernie Ford's Duck Club located along the San Jose Road. I knew it had been pretty quiet in that area most of the morning for duck hunting because of the bluebird weather we were having. I figured the shooting had to be coming from pheasant hunters in the area working the edges of the marshes by that duck club. Loading up Dog, off we went once again to the sounds of the guns.

Stopping just north of "The Little Ole Pea Pickers" duck club, I got out my Big Eye 60 power spotting scope for a look-see as to what was going on. In that scope's field of view I observed five chaps obviously hunting pheasants in the deep rushes alongside several watered marshy areas. Several times, I observed rooster pheasants rising above the rushes in exploded flight, then a shot, a cloud of feathers, and the aerial acrobatics pheasants were famous for were no more. It was obvious the shooters had the right formula for a good pheasant hunt. As my shooters hunted, they were using their stoutly built Labrador retrievers to bust through the dense rushes where the pheasants were hiding and man, were they having a good shoot. Especially with those stout, brush busting dogs pushing out the deeply hidden birds.

What the hell? I thought. *That last bird that went airborne was a tan colored one! And it had been killed just slicker than cow slobbers.* Really crawling into my spotting scope to see what was actually going on with my shooters, out came my trusty notebook. From what I could tell, no matter whatever sex of pheasant went up into the air, they all came down! *Those five guys are killing everything that is going airborne that is good to eat!* I quickly realized.

Seeing that my outlaw gunners were putting everything that they shot into their game bags, I put my enforcement plan of action into gear. Dog and I bailed out and off we went at a trot on "Shank's mare" using what little cover was offered leading towards the illegal pheasant shoot. Twenty minutes later, Dog and I were within striking distance but we faced a major problem. There was a lot of open in-between ground and if we chose to sprint across those areas, it was just a matter of time before we would be spotted before we even got onto the shooting site. That would not do. Here I had a mess of outlaws who were flagrantly breaking the law by killing hen pheasants. I wanted every man of that group of outlaws and missing any of those killers would not fill the bill if they ran off and escaped.

Additionally, knowing if I grabbed off one man and that action was spotted by the rest of the shooters, the guilty ones would ditch their hens while out of my sight in the dense rushes and my case would then be shaky in any court of law if they were charged without the damming physical evidence. That would be especially so if Shadow could not find the hidden birds. Then I got a devilish idea. One of the shooters with a game bag full of hen pheasants was not that far from me. So, Dog and I put the sneak on him as best as we could. Belly-crawling the last 40 yards to my chap who was so intent on his pheasant shooting that he never saw me coming, Dog and I sprung our trap once in grabbing-range.

Rearing up in the rushes as he passed by, I hissed at him. "What? Who the hell are you?" said my shooter in complete surprise.

Quickly moving over to him but remaining in a low crouch, I quietly verbally identified myself and told my chap to sit down. Boy, his butt hit the marshy ground like he had been dropped from an airplane. Identifying myself once again because I was wearing a hunting jacket over my uniform shirt, I asked for his shotgun. With that safely in my possession, we got down to the 'business at hand' while his buddies kept stalking pheasants and shooting up a storm in the adjacent stands of dense rushes.

"Let me see your pheasants," I instructed.

Soon laying before me were three roosters and three hen pheasants. *Nothing like having an over limit and the wrong sex of birds lying out in front of God and everybody,* I thought. You could also tell that my chap was now getting almost physically sick. It was obvious he had never had any run in with game wardens and his first experience with one was not going all that well.

Gathering up his driver's license, I put the rest of my little plan into effect. "Here is what I want you to do," I said in my gruffest sounding voice. "I want you to stand up and call all your friends over to you. I want you to tell them you have found something and then you drop back down out of sight and wait for their arrival. If you try to warn them that a game warden is at your feet, you will be the one arrested and carted off to jail. Do we have an understanding?" I demanded as I eyeballed him with my sternest of looks.

My poor chap. I guess I was a little harsh with him because he puked right them and there over his laid out on the ground illegal pheasants! When he finally got through puking and got hold of himself, I repeated my demand all the while steering away from the spew of anymore forthcoming vomit.

"O.K., Mr. Game Warden," he bleated out. With that, he rose sighted his friends, and yelled at them. Getting their attention, he told the guys that he had hurt himself and needed help. That was when I pulled on his pant legs and he dropped to the ground like I had shot him. It was pretty apparent that I had scared the hell out of my poor chap.

Soon I could hear voices coming asking, "Where did you last see him?" Moments later, I had four other chaps with bulging game bags that were also full of hen pheasants sitting on the marshy ground all around me. After making sure the men had been properly greeted, their guns emptied and I had identified myself, the counting of their misdeeds began. One man had four roosters and two hens, one had three roosters and four hens, one man had two roosters and one hen and the last of the gang of four just apprehended had four roosters and two hens. Before the smoke had died away in the marsh that fine day, I had four of the five with over limits of rooster pheasants and all five for taking protected game birds, To Wit; hen pheasants. Talk about five chaps who all looked like a rather large gator had chomped off their last parts over the fence. There they were and not an excuse for the error of their ways existed among the lot as they sadly looked at the mess of dead pheasants laying around them on the ground.

'Greetings from the State of California' were issued all around and then I struggled off carrying 26 illegal birds towards my hidden vehicle. One of my lads only had two roosters which was within the limit and he was allowed to keep those but he was cited for the hen pheasants he had killed. However, all the rest of the group's birds were seized and hauled off. Then it was back to the federal agents' freezers to store my recently seized birds since my state evidence freezers were already full of other illegal game animals. When that mess of citations finally cleared the Williams Justice Court, the State of California was $2,750 richer!

Later that evening found Dog and yours truly staked out in the Lambertville area homing in on two late waterfowl shooters. Before that little escapade was over, Dog and I had corralled two shooters who were late shooting ducks sixty minutes late. When that little matter cleared the Williams Justice Court docket several weeks later, each chap forfeited

$145 for their little inability to be able to tell the correct time. The going rate for such an offense was $25 for the offense of late shooting and $2 dollars per minute for each minute late shot. Man could get into a lot of trouble dollar and cents wise if he got carried away late or early shooting of migratory game birds in Colusa County in those days.

Dog and I still had not finished our workday. We were in with and staking out ten to twenty thousand mallards and northern pintail that were streaming off the Sacramento National Wildlife Refuge and had headed northwest into southern Glenn County. My counterpart in Willows, Warden Jim Hiller, had been sick for several days so I had promised him I would watch that corner of both of our counties and their masses of feeding waterfowl for illegal night shooters. It was a good thing I did. Just north of me on the Colusa and Glenn County line, I heard three distinct drags round about midnight. I was too far away to do any good other than echolocate on their approximate areas where the shoots had occurred. Then like McArthur had said when he got his butt kicked out of the Philippines by the Japanese during the first part of the Second World War, I said to myself, "I shall return!" And as you shall see in the following story, I did and just like McArthur, I got my butt kicked, BIG TIME!

As for any Flowers or Tombstones gathered that fine November day in the Sacramento Valley so long ago, there were many. As for the Flowers, my memories of working with my dog, Shadow, and the hordes of ducks flowing over us in the darkness like a 'feathered river; remain priceless to this day. Gosh, we really had ducks in those days. When alarmed at night in the rice fields as they fled any form of danger, the ducks provided any close at hand listener a living soft-sounding thunder when they rose into the air. Many times a few seconds later, if I was the close at hand fortunate listener, I could feel the wind on my face from the thousands of frantically beating wings! Then the subtle airborne smells of rotting vegetation, sour mud and dead crawdads that had earlier inhabited the once flooded rice fields wafted through the air. The memories of Dog, Mother Nature and me doing our thing during those days of 'living thunder' came richly flooding back as these lines were written in 2015, some nearly 50 years later. Truthfully, I was blessed to experience many of the things I saw in those days or heard in the rice fields at night. I can't ask for anything more than that when it comes to many of my living memories!

Other Flowers included apprehending 28 individuals who were doing to Mother Nature when they shouldn't have that fine November day. It was always satisfying to me when removing those from the ranks of evil doers when they were doing evil things. Another Flower gathered during that fine November day was the $13,685 gathered in fines for the State of California and their NRA Hunter Safety Training Programs. (Coincidentally, I made more money that day in fines than I earned as my salary for a whole year as a state fish and game warden.) That was one of the best days I ever had as a fish and game warden when it came to catching and prosecuting lads in the Sacramento Valley. I never surpassed that total amount of fines for one day's work until I became a federal officer a few years later.

As for the Tombstones in this story, there were many. As far as the so called hunter ethics on display to me that day so long ago, they were pitiful. I checked a total of 28 individuals shooting afield and wrote every one of them for fish and game violations that they had committed! Additionally, a large number of those chaps were issued multiple citations for multiple violations! That was a pretty pathetic thing to be experienced by an officer of the law. I also seized 84 ducks taken before legal shooting hours and a ton of illegal pheasants. Not to mention, the 26 dead pheasants Dog discovered in a field shot over where the birds were left to rot by that second bunch of outlaws I ran across who were shooting in that huge fallow field just northwest of Princeton. That same field where I rounded up 13 of their cohorts in crime in its southern portion before the rest scattered to the four winds and got away...

Look at all the lost pheasant production as a result of those lads killing all those hens that I seized. With the pheasant population way down in Colusa County in 2015, I would bet the local sportsmen and sportswomen wished they had that potential production back that was lost in the birds I seized that day so many years ago. Then. I lost all those chaps pheasant shooting on the north end of that big field just northwest of Princeton. There were at least 20 chaps shooting that area that sure deserved some of my attention. But even as big as I was, I could only spread myself just so far, so I settled for the group shooting the southern end of that huge weed field. Oh well. In God we trust and all you other folks breaking the laws of man and nature can pay in cash...

The last Tombstone during this November adventure occurred later that evening. I was working north and west of the Sacramento National Wildlife Refuge. As the luck of the Irish would have it, there were about ten bunches of feeding ducks scattered about, each numbering about 10,000 to 15,000 birds! As my luck would have it, there was only one conservation officer on duty that evening. When darkness fell, I picked a bunch of ducks that looked like they were just inviting a drag due to their nearness to a handy escape farm road and staked them out. As it just so happened, the duck draggers got into three different bunches of those feeding ducks around me and blew them up! Not having the luck of the Irish being German and all, my rotten luck surfaced its ugly face once again as no one shot my field. So, all those other ducks were killed and there wasn't a game warden close enough to make anyone pay. That was a very big Tombstone and a personal disappointment for me that evening for all the death and destruction that was caused and not addressed by me or anyone else who was credentialed to do so and didn't...

The last Flower that day I did not discover until I returned home at midnight after a twenty-two-hour long day. There asleep on our couch lay my wife. She had fallen asleep waiting for me to return figuring I would be home shortly for supper. Especially since I had left around two that previous morning. When she awoke, she was glad to see me and, then without another word, got up and fixed me a very nice meal. Man can't go wrong with that kind of wife. Course, I knew that. That is why I fell in love with her in the eighth grade and married Donna a number of years later when we both were still in college. We have been married a total of 53 years and counting as these words are being edited in 2016. How is that for being a perfect example of a Flower?

GUNS OF DEATH AND A 'THUNDER' OF WINGS

The cold Sacramento Valley winter rains had been softly falling for most of the morning. I had been sitting central to several huge flocks of feeding ducks that had poured off from the nearby Butte Sink and flooded out onto the Sartain and Boggs ranches previously harvested rice fields. It had already been a long day for this tired old game warden with no end in sight. I had been working alone and out on foot since about one in the morning, 'sleeping' with my ducks, attempting to keep my illegal night shooters at bay. By daylight, I had no illegal night gunners disturbing the masses of feeding ducks, was wet as a muskrat and shivering like a dog passing peach pits. At that point, enough was enough and I bailed out from my hiding place in the field in order to live to fight other battles in the world of wildlife.

Walking out to the hidden county fish and game unmarked patrol truck (paid for with Colusa County Fish and Game fine monies generated from previous citation issuances), I cranked her over and headed for home. There I showered to warm up, had breakfast with my wife before she went off to teach elementary school in Williams and then Dog and yours truly went back to another day facing the "Wildlife Wars". Only this time, we went back to the Wildlife Wars with a set of dry clothing and a full belly. It was a good thing I ate like a 'lumberjack' that morning because I never saw another plate of grits for the next 21 hours due to the wildlife law enforcement work at hand!

Because I had strong northwest winds 'a-howling' and rain coming down in sheets, the two most necessary weather elements needed for the valleys' many shooters to have an excellent duck and goose hunt, I ended up working my waterfowl shooters throughout my district all day until long after dark. Then it was on to the illegal late shooting crowd of outlaws that I knew from past like weather experiences, would be in abundance that evening. My last seven late shooters shooting ducks an hour and half after legal shooting hours, all of whom I had previously apprehended for the same type of violation, were captured just northwest of Williams off Marengo Road. After wrapping up that little late shooting affair, I called the Colusa County Sheriff's Office and asked them to call my wife and let her know I would not be home for a while. With that bit of housekeeping out of the way so Donna would not worry any more than she normally did, I headed north on a maze of back roads until I arrived at West Glenn Road on the Glenn County line. (Glenn County was the county lying just north of my home county and was heavily agricultural with loads of wintering waterfowl and fields of rice just like that in my assigned patrol district in Colusa County directly to the south.)

Hiding my unmarked county truck, Dog and I ventured out into one of Glenn County's extensive rice fields located just north of West Glenn Road. By that time of the night, the air was literally alive with every kind of duck known to North American man (there are different duck species around the world) winging their way into those adjacent rice fields. Those great numbers of ducks I was now experiencing were flooding off from the nearby Sacramento National Wildlife Refuge by the tens of thousands as they headed for the nearest Glenn County 'rice bowl' and their supper.

Standing there in the winter darkness, I just had to shake my head in wonder over what I was hearing and experiencing! The airways were literally alive with tens of thousands of ducks and geese! So much so, that I could constantly hear their wings slapping as the heavy masses of birds often collided in mid-air in the darkness and heavy rains! Dog and I were wonderfully soon to be right smack dab in the middle of many of those birds as they began descending all around us like huge silent living tornados into the harvested rice fields to feed.

My warden counterpart and squad mate in Glenn County, Jim Hiller, was under the weather and had asked if I could take a turn through some of his western rice ground at night, attempting to keep his wildlife outlaws at bay and I had agreed. Jim had been one hell of a good game warden in the 40's and 50's when most state fish and game wardens were REAL men.

(For my questioning female readers out there, be aware that there were no female California game wardens in those sometimes deadly, man versus man 'hunting the lawless' times. That kind of a physical and often dangerous job was just not the kind a female in those days ever considered doing. Jim, like many others of his breed, had fought in the earlier Wildlife Wars when it took real men not afraid to swing a fist or the end of a gun barrel alongside a wildlife outlaw's head in order to get one's attention. The outlaws of that period sometimes used even deadlier means such as a face full of lead shot to slow down fast approaching wildlife officers. Such was the case of U.S. Game Management Agent Victor Blazevic when he confronted a night-shooting duck poacher in the cornfields of Illinois! In that deliberate shooting instance, when the pursued turned and shot at his pursuer, Vic was lucky he wasn't killed. Many number four sized pellets had missed his jugular vein by just one-half inch when the poacher had chosen to shoot Vic in the face from close range! The poacher was later caught and sentenced to just three years in a federal pen for attempting to kill a federal officer! Bottom line, shooting waterfowl after hours, was a victimless crime and shooting conservation officers was only a notch or two above that! Hence the absence of females in those days wearing the game warden greens.)

On that particular day, Jim's aging body had said no to his venturing forth into the winter rains and cold so he stayed home and nursed a terrible head and chest cold. After all, he had a squad-warden counterpart from the neighboring county to the south (me) who had agreed to leave his own district and provide some top-cover in Jim's area of responsibility. Brother, if I had only known then what I was getting myself into by being a good neighboring officer, I may have stayed home... Naw, not really when it came to the 'staying home' department, especially when the outlaws were out and about just waiting to be caught...

Standing there in the darkness and cupping my ears so I could better listen in order to echolocate in on the numerous bunches of feeding ducks already on the ground, I got a surprise. There had to be at least ten bunches of feeding ducks in the immediate area that I could individually identify numbering a minimum of 10,000 noisily feeding birds to the bunch! *Which bunch do I sit on?* I asked myself as I shook a wet head with rain running down my face.

To my knowledge, there was only one wildlife officer on duty that cold and rainy night in the ENTIRE northern Sacramento Valley, namely yours truly! That point of knowledge was backed up by my own personal knowledge of those officers who might be on duty that evening and the total radio silence on the fish and game frequency attesting to my lone heartbeat out in the wilderness! That lack of nighttime protection in the northern Sacramento Valley had to potentially impact the safety of at least 6,000,000 ducks and at least 1,000,000 wintering geese! Not a federal agent or state officer stirred that evening in an area historically known for its night poaching outlaws when the ducks and geese were in the valley! However, that lack of an enforcement presence in the valley during the late wintertime was not surprising. The waterfowl season in California ran for 107 straight days that year! By late winter, most officers were physically worn out from numerous long days working in the winter weather or were nursing a sickness brought on from abusing one's body for days on end working the various open hunting seasons. However when it came to that evening in question, there was one rather large crazy standing out in the middle of a rice field with waves of heavy winter rains washing over him. That lone game warden sentinel standing in the wet rice field was facing somewhat of a serious problem. He was still just a single rookie when it came to working the oft times deadly commercial market hunters and duck-draggers plying their ugly trade within the Sacramento Valley, always in numbers greater than one.

That inexperience and the historic dangers laid aside, I still had a job to do, so, I did what I thought was best for the critters. In that inexperience, I tried picking a large group of ducks central to all the other feeding bunches of birds and slowly worked my way in their direction using the numerous rice checks in the fields for cover. For to make one's self known to such feeding hordes of birds, would send all of them quickly skyward in a thunder-clap of wings. When the nearby alarmed flocks lifted off in such thunderous roars, it served as a warning and alarm to all other feeding flocks within hearing distance. Those roars of alarm from other fleeing birds would quickly send others nearby skyward in alarm as well. Especially during the latter part of the hunting season when the birds were exceptionally wary after having been shot over so many times months previously. When that domino warning effect happened, one would find himself standing alone in the now deserted rice fields with a hand full of wasted effort and a wet hind end as his reward for venturing forth in the cold winter rains and for being so damn clumsy all at the same time.

Keeping that 'duck-fright and flight' behavior in mind, Dog and I crawled carefully through the mud and dripping wet grasses on the rice checks until we were where I figured we ought to be for the best chance to catch a night shooting duck-dragger or commercial market hunter if one was to show his face. Arriving at my chosen spot, we buried onto the dense water grass side of a rice check and tried to make ourselves as comfortable as we could in the sticky wet mud, rotting vegetation, stink of dead crawdads and the heavy sheets of rain that kept periodically flooding our way.

By now, I had learned one valuable lesson when working night shooters and that was trying to keep myself (and Dog) as comfortable as possible for the long haul ahead. Carefully gathering up several arms full of rice straw previously left in rows by the harvesters, I laid it alongside my rice check to act as a bed and insulator from the ground's damp cold. Soon, Dog and I were one with the mud, cold rains, wet rice straw, and the world of hungry waterfowl continually storming into the rice fields and landing all around us in the dark of the night.

As more and more ducks flooded into my area attracted by all the other noisy hoards of feeding waterfowl below, it soon was like the world of wildlife was at Grand Central Station on a Friday afternoon. Even in my inexperience, I had picked the right spot for a stake out because we had ducks everywhere! We had so many ducks in such close proximity that I couldn't get up and move around to a better position even if I had wanted to. Not without sending 50,000 nearby feeding ducks thundering airborne all at once that is. If one wanted to apprehend the killers of the madly feeding ducks, one had to 'sleep' with the critters for the best chance of capturing said illegal gunners. (As an aside, a good game warden moved to where the wildlife was gathered in its greatest concentrations. That is where he would often find the greatest predator on earth, namely Man. Mixing man and wildlife is historically many times is like mixing a blazing fire with an open container of black powder!)

By two in the morning, Dog and I were wet as hell, stiff as a poker and bone cold. Even wearing my heavy rain gear, the cold drops of winter rains always seemed to find my only remaining dry spots. But we held our 'sand' because the duck-loaded area we were in provided an excellent chance of running across illegal night shooters based on the attraction of so many feeding birds. Bottom line, you couldn't catch a bad guy, especially the night shooters, unless you were within arm's length of the rascals. That was because my illegal night shooting outlaws were all related to jackrabbits once they discovered the law was close at hand and in country.

By late in the morning, I had already heard four different shoots blowing up the ducks' in Colusa County to my south. That illegal duck-gunning activity really pissed me off! By being further north up in Glenn County, I had forfeited any chance of catching some of my own night-shooting duck killers in my district. But wildlife outlaws didn't respect legal boundaries and catching a dedicated night shooter, no matter where the apprehension took place, was always a good thing to my way of thinking. So, I just burrowed further into my rice check for the slim cover it offered from the sweeping rains and tried to ignore the cold rainwater trickling down the back of my neck and running all the way down to the area of my gun belt, where it just soaked in.

Then I heard Shadow quietly rumble-growl! She had been soundly sleeping alongside me but now was sitting up and looking intently to the east. Pointing my binoculars in the darkness in that direction, I saw nothing. Laying them back down on its strap hanging around my neck, I waited. I did so because Shadow was an excellent early warning system when afield in the dark. If Shadow growled quietly and was looking in a certain direction, I knew something was out of place in that area. About then my guardian angels (or sixth sense) began stirring as if they knew something I was acutely unaware of and they were attempting to get my attention. Reaching back into my game bag in my hunting jacket, I made sure my five-cell flashlight was within easy grabbing distance. Then Dog and I quietly waited alongside our rice check listening to the soft rains pelting off my rain gear amid the sounds of happily feeding ducks all around us.

About fifteen minutes later, I thought I heard a slightly unusual sound other than that coming from the nearby feeding ducks. Then once again, nothing but the sounds of feeding ducks, the whirring of wings closely flying overhead, incessant calls from the incoming ducks, the falling rain pelting off my rain gear, sounds of the wind rustling through the dense water grasses on the rice check, and Shadow's continuing low warning rumbling growl. Lying alongside my covering rice check with my eyes and ears searching hard for what was bothering Shadow and my heart beating like someone practicing on a set of kettle drums, I was doused with another torrent of rain splashed across my face by another fresh wave of the winds.

THEN THERE THEY WERE! Not twenty-five feet away moved the faint shadowy images of three humans slowly sneaking along paralleling my rice check in a stooped over position in order to avoid scaring the nearby feeding ducks on the other side of the check. Moving behind them was a smaller image, which I figured had to be a dog. Since no laws were being broken by my suspects walking in a stooped over fashion in a rice field in the dead of night, I let my three chaps and their dog disappear into the gloom of darkness. It was then that I realized my heart was beating more than a mile a minute by the 'fellow' beating the set of kettle drums! In the meantime, Dog, now standing up alongside the rice check, kept quietly watching in the direction where my three chaps and their dog had just disappeared.

Occasionally I could hear small bunches of ducks taking to wing in the direction in which my chaps had disappeared and I just figured it was their presence sneaking by that had disturbed those smaller flocks of critters. However, that was a good thing. The fleeing sounds made by those ducks gave me an indication of the ultimate direction in which my night-shooting suspects were traveling and their approximate changing locations. Those moments also gave me time in which to think just how I planned on rounding up three chaps all at once after they had pulled their 'shoot.'

The rains had abated somewhat and now it was a little easier to see with my binoculars without the raindrops splashing annoyingly across the lenses. As I continued scanning the area, night vision was assisted by the faint down-lighting effect from the nearby city lights of Willows. For my readers' edification, that faint down-lighting effect I am describing, was caused by the cities lights shining upward into the overhead low-based rain clouds. Once that lighting effect reached the bottoms of the rain clouds, it would be faintly reflected back earthward. That was the down-lighting effect that was now aiding me in looking for my suspect night shooters and would especially do so once my suspects 'blew up the ducks'. Watching in the direction my mystery shooters to be had taken, I could see and hear the occasional lift- off from smaller bunches of surprised ducks but not much else. By now I figured my three lads had moved almost directly due north of my position. We now had about 20,000 unsuspecting ducks feeding in a large rice field in between my suspects, Dog and yours truly.

It was at that moment that I realized the wind had shifted. It was changing from blowing out from the northwest to that of now coming from due south. Moments later, I could tell the large flock of ducks noisily feeding between us had shifted from their original direction of feeding into the north wind and were now feeding more towards my position in the south. The ducks naturally did that in order to be feeding into the wind. That way if they were disturbed all they had to do was launch upward into the wind and, with that assist, were easily airborne and on their way away from any real or perceived danger. Still learning the ropes about feeding masses of waterfowl facing into the wind, I continued kneeling there on my rice check all fat, dumb and happy waiting for what I figured was soon to come in a thunder of wings and the rolling-thunder of shotguns firing in unison...

BOOM, BOOM, BOOM, BOOM... went about twelve to fifteen shots that came so quickly I could not even get an accurate count as to their exact number! In fact, that rattle of shots sounded like someone was ripping a thick heavy bedsheet they came so fast! A micro-second later, the sounds of massed shooting was followed by a thundering roar of thousands of panicked and terrified ducks storming into the air! Immediately following, came a discernable rush of air from forty thousand frantically beating wings from just 35 to 40 yards away. It brought to me the distinctive smells of rotting mud and decaying crawdads. And now, like whistling cannon shot of the same intensity of that in 1863 at the final battle of Gettysburg during General George Pickett's charge, came thousands of terrified ducks moving away from the thundering guns of death. Ducks who just moments earlier had been happily feeding on rice grains left by the harvesters and were now fleeing for their lives in intense terror from the streams of killing lead shot.

The thunderous roar of 20,000 terrified ducks lifting off all at once will be a memory that I will keep next to my soul until the day I die. So will the roar of three fast firing shotguns and then the intense silence that immediately followed that barrage for just a split second before the masses of feeding ducks lifted off! Truly, those were the sounds of the guns of death and thundering wings. Like the inexperienced dummy I was in that first momentous event in my lifetime, I jumped up to see if I could make out my nearby shooters with my binoculars, get an exact fix on their location and make ready for the pursuit that was to follow.

WHAM!!! Standing up like a human-sized highway billboard on the side of my rice check, I took a madly fleeing mallard duck dead center in my left breast and was literally blasted clean off my feet and lobbed backwards off the rice check by the impact! No matter my size, struck by a three-pound duck going forty miles per hour had to have the same force and effect of being shot! I hit the ground so damned hard that the impact literally blasted the wind out of me! Stars, I saw more damn stars of shapes and sizes that I didn't even know existed as I laid there on the muddy ground in agony... In fact, I distinctly felt the force of that impact, literally had my heart skipping several beats as it tried to readjust to its normal rhythm.

In the following seconds after impact, my training kicked in and wanted me to scramble to my feet so I could pursue my shooters and do battle. However, all my physical being did was allow me to crawl around on the ground on my hands and knees in agony trying to get my breath back, the heartbeat regulated and stifle the now intense pain shooting through my chest like I was having a heart attack! Damn, I hurt and no way could I get my breath nor do anything other than crawl around on the muddy rice ground in pain from the impact of that 'flying feathered cannon shot'!

Fortunately for me, when working the rice fields alone at night, I always carried two handguns because of the associated dangers in making apprehensions of armed individuals, while usually outnumbered. On my hip rode a .45 semi-automatic and in a shoulder holster over my left chest (I was right handed) rode my big Smith and Wesson, model 29, .44 magnum with a 6 ½ inch barrel. With that weaponry, I figured I could just about handle any kind of danger thrown at me come hell or high water. However, I had not counted on a three-pound duck sailing along at 40 miles per hour drilling me almost center of mass! One that had whanged into my left breast with almost the same intensity of a stray cannon shot from the historic battle of Gettysburg.

As I continued wallowing around in the rice field mud sucking air and trying to gain my breath over the still intense chest pain, Dog had disappeared. Shortly thereafter, she returned and tried nuzzling me in the face with a just retrieved dead mallard duck as I still crawled around in agony on all fours. She was making typical Labrador dog sounds of being so happy that she had just brought me that damn duck that had ploughed 'dead-center' into me, with its broken neck and all. You know, that same damned duck that had knocked me head over heels off my feet and into the rice field mud. Me? I just wished for my wind back and the throbbing pain over my left breast to diminish so I could get to my feet and race after my shooters. But, that took a long while since the intense pain spasms still felt like I was having a heart attack.

Eventually starting to get my wind back and feeling that my now sore as a boil left breast would allow me to live, I came to a sudden and happy realization. That damned duck had squarely sailed into my shoulder-holstered .44 magnum. In short, the impact from that flying duck had been mostly absorbed by the heavy handgun and its thick leather shoulder holster I always carried. Then the realization came that I was one damn happy chap that the low flying duck had not 'head shot' me.

Finally getting my sea legs under me once again, I crawled back to the top of my rice check and with my binoculars tried establishing where my shooters were located and what they were doing in the now dim light of a cloud scudded quarter moon, aided by the down lighting effects from the nearby city of Willows. A quarter moon was now forthcoming in the clearing cloud-studded skies along with the cessation of the rains with the advent of the wind change coming in from the south. Looking long and hard with my binoculars, not a damn human associated thing greeted my searching eyes in the just shot-over rice field! All I could see was a 'blanket' of white-chested male northern pintail ducks strewn across the rice field with other ducks crawling 'maggot like' for the cover the nearby rice checks offered… I was truly looking at a field of death caused by humankind and a battery of rapidly firing shotguns!

Talk about me being acutely disappointed over the scene of death greeting my eyes! I had been right there almost in the field of fire and had not a single miscreant in hand to show for my efforts or what they had done to the world of waterfowl in a micro-second of time. However, I was not done with the moment at hand as of yet. Kneeling back down behind my rice check, Dog and I stayed as still as death waiting in the hopes our shooters would walk back the same way they had entered in the morning when they had sneaked right by Dog and me. That wishful thinking did not produce the desired effect of my shooters passing by 'on parade' any time later. I was beginning to learn that historically when intelligent Sacramento Valley shooters pulled off such a duck killing act, many times they came in one way and left by another. No dummies in that class of duck-killing folks when it came to avoiding being 'hammered' by the long arm of the law. It seemed to me the only dummy in the rice field that morning was the one wearing game warden greens. One who was still tenderly nursing his torso because of the continuing stabbing chest pains from his collision with a low flying mallard duck.

The irony of it all, was that I was there to take care of the ducks and arrest any of their illegal shooters in the event of any such night-shooting action was to occur. Yet, it was one of their 'own' in the form of a three-pound mallard duck, that was the one that took out the ducks' protector. I think that God teaches us sad humans a life's lesson sometimes in such a manner, that we never forget the teaching moment that went along with it!

From my still hidden position come daylight, all I observed were a few stragglers of ducks working the rice fields around me and not another human was seen. Finally realizing I was beaten by someone sharper than I was, I stiffly rose, rubbed my sore left chest tenderly and began walking the area from whence the shooting had occurred hours earlier. It didn't take long to find the early morning duck-drag killing zone based on the lay-out killing zone of the now lifeless ducks.

Scattered in among the many thousands of duck tracks in the soft, rain soaked rice field mud were duck feathers, squirts of poop everywhere and dark reddish-brown blotches of spilled blood where a duck had fed his last moments on earth. Also in evidence were numerous sets of human footprints spread across the area just shot over which I assumed was the stark evidence of mankind picking up the duck-fruits of his labors! I was sure pissed over my stupidity and lack of skill in capturing anyone associated with that shoot! Also scattered about were numerous dead ducks that had either been overlooked by my shooters, left behind because my shooters had all they could carry or drag from the field of death, or the shooters had somehow become aware of my presence and scattered to the four winds and left without picking up any more of their remaining kill.

Sometime later, Dog and I had amassed a rather large pile of mostly dead northern pintail and mallards. Also scattered among the previous two species was a sizeable number of American wigeon which are medium sized ducks obviously left behind because of their lesser size and poorer eating qualities. Those numbers of dead in that pile came to 67 birds! Then Shadow began working the adjacent rice checks and soon the number of dead and dying ducks rose to 129! It was then that I realized the tremendous secondary death toll such illegal drag shooting had on a species population. Hell, it now looked like they had left more ducks behind then they had retrieved.

(Years later while working duck hunters in the Stockton Delta area of California as a United States Game Management Agent, I witnessed a very rare duck-drag occurring during daylight hours in a harvested and partially flooded corn field in which I was staked out. Immediately after that illegal shoot by three individuals whom we later caught, I personally witnessed over 100 ducks falling to their deaths as the remaining flock of birds flew away. Many of the wounded ducks could just fly just so far away from the shooting scene, only to die in the air from their wounds and then dropped over their flight path away from the killing field.)

With a little more looking, I discovered where my three shooters had crawled along the backsides of several rice checks after they had passed by me and finally had found the shooting position they desired. Lying there in the mud were fifteen freshly fired Winchester shotgun shells behind the rice check my shooters had hidden behind just seconds from the initiation of their slaughter in the Sacramento Valley.

Realizing I had accomplished little other than learning a damn good lesson about not standing up right away after a shoot and getting clobbered by errant flying lead shot from my shooters or panicked low flying ducks, I got down to the business at hand. First, I gutted all the ducks in order to lighten the load I had to carry from the field back to my truck. Then stuffing the game bag in my hunting coat clear full of duck bodies and carrying two filled duck straps I routinely carried for just such situations, I made six trips to my hidden truck. Following that, I made a short trip back to the Sacramento National Wildlife Refuge to fill up one of the federal agents' evidence freezers so full that I had to lay a tire and its rim on top of the freezer to keep the lid shut. I wondered what the feds thought when they discovered that the local game warden had completely filled up one of their freezers with seizures from cases he had made while they were just waltzing around looking beautiful or not present on the waterfowl nightly field of battle for whatever reason.

Until the writing of this story in 2015, I never told anyone about me getting my butt kicked on one of my numerous attempts to put those in the business of extinction out of business. Getting my butt kicked by one of those very critters I was trying to save. Nor did I explain to any of my compatriots how I got such a large bruise on my left chest that looked distinctly like the outline of a sizeable pistol holster. When my wife asked what had caused such an injury, I just told her I was chasing an outlaw and had stumbled and fallen down on top of the big magnum and it left a large bruise. I always found it best to leave one's stupidity hidden under a rock and to learn a damn good lesson from such a mishap than to spread the word around regarding one's ignorance.

Like General McArthur in the Philippines, I got my butt kicked by chaps better than me. But I wasn't done yet with those in the Sacramento Valley doing to Mother Nature what they shouldn't be doing. Like General Douglas McArthur said, "I shall return". I did return many times later throughout my seven years stint in the Northern Sacramento Valley during the long waterfowl season. I never again ever took another madly fleeing mallard duck in the chest going 40 miles per hour either...

(I took a load of #4 lead shot in the back in 1967 while chasing duck draggers not realizing they had a drop-off protecting their thieving, duck-killing backsides. If any readers are interested in that story, it is found in my e-book titled, *Wildlife Wars—The Life and Times of a Fish and Game Warden*, in Chapter 12, titled, 'Taking a Load of 4's'. It is an example of another rookie mistake that ended happily once the wounds healed over and I got over having my butt kicked once again.)

As for the Flowers in this adventure, there were many. I was fast learning the tips of the trade associated with the Sacramento Valley and the tricks of the trade needed to catch that particularly difficult breed of night-shooting outlaws, namely the duck-draggers or commercial market hunters. I also learned never to stand up immediately after a drag had occurred in order to avoid the flying lead shot inadvertently coming my way or being 'canon shot' off a rice check by a madly fleeing duck in the dark of the night. However, one has to admit that a madly fleeing duck going 40 miles per hour flying into a shoulder holster filled with the absorbing steel of a big magnum handgun had to be one of the sweetest Flowers going. After all, that duck could have struck me squarely in the face. There goes that God loves little children, fools and game wardens thing once again. I was also learning to dress better when working the cold and damp rice fields at night. All that took was the experience of one cold and wet night in Glenn County in a muddy rice field in a driving rainstorm in learning a life's lesson.

Another Flower associated with this adventure was that I soon discovered that those outlaws night-shooting waterfowl were always moving and could dress lightly when stalking the night feeding ducks because of their physical exertions in so doing. But the officer of the law had to dress more warmly in order to remain still and not be detected over long periods of time in the rice fields' damp of the night. When the officer dressed more heavily in warmer clothing, it kept him warm but slowed him down when pursuing outlaws. Hmmmm, was that another life's lesson learned or just a tip of the trade? I also learned that after lying for long periods of time in the damp rice fields, one could not just get up and quickly chase the night shooting outlaws with any great chance of success. One had to quickly warm up his legs in order to be able to run with the best of them to have any chance of capture. And let me tell all you readers out there, those illegally pulling the triggers after dark, could run like the wind if they thought they were being pursued.

As for the Tombstones in this adventure, there were a few. First the numbers of ducks illegally killed in such killing actions had to be considerable. Those taken by my shooters and the 129 I later discovered in the shot over area represented a sizable kill. And my dear readers, remember half statistically were females and half were males. Then multiply those numbers by an average clutch size of ten and those would have been the real losses that morning had all the next year's production lived to tell their tale and been able to successfully reproduce.

Another Tombstone was the fact that I never caught a single chap doing the shooting on that occasion in Glenn County. My own damn stupidity precluded me from doing so…

(I am told that today in the Sacramento Valley, those great numbers of ducks I experienced in the 1960's are no more. Believe me, to see a 100,000 ducks in the air or feeding on the ground was a sight to behold and remember. I am sorry my readers will probably never again see such feathered riches of our national heritage in the Sacramento Valley, which at one time literally was a wildlife Horn of Plenty.)

The last Tombstone from that morning so long ago is that of my friend, Jim Hiller. Jim passed over the Great Divide a few years later without leaving a discernable ripple in the water in this day's busy world. That was unfortunate because men such as Jim Hiller wearing the game warden's greens, made it possible for what many of you readers are able to see today in the way of what is left of our wildlife heritage. Thank you, Jim, for your service to the American people. You left a ripple of learning in my life, Jim, and I thank you for that. That ripple of knowledge shared with me on later joint patrols went on to serve me well during my 32-year career as a wildlife officer. I can only hope that my successes because of your teachings went on to made you proud wherever you are.

"LIONS ONE, CHRISTIANS NOTHING"...

Quietly sitting on the north end of McDermott Road in a 'hide', I watched thousands of ducks streaming off from the distant Delevan National Wildlife Refuge, crossing the I-5 Interstate, and coming down like huge silent tornados in the Lenahan Road area of Colusa County. Soon the rice fields north and south of Lenahan Road were swarming with numerous clouds of ducks rising and lowering in an undulating fashion, as they flooded across the harvested rice fields looking for safe places to land and feed. It was always an exhilarating experience to see the grace and beauty of such a natural wonder in full display moving all around me! Those flocks of ducks represented a wonder of nature of which I never tired of watching during my entire law enforcement career in the Sacramento Valley of California.

Those ducks had been feeding in that area for the last two days and that could be savagely unfortunate for them. If I could see such huge clouds of hungry milling ducks in many of the rice fields, so could my local night shooting duck draggers and commercial market hunters. In fact, I had already quietly sneaked up on a sitting carload of known wildlife outlaws from

424

Maxwell and another one from the Williams area an hour earlier, as they sat and watched the ducks with rapacious eyes, black hearts and itching trigger fingers. I purposely surprised all of those lads by making my immediate presence known and in so doing, took a law enforcement 'dump' in their night time duck killing mess kits. I knew they were looking for a close at hand group of ducks to blow up, so, I just figured I would blow up their little duck-dragging plans before they could pull a trigger. I had more potential night-shooting problems than I could handle during that time of the year and once again, had no close at hand state or federal help in the valley. So, I just up and pulled my 'trigger' early and ran off my close at hand outlaws with my much hated but beautiful and beaming presence.

With my surprise entrance, I made sure that my two carloads of outlaws knew there were visiting game wardens from other parts of the state and a healthy dose of federal agents behind every blade of water grass in the Sacramento Valley that evening. That verbal maneuver was a little trick of the trade that I called a force multiplier. By making my outlaw lads think there was an army of law dogs behind every blade of grass, that made most of them scurry back under the pile of dung from whence they had emanated. In the instant situation I found myself in, that was all it took for those two carloads of cockroaches to scurry back under their leaf litter from where they had originated. When those two car loads of outlaws had left the area, I called that a mission accomplished.

However, I didn't say anything to a young Italian fellow living in the Delevan area some thirty minutes later as he also slowly cruised by the feeding duck-loaded rice fields looking at the birds with a rapacious eye. I just figured that chap was historically long overdue for some of my personal law enforcement attention so, I gave him a pass. I just let him look as I kept my eye on him from my place of hiding in case he later got an itchy trigger finger and a hunger for a plump rice fed northern pintail or mallard duck dinner. Man, if he only knew that he had driven within yards of where I was hiding that evening quietly watching him as he passed by. You just never knew just how lucky you were that evening, Tony, especially when you didn't show up later in the dark of night.

Later that evening just north of the small valley town of Williams, I could hear my usual boiling tea kettle of late shooters hammering the ducks until it was an hour and a half past legal shooting time! Dad burn it, it never failed! Every time I 'zigged' in setting up a law enforcement ambush operation, it seemed that my local outlaws would 'zag'. Gritting my teeth over the flagrant late shooting violations going on south of my position, I logged the same in my memory banks so I could address any like situations in the future. In the meantime, regardless of those constant late shooting violations being heard to the south, I continued 'holding my water' and watching my huge flights of constantly incoming ducks. I just kept looking for any suspicious signs of a potential and unsuspecting drag shooter in the area who was unaware that the law was so close at hand.

Deep darkness soon overcame the area and emerging from my 'hide,' I ran across McDermott Road and into the nearest harvested rice field holding a pile of feeding ducks. Jumping behind the first rice check that Dog and I came to, I turned around and looked for any obvious signs of discovery by anyone driving down the road. Seeing none, Dog and I began making a careful sneak towards a huge flock of ducks already madly feeding on the ground that we could stake out. Slowing down my sneak and finally changing into a crawl, Dog and I managed to gain the cover of the nearest rice check without spooking my close at hand feeding ducks. We had no more than arrived, when with Dog and me pressing closely to the rice check to avoid discovery by the birds, had a flood of feeding ducks move over the top of us as they moved from one field to the next like a living feathered carpet! That kind of event really bothered my constant companion in the field, namely Shadow, my Labrador retriever! She just quivered the whole time the two of us were inundated with the flood of madly feeding ducks, as they changed from one rice field into another holding better grits. Shadow knew those things crawling all over her were to be retrieved and not tolerated squirming all over her. However, she also knew better than to move and minded her boss in lying as still as death when such events occurred. Retrieving my comforting arm previously laid over her to assure and help in keeping her quiet until the feathered flood had left, I whispered, "Good girl, Shadow. Good girl." When I did, I got the usual Labrador 'thump-thump' of a heavy tail hitting the ground next to the two of us. What a wonderful dog she was and a wonderful moment in time for the two of us to enjoy together! The day she passed away years later of cancer, I flashed back to some of those moments in time when we enjoyed working the ducks in the Colusa County rice fields together and cried like a baby. Even today in 2015, some 40 years after her death, I am finding it hard to write these lines…

Then it was back to 'sleeping with the ducks' as my hordes of waterfowl fed throughout the nearby rice fields that Shadow and I had chosen to stake out. Lying up onto the side of the rice check where I could see and yet not be seen, I continued glassing the area around my feeding ducks as Shadow snored loudly away in her boredom as she laid by my feet. (Bored because I wouldn't let her retrieve one of the ducks that had flooded over us and squirt pooped on her head earlier in the evening.)

To me, the weather that evening was perfect for a 'duck dragger ambush'. It was partially overcast but still allowed me to use my binoculars rather effectively in the fleeting moonlight. But the breeze now moving from out of the northwest portended the possibility of a weather change, namely more winter rains soon to follow. For now, I was dry, could see rather well with a binocular assist from the low cloud down-lighting effect from the nearby town of Williams and had a field of living targets all around me in case some son-of-a-gun dared to lay a round or two illegally in their direction. However, like many of my previous waterfowl stakeouts, that quiet was soon to change. Around midnight, the breezes from the northwest strengthened into a rather stiff blow and a short time later, I felt my first raindrop hitting my exposed hand.

THUMP, THUMP, THUMP, went three quick shots by a duck dragger south of my position somewhere near Lurline Avenue and Bowen Road! Those sounds of distant shots brought Shadow to her feet and me back from being about half-asleep. I had been working a number of 16-18 hour days, seven days a week stints and now those days and harsh winter weather labors were beginning to wear on me. I had recently discovered due to those long hours and days worked, that I could find sleep in a muddy, dead crawdad infested and sometimes even dead carp strewn, previously harvested rice field like it was my great king sized bed back at home. In so doing, being able to sleep lightly in the damp rice fields just extended my time and opportunities in which to catch some of my wildlife outlaws on the loose. Listening to see if I heard any more shooting from that area, the darkness of night and the opportunity of discovering a local outlaw in action, told me no such luck. They weren't that dumb to keep shooting so I could echolocate in on them and then move to the sounds of their guns. That and the fact that the shooter was pretty far away, made capture problematic.

With the sounds of that shooting to my south, my nearby fields of ducks quieted for the moment as their uneasiness over being previously shot over many nights earlier became apparent. That degree of awareness and uneasiness on the part of the feeding ducks increased as they were shot over more and more as the illegal night gunning season progressed. Soon I could tell that my chosen field for the night was beginning to empty of ducks as the rains increased and a number of the birds that had already fed up, were now departing for the safety of the nearby wildlife refuges. However, I figured I still had a good 10,000 ducks feeding around me and that would be more than enough of a lure to suck in any unsuspecting duck dragger. So with that in mind, I quietly held in my stake out position. Did so because the local outlaw lore based on the valley's market hunting history, was that it was wise to avoid shooting the larger bunches of ducks because those flocks of birds would be the ones the much dreaded federal wildlife officers would be 'babysitting'. Hence, I would sit on my remaining smaller flocks of ducks in the rice fields around me, rain or no rain, until I froze out.

One o'clock came and quietly went on the staked out rice field. The rains had increased to the point that I knew I still had fields of ducks nearby but with the increasing intensity of the rains, my feeding birds had grown considerably quieter as they fed. That was another valuable lesson I had learned early on during one of my many stake out ventures. When the rains came, it seemed to me that many times the ducks fed up and left for the refuges and those that remained got quieter as they fed. (Who knew, with the scope and degree of what I was now learning about the wildlife tricks of the trade, I just might make a good Sacramento Valley game warden yet.)

BOOM, BOOM, BOOM, BOOM, BOOM, BOOM, went six quick shots into my field of ducks! For the first and only time in my 32-year law enforcement career, I was looking in the right direction at the right instant and saw the winking-streams of muzzle flashes the very moment my shooters let loose! As it turned out, I had been sweeping my fields of ducks as best as I could with my binoculars in the light rains, looking for any kind of movement that I considered out of place. I had earlier quietly moved across a series of rice checks in order to stay closer to the feeding masses of birds just as my shooters had let her rip. Quickly looking at the luminous dial on my watch, I saw that my shooters had opened up on my ducks around one-fifteen in the morning. By now my faithful partner, Shadow, was up and looking in the direction from where those six shots had come from as well.

Zeroing in on the spot where I had seen the muzzle flashes, I watched that immediate area like a hungry red-tailed hawk would a small out-in-the-open California ground squirrel. Nothing and no signs of life or movement graced my eyes regarding my suspect shooters at hand. However, the thunderous roaring of thousands of ducks' wings told me my just shot over critters had now lost interest in putting on the 'feedbag' and were just getting the hell out of Dodge and onto the nearest national wildlife refuge for the safety that offered! That fleeing the scene also included many of the nearby surrounding bunches of previously feeding ducks not directly affected by the duck-drag at hand as well.

Then from a distant location north of my position, I heard at least ten quick shots adjacent the Dirks Road area. "DAMN-IT!" I yelled inside. "Another damn drag to go along with the first one I had just witnessed earlier in my set of fields". Gritting my teeth over my inadequacies, I just shook my head and hoped I would soon at least have my field of shooters clamped in irons. Well, no such luck. I couldn't make out any sign of my trigger-pulling son-of-a-guns through my now raindrop impaired binoculars. 'Low-sweeping' the binoculars back toward my field location, I memorized the ground and the several rice checks I needed to clear in order to get to where I had seen the earlier muzzle flashes. Then Dog and I hit the 'bricks' and began moving forward like a couple of Marine commandos.

Moving as quietly as we could and in a crouched over position, Dog and I swiftly moved along the backside of my rice check. If nothing else, I was in the process of warming up my near stone cold legs in case I got into a foot race with any of my shooters. Then dropping onto my belly in the wet rice field adobe-like mud, across the field I crawled like a Marine sniper going across an open area on Iwo Jima during the Second World War in the Pacific Theater. Man, I even surprised myself, as I quickly scooted across that open area like a giant mud turtle, only faster. Gaining the cover of the next rice check, I turned south and began sneaking along the backside of that rice check towards the location from whence the recent shooting from my duck draggers had emanated.

Then I stopped dead in my tracks. I could smell cigarette smoke! *Damn, I am so close to my shooters that I can smell them smoking or at least the nicotine stink on their clothing in the dampness of the morning,* I thought with a renewed grin of anticipation.

We were now right at the corner of a rice field with a farm road running closely along the eastern side of the field that Dog and I now occupied. With that geography in mind, it became apparent my shooters had let the feeding ducks cram into that corner of the field and, before they could swarm over the rice check into the next field, had opened up on the feeding birds. Well, that was all good because less than twenty yards away still sight unseen knelt The Great Grotz (that's me) in all his Teutonic magnificence! After hearing three drags that evening all around me, you could bet if God ever made green apples, I was going to have one or both of my close at hand duck draggers in my clutches shortly.

It was at that very moment that my two shooters stood up from the backside of their levee and appeared to be looking all around to see if the coast was clear. Sensing no danger, they boldly streamed out into the rice field and began picking up dead ducks and appeared to be biting across the heads of those that were still alive. (For my reader's edification, a number of the old-timer duck draggers would bite across the heads of any

431

retrieved wounded ducks. That allowed the ducks' heads to remain attached to their necks and made for easier transport from the fields. In short, a neck-wrung headless duck did not transport well on a duck strap.) Once my lads had all they could carry, they made swift trips back to their rice check, dropped off the birds in a pile at the corner of the rice field and went forth to gather up even more dead ducks. Every-time they ventured back out into the rice field for more ducks, guess what handsome son-of-a-bitch kept crawling closer and closer to their pile of ducks? You Folks guessed right on that one, it was The Great Grotz! In so doing, I clamped down harder and harder on the bit in my teeth the closer I got to my two shooters. "These two shooters were going to pay the price for blowing up my ducks if I had my druthers," kept crossing my mind. "Blow up my ducks and, if I was ever in country, someone was going to pay the price for being so damned stupid," type thoughts kept streaming through my mind like there was no tomorrow!

I finally decided it was time for me to spring my trap. It was taking my two lads longer and longer to come back to their pile of birds because the dead and wounded ducks further out in the field of fire were getting harder and harder to locate. Since I had let my shooters do all the work in gathering up the dead and dying birds, I figured they would be winded after having to run constantly across that muddy rice field after their quarry. With that in mind, The Great Grotz would then be on the top of his form and hopefully in the middle of his shooters before 'Christ made corporal'.

When both men arrived back at their bird pile about the same time, I sprung my trap. Over the rice check I stormed like the Marines did on Tarawa when they landed on the beach behind the sea wall and in so doing, reached for the closest of my chaps dumping his ducks. Surprised at this huge shape lunging at him from such close range bellowing, "Game

432

Warden! Hold it right there!" he took a swing at me in an instinctive and defensive blocking reaction to my near at hand and quickly closing presence. When my chap swung his fist, he hit me squarely in the mouth! That was the last punch he threw before he hit the ground with a more than violent sounding THUMP! (For my readers' information, I did not file assault charges on the man because I was sure he had swung at me purely out of his extreme surprise and fright of a monster sized person being launched unexpectedly his way from just feet away.) His partner, who was a few feet further away, instantly took off running for the farm road near the corner of the field with me in hot pursuit. We both hit the road berm at the same time but I slipped in the mud and stalled out in my pursuit. In the meantime, my fleeing chap hit the road berm at full stride, gained the road surface and took off running like a shot down the road to the north. Gaining the road myself, I took off after my chap like a cheetah. Alright, alright, you darn readers who are aware of my more than ample size, maybe a slow cheetah.

OOOFF, yelled my runner as he took a spectacular spill seen even in darkness of the night. Realizing my chap had slammed into an unseen barrier that I was rapidly approaching, I slapped on the brakes because even if I landed on something soft, 320 pounds flying through the air at the speed of light will always hit hard no matter what I landed upon. WHAM! Out went my feet from under me on the muddy road surface, landing me violently flat on my back! I then found myself sliding forward about ten feet in the soft mud and through a mud puddle because of my inertia chasing my culprit. When I did, I realized I had just slid under a cable that was strung across the road about two feet above the roadbed. Some dirt farmer wanting to keep unwanted people out from his field, had strung the unseen cable across his farm road and, in the darkness, my runner had barreled right into it running full bore! As such, he now lay groaning in the mud of the road in a hell

433

of a heap. Me? I had just slid about ten feet in the mud after losing my footing when I slapped on the brakes and had slid cleanly under the cable and remained uninjured. Well, I can't really say that. The Great Grotz had his feelings hurt since he had taken a not-so-graceful tumble as well after slapping on his binders. Jumping up and reaching for my .45 semi-auto handgun carried on my hip in case my chap went for his shotgun, I FOUND IT MISSING! Apparently, when I had plowed onto the ground on my back at Mach 3, the force of the impact and the mud I was plowing through, unsnapped my holster strap and the .45 slid out into the mud, the blood and the beer in the dark of the night!

But, I still had my second gun, my big magnum in its shoulder holster, so I tossed open my hunting jacket, grabbed my flashlight out from the game bag and announced my official presence once again all in the same fluid set of motions. As it turned out, my defensive actions were unnecessary. My chap had really barked his shins when he hit the unseen cable across the road and could barely walk. Not realizing that, I grabbed him up off the ground by his stacking swivel, told him he was under arrest for night shooting waterfowl and somewhat roughly saw to it that he was returned to where his partner had been laid out earlier when I returned his punch with a bit more force then his taken at me.

Arriving at the scene of the crime, I found my previously struck-in-the-head chap starting to come to. When he regained consciousness, I had both he and his partner in crime sit their 'tail-ends' down on the rice check after they had handed me their driver's licenses. As Dog sat next to their two shotguns lying now unloaded and off to one side a few feet away in the mud where I had laid them, I shined my flashlight onto their licenses. Lo and behold, I had Pauli Lee Dutra from the town of Orland and Franklin Ernest Pagani from the nearby town of Willows. As it turned out, both men were truckers and had wanted to take a mess of freshly killed rice fed ducks to some of their clients in return for the business those clients had provided the two men in their independent trucking business. Either way, the two men would not be trucking any rice fed ducks soon and neither would their clients be eating any if I had my say.

Looking over the wimpy chap who had slugged me in the mouth when I had hammered over the top of their rice check in surprise, I could see that my strike had been much more effective than the little pop in the mouth he had given me. David had a goose egg over his right eye that was fast on its way to becoming a swan egg. As for Frank, he was so crippled up from tearing into that unseen cable strung across the road, his battered and bloody shins were not going to give him any easy walking miles any time soon.

I counted out the 83 ducks the men had piled up at the foot of the rice check and Shadow had discovered another 48 dead and dying ducks in the weeds on the adjacent rice checks surrounding the field just 'shot over'. Deciding both men had suffered enough, I dug out my citation book from my muddy hunting coat's game bag and commenced issuing citations on the spot. In the end, both men received citations for early shooting migratory game birds, using unplugged shotguns and jointly taking and possessing over limits of migratory game birds, To Wit:131 ducks over the legal limit. I also seized their shotguns as evidence and for possible forfeiture to the State of California. With that, I sent both men packing. As the two men walked out of sight, I ditched their shotguns along a rice check to reduce the weight I would be carrying on my half a mile walk back to my pickup. When I was satisfied that both men had walked and limped out to their hidden vehicle and had left the area, Dog and I hiked out to my 'hidden-in-plain-sight-with-the-broken-down-note-on-my-window' vehicle.

Driving back to the field in question, Dog and I spent the next hour or so in my truck's headlights gutting out the ducks.

Well, I can't say that. I gutted out the ducks and Dog ate all the innards that she could handle. Then using the headlights from my truck to illuminate the roadbed so I could recover my .45 pistol, I soon found it rolled up in the mud when I had slid under the unseen cable. By then it was daylight, so, I drove up to Maxwell and in my muddy clothing, had breakfast in Charlie Dennis's cafe with Charlie and his son Tim. I soon discovered I had a lot of locals looking at my recent duck seizures in the bed of my truck parked outside in front of Charlie's cafe. That kind of public display in the local game warden's truck was always another force multiplier for all the local outlaws to see. If nothing else, it was a reminder to those walking on the wild side in the town of Maxwell that sometimes the bear would eat you if you were not too careful.

From there I headed south to Williams and filed my citations with the Williams Justice Court. I then got the O.K. from Judge Gibson to dispose of the seized birds as I saw fit since it was a slam-dunk case. Driving home, I let my wife know via a landline call from the Colusa Sheriff's Office, that I was OK but still going to be afield for a few more hours. (Boy, I loved coming home to that woman. Hell, I still do and will love her forever and a day for putting up with me and the all-demanding wildlife law enforcement profession! A profession known for all the divorces it causes throughout the ranks of the men in green during their careers.) Then I got ready to play Santa Claus with the good eating rice fed ducks.

I delivered a pile of ducks to five Mexican farm families living on the east side of my district, each with a passel of kids. Following that, I gave away three limits to three sets of black folks fishing along Butte Creek who were all too happy to receive such bounty since the fishing was so poor. Then I drove back to Colusa where I gave a limit of fat northern pintail to Mrs. Sada Yamamoto because she and her husband, Tom, loved eating game birds. Finally, I went back to Williams where I dropped off the remaining birds to two needy families whom I knew were struggling just trying to keep the wolf from the door. As I have stated numerous times before, I loved playing Santa with Mother Nature's critters every chance I got.

By then, Dog and I were ready for a few hours of sleep and that we did. By four in the afternoon, I was again watching the flights of waterfowl exiting Colusa National Wildlife Refuge as they headed for harvested rice fields in the area of Lone Star and Hahn Roads. Thus began another round of trying to protect those in the world of wildlife who had little or no voice from those walking on the dark side of man.

Now for the Flowers and Tombstones generated by this adventure in the storied Sacramento Valley during the height of the winter migration of millions of migratory game and non-game birds. As for the Flowers in this adventure, I, like the R.C.M.P., finally got my man. In the ensuing chase, I did not get injured as did one of my duck-dragging outlaws. Once again, I experienced another of God's aerial wonders up close and personal like as the ducks hungrily fed in the rice fields around me and did so with my ever-faithful companion, Shadow, who is now a memory...

Another Flower was that I never again crossed swords with Pauli or Frank. I am sure they never quit gunning illegally but they just did their dirty deeds elsewhere other than in my patrol district. And, I was continuing to learn more and more about how the job was to be done when it came to my many night shooters. A set of outlaw captures and a well-earned Flower in anyone's bonnet if I say so myself. Another set of Flowers derived from this adventure were the legal happenings that followed in the Williams Justice Court. Neither Pauli or Frank appeared to contest their charges against them. They just chose to forfeit the bail for such violations. As such, Judge Gibson levied $1,000 fines upon each man and forfeited their shotguns to the State of California. I would think there had to be a lesson learned in that legal event by both men, which counted as another Flower as well.

Lastly for this adventure's Flowers, I got to play Santa Claus to a lot of well deserving folks through the distribution of those ducks taken illegally. In several cases involving the poor Mexican laborers, the blessing of having meat on hand for their meals had to be a God send. Then as it turned out, guess who started turning invaluable information over to me about wildlife outlaws doing their thing? You got that right. The grateful Mexican farm hands... I guess one could throw that bit of quiet assistance in the form of valuable information about on-going violations into the category of Flowers as well.

As for the Tombstones in this adventure, there continues to be a litany of death and destruction of our waterfowl national heritage. One cannot expect such gross illegal takes of myriads of waterfowl for it not to eventually have a profound negative effect on our natural resources. Between California's great droughts in 2013-2015, habitat changes, illegal gunning and changes in farming practices on the Prairie Provinces or what are known as 'duck factories' for the thousands of ducks and geese they produce, waterfowl numbers have taken a dive. Today in 2015, no longer does one see hundreds of thousands of ducks streaming from the Sacramento Valley's national wildlife refuges into the rice fields at night to feed. No longer does one see tornados of ducks by the tens of thousands slowly spiraling down from the heavens to land and feed as they once did. As a direct result of those population reductions and a sub-cultural change in the Sacramento Valley's peoples, no longer do the illegal guns of night thunder as they once did. I rest my case when it comes to that field of Tombstones now silently overseeing the natural history dust of the sins of man from yesteryear. A dust that will forever shadow man's sins and cause regrets in the lives of those Americans yet to come.

A THREE POUND TRIGGER PULL AWAY FROM
ETERNITY

Late one summer Friday night, Dog and I were checking our perennial warm water game fish fishermen southeast of Colusa fishing in the waterway along the Butte Slough Road. It was the familiar start of a typical weekend evening with dozens of my African-American fishermen and women trying out their angling skills after a hard week at work. Most of those folks had come up from the Bay Area to sample the warm water game fish bounty typically offered by Colusa County's many open-to-the-public waterways. That evening was little different from many other previous weekends when it came to my fishing fraternity. I had dozens of black fishermen and women camping in groups along my waterways in small tents or just in their automobiles but all of them were having a good time. The fish were biting, the mosquitoes seemed to be about in less than their normal numbers, and the drinking and hellraising by my some of the fishermen was more or less under control.

My usual patrol procedure was to drive in the darkness without using any lights along the numerous levee and farm roads until I came to a large, strung out number of campsites of folks fishing along many of my open to the public waterways. Stopping, I would first glass the scene with my binoculars through my front windshield for any obvious signs of fish and game violations like using too many fishing lines and such. Seeing the waterway clear of any obvious fishing violations, I would then get out from my truck and walk off the levee in clear view toward my fishermen. As my presence became known up and down the line of fishermen, many folks watched my obvious approach with interest and of course, some with suspicion. Watching me closely with suspicion would be those fishermen who had no fishing licenses or were in some other kind of violation of the fish and game regulations. Many times I would have from a dozen to as high as 30 black fishermen in groups strung out along those waterways, all punctuated by a number of small campfires illuminating the fishing action. Once having walked off the levee and down among my folks, I would hesitate in plain view for the effect it would have in getting everyone's attention without making my actions too obvious as to what was coming. Turning, I would give a low and very much obvious whistle back towards my patrol truck and with that action, I would now have everyone's rapt attention

As a history lesson for my readers, I was very much aware that this was during the turbulent 1960's when there was so much unrest in the nearby Bay Area cities between a number of the black folks and the law enforcement communities. For a number of those people fishing along my waterways, there was an intense hatred of law and order and of those enforcing the laws of the land. Rightly or wrongly, there was an intense suspicion of anything related to anyone wearing a badge called "Pigs" in those days and what they stood for. That went double with some of my black folks when they had come up into the outback to get away from the troubled cities in order to just relax and get in some fishing. So, when an officer of the law happened upon their fishing scene, a number of the more radical folks, especially the younger ones, would exhibit or develop an attitude that would showcase the gap of trust that existed between the white and black cultures. However, I had been raised and subscribed to the theme that I would treat everyone like I would like to have the members of my own family treated in similar situations. That didn't mean however, that I wasn't aware of the underlying resentment problems in the big cities and went around with my guard down. If a badge carrier ever subscribed to waltzing around without being cautious in such situations, he or she would be quite possibly retired early or never live see another sunrise…

With that problematic background not of my doing in mind and my now obvious whistle, out from the back of my truck would come a 100 pound, all black Labrador dog running towards me in the dark of the night like hell was on her tail. When Dog got to my side, she would immediately skid to a halt, sit and wait for my next command. Now that I had the attention of anyone who might have an attitude, I would start with the black ladies first and treat every one of them just like the ladies they were during my routine fish and game inspections. I would laugh with them, joke around, tease them, share my always handy can of mosquito spray, tell them what was the best bait to use, admire their catches and just generally have a good time jaw-boning with them. (Now keep in mind, everyone saw that big dog jump from the back of my truck and run down to the fishing area to be with me. Throughout my talking and checking licenses with the females, Dog never moved from where she had earlier seated herself. She just quietly watched me for any sign of a given command.)

Then I would turn my attention to the males or some of the more militant members of the fishing community at hand. As mentioned earlier, the younger ones, especially those in the 20-30 age groups, seemed to have a chip on their shoulders or an ax to grind because of real or perceived slights by some members of the San Francisco Bay Areas law enforcement community. In so doing, I then walked up to my male fishermen in full uniform with the same friendly attitude as I exhibited around their ladies. I very professionally would begin checking fishing licenses and respond to any questions any of the men might have and in the process, treat them like I would like my family members treated under like conditions.

As was usual, a number of them would be grumpy over the fact that they had come to fish and not be hassled by a Pig. Having been there before, I put on my best face, as I ignored and accepted the attitudes and subtle slights as a thing of the times. I had a job to do and got it done as fast and professionally as I could so I would not interfere too much with my folks and their hoped for fishing experience. I did so because I always had an ace in the hole. I had rightfully treated all of their women like queens. So, if any of the men got loud or mad at me for hassling them as they called it, the ladies would come to my rescue and let the men know they had better be nice to Mr. Game Warden or...

In that first bunch of fishermen I checked on that particular evening, I apprehended six men fishing without licenses or for using more than one fishing pole in inland waters. During the time it took to issue the citations, I noticed five very beautiful, somewhat scantily clad white women 'working' a number of the black men. I also noticed there was a HUGE black man who was collecting all the money paid for the services rendered by his ladies. My huge black man had to be all of at least 6-foot 7 or 8-inches tall and weighed in at least 400 pounds! Damn, he was one BIG black man! Another thing I noticed was that he was all eyes when it came to watching his ladies and their interactions with the interested single men fishing along the waterways. I also noticed that once a 'deal' was struck, the pair would adjourn to a rather large tent pitched at the south end of the waterway and disappear inside together.

Realizing that prostitution was illegal in California in those days, I put that gem of information into the banks of my mind for later action with the Colusa County Sheriff's Office. But for the moment, I was more interested in my wildlife and how it fared and not the huge black man's form of 'wild life', so, I ventured on. Bottom line, they weren't breaking any fish and game laws so I didn't get too excited. To be certain, there was a line of hopeful candidates also lined up at the entrance of the tent so everyone seemed happy and it didn't call for any Penal Code interference on my part at that time.

Finishing with my fish and game business, I bid everyone good-bye and good luck, then walked back to my truck, turned and looked back. Almost to a person, all my folks were still looking at that big black dog I had left behind still sitting there quietly in the middle of the fishermen. I could just see the concern written across some of their faces indicating, *The game warden has just left his BIG black dog behind!* Grinning inside, I gave a low whistle and here came Shadow at a dead run. "In the truck," was my command and she was instantly happily airborne and reunited with her patrol vehicle. (I shortly thereafter contacted the Colusa County Sheriff's Office and soon had Undersheriff Joel McDermott on the radio and informed him of the action on Butte Slough. Joel decided to leave well enough alone since there didn't appear to be any need to officially interfere and create a scene with his limited number of officers currently on duty. So, he let sleeping dogs lie, in a manner of speaking.) With my fish and game business finished, I moved on to the next large camp of warm water game fish hopefuls up the line and began checking their licenses just as I had done in the last big fishing camp.

I continued checking my fishermen from the southern part of my assigned patrol district all the way north to the end of my patrol area where it butted up against Butte County and Warden Fred Brown's territory. Then I did what most outlaws figured I would not do. Since I had already checked my fishermen once, why would I come back around later? Well, that is exactly what I did. After fishermen were checked once and left alone, many times they got a little wild figuring the fox had left the hen house and now they could begin breaking the fish and game laws as they pleased. Every time I instituted such a surprise second return patrol, I always made money from a goodly number of those previously checked. When I did, it was common to discover my previously checked chaps fishing with more than one rod, running drop-lines, putting out set-lines, littering or taking more fish than the law legally allowed. That 'checking it twice' trick of the trade was a very effective and many times successful type of 'serious game' that I played over my years as a fish and game officer in the Sacramento Valley. And in the process, made many thousands in fine monies for the county and the State of California, not to mention, taught a lot of my outlaws a new trick.

With that plan of action in mind, back down along my many waterways I went visiting my previously checked fishermen once again. My plan was to visit my folks and if they were legal, chew the fat with them, let them know where the best fishing was, what was the best bait to use and the like. However if they were in the wrong, they would be cited or booked depending on the severity of the crime and the circumstances surrounding the violation.

Around three the following morning, I finally was able to get back to my first checked, original group of fishermen where the giant of a man had his little on-going whore house in the tent operation along Butte Slough. By that time of the morning, most of the folks would normally be sleeping in their cars, tents or lying in rolls of bedding alongside their campfires. In fact, I didn't see a single person awake throughout the entire original camp of about thirty fishermen as I pulled into view for a second time. For most, their fishing gear was still out and fishing for warm water game fish at all hours of the day or night was legal (unlike fishing in inland waters for salmon, trout, mountain white fish and char, which was only allowed an hour before daylight to one hour after sunset).. Checking with my binoculars from a discreet distance as I always did, I did not see any evidence of violations and was just getting ready to leave when I spotted something unusual.

Taking a better last look at the tent holding its beautiful women and their huge black pimp, I saw what appeared to be the butt of a fishing pole lying on the ground on the far side of their 'well visited' tent. The tent was adjacent to the main waterway and the fishing pole lying on the ground had a line in the water. That wasn't the case when I came by the first time and checked. None of that group had been fishing during my first visit the evening before. Then I wondered if my little return visit was going to be successful and pay fish and game violation dividends. No one from that particular tent had been checked for their fishing licenses during my first visit because they weren't fishing. That and a 'fishing license' wasn't required for what they were doing during that first visit... Now it appeared someone from that group was fishing because a fishing pole was laid cleverly on the far side of the tent almost out of sight, with a line in the water and a little bell attached to the end of the rod to notify the fisherman when a fish was on. Figuring I might have a violation but needed to get a better look, I left Dog in the back of my truck and quietly headed down off the levee to my suspect tent, its sleeping occupants, and the fishing pole in question.

It was pretty damn dark next to my suspect's tent so I now had my flashlight in my left hand in case it would be needed in checking out my suspect fishing pole. Quietly walking up to the front of the tent and careful not to awaken its sleeping inhabitants, I stepped over to the slough side of their tent and took a look. Sure as all get out, there laid not one but six fishing poles! All were cleverly laid out of sight on the backside of the tent housing the five white women and my huge black man. Additionally, every one of the fishing pole's handles were tied to wooden stakes driven into the dirt. That was so if a large fish was hooked on the unattended rod, that fishing pole would not be dragged off the bank and lost into the deep waters of the slough. There was a small bell attached to the tips of each fishing pole so if a fish struck, the fisherman would be alerted to that fact and he or she could attend to landing the fish. That whole fishing pole layout behind the tent was well thought out and 'slicker than cow slobbers' when it came to evading the searching eye of the fish and game law.

Taking my flashlight and letting just a sliver of light shine through my fingers, I confirmed that all six of the fishing poles had lines in the water, were baited and actively fishing. Sensing I potentially had my ladies and their pimp on my 'hook and line', I walked back to the front entrance of the tent. Once there, I made sure I was positioned about ten feet away from the front opening of their tent in case everyone came streaming out all at once, after I had announced my presence. **THAT QUIET DEFENSIVE MOVE ON MY PART ULTIMATELY SAVED A HUMAN BEING FROM SLIPPING OVER THE GREAT DIVIDE INTO ETERNITY!**

Turning on my flashlight, I said in a fairly-loud voice, "Good morning, State Fish and Game Warden. I would like to check some fishing licenses if I may." After that rather loud announcement, I heard no sounds coming from within the tent. Again, I loudly announced my identification and the reason for me being there. That time I could hear stirring sounds coming from within the tent. Then silence. That following silence kind of made me think everyone had just rolled over after hearing me and had gone back to sleep.

"GOOD MORNING. STATE FISH AND GAME WARDEN," I informed those within the tent in a louder tone of voice. That time I heard a woman's voice saying something inaudible and then more stirring about from within the tent. It was also at that very moment my guardian angels began stirring about within my carcass. Sensing the uneasiness of my guardian angels, I reached down and unsnapped the catch on my holster freeing my pistol in case I would have need for its hasty withdrawal. I then sensed there was more stirring about in the tent but no more women's voices talking did I hear.

Suddenly, the tent flap was explosively thrown back and out stepped my huge black man! What followed sure as hell got my undivided attention in the following heartbeat! My huge black man quickly lunged my way from the tent in a crouched over defensive fighting position! In the soft light of my flashlight, I then saw the glint of a large knife in the man's right hand! Large, hell! The knife appeared to be about a ten-inch-long commando type knife and from all looks and appearances, my black man knew what to do with it and was about to commence his actions…

"HOLD IT RIGHT THERE!" I commanded, as I felt the comforting handle of my heavy .44 magnum filling my right hand in a millisecond! "STATE FISH AND GAME WARDEN! HOLD IT RIGHT THERE OR YOU ARE A DEAD MAN," I bellowed loudly enough for even God to hear.

Upon hearing my latest command, the huge black man stood up to his full height, thrust his knife forward in an attack mode and stepped towards me in a flash! (I still remember just how fast that big man moved toward me and my surprise over his speed.) Then it dawned on me, *Terry, you had better get your ass in gear or you are a dead man.*

Now in those days, the Smith and Wesson .44 magnum I carried as my service weapon was the most powerful commercially manufactured handgun made. As for my magnum, it had a six and one-half inch barrel and was loaded with 255 grain Keith-Thompson semi-wad cutter bullets, powered by over 20 grains of 2400 Rifle Powder. [I made my own ammunition because of the high cost of commercially manufactured .44 magnum ammunition.] That particular hand load was moving along at better than 1,200 feet per second. As such, a center of mass hit would open up anyone no matter how big they were with the same results one would expect to see when one shoots a watermelon at close range! I think you readers get the picture. I routinely shot distinguished expert on the pistol range using full house loads with that big magnum, so, there was no issue in hitting a target, especially one that big and close. To all my readers out there who are pistol- shooting aficionados and familiar with that big magnum, you understand what I just said and what those words would have meant had I pulled the trigger, while confronting my huge black man in the instant case!

In the morning's darkness on that day so long ago, that black man still coming my way with the large knife was more than filling my sights! My magnum had a crisp, honed and balanced, three-pound trigger pull and in that very instant, I clearly remember that I had already pulled about one and a half pound's worth on my trigger and was heading for more as my huge black man with the knife continued fast-walking in a crouch towards me!

Now, not more than two feet away from the tip of the man's knife and the end of my gun barrel, the huge black man suddenly stopped his charge! I remember thinking that I would let the man with the knife get right to the very end of my pistol barrel before I 'touched her off'. I knew the kinetic energy of that big magnum's bullet striking him center of mass, would blow him backward ass over tea kettle and put me out of harm's way in the following micro-second. (Looking back on that moment today as these words are being written in 2015, there couldn't have been more than one pound of trigger pull remaining on that big magnum before that chap stepped over into that faraway place called eternity.)

All of a sudden, the man bellowed, "Whose you?" The strong heavy smell of stale whiskey filled my nostrils and the early morning's summer moist air around me when he bellowed out those words. (That should tell all your readers out there just how close that man was not only to me but to stepping over the great divide.)

"State fish and game warden. Drop that knife or you will die right where you stand!" I said in such a tone and tenor that I even turned God's head, causing him to look earthward.

Now fully illuminated in the light of my flashlight held in my left hand and letting him clearly see my right hand holding the handgun with the muzzle aimed directly at his chest, my black man froze in his actions. With his observation of the end of a gun barrel aimed directly at him from two feet away along with the realization that eternity was staring him in the face, he carefully bent over and slowly laid a ten-inch military-like knife down at his feet.

"Now, kick that damn knife off to one side", I commanded without moving my gun's point of aim from the center of his massive chest in case he still decided to rush me. The man did as instructed and by now, I had several women peeping out from the tent looking at the commotion in front of the tent. "Now, sit your big hind end down and don't move," I instructed, as I started coming down from the adrenaline rush of the moment.

"Come here, Shadow," I yelled without taking my eyes off my monster sized black man sitting in front of me. My command was instantly met with the sounds of Shadow's toenails scratching on the side of my truck as she bailed out and made for me like a freight train. When the 'cavalry' arrived, I had her sit by me so she could be part of any future play from my black man. When she did, I could tell from the worried looks on his face in my flashlight that the entry of Dog into the picture had more than gotten his attention.

"May I speak, Officer?" quietly asked my black man.

"Go ahead. But you remain seated just as you are," I said, as I slowly holstered my pistol. I left the retaining strap off the handgun just in case I had to unlimber that piece of artillery again if things went quickly downhill from there. Then I took three steps backward to increase the distance between my black man and me for the safety that extra space offered.

"I have been drinking a lot over my ladies successes last night and I didn't hear you until you called out. In my foggy haze, I jes' figured youse were one of those other black men trying to get at my girls without paying. And that ain't a-goin' to happen if I has my say," he continued.

"Well, that didn't give you cause to erupt from the tent with a knife in hand and making a menacing move at whoever was confronting you," I said in a tone of voice not meant to be to misunderstood.

"Yes, Sirs, Mr. Game Warden. I sees what you are saying. But I jes' wanted to protect my girls, and I jes' let the whiskey speak for me and my behavior," he continued.

"Let me see your driver's license," I said.

The man dug around in his wallet, which I noticed was full of paper money and handed the license to me. Looking over the license information, I saw I had David Jackson Billit from Oakland, California seated in front of me.

"Mr. Billit, do you have any priors or warrants on you as we speak?" I asked as I stood a short distance away still in a defensive position in case he changed his mind and rushed me.

"No, Sirs, Mr. Game Warden. I don't give nobody any cause to be out and hunting me. My mother didn't raise no fool," he continued as his voice revealed that he was also coming down from his initial fright over being confronted by me, another large man, a man who had come into his world through the whiskey fog in his brain from out of the dark of night.

By now, with all the earlier commands and loud voices, the rest of the fishermen along the slough were wide awake, bunched up and looking in our direction. But none of them moved or appeared to be wanting to get involved. Especially in light of me earlier holding a rather large handgun on the giant of a man in the glaring light of a five cell flashlight!

The women in the giant's tent were now all awake and wondering aloud among themselves what was going on. Finally getting everyone all calmed down, I left Dog to watch my large chap as I walked back up to my patrol truck. Driving it off the levee, I brought it down to the suspect's camp and illuminated the whole scene with my headlights. From where he could hear me and I could keep a close eye on my previously knife wielding chap, I called the Colusa County Sheriff's Office and requested a "10-28' and a "10-29' on my lad. Surprisingly, he came back clean with no outstanding warrants or serious convictions. I didn't bother running any of the ladies to see if they had any warrants, nor did I have any reason to really do so. Now that I had a moment to think over the events that had just occurred, I decided not to charge my knife wielding man criminally. I figured he had been spooked and influenced by imbibing to much 'John Barleycorn', which had hazed his thinking. As such, there was no need in proceeding criminally against the man for the threat he had earlier posed to me as a peace officer of the state. Besides, my giant of a man still had two feet to go to get to the end of my gun barrel and a place called eternity, before I touched her off...

However, I did run a check on everyone regarding possession of fishing licenses and would you believe it, everyone in the party had a fishing license! Here I had damned near killed another human being over a non-violation of the fishing regulations. Well, that and the small issue of a rather large knife wielded in what I considered a somewhat aggressive and inappropriate manner...

By then it was almost daylight and since everyone was up, my little group relit their campfire and began preparing to make their breakfast. That was when my giant came over and extended his monster hand and asked if I could forgive him for being so stupid to think that he had to use a knife to defend himself. I shook the man's hand (left handed of course as I kept my gun-hand free) and found his handshake to be firm and genuine. Then came the surprise of the morning.

"I tell youse what, Officer. Youse can have any of my girls for free to make amends for me trying to stick you with my knife. Any of them, jes' take your pick. Youse can take even more than one if you feel up to it," he said with a big toothy grin. It was then for the first time, that I noticed my huge black man had a rather large diamond firmly affixed in the space between his two front teeth...

Floored by the unexpected offer, I thanked the man and told him I had a great little wife at home waiting for me and I had better get it in gear if I wanted to have a sit down breakfast with her before she started her day.

However, my black man persisted unfazed over my statement of denial when it came to his more than surprising offer. "She won't knows unless you tells her what you did. Jes' think what you are missin'," he continued with a twinkle in his eyes.

"Thank you anyway but I have to get home and let my wife know I am alright. However, I see a lot of your fellow fishermen looking covetously in this direction and, instead of messing with me, you have some paying customers over there," I said with a grin and a flourish of my hand in the direction of the many expectant looking fishermen. With that, we laughed and shook hands again. Then like nothing out of the ordinary had happened that morning, I loaded up Dog and we drove off. As I did, I just had to chuckle over that morning's events. First, there was a possible fishing violation that almost turned deadly. Then receiving an offer to 'get friendly' with a mess of 'Ladies of the Night' from a man who almost became a target because of his hostile actions. My how God throws funny and sometimes serious situations at us game warden types, 'kind of willy-nilly'.

I didn't get too excited over the man for being so ingenious and bringing the ladies of the night up onto the fishing grounds for some monetary gain. What the hell! This was America and many a person had made their fortunes by being inventive, sometimes illegally and for often times thinking out of the box. I guess one could say my huge black man had come up with one hell of a good idea. One could fish and dally around all on the same stream bank and forget one's woes back in the big cities' concrete jungles.

However, all smiles aside, I was sure glad I had that big magnum that morning and that it had a **three-pound** trigger pull instead of one that was just only **two-pounds!** (I learned in later years from my law enforcement police officer younger son, Chris, who was a nationally recognized ground fighting and a knife-fighting expert, just how dangerous a man can be with a knife. Chris taught me that an expert in knife fighting can cover 20' feet of ground and be on you before you can pull the trigger of a gun pointed right at your knife wielding assailant! My faith in the big magnum and its abilities was well placed. Bottom line, if that man confronting me with his knife that morning had wanted to take my life and was good at what he did as a knife fighter, he more than likely could have done so before I could have pulled the trigger in self-defense.)

As I have said so many times in my previous writings, 'God loves little children, fools and *game wardens.'* It is now obvious that He appreciated me and the work I did in protecting His critters that fine morning so long ago. Otherwise....

As for the Flowers in this story, they should be obvious. A huge black man had been graced by God and given a second chance when it came to his life after pulling a stupid stunt such as he did. Thank Heaven for a three- pound trigger pull instead of a two- pound trigger pull...

As for any Tombstones, there thankfully were none. **For both men, but for the grace of God go the two of us...**

THE STRATEGIC AIR COMMAND

The winter's night air was rice-field damp and cold. Looking skyward, I could see that I had a quarter sized moon with a ring around it portending another coming winter storm.

Just the right amount of light if someone wanted to blow up my ducks and plenty of light for me to use my binoculars in apprehending the shooters, I thought with a grin of satisfaction. In several harvested rice fields to my front were about 10,000 noisily feeding ducks not far removed from Lone Star and Ware Roads. Since they were such easy and tempting targets to the ear and eye for any potential night shooters, I had chosen those flocks as my stake out birds for that evening's duration. Well, that and the fact that my Colusa County counterpart from the town of Williams in whose law enforcement district I was now in, was sicker than a dog from too many long hours in the damp rice fields during the valley's winter season. Bottom line, not feeling worth a hoot, Warden Chuck Monroe did not have the strength to sleep with the ducks in his patrol district. With that information regarding the Williams' warden's sick down time, it didn't take my local outlaws long to figure out where fish and game's weaknesses were and take deadly advantage of that by illegally blowing up the ducks at night in his district. Under those circumstances, I just figured, one duck dragger's surprise deserved a beautifully handsome 320-pound surprise in the same field when he decided to pull the trigger and blow up the ducks in a sick officers district. Not only that, but one of my better informants had warned me that the ducks were feeding in the Lone Star Road area by the tens of thousands and I had better keep an eye out if I didn't want the critters in that area blown to kingdom come by local duck draggers from the nearby towns of Williams and Colusa.

With a 'battle plan' in mind, Dog and I had hidden our patrol truck in between two bank-out wagons and a Hardy harvester sitting idle in a nearby freshly harvested rice field shortly after dark in the Ware Road area of my sick counterparts district. With my camouflage parachute tossed over my vehicle for good measure, Dog and I were set for the evening and the following morning's duck dragging activities were they to occur. After Dog and I had hotfooted it into an adjoining field and laid down behind a rice check for the cover it offered, we didn't have long to wait for what was next to come.

BOOM, went a single shot in the darkness to the northeast of my stake out position from the Abel Road and Colusa National Wildlife area! Looking in that direction and running the geography of that area through the mental processes in my mind, I figured that shot had come from somewhere within that national wildlife refuge's boundaries! Even more worrisome, the sound of that shooting had come from a hunting rifle and not a shotgun!

(To those of you who are wondering how the dickens the difference could be told between the two, simple. Most game wardens in those days were also outdoorsmen of the hunting and fishing variety. It doesn't take long to be able to differentiate the difference between a rifle and shotgun being fired when one comes from such a sporting background. When discharged, a shotgun has a booming sound and a rifle makes a sharper 'crack' sound. Since game wardens make their living with their eyes, ears and other primal instincts, hence my quick identification and distinction of the sound. With the above fodder as part of my life history background, it is easy to tell the difference between the two shooting sounds, even from long distances.)

What the hell? I thought. *Someone would not be stupid enough to try and blow up the ducks on the refuge with a rifle.* (Some waterfowl hunting was allowed during the daylight hours on a small portion of that refuge but not at night and certainly not with a rifle.) Puzzled over that single shot, for the longest time I listened intently for any further repeat clues as to what was going on. Nothing in the way of any further suspicious activity greeted either my scanning eyes through my binoculars or my ears. As was many times the case, planned stakeouts could be busts and that one was when it came to any duck dragging activities that evening. That was except for the mystery of the lone rifle shot on the adjacent national wildlife refuge taking place in the dark of the night. Around four in the morning, I broke off my quiet stake out and headed for home to get some much-needed sleep so I could hit the 'bricks' the rest of that day after waking.

Knowing my informant's information about a pending duck drag somewhere along the Lone Star Road was good, I let my Williams counterpart know I would be staked out in his district the following evening as well. With that bit of formality out of the way, somewhat later Dog and I ventured forth into the damp darkness from our usual hiding place among the idle pieces of farm equipment the following evening. It was now Saturday night and a good time for an illegal night shoot being that the local outlaws did not have to work the next day and there were dozens of large bunches of feeding ducks scattered everywhere surrounding the Lone Star, Abel, Ware and Myers Road areas. In short, those areas were historically easy access sites for local duck draggers to ply their evil and deadly time worn trade and all too frequently, thousands of ducks obliged those shooters by concentrating heavily in the area.

Looking skyward as I moved into my stake out area in a rice field alongside a rice check, I could see scudding winter rain clouds were just now moving into the Valley from the northwest. However, I still had enough good light conditions from a quarter-moon to carry on, so carry on I did. Long minutes later, Dog and I were smack dab in the middle of a wonderful mess of the feathered-ones in the world of waterfowl. Other than the carrying-on of all the feeding ducks scattered throughout the area, it was as quiet as an Egyptian tomb until about one-thirty the following morning,

As if on cue, BOOM, BOOM, went two quick shots from a heavy rifle in the area of the Colusa National Wildlife Refuge a second night in a row! Brother, that sound of shooting and its location sure got my attention! Standing up and cursing the scudding rain clouds now obscuring the partial moon that I had relied upon earlier, I continued glassing the area to my northeast from whence the mystery shooting on the refuge had come. (That evening I was even closer in location to where I had heard the one shot fired the evening before just in case there was a repeat performance of my mystery shooting.) Looking for anything that suggested human activity on the refuge, I saw no evidence of flashlights being used or lights from a nearby automobile moving suspiciously on that portion of Abel Road crossing by the southern end of the refuge. As was the case, nothing of a suspicious nature greeted my eyes. Then, the sun finally shone on the manure pile behind the barn...

I recalled that three weeks earlier, Deputy Sheriff Peter Grevie had apprehended several individuals as they were illegally leaving the Colusa National Wildlife Refuge in the early morning hours. As it turned out, Deputy Grevie had apprehended several Bay Area chaps who had been illegally trespassing and hunting wild hogs found on the refuge as a matter of course in the dark of the night. That group of outlaws had been apparently commercially booking illegal hunts with clients who wanted to experience the thrill of hunting wild hogs in the dark of the night on a closed national wildlife refuge with the use and aid of dogs. (The time those folks apprehended by Deputy Grevie later spent in court sure as hell let the air out of the balloon of their little illegal hunting trips on the Colusa National Wildlife refuge after that. As it turned out, that group of wildlife outlaws caught shooting feral hogs at night, after paying their high fines and losing all their hog-killing weaponry, were never seen again in the area.)

Feral hogs running wild on a national wildlife refuge you ask? You got that right. The Colusa refuge had a very healthy population of feral hogs living within the confines of the refuge's external boundaries. As the local story went regarding the hogs' genesis, during the Great Depression a bank was about to foreclose on a local hog farmer. Mad because the bank would not extend his credit, the hog farmer turned his hogs loose so the banker could not have them when they finally foreclosed on his farm. The hogs quickly reverted-back to their wild state and took up their new home on the nearby swampy national wildlife refuge. There they had lived peacefully and numerically flourished for many years until local wildlife outlaws discovered the illegal shooting and culinary opportunities that existed right under their noses on the refuge. With the bit in their teeth, a number of local outlaws began poaching those feral hogs on the national wildlife refuge like there was no tomorrow. As a result of those illegal night time hog shooting activities, for many of those hogs, there was no tomorrow! For years, the illegal night hunting activity had gone on unnoticed right under the noses of the old time local game wardens. I think that was due to the fact that the critters being killed were just plain old feral hogs, not wildlife. Additionally, those few Sacramento Valley game wardens in the days of old, had their hands more than full with the illegal commercial market hunting and duck dragging activities being carried on by many of the locals. Bottom line, killing hogs on a national wildlife refuge just did not get top billing in the law enforcement efforts over the other more pressing issues of the day protecting migratory waterfowl from the gross illegal take and sale by waves of commercial market hunters. That was until many years later when Deputy Grevie had stumbled across a mess of hog hunters and promptly arrested the lot for illegally hunting on a national wildlife refuge at night.

Now I suspected I had a return of illegal night stalkers attempting to take the elusive but fine eating wild porkers within the boundaries of a national wildlife refuge. (As an aside, I had just recently discovered that wild hogs were damn fine eating. Their flesh is not as fatty as that from pen raised hogs, the taste was unique and truly wonderful. Just saying... No, you darned readers, I did not go out and illegally take a hog so I could try it. Over the years, federal officers would stalk the refuge in an organized annual hunt and cull down the feral hogs' numbers. That killing was performed because the hogs were terribly destructive to the flora and fauna on the refuge, ate nesting birds and their eggs like crazy and rooted out many of the earthen dikes used in regulating water flows in the marsh. Then the gutted hogs would be loaded into a truck and shipped off to local sheriffs' offices so they could help feed the prisoners and reduce taxpayer costs. On one of those occasions, Refuge Manager Ed Buria gave a chunk of wild hog meat to me to cook and taste. It was wonderful! Since that day, I never turned down the offer to take or eat a young feral hog. The wonderful texture and taste are two of the allures why so many folks chance taking a feral hog off a national wildlife refuge that had a thriving population of such good eating critters.)

Still concerned about my ducks getting' blown up' over the issue of the illegal rifle shooting on the adjacent national wildlife refuge, I held my ground and continued watching my winged critters as they fed up for the night. However, my mind was now racing over this new night shooting challenge and how could I successfully address such an issue. Especially since that potential lot of night stalking, hog shooting outlaws had to be slick as cow slobbers, bold as a hippo-sized hornet, and not conducive to any form of easy capture. Then as if I didn't have enough problems in the conservation arena, I had ducks galore feeding in the rice fields at night by the hundreds of thousands in my own law enforcement district and a mess of my local outlaws taking advantage of such natural riches on an almost nightly basis.

I quickly discovered that this challenge of catching night shooters illegally shooting feral hogs on a national wildlife refuge, was fast becoming my personal pick of the poison. Again without any activity on the part of my duck draggers during that evening, I broke off my stake out around four in the morning and headed home for some much needed sleep once again. But once in bed, I found sleep hard to come by as my mind raced over the night shooting on a national wildlife refuge by some very dedicated savvy killers and me coming up with a plausible law enforcement solution.

Do any of you good folks out there reading these lines realize just how hard it is trying to catch an outlaw out in the middle of nowhere who does not want to be caught in the dark of the night? I rest my case. I think you readers are now beginning to see a 'standard bomber turn' pattern developing when it comes to the complexity of this wildlife law enforcement 'thing'. Just because one stakes out outlaws does not mean they cooperate and apprehension is a daily occurrence. To my way of thinking, most serious wildlife outlaws are a lot like child molesters. They don't advertise their trade and many times are as slick as greased lightning or as silent as a garden snake sliding across a wet lawn when it comes to ducking their heads and avoiding the capturing long arm of the law. Therefore, many a lonely stakeout in the world of wildlife is for naught. But, you can't get your feet wet unless you cross the stream. And to be quite frank, the journey is what makes life sweet, therefore, the many long hours yours truly spent afield hunting the lawless.

After getting four hours of sleep, I was up and moving again. The anticipated winter rains had since arrived and Dog and I found ourselves out in a heavy rain and windstorm as we headed through the front gates of the Colusa National Wildlife Refuge. I talked to Ed Buria and Ernie Ambrosini, the two facility managers, to see if they had heard or observed anything out of the ordinary on their refuge recently. Neither man was aware of anything out of the normal scheme of things occurring on their wildlife refuge in response to my questions. I didn't expect the refuge managers would be out and about in the dark of night and early in the morning like I was, so, I wasn't surprised over the lack of information from the two men about those I was now stalking.

Driving around the refuge public access roads after my meeting with the two refuge managers, all I got was a wet face for my efforts because of the heavy rains. With that, Dog and I headed north into the Four Mile Road area to check our always numerous duck and pheasant hunters. The rest of that week, I had all I could handle in my own law enforcement district, so, I didn't venture south of Highway 20 into the Lone Star Road area into the Williams' warden's patrol district. But no matter, the mystery shooting was not far from my mind as well as the need to catch those illegal shooters pulling the rifle's triggers.

With improving winter weather at the beginning of the following weekend, I was back in the saddle only this time, in the area immediately south of the Colusa National Wildlife Refuge. In the darkness of night, that Friday I slid into my familiar hiding spot by the idle farm equipment, hid my truck and raced into the adjacent rice fields full of thousands of noisily feeding ducks. (To all my readers out there unfamiliar with what sounds thousands of feeding ducks make, it's a piece of cake. Tens of thousands of moving bills through the harvested rice fields searching for rice grains in the darkness sound like flowing, moving water in a rocky trout stream. The sound is so unique that experienced duck draggers or commercial market hunters can hone in on it immediately by just cupping their ears and quietly listening in various directions of the compass in the dark of the night. Within moments, that flowing water sound will lead many an experienced night shooter to the exact location of his feathered quarry and then look out!)

Quietly heading north sneaking further into the interior of my fields of feeding ducks, Dog and I finally burrowed onto the side of a rice check and waited for anyone stupid enough to sneak into and shoot our bunches of winged critters. That evening I saw several slow moving cars traveling north and south on Lone Star Road and a few along Ware Road as if looking over the area holding thousands of noisily feeding ducks. But once again, I had no takers on my immediate field of dreams full of happily feeding waterfowl.

BOOM—, BOOM, went two quick rifle shots from two different guns just to the north of me on the southern portion of the refuge! "Damn it!" I yelled out loud in frustration into the dark of the night like a damn old knot head. The sounds of that shooting had come from two heavy rifles, no two ways about it! For the next three hours long into the dark of the next morning, I looked for any sign of lights to the north of me on the national wildlife refuge. Hell, I didn't even see any vehicle lights running around on any of the adjacent farm roads or trails surrounding the area much less on the refuge. But you know something, Folks, one doesn't throw down a challenge glove in front of a good game warden unless he is a damn fool. For those good officers wearing the game warden greens, having a challenge glove dropped at their feet is like saying, "Catch me if you can". As of that moment in time, I now found myself holding that glove of challenge in my business (or gun) hand.

The next morning found me driving around on the roads within the refuge's external boundaries. I now had better weather and I was looking for anything out of place..., anything. In addition to a zillion resting ducks and geese on the closed zone of the refuge, all I saw were a pair of turkey vultures lazily circling around in the sky over the southwestern portion of the refuge. That flying around by turkey vultures in the area was not unusual though. Lots of ducks and geese, shot, maimed or wounded elsewhere and who made it back to the safety of the refuge, ended up dying there many times from their wounds. Because of that, the vultures and quadruped predators routinely feasted in that portion of the refuge. However, on that morning, I was truly on the hunt for what was buggin' the hell out of me! Being that vultures were always one of my key indicator species of something gone badly wrong in the world of wildlife, I slid my truck to a halt.

A good game warden always watches his birds for what they might telegraph about what is going on around them. Birds like vultures, crows, ravens, jays and magpies, will always find a fresh kill before anything else does. So, if an officer is on his toes, many times certain birds will lead him to a kill site. And since I was on the hunt big time, I tried not to miss any of Mother Nature's call signs of death. For sure, the highly developed sense of smell of a vulture which aided that critter in finding a fresh kill site was also a good 'tell' for me to be aware of and react to.

(Just to give my readers an idea on how well developed a vulture's sense of smell truly is, I offer the following. In 2003, a movie was made by The Discovery Channel for the Animal Planet Series based on some of the stories in my previously written wildlife law enforcement adventure books. One of the stories covered an adventure that occurred later in my career when I had apprehended three hog hunters on the Colusa National Wildlife Refuge in the dead of night. In that adventure, I ended up apprehending several Penal Code law enforcement officers who were commercially hunting hogs illegally on the refuge. In one sequence in the movie making during a windy afternoon pending an oncoming storm, the movie crew dumped out the innards from several hogs for an up-coming action scene. In the howling wind and incoming rain storm, we had four turkey vultures with their wonderful sense of smell circling the immediate area within twenty minutes after the guts had been dumped out onto the ground!

Hell, with as hard as it was raining and the wind blowing, one couldn't have even smelled the stench of a nearby pulp mill much less one hundred pounds of fresh hog guts. But with their unique abilities to 'smell a dinner in the making', those remarkable vultures found that gut pile in record time! Hence to a good game warden, the vultures are a good 'tell' when death abounds.)

After parking the truck along the road, Dog and I exited and began walking across the swampy area heavily covered with brush, swamp grasses and rushes. Splashing across several shallow ponds, Dog and I were soon under the lazy circles the vultures were making in the sky above us. Then a mess of yellow-billed magpies silently exploded into the air in alarm from a spot ahead of us as we approached. Moments later, Dog and yours truly were standing over the fresh remains of a very large hog's carcass, one weighing in at over 400 pounds! Whoever had killed that animal, had partially skinned out the critter, then removed the hams, back straps, and the front shoulders for the eating that was to come. The rest of the partially butchered hog was left to rot! Digging through the remains, I tried to find a bullet hole and hopefully a bullet in the carcass for later forensic comparisons. No such luck did I have in that messy endeavor. Whoever had killed the hog was a smart one. The killer had also located the bullet hole and had dug out the slug as if to preclude anyone from ever using that spent bullet's slug against the shooter. That was one for the books and an indicator or 'tell' as to what kind of a cunning outlaw or outlaws I was now stalking.

Finding nothing more of evidentiary interest around the kill site, Dog and I began looking over the immediate area for any additional clues. It was plain in the mud from the footprints that my hog killing party numbered three scoundrels. Backtracking their point of travel from the dead hog's carcass, I made several discoveries. Firstly, the tracks led to the kill site from the southwestern corner of the refuge, probably entering the area from off Abel Road. Secondly, the area I was now traveling through was a hog heaven. The ground was slightly higher than that of the rest of the Colusa Refuge and, being that it was on the higher ground, there was evidence of feral hogs everywhere. There were hog trails leading to and from every point on the compass. Scattered throughout and in greater numbers were hog nests. Many appeared to have been in use for a long time. Additionally, I bet I observed at least 40 feral hogs quietly moving throughout the area that I was slowly traversing. No two ways about it, this was hog central. It was readily apparent as to why my hog killing outlaws had concentrated their efforts on that area of the refuge that was so hog favorable. That observation was backed up by the fact their tracks had crossed this higher ground area many times in their previous hunts for the hogs.

In traversing that area following the numerous sets of human footprints, I discovered three additional hog kill sites that were older in nature. From the numbers of hog hoof prints around each kill site, in every case other hogs had also feasted on what had been left of their brethren. About all that had been left at each earlier kill site were a few of the larger bones and a much chewed on skull from each kill. It then occurred to me that my hog poachers had probably depended on the remaining live hogs to do away with any signs of evidence of an illegal kill.

Leaving the main hog nesting area, and, yes, my readers, that bunch of wild hogs had made nests in the dense thickets of rushes just like a big bird would, I continued back tracking my outlaws. Twenty minutes later I lost their trails. The poachers had cleverly hidden their tracks and ultimate final direction of travel by moving through several low, densely marsh grass matted areas. In so doing, their tracks totally disappeared. And for me, that was going some. I had been raised as a young man by my step-dad, Otis Barnes. Dad had been raised as a young man with the local Maidu Indians in northeastern California. Befriending many of the young Indian men, Dad was privileged to be taught many of their everyday survival skills. One of those skills was how to track critters. Dad was great at that tracking skill as was now yours truly. So for me to lose the trail of my hog poachers so easily was unusual. But they lost me by walking through densely matted stands of marsh grass in shallow water leaving little or nothing in the way of tracks. It almost reminded me of someone who had been trained by the military in the skills of escape and evasion. Almost...

Returning to the main hog nesting and home-range concentration area, I ran across at least 30 hogs moving about including one rather large boar that had to top the scales weighing in at over 600 pounds! And when I ran into my "Boss Hog", he wasn't impressed with my size or, for that matter, me trespassing in his domain. Standing and looking at one another, I slowly unzipped my jacket and made sure the hammer strap over my .44 magnum was unstrapped in case I had to clear leather in defense of my miserable carcass.

Realizing that I wasn't worth the bother, Boss Hog ambled off in the company of two sows and a mess of squealing and wiggling piglets. Me? I was glad I didn't have to unlimber the big magnum. For once, I wasn't too sure I could have stopped Boss Hog if he had decided to charge me in an attempt to alter my beautiful carcass. But you readers can bet your last parts over the fence that faced with such a challenge, the big magnum had six 255 grain answers for such rude behavior on the part of the big tusker had he decided to do the 'swamp dance'.

Walking back to my truck looking for any signs of shell casings left behind after a shoot, I detected the sickly sweet smell of death nearby. Following my nose for about twenty yards off into a stand of dense brush, I found that source of death. Dragged off to one side of a dense brush patch laid a headless California mule deer. The kill was at least several weeks old and had been partially eaten on by some hogs. However, the destruction of the carcass by the hogs did not hide the fact that the big bodied deer had been apparently taken just for its trophy set of antlers. Sure as God made grasshoppers good trout bait, there laid what had been a huge bodied deer with the obvious signs that its head had been sawed off at the base of the skull. As for the meat, it had been left to rot. Now, I was really pissed! I now not only had illegal poachers stalking wild hogs on a closed national wildlife refuge but there were what appeared to be trophy collectors or maybe even commercial market hunters out and about in my backyard killing the refuge's largest trophy deer!

Taking a picture with my point and shoot camera of the deer carcass's remains minus its head, I headed for my patrol truck in a funk. Here I had way more wildlife related law enforcement problems than I could handle in my own district with wintering waterfowl and didn't need to go meddling around in another game warden's district like I had nothing better to do. But I just couldn't pass up such flagrant violations such as this deliberate hog killing on a national wildlife refuge. After I had visited with Refuge Manager Ed Buria about my findings, I headed for the small Sacramento Valley town of Williams. There I shared my refuge poacher's findings and information with Warden Chuck Monroe in whose district the problem was occurring. Chuck assured me he would give the problem his undivided attention once he got over his sickness and off I went to fight my own district's world of wildlife battles.

Come January of that year, like most hard working game wardens in the Sacramento Valley, I was now running on fumes. Numerous seven day weeks with 16-18 hour days as an appetizer and my old carcass energy level was just about on zero. A number of the hardworking wardens in my squad were also physically run down because of the lengthy on going duck-goose-pheasant hunting seasons and the many thousands of sports who pursued such species almost on a daily basis in our law enforcement districts. Then throw into that mix the wet winter weather, eating spotty meals, getting little rest and one had a sure fire recipe for a mess of ailments leading to a mess of run-down officers. As a result, Chuck Monroe, the Williams game warden, was flat on his back with almost pneumonia again, and I found myself now doing double duty in both of our busy Colusa County districts.

Once again on a weekend evening, I found myself looking at the tornados of tens of thousands of ducks working every rice field along the Lone Star Road area, south of State Highway 20 and north of Hahn Road. Brother, I had upped my efforts to an 18-hour day and now here I found myself looking at thousands of tempting targets in a county known for its plethora of duck draggers and a few remaining old-time commercial market hunters. With my counterpart Warden Monroe flat on his back sick, someone had to give it a go and that left me as the only game warden standing in the county. Waiting until it was dark, I slipped back into the Lone Star and Abel Road areas and quickly hid my truck behind a broken down Hardy Harvester in an adjacent rice field. Tossing my camouflage parachute over the truck for good measure, Dog and I took a fast look around to make sure we hadn't been discovered and then thundered into an adjacent harvested rice field full of feeding ducks.

Finding the first convenient rice check, the two of us bailed into the water grasses covering the levee for cover and then again looked all around in the darkness with my binoculars for any signs of discovery. Seeing no one driving by or looking at the ducks and hearing a huge mass of feeding birds to our immediate east, Dog and yours truly, trying hard to stifle my bout of coughing from a cold I couldn't shake, began crawling to a different location. One in which if anyone shot into the mass of ducks I was currently overseeing, I would have a better chance at running them down and effecting an apprehension. Especially since I was so physically run down and could no longer run as fast as a cheetah, I needed to make sure I was close to any potential forthcoming illegal action and the expected foot chase to follow.

BOOM, went one rifle shot to my north in the central area of the Colusa National Wildlife Refuge! "Damn it," I uttered under my breath as I continued crawling towards my mass of feeding ducks. Once again I had heard the familiar single rifle shot coming from within the refuge. Crawling onto the backside of another rice check, I unlimbered my binoculars, peeked over the check and looked north towards the refuge and the suspect area from whence had come the single shot. Nothing greeted my eyes in the quarter moonlight in the way of any artificial light in the area of the shooting. (And to my readers out there, one can see the light of a candle from ten football fields away even with the naked eye in the dark of the night. Throw the use of a set of binoculars into that arena and one can see why I extensively used such devices looking for an outlaw lighting up a cigarette or using a small hand held light, in my efforts to locate my quarry.)

In the meantime, my group of ducks feeding to my front decided to change rice fields and they stormed over my entire levee. So, I laid back down and remained as still as death in order not to spook the birds. It was at that very moment that I heard another single rifle shot coming from the Colusa Refuge! Now I was really pissed off! Well, not really, I felt more like with that last rifle shot taken on the refuge, that I was really being pissed on!

But there I was smack dab in a mess of ten thousand feeding ducks and some damn knot head was blazing away on the national wildlife refuge some few hundred yards to the north of my location. My refuge poacher was safe in what he was doing because I was too far away to have any effect on shutting the trigger pulling SOB down. But I had been here before and just held my water and did not let it boil.

However, we only had seven more days of the waterfowl season remaining. And since a lot of my waterfowl were already feeding on the new grasses instead of the now almost fed-out rice fields (meaning they did not taste as good), I could slack off a bit on my night shooting, duck dragging SOBs and devote my time to my knot headed refuge poachers. Folks, one needs to remember, it is not nice to piss off Mother Nature or her minions. Remember, I still had that challenge glove in my hands that had been tossed down in front of me that first time I had heard someone illegally shooting on the refuge at night. For me, once the waterfowl season had ended for the year, the hunt would be on for my hog hunters BIG TIME! And let me tell all of you out there reading these lines, there is nothing quite like hunting your fellow humans, especially when you have the bit in your teeth.

Waterfowl season came and went that year and so did the local Colusa warden. That was, straight down to my old hiding place along Lone Star Road and this time into the fields just below the Colusa National Wildlife Refuge and its southwestern boundary. I still didn't feel worth a damn physically with a bad chest cold hanging on for all it was worth but the hunt for my hog shooters was full on and a damn measly cold be damned! However, it was a good thing that damn cold was hanging on for all it was worth because I was now hot footing it across a rice field so I would be just outside the southwestern external boundary fence of the refuge. I had finally deduced that my chaps had to be coming out that area of the refuge after making a kill. And if they did that evening, guess which SOB would be hanging onto their last parts over the fence like a pit bull with nothing better to do?

The last time I had been on the refuge, the suspects' three sets of tracks seemed to be heading in my current stake out direction after they had left with the meaty portions from the freshly killed hog I had discovered much earlier thanks to the circling vultures. And since I had never discovered any type of vehicle hidden in the immediate area for my suspects to use in their flight from the refuge, I figured it best for me to head them off at the pass in their last known direction of travel. So that evening, I was at the southwestern corner of the refuge with bells on my toes and a set of empty arms to welcome any shooters whomever they might be, if you get my drift. Well, like many other stakeouts, nothing happened that evening. In fact, nothing was to happen on the refuge for the next three weeks either! Man let me tell all you readers out there, the nights sure get long, lonely and plenty cold on stakeouts like that one. But, I still had that challenge glove in my hand...

With things calming down in the world of waterfowl now that the hunting season was over and the ducks were on the grass, most of my problems revolved around the illegal spotlighting of my mule deer in the western foothills of my district and my oodles of warm water game fish fishermen and froggers strung out along most any waterway at any time of the day or night. Other than that, I was down to a fourteen-hour day. And by that time, I had that damn challenge glove now in my gun hand!

Many Friday nights later, Dog and I staked out on the southwestern corner of the Colusa National Wildlife Refuge for the umpteenth time. I was using the county undercover truck because it was unmarked and was a four-wheel drive. (My state patrol truck was a two-wheel drive, one mouse powered Chevy pickup and worthless as teats on a side of bacon when it came to traversing Colusa County's sticky damn adobe rice mud farm trails.) With that four-wheel drive aid and assist, I was able to get off Lone Star and Abel Roads and out into the middle of nowhere on a muddy farm trail near the southwestern end of the refuge boundary. Parking and hiding the rig under my camouflage parachute, Dog and I headed off for our usual stakeout point. As was becoming a boring pattern, nothing illegal happened that caught my eye later during the morning hours. I broke off that cold and damp stakeout around four in the morning and headed home for some sleep and a damn big shot of Wild Turkey 101 proof whiskey—for medicinal purposes of course...

Saturday morning I was once again out and about on the national wildlife refuge's public road system. I had come following a hunch and I was beautifully rewarded. Near the nesting area of the various feral hog families, I observed several vultures warily circling in the sky. Only that time I had four turkey vultures telling me through that circling behavior, their tale of woe was lying somewhere below. Once again a trip into the marsh was called for and duly rewarded somewhat later. As the vultures warily circled Dog and me overhead, we discovered the signs of another fresh kill. The kill had been stripped of its best parts and the rest left to rot or be eaten by the scavenging hogs as they are known to do in the presence of any food item.

(Just for my readers' information, wild hogs will eat just about anything, including dead humans! There are plenty of firsthand accounts during the American Civil War in which the dead from both sides were many times scavenged by local farmers free roaming hogs. Many hog farmers refused to eat their own hogs after they had savaged the soldiers' bodies but chose to sell them to the unknowing folks in distant towns that were distant from the recent and bloody battle sites.)

Again, the birds had led the game warden to a site of death. The vultures had once again provided a 'tell' that would soon be put to use. Plus, I was now aware whoever those hog hunters were, they were deadly serious and damn good at what they did, plus, they were back! I had staked out the refuge the previous day until around four that morning and then left for home. In that period of time from when I had left until daylight, my killers had apparently struck based on the freshness of the kill I saw. Now I was really angry at myself for being a wimp and going home to get some rest instead of remaining in the wildlife field of fire!

That next night, Dog and yours truly were on our usual refuge stakeout spot. I figured since the vultures had spoken, it was time for me to do the same. The previous times I had heard shooting on the refuge at night, it had been over the weekends. A trait and weakness exhibited by the poachers that clearly violated one of Grosz' Rules and one I now hoped to exploit. Grosz's Rule: "If a poacher is successful and has no interference in his illegality, many times he will come again under the same circumstances to do unto Mother Nature what he should not be doing." And if my killers returned to Mother Nature's well just one time too many, hopefully I would be there. Hence my wonderful and beautiful appearance that Saturday evening with plans on staying until very late into Sunday morning. However, no other heart beat showed his ugly face so during that stakeout, so home I went for some sleep late on Sunday morning. (Are any of you readers getting tired yet of this exciting life a game warden routinely lives when on one of his many stakeouts?)

Sunday night around nine after I had finished some patrol work along Butte Creek checking my warm water game fish fishermen, I drove over and slid into my hiding spot off Lone Star and Abel Roads at the end of my muddy farm trail. Thirty minutes later found Dog and me staked out at our new intercept point where we could look over a large area of the southwestern corner of the fenced refuge in case anyone took me up on the reason for my lonely stakeout. Besides, I had now changed the timing of my old plans. Heretofore I had managed to utilize my stakeout times over the weekends. Now for the first time, I had changed to staking out my area on a Sunday night in the hope that a change of my habits might just yield outlaw gold. Nothing but the usual sounds of night greeted my ears and eyes for the longest of times. *But the night is young,* I thought, *so patience is the word of the day.* Meanwhile, Dog snored away her portion of the night as her master kept the enemy of sleep bayed at the front door with the addition of his many helpful chews of his favorite chewing tobacco.

BOOM! That close at hand single shot on the refuge blew both Dog and me wide awake and bushy tailed in our place of hiding. Throwing my binoculars up in the direction of that lone rifle shot allowed me to see for the very first time a very faint light occasionally working its beam near ground level. My thought of wanting to rush into the refuge in the darkness and try quietly to move into my poachers for the on-site apprehension was quickly discarded. I decided I had a better chance at apprehension if I could somehow intercept my three poachers (based on the earlier discovery of three sets of tracks leaving a previous fresh hog kill site) as they exited the refuge instead of thrashing noisily around in the marsh in the dark. Especially since my three lads had shown they were after the great eating hogs for their meat. That being the case, they would be packing out heavy loads of said meat as they exited from the refuge. If they did and I was able to intercept them at their exit point, you could bet your bottom dollar some of those three, if not all, would soon be paying for their crimes. I continued watching the small only occasional use of the light in the brushy portion of the refuge moving around until it finally went out and then all was then quiet on the western front.

Fifty minutes later, Dog began the coming event with her quiet rumble-growl of warning. By now, I too could hear what sounded like humans' heavy plodding sounds of movement in the marshy grasses, mud and shallow water coming towards our point of ambush. As the heavy walking sounds got closer,

I could smell the odor of stale tobacco wafting through the damp air. (Man, let me tell all your readers out there that when hunting humans, it is surprising just how acute ones' senses become. Especially when trouble comes directly at the badge carrier in the form of a capital "T"!)

Moments later, I could make out three darkened shapes slowly moving my way. They appeared to be struggling under heavy loads as they slowly and quietly made for the refuge's external boundary fence without a single word being spoken among them. In short, the poachers were 'cat-quiet and wolverine-cautious' as they moved my way! Every few steps they would stop and just quietly listen. Then they would move a few more yards, stop and listen again. *These cats are sharp,* I thought. Almost military like in the precision of their evasion procedures which for some reason once again flashed 'Military Targets' across my mind's eye.

Moments later, my chaps quietly arrived at the refuge's barbed wire external boundary fence, knelt down and for the next fifteen minutes remained silent as a tomb as they carefully surveyed their darkened surroundings. In the meantime, Dog remained as quiet as a tombstone and I hardly dared to breathe because the Great God for once, had placed Dog and me just a few short yards away from what had been a rather elusive quarry over the many previous weeks! When that happened, the memories of all those long, lonely and cold numerous stakeouts melted into nothingness. By the grace of God, I had chosen my intercept spot beautifully and now I was just waiting to spring the trap.

In that trap soon forthcoming, I had a plan. I would wait until the last chap had cleared the refuge fence. In their process of climbing over the fence and after hefting over their loads of what I assumed would be slabs of fresh pork in their backpacks, I would make my move. When my chaps were making the most noise coming over the fence, I would be slowly crawling the last few yards their way. Then just as my lads finished climbing over the fence and were gathering up their backpacks, I would be upon them like Grant took Richmond! At least, that was my plan.

Have any of you readers thought about what the hell is REALLY about to happen? Here you have a single officer with no hope for any kind of backup about to take on three armed and deadly serious outlaws in the dark of the night. Well to be quite frank with all of you out there reading these lines, that sure as hell wasn't on my mind! I had worked so damned hard to get this human adventure to a point of capture and any deadly threat was sure as hell not a consideration at that moment in time. I was only mindful as to how I could capture every one of these chaps that had caused the hogs and me such misery. (No wonder we goofy damn game wardens have such a high mortality rate according to FBI statistics, when we try this kind of crap alone, eh?)

However, instead of noisily crawling over the four strand barbed wire fence, my first two outlaws quietly crawled under the fence. There went my original battle plan in a New York minute. *Pretty damn smart move,* I thought. That way they made no noise going over the fence and were ready to flee at a moment's notice by crawling underneath instead of being hung up on a fence. Once those two were on my side of the fence, the lone man on the refuge side of the fence quietly passed the three heavy appearing backpacks over the top wire. That done, he too crawled under the fence to the other side. *Man, those guys are sure slick,* I thought. Now that my three chaps were over the fence, they began shouldering their heavy packs without a word being uttered. When they did, they made a fair amount of low sounds while shuffling their heavy packs about on their shoulders. With that as my cue, I crawled quietly the last few feet towards my targets.

Quietly raising up from the deep like the Creature from the Dark Lagoon, on went my flashlight with its beam held head high in order to temporarily blind the men. "HEY-HEY!" they yelled in unison as my light went on, exposing three men completely dressed from head to toe in military camouflage gear and sporting paint-blackened faces. On each man's back was a military style camouflage rubber lined backpack that appeared to be heavily loaded.

Quickly I yelled, "**HOLD IT RIGHT THERE! STATE FISH AND GAME WARDEN! YOU ALL ARE UNDER ARREST!**" Those commands did me one hell of a lot of good. All three men instantly tried shucking their heavy packs in preparation to bolt and head for the hills! Well, my mother, God rest her soul, didn't raise a turnip. I grabbed the chap closest to me by the nape of his neck and made sure his last part over the fence married the ground rather abruptly. As I did, I kept on moving toward my second grabbing choice. However, I kept one foot on the body of my first choice so he could not scramble to his feet and fade off into the darkness. Grabbing my second choice by the front of his camo shirt, I yelled, "**STATE FISH AND GAME WARDEN! HOLD IT RIGHT THERE!**" When I uttered those words, I felt his body tighten up in my right hand as I sensed him preparing to jerk away from me and trying to run. That was the last thing he did in a standing position! Feeling his body tighten up under my grasp in preparation to make good his escape, I pushed him clear off his feet backwards, slamming him to the ground rather rudely! With that, my now struggling first choice still being footed by yours truly and my second choice ending up struggling in a heap, I made ready for my next move.

With both men struggling in a pile at my feet, I quickly turned my attention to my third choice. When the light from my flashlight had first splashed across the faces of my three men, my third choice had a rifle in his hands. Without missing a beat since I did not have him and his weapon under control, my right hand sped to my sidearm as a matter of course, training and precaution. However, there was no need. **HE**

WAS LONG GONE! But I still had two out of the three outlaws and that was fine with me for the moment.

Flashing my light quickly back onto my two grounded chaps, I discovered both of them still trying to get untangled, rise and have another go at running. "**First man moves, I will shoot him dead! The second man to move and I will have my dog take him. And if that happens, I will be slow in pulling her off so you will have something in the way of a hatful of scars to remember her and this moment in time!**" I bellowed. I really did not intend on shooting the first at trying his hand in escaping but it sure sounded like a good thing to say and threaten at that moment. With those words of warning, my two lads married themselves onto the ground and froze. I took one more quick look with my five-cell flashlight but my third man escapee was in the next county by then. Since my two men appeared to be unarmed, especially when it came to a long rifle, I assumed my runner had taken the firearm with him that I had heard shooting earlier.

"Alright, gentlemen. You know who I am. Now I need to know who the hell you are and what you are doing on a national wildlife refuge packing out a ton of fresh hog meat in your packs?"

Neither man said a thing. Then a strange feeling came over me as it had earlier and I began wondering if these two lads were active duty military. I had that feeling from just the way they acted being so careful and secretive upon their return, almost military like. That and all the men were wearing military style camouflage clothing and sneaking around like they were on a survival mission. And finally, the two were remaining as quiet as a mouse pissin' on a ball of cotton with uniquely strange looks of worry splashed across their faces. I had seen this type of behavior before when I had arrested active duty military personnel, especially those holding sensitive positions or special clearances. Being in the military and apprehended, had always caused noticeable changes in those I had previously caught walking across the lines of legality. I was not sure what it was like in those situations but I suspected that once their superiors got wind of their arrest, the crap would hit the fan in the military in the form of being reduced in rank, face a court martial or even worse if one was a member of the Strategic Air Command. (In those days, General Curtis Le May was in charge of the SAC bomber groups and he tolerated no mischief on the part of those under his command and his men were well aware of that.)

As an aside, I had met Le May and Doolittle in Alaska on the Nak Nek River in the summer of 1962. I also had the opportunity to see General Le May in action several days later at the U.S. Air Force non-commissioned officers recreation and fishing camp. To read that story, you readers will just have to acquire my EBOOK story titled, *Genesis of a Duck Cop,* and read chapter twelve, titled Alaska.

"Gentlemen, I need to see some identification." Then out of the blue and on a whim I said, "I will also need to see your military identification cards."

Man, did those last words elicit funny expressions on the faces of my two sorry looking lads in the light of my flashlight. Those forms of identification were soon forthcoming, which surprise, surprise, INCLUDED THEIR MILITARY IDENTIFICATION CARDS. Reviewing the documents under the light of my flashlight, I saw that my two captures were in fact, active duty officers from the Strategic Air Command! As it turned out, both men were pilots from the 5th Bomb Group stationed at nearby Travis Air Force Base near Fairfield, California.

"What is the name and rank of the lad who bolted when I first announced my presence?" I asked.

"Sir, we can't give you that," replied the man with the handlebar mustache.

"Can't or won't?" I asked.

"Sir, try to understand the predicament we are in. We both are from a branch of the U.S. Air Force that has a zero tolerance policy on outside legal problems. We very well may lose our jobs if the Air Force finds out about this. Please understand our reluctance in giving up a fellow member of the Strategic Air Command, especially since he is a superior officer in rank. We will tell you everything we can without getting others involved. But please don't insist that we give up our partner. He still has a career ahead of him, a family of five to support and is an Air Force Academy graduate. If we give him up, he may very well lose his job as a senior command pilot," continued a very worried man sporting the handlebar mustache.

Realizing I had a cat by the tail and although they were in semi-serious trouble, I didn't feel like having them hammered by the system twice for their single misdemeanor offense under The Refuge Systems Act. So, for the moment, I backed off. "Alright for now. What is in the three backpacks?" I asked. (My escapee had shucked his and left it behind when he took off so he could lend additional flight to his feet.)

"We killed a huge pig back on the refuge earlier in the evening. We butchered it out and each pack is full of meat from that animal. We even brought out the head so we could have it mounted," continued the man I now had named, "Captain Mustache".

"Alright, step back and let me take a look," I said. With that, the three packs were opened and, sure as all get out, they were chock full of boned out meat presumably from a big pig just killed on the refuge. And surprise of surprises, in one pack sack was the head of the huge 600 pound plus boar Boss Hog I had confronted many weeks earlier. I could see why the men took him as a trophy to be mounted. Its tusks were at least ten inches long and wickedly curved. Then still curious as to their commando clothing, gear and military precision in their operation, I continued with my questioning. "Alright, Gentlemen. Tell me the story behind this pig killing operation on a national wildlife refuge. Why did you do it and why with all the military type secrecy?" I asked.

"Well, Sir, it is a long story. It all started with out escape and evasion survival training two summers ago. First a little background. The three of us went through the academy together and have become good friends since then as have our wives. As part of our training, all of us went through numerous stages of survival training in case we get shot down behind enemy lines while ferrying our B-52s on an attack bombing mission during a state of war. Several years ago, all three of us were air dropped into northeastern California in Plumas County. We were parachuted into places called Clover and Squaw Valleys and were expected to remain in the wilds surviving with the survival skills we had learned in training for ten days. While there, other military patrols tried to actively seek us out and take us as prisoners. Those recovered as prisoners were taken back to a mock prisoner of war camp near Reno, Nevada at Stead Air Force Base and poorly treated and interrogated almost constantly. That type of training was to prepare all of us for any eventualities if any of us were shot down behind enemy lines and captured during times of war between the United States and our enemy combatant," said Captain Mustache.

Then the captain after a short interval as if gathering up his breath, continued. "All three of us survived that training and, upon return to our base at Travis, the officer who got away wanted to get the three of us into a hunting club in the Sacramento Valley. So, all of us being hunters, we applied and were excepted into the Richmond Hunting Club in Colusa. There we could hunt ducks, geese, dove and pheasants. Well, one day all three of us were duck and goose hunting on some Richmond Hunting Club lands south of the Colusa National Wildlife Refuge. While sitting in our duck blind one afternoon, we saw a line of feral hogs streaming back into the south end of the refuge."

"With the shooting being poor that day, we all got to figuring how good some of that wild pork would taste and got the idea to use our survival skills, sneak into the refuge at night and kill some hogs. Push came to shove and we gave it a try. We figured it best to hunt the refuge late at night plus it would allow us to more accurately test our survival skills. To be quite frank, we have been doing this now for over two years and never once has anyone ever even come close to catching us. In fact, one day, it got daylight on us before we had finished cutting and gutting out a hog. We had to hide all day on the refuge and once it got dark again, we got away. Based on your size, I think we even saw you on the refuge looking around by one of our hog kills. You walked within twenty yards of us and never even saw us. So, I guess some of our escape and evasion training must have worked, huh?" said Captain Mustache.

With my head swimming over what I was hearing, I asked, "Where did you guys park your vehicle? I have been all over this area and I never saw any strange vehicles parked near the refuge."

"That is part of the E&E training (Escape and Evasion). We never have any kind of escape vehicle parked near our activities. We always parked our vehicle at least a half a mile away and walked in. That way we could get some great exercise, keep in shape, and no one was any the wiser. Then on our way out, we would walk to the nearest road in the dark, hide our gear and one of us would walk back to our vehicle and come and get the rest of us and our gear," quietly continued Captain Mustache.

By now my head was really swimming! I had been raised in Plumas County and our family deer hunting camp was located in Clover Valley in the eastern part of that county. The same general area in which survival exercises had been held for members of the Air Force. As a 13-year-old boy in the 50's, I can remember the air force survival candidates hiding in among the woods and mountains trying to evade the Air Force patrols looking for them during the height of our fall deer hunting season. In fact, one time several of our family members hid one of the air force lads who had injured himself when he had bailed out and kept him away from the patrols so he could last out the days afield and pass the survival school. "And to be quite frank, their survival skills and E&E tactics had served these three chaps very well if they were able to hunt on the refuge for several years and never been detected," I thought to myself.

"Well, gentlemen, here is what I am going to do. Both of you will be cited into Federal Court in Sacramento. Now, don't hump up. You have been most interesting in your story and I have no desire to have any of you 'shit-canned' by the military for a stupid damn stunt of trespassing on a refuge and killing a few feral hogs. The charges that will be brought against you are all misdemeanors. That means a maximum fine of up to $500 dollars and/or six months in jail per offense. I doubt any of you are facing jail time and, to be quite frank, a misdemeanor wildlife violation is like a traffic ticket in the federal legal system. I doubt anyone in the Air Force will find out about your stupid little act and I sure as hell am not going to tell anyone in the Air Force of your little 'NO-NO' either. To be quite frank, I will find out who your partner in crime was in short order. All I have to do is go to the administrative 'wheels' in the Richmond Hunting Club and I will soon know the identity of your partner in crime based on their enrollment rolls. Especially since you guys more than likely have a house trailer parked there on the Richmond Hunting Club grounds. But don't worry. I will keep that information to myself. I can't charge your friend anyway because I did not get a really good look at him so criminally proceeding against him any further is a legal wash. And I sure as hell don't expect any of you to testify against him, realizing the bad-blood' and consequences to follow. Especially since he is a senior officer to the two of you. However, if I had been able to identify him, he would have been charged as well regardless of his rank. Count on the fact that if I ever catch any of you ever doing this again, it will be a trip to the Colusa County Jail in a heartbeat. If any of you end up in jail, General Le May will certainly find out about that and then moving to Guam will be too damn close for comfort around that general if you get my drift," I advised.

"Lastly, I will need you lads to surrender to me your two heavy hunting rifles because on one of your little evening hunts I distinctly heard two rifles firing. Since your partner ran off with your rifles, it will be incumbent upon the two of you to retrieve them and bring them to me at the Richmond Hunting Club headquarters in two days. There they will be confiscated and more than likely forfeited to the U.S. Government since possession of a firearm on a national wildlife refuge is a violation of federal law. And if you choose not to bring those rifles to me during the allotted time frame, I will see to it that the U.S. Marshalls serve a warrant on the two of you," I continued.

"Yes, Sir," came instant dual responses from my two captures.

Finishing up with the paperwork, the three of us hefted all the backpacks full of hog meat back to my hidden vehicle and then I issued the two men seizure tags for the meat and their rubberized backpacks in order to better help me transport the meat to a locker in Colusa that I had rented in which to store my seized evidence.

I then explained the process whereby the Magistrate's Court in Sacramento would contact the men and give them the option of paying or appearing to contest the charges. Since none of us had any further questions after those explanations, we parted ways with a handshake. Me to take my boned out hog in the backpacks to a local butcher to have it processed, packaged and wrapped for later distribution to needy families and my lads back to wherever they came from. As far as I was concerned, my two chaps could use their E&E tactics and find their own ways back to base. Then it was home and to bed since I hadn't slept for 24 straight hours. Two days later, I went to the Richmond Hunting Club headquarters and discovered the name of my Air Force runner from their membership list. With that, I could see why the reluctance on the part of my two captures who we just captains in the Air Force in identifying their partner in crime. My runner turned out to be a full-bird colonel in the Air Force and what was called a senior command pilot! Then I walked over to my chaps' trailer space and met one of the men previously apprehended having lunch after a morning's pheasant hunt. Without a lot of fanfare, I took possession of the two rifles I had requested earlier to be turned over to me. When I did, I was surprised over what fine rifles they turned out to be. Two almost brand new Remington model 700 BDL's, calibers 30-06 with Redfield 3X9 scopes. Losing those rifles sure had to hurt their two previous owners. While there, I also picked up a five-point set of mule deer antlers drying out on the trailer roof and loaded those into my patrol truck as well. I presumed they were the antlers from my headless deer I had discovered earlier on the refuge. Since I had no solid legal connect in the taking of that animal, either through personal observation at the time of the crime or a subsequent confession, there wasn't much I could do in that prosecution arena. I knew and they knew but in a court of law, I had little solid evidence to go on with that violation. Oh, I probably could have pushed the investigation but I already figured I would let 'sleeping dogs lie' with just a little word to the U.S. Magistrate and let her 'stack the deck.' My air force captain had nothing further to say when I seized their rifles or the set of antlers and neither did I. It was obvious that we both knew what had happened in that little deer night shooting arena. Since as an officer I had the discretion to proceed with an arrest or citation after apprehension, I did as I saw best for all parties, including the hogs.

I just figured my lads had learned a damn good lesson and since my government had paid a $1,000,000 dollars each in those days to train those pilots who were protecting my country, I let it go at that. I just hoped if any of those lads ever got shot down behind enemy lines, they had better run across Russians who were dumber than a damn old broken down game warden like me when it came to apprehending those bombing the hell out of Russia. (By the way for the record, the lad who fled the scene at the time I apprehended the other two chaps, eventually retired from the U.S. Air Force as a Lt. General with a record as a damn fine officer. At least that was the word of the day according to my contacts in the FBI. The two captains have since also retired as full-bird colonels. I guess I did my country a service in not ruining their careers over a bunch of feral hogs and three men trying out their E & E tactics on a dumb-assed game warden.)

Several weeks later, Juanita Hobbs, secretary to Agent in Charge Jack Downs, called me and advised my two air force captains had paid up like slot machines. Both men had forfeited $500 for the trespassing error of their ways, another $500 for possessing a firearm on a national wildlife refuge, another $500 for the illegal possession of wildlife on a national wildlife refuge and both rifles were forfeited to the U.S. Government. Smiling over those words of bail forfeiture, I would say the U.S. Magistrate 'stacked the deck' on my two lads after hearing my part of the story. I just figured the man who escaped could just chip in and help in paying those rather large fines to settle his part in the issue at hand... I never heard another thing from the Air Force about my two very contrite captains or their little 'NO-NO.'

As for the Flowers and Tombstones in this adventure, as is always the case, there were a few of both. As for the Flowers, I think my Air Force chaps learned a damn good lesson. That little lesson surely put a little more thinking into their efforts in their E & E tactics and about obeying the laws of the land. The next time they might have had to use such tactics, it could have been in a foreign country and instead of a game warden hunting them down and issuing them a citation, it may have been a hard- nosed Russian apprehending my chaps, all followed up with a rifle bullet...

Another Flower in that above venture garden was that instead of ruining three careers, they were allowed to Flower and serve this great country of ours very well throughout the lifetime of their careers.

Another Flower was that I was able to donate all the now processed meat from the hog to a number of families in my district that I always tried to help. A father of one large family just broke down and cried when he received such a nice amount of meat. It seems his family had not eaten any meat for over a week because he could not afford to buy any…

Another Flower was involving that of a farm laborer who worked for Terrill Sartain. A Mexican man who routinely worked double shifts or 16 hour days, six days a week. He did so because he wanted to send all seven of his children to college so they would have better jobs than he had. As I later learned, he did in fact send all of his kids to college before it was all said and done. Over those seven years I worked in the valley, both a state and federal officer, I saw to it that I kept him and his family supplied with every kind of meat imaginable that a conservation officer could seize and legally provide.

As far as the Tombstones, there were several in this adventure as well. First of all, my Air Force chaps illegally shot hogs on the Colusa National Wildlife Refuge for over two years without apprehension according to their own words. That is a classic example of the extreme odds all North American conservation officers faced on a daily basis in hunting down and apprehending wildlife outlaws. Really SERIOUS wildlife violators are probably only apprehended about one-tenth of one percent of the time! I say that based on my numerous years experienced as a state and federal wildlife officer across this great nation of ours. There are only about 10,000 conservation officers in ALL of North America! (Many major cities in America today have more local law enforcement officers than that.) Then multiply that by 350 million folks living in North America and you can figure out the odds of being caught breaking the law by just 10,000 working hard conservation officers.

Another Tombstone was that of those feral hogs living on the refuge. For two years they were sniped off on a regular basis by my three Air Force chaps. Well, those three chaps and a number of others throughout the years that we knew were doing the same but couldn't catch them in the process. (Once again, can any of you imagine just how hard it is to catch someone who does not want to be caught, moving around in the dead of night over a space of several thousand acres? I rest my case.)

As for the hogs, I find that their state of affairs turned out to be a final matter of both Flowers and Tombstones. The poachers kept the hog numbers thinned out which helped all the flora and fauna on the refuge with their survival. (Hogs are terribly destructive as were the hogs on that refuge.) So by keeping them thinned out that was a Flower. But conversely, a refuge is just that. It is a place where wildlife can be given a rest away from the constant deadly pressures of man. The Colusa National Wildlife Refuge turned out to be a 'lure and attractant' par excellence and a killing field for those feral hogs as well.

The fourth wildlife Tombstone was that those of us who have sworn to protect and preserve who were ultimately unable to do so. (During a book signing in Colusa in 2015, I was told that all the hogs on the Colusa National Wildlife Refuge are now gone. I wonder who else in my absence slipped in on the refuge and helped himself to some good tasting wild pork?)

As for the final Tombstone in this adventure, the Williams Game Warden, Chuck Monroe, passed before his time. He was a man who had dedicated his life as well as much of his family's quality time to those in the world of wildlife who have little or no voice. Sadly, Chuck was taken seriously ill early in his career and passed. Thank you, Chuck, for your service to those in the world of wildlife who have little or no voice.

THE BOYS FROM GRIDLEY AND THE DIRT PILE

It was long after nine in the evening and Dog and I were slowly driving north on River Road without using any headlights. Other vehicular traffic was light, allowing me to run without using any lights, thereby letting my eyes adjust to the night and not announce my presence to any nearby duck-shooting outlaws. Earlier in the afternoon, I had observed thousands of ducks and geese swarming off from their resting places in the nearby flooded Butte Sink and coming my way. They came in long streams and eventually descended earthward in long living cascades and swirling tornados onto numerous harvested rice fields on Sartain's lands and those areas just east of the Garvin Boggs old home place. Stopping south of Garvin's old home place in the dark along the now deserted River Road, I shut off my truck's engine, got out and cupped my ears in the direction I had earlier observed the swarms of ducks and geese landing into the adjacent fields. Sure as my mother made the finest pickled crab apples in the world (may God rest her soul), I could hear the familiar flowing water sounds made by the many thousands of night-feeding waterfowl in the nearby harvested rice fields.

Getting back into my darkened patrol truck, I started up my engine and slowly idled my way up to Garvin's old home place, sitting just off the River Road. Seeing that the way was clear for a 'sneak-by', I quietly drove alongside his home on one of his farm roads hoping not to be observed. Looking through the living room window of Garvin's home as I quietly drove by, I could see Garvin sitting in a chair watching television. *Good! He didn't see me or even realize that I was in country and on the hunt in his own backyard,* I mused. I had long since learned that when working waterfowl night shooters in the Sacramento Valley, the less anyone knew that I was in the area the better if I wanted to be successful when it came to capturing my night shooting outlaws. Quietly continuing on, I headed due east and then north on several other muddy farm roads until I was almost in the middle of a number of huge freshly harvested rice fields full of feeding ducks.

Hiding my truck in a grove of cottonwoods near the backside of one of Sartain's rice fields, Dog and I got out and just stood there in the darkness drinking in the noisy specter of the world of wildlife swirling around us. I couldn't help but marvel at the thousands of mostly ducks in the area and all the happy feeding sounds they were making in the nearby harvested rice fields. Of course, having such huge feeding and noisy flocks of birds so close at hand to the local outlaws was always a curse and a concern as well. A curse and concern because if I could hear all that racket those feeding ducks made, so could all my local outlaw duck draggers and that portended danger for my birds.

Not sure which bunch of birds to babysit that evening, I finally chose to position myself in between two flocks of birds located a short distance away from a cottonwood tree grove growing on Sartain's property. That way, I figured if someone shot into either bunch of feeding ducks that I had chosen to baby sit, I could move to the sounds of the guns and hopefully gather up my illegal night shooters. The only problem was that after an illegal shoot, a goodly number of duck draggers seemed to melt into the ground or darkness, many times never to be seen again by Johnny Law. Bottom line, one had to be right on the illegal shooters when they 'blew up' the ducks or there would be no cigar for the failed efforts of one lone 'badge carrier' hunter of humans.

Careful to avoid spooking off the numerous bunches of feeding ducks, Dog and I sneaked into the small grove of cottonwood trees and burrowed our way deeply into a patch of brush and leaves in order to avoid any discovery by unseen shooters in the area. Once again, Dog and I were enveloped in the damp of a rice field night, could smell the rotting vegetation and dead crawdads and were totally mesmerized with all the noisy feathered biomass surrounding our hiding place. For once, I was in a neat hiding spot just a short distance away from the feeding ducks and yet could quickly move to anyone crazy enough to blow up the birds in a heartbeat. That 'hide' was located on a small patch of high ground that was dry and well hidden within a patch of tall grasses and rank weeds. Soon Dog and I were very comfortably situated as we listened and looked on to our hordes of feathered charges madly feeding all around us. In fact, the two of us found our little hiding place almost too comfortable... Soon the many long days worked, the deep tired that comes from running on driven energy most of the time and the happy, soothing feeding sounds 20,000 nearby ducks made, lulled Dog and me off into the quiet world of sleep.

BOOM, BOOM, BOOM, BOOM...went 15 or more blazing fast shots fired from at least three nearby shooter's shotguns! Those shotguns were fired so rapidly, that I was not sure of the exact count of shots fired once my senses quickly awakened, drawing me back into the world of the living. In a mental instant, I could just picture those thundering shotguns slinging killing streams of lead shot, 'head high' into the masses of feeding ducks on Sartain's rice field not forty yards to my north! Quickly rolling over and going to my knees in the tall grasses, I used my binoculars to glass in the direction from where the thunderous barrage of shooting had just come. I was instantly rewarded with the darkened shapes of thousands of fleeing waterfowl filling the air and streaming away from the field of death. I also vaguely observed through my binoculars other previously feeding flocks of ducks raising up off the ground in sheer terror like a big living feathered sheet being pulled upward by its corners. That kind of panicked lift-off from just shot over flocks of ducks by outlaw gunners was to be expected. I had discovered early on that when the ducks stormed into a rice field to feed, many times they numbered in the tens of thousands! The bodies of those ducks would then be jammed shoulder to shoulder, as they competed along in the darkness like a big snake with their bills, all the while feeling along in the darkness on the ground for the much sought after scattered rice grains of life. Then if the flock was shot into, only those ducks on the outside of the feeding hordes, because of their bodily closeness, could rise up and flee. When the outsides of the flock rose up in panic, that created room for the next ducks in line to rise into the air so they could flee as well. Hence the appearance of a sequential lifting up of a sheet of ducks when alarmed because of the closeness of all their bodies, interfering with any kind of all-at-once winged explosion of free flight.

Scanning the entire shot-over area to my front with my high light gathering binoculars, I could see many more thousands of ducks still rising to wing. I then became aware of a similar roar of thousands of frantically beating ducks' wings behind me distant fields away from other huge flocks that had been feeding and were now also alarmed. Quickly looking at the luminous dial on my watch, I could see that the time my 'shoot' into the ducks had occurred, was at three-twenty in the morning!

Scanning the field just shot over with my glasses one more time hoping for the scene of running duck draggers picking up dozens of dead and dying ducks, I saw nothing but panicked birds flying every which way and the white chests of many of the dead lying on the ground! But that was O.K. with me, because of my now previously learned history of the area and the duck-killing sub-culture's methods of operation when dragging ducks at night. I had learned that often times duck draggers would shoot into a feeding flock and then lie back down in the darkness and wait to see if they were being pursued by nearby game wardens or federal agents. Having learned that little duck-dragger trick of the trade, I too found that I could be just as patient as the Egyptian Sphinx when waiting for my shooters to show themselves so I could initiate my apprehension moves.

As it turned out, Dog and I watched from our place of hiding until just before daylight! Not one single heartbeat surfaced in the rice field just shot over! Such behavior regarding no one showing themselves as they gathered up the dead and dying ducks, I found baffling. Usually my illegal night shooters would surface shortly after a shoot, pick up a number of ducks and split or gather up all of the birds, stack them and then leave the area from a point different from their entry into the place just shot to avoid detection and apprehension. I knew damn well that no one had earlier seen Dog and me sneaking into the area or they wouldn't have shot the ducks right next to us in the first place. So Dog and I patiently held our sand and waited like a South American bushmaster along a game trail for our shooters to show themselves.

In the meantime, I could see through my binoculars a long swath of dead pintail ducks with the male's white breasts showing against the night's subdued golden color of the harvested rice field about forty yards away! And that did not include the many more wounded and crippled birds moving away from the killing field like maggots off a carcass! In fact, Dog and I had six Northern pintail come crawling into the tall grasses clear over to where we were hidden as they tried escaping from their recent field of slaughter...

By nine o'clock in the morning, not a single shooter had moved or surfaced in the area previously shot over! *What the hell is going on?* I asked myself at least a dozen times. *No one pulls a drag as successful as I could now clearly see in my binoculars in the daylight hours and then just walks away from it and the spoils of the shoot,* I thought. But like the bushmaster, Dog and I continued waiting without hardly moving a muscle for fear of being inadvertently discovered by our out-there-somewhere mystery shooters before I was able to make my move of apprehension.

Noon came and went that day and not hair nor hide of my illegal night shooters made themselves known. Damn, now I was REALLY getting worried. I knew whoever had pulled that shoot had not discovered Dog and yours truly and, as a result, had fled the scene before they picked up any of their dead ducks. Dog and I had carefully entered the area earlier the evening before and had remained hidden the whole time. I also knew that when we had driven by Garvin's house the evening before, he had not noticed my darkened patrol truck moving slowly by. That being the case of not seeing me drive by, he surly had not spread the word that I was in the area. With those factors in mind, I knew damn well we had not been discovered at any time during the whole event. But by damn, no one who had pulled the triggers on that drag killing all those ducks had yet to surface to pick up their ill-gotten gains. Then to make matters worse, I had wounded ducks pouring into our hideout like there was no tomorrow as they tried escaping from the area of the killing field. Soon, I had 19 dead ducks lying alongside where I lay sprawled out and hidden in the tall grasses and rank growth of weeds. Sadly, those ducks that had crawled into where I was hidden, did so only to die by the hand that was there originally to protect them. I just figured dying by a quickly broken neck was better than dying slowly from their wounds, starving to death or being eaten alive later on by a predator, so, they died by the hand of their protector. By now, I was more than pissed off and truly baffled over the non-appearance of my damn shooters! *Who the hell would just blow up the ducks as successfully as they did and then let them lay where they died to go to waste?* I kept asking and second guessing myself throughout the morning. But extreme patience is a good game warden trait and now being pissed over what had happened, I decided that I would now lay there until hell froze over if I had to in order to catch my lads...

Suddenly behind me, I could hear a vehicle slowly coming my way on a muddy farm trail. Soon into my grove of trees drove a Ford pickup carrying three individuals whom I did not recognize as locals. They slowly drove up into the backside of the area where the earlier shooting had occurred and stopped. My three lads then bailed out from the truck and all of them casually took care of a call of nature just like Joe Casual. Looking at my watch, I saw that since the arrival of my three lads, it was now one-thirty-eight in the afternoon. *If these lads were the shooters, they were some sort of cool*, I thought as I continued observing their actions from my hidden in the brush place of hiding.

Still, not one of the bunch of newcomers moved into the nearby morning's killing field or even looked at it like they knew it was there. All three men casually lit up cigarettes and continued talking as they stood around the bed of their pickup like it was an everyday event to do so. However, I did notice that every one of them kept nervously looking all around like they were looking for something to appear out of nowhere.

Maybe they were looking for the local game warden to come swooping in, I thought. *Look over here, you idiots, if you want to see the surprise of your lives by what is lurking in the bushes,* I thought grinning all the while. I finally figured these were the lads who had earlier shot the ducks and were now on the killing scene in order to pick up their illegal booty. *Why else would they be here out in the damn middle of nowhere near a recent duck drag acting all casual like?* I kept asking myself.

Finally satisfied there wasn't a game warden within miles of their miserable carcasses, out my three lads streamed into the killing field shot over at three-twenty in the morning like they owned it to pick up the dead ducks. What each of the men did next was as slick as a mess of 'cow slobbers'. Each man walked around and only retrieved a daily bag limit of eight ducks from the field of the dead and many still badly wounded birds. I assumed they did so just in case they ran into a game warden and would only have a legal limit in their possession to show how honest they were. Then each chap walked back to their truck and began hiding those ducks under and behind the seat like they had done this before. After each man had made two more trips into the field and back to the truck, the area behind the front seat was jammed jug full with 48 dead ducks. Then talk about the men being even slicker, what I saw them doing next was bordering on pure genius! I assumed what they did next to hide their dirty duck killing deed was to foil any game warden's casual subsequent inspection.

Now satisfied that they were alone on the backside of one of Sartain's huge rice fields at the edge of a tree and brush line, the three men picked up their pace in the duck retrieval department. Soon the men were quickly bringing in double hands full of dead ducks and just tossing them into the bed of the truck in a pile and in so doing, leaving them out in front of the eyes of God and everybody. As they did, I hung in my hiding spot just as tight as a tick because it was a lot easier for me if my outlaws gathered in all of the ducks they had killed instead of me doing all the leg work doing the same. Besides, there was a legal aspect to my leaving them alone and letting them hang themselves through their now guilty actions. It would be kind of hard for my chaps later on in a court of law to deny that they had knowledge of the early morning duck drag or had over limits of waterfowl in their possession. Plus, I wanted to see what the hell my chaps were really up to with their 'just throwing' all their ducks into the back of their truck out in the open and all. Hang on, my patient readers, the best of these three chaps pure genius was soon to reveal itself in all of its glory.

The three men were now bringing in so many ducks at a time, that I could not get an accurate count on the number of birds they were dumping into the back of their truck. They were still casually tossing those huge numbers of ducks into the bed of their truck like it was nobody's business because they were so isolated and out of view. After another half an hour of such rapid duck retrieval and dumping the same into the back of their truck, the men ran out of the ducks that had died in their initial series of shots and were the most easily retrievable. Now the greedy lads had down-shifted their efforts to beating the brush and adjacent rice checks for crippled ducks that had struggled off and tried to hide after being crippled in the initial fusillade of shooting.

Following that, came the arrival of their pure 'hiding-the-deadly-fact-in-plain-sight' genius when it came as to how they were going to get such a large and illegal mess of ducks home safely. While one man continued beating the brush and grasses for additional crippled ducks, the other two men grabbed shovels from out of the bed of their truck. Without missing a stroke, both men began shoveling dirt up into the back of the bed of the truck ON TOP OF THE HUGE PILE OF DEAD DUCKS! Suffice to say, when it came to the shoveling department and hiding all those ducks under a dirt pile, those

497

two lads were all business. So for the next twenty or so minutes, the dirt just flew as the two men shoveled like they were in a hurry! I guess I couldn't blame them for working their butts off. As near as I could count, they had at least 200 dead ducks in the bed of their truck, another 48 ducks behind the seat of their vehicle and I had 19 more dead ones lying alongside me as part of their kill of their soon-to-be-ill-fated shoot! *Yeah, shovel away, you guys, because the fact of the matter is, you are in essence digging your own graves!* I thought with a HUGE grin on my face.

Following their furious shoveling activity, it was time for some of my pure genius to surface as I formulated a plan that was made to order when it came to trumping their little 'hide the ducks' genius. I got an idea to trick my lads and just show them how great a good game warden's nose really is. A trick that an officer of the law can only use if he has observed the commission of a crime and the bad-guys don't know the officer had observed the same. The outlaws so touched by such a trick, would have a story to tell anyone who would stand still long enough to listen about their upcoming sad but true, horror tale regarding a game warden's prowess with his snout. (As indicated earlier, this was a trick of the trade that I obviously only used when I had my outlaws stone-cold dead as to the violation in question. But it was a 'funny' that I enjoyed immensely doing just to teach an off the wall learning lesson to my outlaws in the hopes it would slow them down a tad in the future on any such illegal endeavors.)

Finally my single lad in the field had scoured the area for all the crippled ducks he could find and had returned to the truck. And all those birds he was lugging from his discovery in the field, went into the back of the truck on top of the other ducks yet to be covered with dirt. Soon, my now three shoveling lads had a respectable load of rich brown silt from the edge of Sartain's field piled up into the back of their truck.

Since my lads had appeared on the scene without any sign of a shotgun between the three of them and had only a load of dirt in the back of their truck to show for their efforts, that normally would have shooed off and precluded any casual look-see by a game warden. And being in duck country during the hunting season, with no ducks in their possession, they had a sound reason for all their innocence and a dirt solid alibi to boot, no pun intended.

Well, I guess one could say, maybe not quite so 'dirt-solid' an alibi after all, with all things seen considered. Remember that damn bushmaster lying alongside the game trail, my dear readers? Here he comes so all of you need to now 'hang onto the willows' for the finale. Waiting until my lads were all looking skyward at several thousand lesser snow geese flying by, Dog and I rose up from out of the grasses stiff as a couple of pokers from lying still half the night and into the next day, as we then began quietly walking towards my three duck dragging 'field angels' from 40 yards away.

"Morning, Gentlemen. Game warden. What are you lads up to?" I, in a dumb-as-a-stick tone of voice asked. For a moment, the surprised three musketeers-uh-duck draggers, almost bolted in surprise over my unanticipated arrival from out of nowhere and so close at hand. Then their 'outlaw-ness' took over and they quickly calmed down, knowing they had hidden well the evidence of their illegal deed under a mound of dirt. Man, you talk about a perfect cover! (Pardon the pun.) As I approached their truck, they now had a full load of dirt in the back and three shovels stuck into the mound of dirt with their handles sticking up in the air like nothing out of the ordinary was going on.

"Uh, good afternoon, Mr. Game Warden. My friends and I were just getting a load of dirt to help out with putting in my new lawn," said an older man with a pot belly like mine.

"You boys have permission to take dirt off Terrill Sartain's land?" I asked as I kept moving into their personal space.

"Sure do," said "Pot Belly" as he dug out a rumpled piece of paper from his shirt pocket and handed it to me for my perusal.

Like I said earlier, damn near pure damn genius on their parts, with the dirt pile of ducks and all, supported with an 'allowance note'. Sure as all get out, my men had a signed note from Terrill himself allowing them to get a pickup load of dirt from the backside of Section 17 of his land.

Now I figured it was time for "The Great Grotz" (that's me) to pull the wool clear over my three duck-killing lad's eyes. And man, I had a big bag full of wool to pull over the eyes of my shooters, if you readers out there get my drift. "You boys been hunting any ducks?" I casually asked as I hitched my right foot up onto the back bumper of their truck just a scant yard away from over 200 freshly buried ducks in the bed and hooked my arms over the top of the tail gate. When I made that move, I had three sets of eyes from my outlaws glued to my every action because of the closeness of my move to their little secret. I would think if a game warden was on his toes, he could call that cornered look on the faces of my three chaps a 'tell'.

"No, Sir," came three instant denials faster than a spitting cobra could spit.

Casually taking out a chew of Levi Garrett chewing tobacco from a pouch in my front shirt pocket and, without saying another word, I casually took out a big ole wad and placed it slowly into my mouth. I then slowly placed the tobacco pouch back into my shirt pocket without offering my three chaps any like a gentleman would do. The way my lads so intently looked at what I was doing, you would have thought I was starting to eat a big ole garden spider. Without missing that 'tell', I then withdrew my tobacco pouch from my shirt pocket, apologized for my lack of manners and offered it all around like a good sharing Christian man would do. As it turned out, I had no takers from my three outlaws in the chewing tobacco use department. From the looks of concern on their collective faces over my nearness to their little secret, I could see why no one took me up on my nicotine loaded offer. It was obvious, they preferred that I get the hell away from them so they could be safely on their way home rather than my hanging around and just chewing the fat with them.

What happened next my lads never saw coming because I was now starting to implement my little bit of pure damn genius. "If you lads aren't duck hunting and just shoveling dirt, why do you all have dried blood smear marks on your hands?" I casually asked right out of the blue as I shifted the big wad of chewing tobacco around to a more comfortable place in my cheek. With those stabbing words of inquiry, the bushmaster lying along the game trail had struck...

For what had to be one of the longest seconds in those three lads' lives, the men were speechless. Then there was a lot of each man looking at the tell-tale smears of blood (or I guess one could say self-inflicted wounds) on their hands from wringing so many ducks' necks. Those looks of surprise were quickly followed with stark stares of fear and an obvious loss of words over what to say in answer to my rather accusatory question regarding the bloody smear marks on their hands.

Finally Pot Belly tried to save the day. "Mister, we were hunting ducks back by Gridley earlier this morning and cleaned them before we came over here for a load of dirt at Sartain's. Guess being in a hurry to get this load of dirt loaded and spread, we just plumb forgot to wash it off."

Ignoring the man's flimsy attempt to cover up all the fresh bloody smears on their hands, I burrowed into their psyche like a wood tick into the side of a mule deer saying, "You mean to tell me that you did as you say and then didn't wash off your hands? And then you boys came all the way from Gridley with bloody hands just to get a truck load of free dirt from old man Sartain?

You talk about consternation now spreading within the ranks of my three obvious shooters from the morning's field of death located just yards away. I am here to tell you that the looks on their faces spoke to a thousand words.

As an aside, I hadn't seen my lads after the shoot and I never saw their vehicle leave the area. I just figured they had shot the ducks in a remote corner of one of Sartain's rice fields and split the scene by crawling off. Once away from the killing field, I figured that they had quietly walked back to their hidden vehicle and escaped. I guess they thought that no one would discover their little killing secret because the dead ducks were located so far away on the back forty of Sartain's property. That way, my shooters could escape the area and then come back at a later time and pick up their ducks when things had cooled off. A beautiful plan of deception except for one very large problem. That problem being the SOB lying half asleep in the grass and weeds by God-given happenstance near the killing field 'triggered illegally' by my three chaps from the nearby town of Gridley. No two ways about it, my lads were smart and probably well experienced in this duck dragging thing. Being as smart as they were and leaving the field with no ducks in the dark of night and then returning without their shotguns hours later after things had cooled off to retrieve their ducks, was a stroke of pure experience in the round. Pretty damn slick but there was a rather large fly in the ointment. I hadn't been lying there all night just to get all stiffed up, dead-crawdad smelly and cold for the hell of it.

"Well, I will tell you what, Boys. I have one of the best noses in the country. (Here comes MY trick that some would say was pure genius as well.) Plus, at the fish and game academy, they teach all of us on how to learn to smell out the various smells of death that are close at hand. You would be surprised at how much one can smell once you realize what kind of critter you are trying to smell. Speaking to that, right now I can smell freshly killed ducks, lots of them! Boys, that smell is very strong to this old game warden's way of thinking!" Trying to string them along for the finale, I let those words hang heavily in the air for just a moment as I spit out a long spew of tobacco juice, then continued on with my style of pending apprehension. "I think you Boys must have some ducks stashed in the cab of this truck (remember, I had observed my chaps earlier placing 48 ducks behind the seat in their pickup). That smell of dead ducks is just too strong for you not to have a mess of ducks hidden there. Who owns this truck?" I asked in my most serious sounding tone of voice.

A tall skinny lad didn't say anything upon hearing my question. He just raised his hand out of 'momentary fear' like a kid being accused of something by his teacher in the 3rd grade. He painted such a pathetic funny picture that I almost broke out laughing. "If you are the owner, may I have your permission to search your truck?" I asked in a tone of voice that to a guilty party, was nothing short of a question and a death knell all in the same sentence.

Before the vehicle's owner could respond to my 'search' question, Pot Belly said, "What the hell for? We don't even have any shotguns. So, how the hell could any of us kill any ducks clear over here at Sartain's?"

Looking Pot Belly straight into his eyes, I said, "I would like to search your truck because I can smell oodles of freshly killed ducks." (Now remember, Readers, I didn't need a warrant or his permission to search the truck. I had observed every one of the men putting over limits of ducks behind the front seat of their truck earlier in clear violation of the hunting regulations. In reality, no permission or warrant was needed when I had already observed the commission of a crime and the place of concealment. I was just stringing my lads along so as to fit everything into my little battle plan that was soon to unfold like an unstoppable wave pounding up on a sandy beach somewhere on a Pacific isle.)

"May we talk among ourselves?" asked Pot Belly.

"Sure," I said with a knowing grin because I knew what was coming next. I figured after they had talked among themselves, they would act all innocent like and give me authorization to search their truck knowing I would find the 48 ducks behind the seat and would be satisfied in writing the three men citations for those over limits and in that distraction, overlook the 200 plus ducks buried under the dirt pile in the bed of their truck. In short, after issuing a lessor citation, they would probably surmise that I would let them go on their merry way with a monster over limit of ducks in the back of their truck hidden under that pile of dirt. And by falling on their swords over a lesser violation, they thought they could pull the wool over the dumb-assed game warden's eyes and escape a REALLY BIG reckoning over a major violation.

With that, my three lads moved away from me out of ear shot and began vigorously arguing among themselves. Me? I just loaded up another chew of tobacco for the long haul trick of the trade technique I was soon to employ. One that when it came to fruition, my three duck draggers would have a story to tell their grandkids about a part-bloodhound game warden they had crossed swords with earlier on in their lives over a few ducks and had lost the duel. A short time later, the three men returned with concern written all over their faces but with also a tiny spark of hope showing in their eyes, hoping I would fall for the bait they would now dangle my way like a carp would fall for a gob of worms.

The vehicle's owner whom I had dubbed "Skinny" said, "You can search my truck but we have a few ducks hidden behind the seat from our duck shoot we had earlier in the day over by Gridley."

Without a further word, I walked over to the cab of the truck, opened up the door and said to Shadow, "Find the duck!" With that, she was in the truck trying to get behind the back seat like there was no tomorrow. Moments later, I had 48 ducks laid out on the ground next to their truck and three lads with pretty long just captured looks 'splashed' clear across their faces. But to a sharper eye, one could also see sinister looks on each and every face of my outlaws over a secret they harbored within their black-hearted souls. I wondered if they discerned the special look I had on my face as well for what I had in store for them relative to the pile of dirt in the back of their truck?

"Well, Gentlemen, looks like several citations are in order," I said, knowing the best was yet to come. Walking to the back of their truck, I got out my cite book from the game bag in my hunting jacket and let down their tailgate. Then I hopped up and plopped my rather large posterior upon the once again closed tailgate so I could make out like I was going to write them citations for their over limits of ducks discovered in the cab of their truck. Pausing, I let fly a big spew of tobacco spittle over the side of their truck, then made a big gesture of stopping in mid-stride saying, "Say, guys. Do any of you smell that?"

"Smell what? I don't smell nothing other than some dead crawdads," said Pot Belly with a quizzical look on his face. His two partners in crime, seeing me sitting on the tailgate by the huge pile of hidden duck bodies buried underneath the dirt pile, had a look of pure scared splashed all over their faces fearing that I would soon discover their dirty (no pun intended) secret with that nose of mine. I was just too damn close for comfort to what they were desperately trying to hide and, to the casual eye, it now seemed that all my lads were having trouble breathing over my closeness to their secret buried under the pile of dirt.

"Dang, I still smell one hell of a pile of dead ducks," I said as I made much of looking all around from my sitting position on the tailgate for the cause of the smell like I had missed some ducks hidden just off in the weeds or somewhere else close at hand.

"Hell, Officer. If you can smell ducks, you are just smellin' those laid out on the ground behind you," said Skinny in a hopeful tone of voice. However, the look on the faces of the men was one of pure fear. Here I was sitting on the tailgate (purposely, I might add, for the terrorizing effect it would have), less than two feet away from over 200 freshly killed ducks buried under a foot or so of soil. To Pot Belly's way of thinking from the queer look on his face, he just 'knew' I was now smelling those buried ducks under the pile of dirt in the back of their truck. And to my way of thinking, it was apparent that he was having a hard time just keeping his heart working normally.

Then I spotted something that I could handily use in my ruse against those three chaps. Looking at the side of the truck from where I now sat, I could see just one drop of fresh blood. Apparently one of the ducks thrown into the back of the bed of the truck had been bleeding. In the loading process, it had dropped one drop of its blood onto the side of the truck. With my three outlaws watching me intently looking at the now very obvious drop of blood, it was apparent I had their undivided attention over the crime at hand. Taking that as my cue to continue this act of a game warden's almost mystic sensory prowess, I reached over and drew my finger across the blood drop. Lifting up my index finger with the fresh smear of blood on it, I said, "Well, well, well. What have we here?" But before I could answer my own question, my roving eye caught another 'tell' that I could use to snap the proverbial bear-trap's jaws across my outlaws last part over the fence and do so in short order.

I then spotted a blood smear on the handle of one of the shovels sticking up in the pile of dirt in the back of the truck. Slowly reaching for and removing that shovel and carefully taking my time looking intently at the handle for the effect that had to be having on my chaps' anal sphincters, I slowly laid the shovel down across the tailgate. Turning, I said, "How do any of you suppose this fresh blood got on this shovel handle?" Man, with that question hanging in the air, one could have heard a mouse passing gas in the next county because my lads were so silent. Stepping off the tail gate and back onto the ground, I turned and paused for a long, hard second look at each and every man. It was then that I dumped them with a favorite trick of the trade of mine. After looking intently at each man one at a time, I turned, bent over the side of the truck and took a long drawn out noisy smell from over the dirt pile. When I did so, I acted as if I could strongly smell something of interest contained underneath that pile of earth. When I did, I turned and took a quick look at my now almost frozen in time chaps. Not a one of my three chaps seemed to have what a good medical doctor would call a discernable heartbeat.

"Whooo-eee! That is where all that very strong dead duck smell is coming from," I said as I looked and pointed at the dirt pile. With that, I quickly turned and looked at my lads. When I whirled around so rapidly, every man jumped like a bug on a hot rock. Every one of them had a look on their faces that seemed to be saying, "Lord, help me. I will never sin again if you get me out of this mess." However, He was one Chap who couldn't help them at this stage in the game. (Anyway, wasn't He the One who created all the critters that needed the protecting from the chaps like my three shooters in the first place by a fellow like me?)

"Well, Lads, if there are a mess of dead ducks buried under this pile of dirt and I have to dig them out, everyone here goes to jail. However, if you lads want to dig them out, I will just issue citations for the over limits." Then I hit them with the ringer that had been bounding around in my mind for some time on a whim. I had earlier figured that my lads had shot the ducks, hidden their shotguns in case the warden stopped them walking out after hearing the early morning shooting and would allow them to continue walking out because there would be no evidence of foul play (no pun intended). So, I gave my whim a whirl and took a long 'verbal' shot at my chaps in the hopes I could retrieve their shotguns used in the early morning drag.

"Additionally, in order to preclude all of you going to jail, one of you lads needs to walk over and retrieve your shotguns for me which you have more than likely hidden nearby after you shot the ducks in Sartain's field earlier this morning," I quietly requested like I knew what I was doing. The application of that off the wall request was an old trick Arcata Warden John Finnigan had taught me at my first duty station in Eureka, California (may God rest his good hearted ole Irish soul). And before my words had dissipated into the damp afternoon air of the rice fields, Skinny walked off and returned shortly bearing three Winchester model 12 shotguns. Those shotguns were silently handed over to me as the other two men began digging out the dirt from the back of the truck without being asked a second time.

A half hour of digging later produced 212 freshly killed, slightly dirty ducks of several assorted species and three of the longest faces from a collective set of outlaws from the town of Gridley you ever saw. One could just see in my outlaws' eyes the wonderment over how such a well-planned shoot had become so screwed up. Then just to make sure I had them by the stacking swivel, I said, "That's what I was talking about. I knew I was smelling a very large pile of dead ducks other than the 48 I dug out from behind the front seat of your truck. See, it was just like I said earlier. Dead animals give off a certain smell and, if one is trained like I was at the academy, that smell can be detected even when they are buried under two feet of fresh soil."

Then the work began. I had my three lads walk the fields and ditches surrounding their shoot area again. With the help of Dog, we discovered another 33 dead or crippled ducks from

508

my lads' deadly shoot! That now made a total of 312 dead ducks my three shooters had executed that fine morning so long ago! For the next hour, the four of us gutted all the ducks so they would not sour from their wounds or spoil. That way I would have a good product to give away to those less fortunate living throughout the valley once the county prosecutor gave me the go-ahead for such a disposal.

After interviews of my lads and their subsequent admissions that they were indeed the ones who had pulled the drag at three-twenty in the morning, citations were in issued. Each man was issued citations for early shooting and for collectively possessing over limits of ducks, To Wit: 312! In addition, their classic Winchester model 12 shotguns were seized and held as evidence with forfeiture ultimately in my mind. Seizure tags were issued all around and, with no further questions regarding the legal process, my three lads split the scene on what had to be a long ride back to their nearby Sacramento Valley home town of Gridley.

Gridley was a town that had produced large numbers of market hunters and duck draggers in the days of old. Seems even in its modern days, it still had its share of duck draggers and a few remaining commercial market hunters. I guess one could say that old habits die hard when it came to illegally killing ducks in the dark of the night. Just like the ducks did when they faced a stream of lethal lead shot in the dark of the morning fired at them from ambush just yards away from where they were happily feeding.

I waited until I was satisfied that my three chaps had left the area for good and then a very tired dog from all the retrieving of cripples and yours truly walked back to my hidden patrol truck. After driving back to my pile of ducks, I loaded them into my pickup for transport so I could dispose of all of their carcasses. That afternoon, I got clearance from the county attorney for disposal and then off I went to play Santa Claus so the seized ducks would not go to waste. I saw to it that every poor Mexican I knew on the east side of my patrol district who had children received a mess of great eating, rice fed ducks. Then I drove to Colusa and a number of needy families there received some of those ducks as well. The rest were later given to needy families in the town of Williams.

That night I was home for a rare family supper. Knowing I would be home for that meal, my bride made my favorite supper. Crispy fried chicken, mashed potatoes with thick chicken gravy, fresh garden peas, homemade buttermilk biscuits and for desert, one of my wife's world famous homemade apple pies. Man, I thought I had died and gone to heaven with a dinner like that and the love from my bride that prepared the feast! (But, I knew that when I met that little gal in the eighth grade and later married her while we were still in college. We are still together after over 53 years of marriage as of the date of publishing this story in 2016.) I had been blessed to say the least when the good Lord gave me an Angel, namely my wife, Donna, in the eighth grade...

Later that same night, found me and Dog sleeping once again with my beloved ducks in the rice fields of Colusa County. Only this time, I was staked out just north of the Linc Dennis Farm on the Newhall Farms properties. Man, let me tell you, I had ducks once again all around me, thousands of them! Once again, Dog and I hid my vehicle by some currently unused farm equipment, covered it with a camouflage parachute and then we slowly crept out into a harvested rice field loaded with happily feeding ducks. Sneaking up to an appropriate rice check for the dense watergrass cover it offered, Dog and I burrowed in and got as comfortable as we could. Looking around from my place of cover, I could see we had a quarter moon for the helpful light it offered, a soft breeze from out of the northwest portending another storm and about 10,000 feeding ducks immediately to our south as they fed my way. Settling back down behind my rice check, I turned around and laid my back up against the check's berm as I crawled more deeply into my jacket. Looking skyward, I thanked The Chief Game Warden in the sky for all of the blessings I had received in life and quietly realized just how fortunate I really was. I had the world's best wife, two great kids (that number went to three several years later with the adoption of our Kimberlee, a Vietnamese air-lift baby) and was out in the wilds with my world of wildlife. My journey getting to where I was had been sweet and Heaven sent. My reason for such a journey had been to make sure I got to go there before it was all gone. And now I was there in my world and loving every moment of it...

Then the happy sounds of the feeding ducks, a soft breeze, the rice field damp and realizing that life was not measured in time but what I did with that time, I knew I was home...

Weeks later, none of the men who had pulled the early morning duck drag on Sartain's chose to show up in court but just forfeited bail of $1,000.00 each. That was the maximum dollar amount fine in those days for their offenses under state law for violation of regulations pertaining to the illegal taking and possession of migratory waterfowl. All three shotguns used in the crime were forfeited to the State of California and later sold at a general auction held regularly to sell off seized and forfeited property used in the commission of wildlife crimes.

As usual, there were plenty of Flowers and Tombstones to go around in this story. As for the Flowers, I was getting better and more successful in my chosen profession when it came to not only catching the run of the mill outlaws but to catching some of the really serious killers like the three caught in this story. (A later records' check indicated this wasn't my three lads 'first rodeo'. Hence the rather stiff fine for each man.) I was never good enough to catch every trigger-pulling outlaw but I caught enough to make a dent in their numbers in the Sacramento Valley during my time in the saddle. I just figured

I'd let God, the Creator of all living things, attend to those who slipped through my fingers as he saw fit and at a time of his choosing.

Another Flower had to be the lesson, albeit a goofy one, about one game warden's tremendous sense of smell. I would have loved to have been a fly on the wall and listened to the stories told to their fellow workers by my three outlaws on how the Colusa game warden had smelled out their over limit violations from behind the seat of their truck and from under two feet of dirt piled up in the bed of their truck as well. If nothing else, maybe that story told to other outlaws, forewarned about my wonderful properties of smell, caused them to stay the hell out of Colusa County and do their killing elsewhere. Or, who knows? Maybe some stopped such illegal killing practices altogether. (At least I can hope so.)

As for the Tombstones, there were 312 ducks killed that morning so long ago. Statistically one half were females capable of producing approximately 8-10 young of the year per hen had they lived to nest the following year. So instead of just losing half of 312 birds, one potentially lost from the waterfowl population approximately 1,200-1,500 young! And since most of those ducks killed that day were northern pintail, a duck whose population numbers have drastically declined at the time of this writing, the loss from this illegal shoot on future populations, accounted for a considerable field of Tombstones!.

BLOW THE DUST OFF MY SOUL, LORD, BECAUSE, LIKE THE WIND, I WILL NEVER KNOW MY PLACE. (TERRY GROSZ, 2015)

THE END

Terry Grosz

A Sample Chapter from Wildlife Wars by Terry Grosz

Preface

Originally, I hoped to leave behind some form of written word as a record of my days as a California state Fish and Game warden, then as a U.S. game management agent, and finally as a special agent with the U.S. Fish and Wildlife Service. Initially, this dream of short stories was committed to loose stacks of paper in a forgotten corner of my office, which were someday to act as a reminder to my children and grandchildren of what their father and grandfather had done with thirty-two years of his life. However, as the work in progress grew and others shared in the reading of those stories in those loose stacks of paper and began supplying encouragement for publication, another dream began to grow. Today those dreams and paper stacks have metamorphosed into this and many other like books and EBOOKS of mine you may now be holding in your hands. This book traces my footprints across the face of time in the world of wildlife as I tried to protect those natural

514

resources, our national heritage, if you will, against evil forces hell-bent on their destruction.

In this book, and others that followed, I have tried to describe the very essence and soul of the wildlife protection trade through the many faces of human conflict, as my ship of life crossed across the great sea of our natural environment. I was very fortunate in my years as a wildlife law enforcement officer to have seen and experienced the end of the very best years of the California Department of Fish and Game as it related to its officers and their chosen vision quests. I was also fortunate to have witnessed the end of the very best years of the U.S. Fish and Wildlife Service as those staid officers fought against more than challenging odds that would have made Custer proud. Suffice it to say that in over my three decades of wildlife law enforcement, one sees many changes in the world and, as is to be expected, many of those changes are not for the better.

I was also fortunate to be blessed with a body that more or less held up to the rigors required by the wildlife law enforcement profession in the form of long hours, lousy food (usually sat upon by my Labrador retriever), dangerous animals, inclement weather, poor supervision, budgets designed not to allow one to do the job one was trained to do, national politics skewed toward private interests, wildlife that would not cooperate, equipment purchased from the lowest bidder, unsympathetic government attorneys, juries that did not have an ounce of common sense, judges who had no sense of history, more long hours, crooked state politics, sometimes useless state and federal help, occasionally bullets flying to close at hand, taking risks that never should have been taken all for a defenseless critter in its time of need...

I was also blessed with a wife who had a deeply unique sense of her husband and understood what he was trying to accomplish long before he knew himself. Over those thirty-two years of law enforcement, she quietly assumed the position of second love and patiently waited until I retired to assume her rightful place as my first love. I also had two sons and a daughter who, like their mother, realized Dad was on a vision quest and, also like their mother, provided unmitigated support and love in order that the vision quest might be fulfilled.

I was also blessed over the years with some of the best staffs and officers in the nation to assist me in achieving the many goals I set for preservation of our natural resources. Most of these folks were of such quality that no accomplishment was impossible as long as you gave them a little time to figure out how to administer the program or run the bad guys to the ground. Those 'law dogs' were so good that I often teasingly told them if they ever got on my trail, they should expect a bullet. That would be the only way I could get them off the trail once they set their sights on their target. The American people truly owe those folks a debt of gratitude for what they did to preserve the natural resources of this land for those yet to come. It is a fact that the wildlife one sees today in this country is a tribute to those wildlife officers who came before and those who currently hold that position, representing the "thin green line," and their much dedicated front-line staffs.

It might be surprising to learn that my career all started with the malicious tossing of a snowball. In 1954. I was a twelve-year-old boy living in Quincy, California, a town nestled in the northeastern Sierras about eighty miles west of Reno, Nevada. It was the dead of winter, and in those days the snow in that lumbering community was higher than the shoulders of Babe the Big Blue Ox. I was walking home from school that winter day and chanced to see a bunch of out-of-work lumbermen tossing snowballs at a covey of mountain quail huddled under a manzanita bush alongside the highway. The snow was so deep that the only place the quail could go was under some of the deeper stands of brush in order to find some ground to stand on. One of the men, called Gabby by the others, whanged a quail on the head with a snowball, killing it instantly. The men ploughed through the waist-deep snow to retrieve the dying, fluttering quail as the rest of the covey flew off into the ponderosa forest to safety.

Well, I was a ragged-assed kid in those days and was able to talk the men out of the quail so I could take it home to share with my family. However, once I had the quail in my hand, I turned around and walked back into town and straight to the local game warden's house. There was just something about fair play, deep snow, and starving quail that hit a nerve, even for a twelve-year-old hungry kid. The game warden was a stoop-shouldered man, the stoop having been caused by a poacher's rifle bullet, but a damn good man and an excellent game warden. Paul Kerr listened to my story, then loaded me into his patrol car and headed for Gabby's home. In those days everyone knew everyone in such small mountain communities.

Driving up in front of Gabby's house, Paul knocked on the door and was invited in. I often remember that in those days the law was a welcome and respected sight. Shortly afterward, Paul came out of Gabby's house, got back into his patrol car, and took me home. He had written Gabby a ticket for taking a game bird during the closed season and seized the quail for evidence. However, before he took me home, he took me by his back porch, opened up his evidence freezer, and pulled several packages of deer steak from it. He placed the meat in a paper bag, telling me to take it home for my mom to cook up for us kids. He also thanked me for obeying the law and turning in those who took advantage of wildlife in its deepest time of need.

I never forgot those words. Years later I went to college at Humboldt State in Arcata, California. In 1966 I graduated from Humboldt with a Master's of Science degree in wildlife management. Shortly after that I took the California state Fish and Game warden's exam along with 1,400 other hopefuls. Forty-five of us were selected for the physicals, and ultimately twenty-five of us were selected as game wardens, of whom twenty-three were sent off to a training academy in southern California. Upon graduating from the academy, I was assigned to a warden's position in Eureka, California, and spent a year and a half there. In 1967 I was transferred to Colusa, California, in the heart of the Sacramento Valley, about eighty miles east of Sacramento. I worked in that area until May 1970, when I resigned my state commission and accepted a position as a U.S. Game Management Agent with the U.S. Fish and Wildlife Service. From that day on, I never looked back.

This book, which is one of a number of like books, deals with only a small portion of my state wildlife law enforcement career and experiences. Even though these events are true, they have been altered so that no one will be able to identify any of the real-life characters. I have even incorporated some blind alleys into the text to throw off the really astute students of wildlife law enforcement history, be they pursuers or pursued. The places described in the book are very real, but the names of the characters have been changed to protect any who remain living or their families. You may find many of these tales sad, disgusting, evil, funny, moralistic, or just plain and simply gross. However, they all come from the actual fabric of my life's adventures, and the events they depict are still ongoing in many new forms and places as you read these lines.

Regardless of your reactions, bear in mind that these events actually occurred and that they are the adventures of just one officer. There are almost ten thousand like officers, state, federal, Tribal, Territorial, and provincial, across North America who could tell similar tales. That being the case, imagine the scope and degree of illegal activity and the actual soul and essence that meets such activity on a daily basis in the world of wildlife all across North America.

I hope that you will be able to read between the lines and realize the amount of destruction that takes place daily among your plant and animal communities, nationally and internationally. There are fewer and fewer natural resources over the horizon because of mans' inhumanity to man. In fact, for the most part, many resources are going or gone. Also, I hope you will understand the dangers met by those wearing the badge and those left behind on the home front. They are tremendous and many times requiring of the ultimate sacrifice, be it an officer's life, injuries or that of his family through divorce from one's partner.

Bear in mind that the business of extinction is alive and well. Let us hope and pray that we do not all go the way of the passenger pigeon. Then again, maybe that would be the way to go, and let Mother Earth heal and start all over again—perhaps this time with better results.

About the Author

Whether as a professional in the field of wildlife law enforcement or as a prolific writer, Terry Grosz has distinguished himself with a kind of passion, dedication, integrity and professionalism that often exemplify Humboldt State alumni. The beginning of his 32-year career in wildlife law enforcement began in 1966 with the California Department of Fish and Game in Eureka as a Fish and Game Warden. After several years and a transfer to Colusa, he was subsequently hired by the U.S. Fish and Wildlife Service (FWS), moving into increasing responsibility for conservation and wildlife law enforcement in successively larger geographic regions, from jurisdiction over the central half of Northern California to finally Special Agent in Charge, where he supervised FWS's wildlife law enforcement programs whose jurisdiction encompassed three-quarters of a million square miles within the States of North Dakota, South Dakota, Nebraska, Kansas, Montana, Wyoming, Colorado and Utah!

In 1998, Grosz retired from the FWS and began a second career as a prolific writer, and has since authored and published eighteen books, with several more on the way. Additionally, Terry has a two-hour movie credit with Discovery Channels Animal Planet series based upon a number of his true life action adventure stories. Clearly, he's got a lot of material to work with. Many of his stories have hilarious moments and hair-raising adventures, some others are sad and tragic, twelve of his books are all about the men and women who work as wildlife conservation officers trying to preserve our natural heritage for future generations. The two critiques most commonly received about Terry's books are, the books aren't thick enough (they run around 350-400 pages generally) and once you pick one up, you can't put it down.

48985550R00328

Made in the USA
San Bernardino, CA
09 May 2017